ILLICIT FLOWS

AND CRIMINAL THINGS

TRACKING GLOBALIZATION

ILLICIT FLOWS AND CRIMINAL THINGS

States, Borders, and the Other Side of Globalization

Edited by
Willem van Schendel
and
Itty Abraham

Indiana
University
Press

BLOOMINGTON AND INDIANAPOLIS

Published with the generous support of the
Social Science Research Council

This book is a publication of

Indiana University Press
601 North Morton Street
Bloomington, IN 47404-3797 USA

http://iupress.indiana.edu

Telephone orders   800-842-6796
Fax orders   812-855-7931
Orders by e-mail   iuporder@indiana.edu

Manufactured in the United States of America

Library of Congress Cataloging-in-Publication Data
Illicit flows and criminal things : states, borders,
and the other side of globalization / edited by
Willem van Schendel and Itty Abraham.
     p. cm. — (Tracking globalization)
  Includes bibliographical references and index.
  ISBN 0-253-34669-X (cloth : alk. paper) — ISBN
0-253-21811-X (pbk. : alk. paper)
  1. Transnational crime. 2. State, The. I. Schendel,
Willem van. II. Abraham, Itty, date III. Series.
  HV6252.I448 2006
  364.1'35—dc22
                                        2005010917

1 2 3 4 5 10 09 08 07 06 05

Contents

Acknowledgments

Country boats floating down the river Ganges with cargoes of contraband cattle, motorcycle parts, people, and heroin. Border guards in civilian clothes receiving the smugglers to count their goods and collect pocket money. A border that was officially closed but at the same time clearly an important site of trade and migration, facilitated by collaborating state personnel and smugglers. . . . This is how, many years ago, the subject of this volume first took shape for one of the editors. The roots of our fascination with "illicit" flows across international borders and with processes of globalization "from below" come from intersecting questions drawn from international relations, anthropology, geography, history, security studies, and cultural studies, and each of us has attempted to make sense of these in different geographical and historical contexts. However, the intellectual trajectory that led to this volume was, from the outset, a collective one, shared among scholars from a variety of countries and disciplines, aided by the support of a number of institutions.

In the first instance, this volume developed out of conversations among scholars involved in the last Joint Committee on South Asia at the Social Science Research Council (SSRC), New York, which led in turn to the formation of an SSRC collaborative research network "Illicit Flows and Criminality," and finally to the project's last home, the program on Global Security and Cooperation. This project has received financial support from grants from the Ford Foundation, New York; the MacArthur Foundation, Chicago; and the Hewlett Foundation; for which we are very grateful.

Following initial discussions, false starts, and other hiccups in New York, workshops and planning meetings took place in Amsterdam (1999), Paris (2000), and Vancouver (2002) with different themes and participants, not all of whom are represented in this volume. In particular, we would like to thank the following colleagues who both advised and contributed substantially to earlier stages of this project: Bernhard Bayerlein, Mamadou Diouf, Michael Kearney, Al McCoy, Carolyn Nordstrom, Douglas Sanders, Chris Smith, Heinz Steinert, and Neil Smith. Others who attended and/or wrote and presented papers at one of these workshops include Belinda Bozzoli, Marc Epprecht, Peter Vale, Sun Laichen, David Atwill, David Feingold, Guy Lamb, Laurent Laniel, Robert Karniol, Eric Tagliacozzo, Jonathan Goodhand, Kathi Austin, and James Scott. Our sincere thanks to them all, and to Thomas Trautmann, who was supportive of our desire to

Acknowledgments

publish a selection of papers in *Comparative Studies in Society and History*. We were also fortunate to have, at the Paris meeting, the assistance of the faculty and staff at the Centre d'Études et de Recherches Internationales (CERI). Especially given their imminent move to new quarters, we are particularly grateful to Janet Roitman, Christophe Jaffrelot, Roland Marchal, and David Camroux for taking time off from their weekend to participate in our workshop. Institutional support was also received from the International Institute of Social History, Amsterdam, and the University of British Columbia, Vancouver.

As always, enormous amounts of semi-invisible, though hopefully not illicit, labor made the many iterations of this project far easier to manage and finally complete. We were fortunate to have a series of dedicated, smart, and hard-working project assistants who included, over the years, Mathew King, Christina Harris, Munmeeth Soni, and Maggie Schuppert. Veronica Raffo, program coordinator at the SSRC, was indispensable in keeping this project on track and for not losing sight of all the thousands of details that go into getting a manuscript to press. Indiana University Press, represented by Rebecca Tolen, and Robert Foster, who heads up the Tracking Globalization series, were very supportive of our initial queries and have made the process of publication relatively painless. Our thanks to them all, and to all those who may be reading this.

ILLICIT FLOWS

AND CRIMINAL THINGS

Introduction

The Making of Illicitness

Itty Abraham and Willem van Schendel

Around the world, the mass media have turned talk of transnational crime into a major cottage industry. You only have to take a cursory look at the World Wide Web to find news stories of transnational crime in many forms. Endangered animals and exotic birds are smuggled to collectors overseas from the Pramuka pet market in Jakarta and Moscow's Bird Market. Banned ozone-depleting chemicals are transshipped between India, Nepal, and Bangladesh. Snakeheads in China are accused of smuggling thousands of migrants into the United States for fees of up to US$20,000 per person. The fall of the Taliban regime is linked to a startling increase in the flow of opium and heroin from Afghanistan to Russia and around the world. The meat of humpback whales, a species that has been protected since 1966, is reported to be freely available in a Hiroshima fish market. A nuclear black market connects countries as diverse as Pakistan, North Korea, Iran, and Libya. And perhaps most alarming of all, innumerable stories of sexual trafficking and slavery: Moldavian women to Germany, Nigerian children to England, Nepalis to India, Latin Americans to North America, Burmese to Thailand, Thais to Germany, and Filipinas to Japan.[1] The horror is multiplied when some of these illegal practices merge, as when illegally trapped animal pelts are filled with cocaine, or when illegal migrants are "mined" for their organs.[2]

Adding to the newsworthiness of these stories is the apparently enormous financial scale of transnational illicit activities. The United Nations Conference on Global Organized Crime (1994) estimated the value of the world's trade in illegal drugs alone at US$500 billion annually. Manuel Castells feels that number should be doubled.[3] The annual illicit trade in small arms has been estimated to be worth US$2–3 billion, or roughly 20 percent of the total world trade in small arms.[4] In the closing years of the twentieth century, estimates of the world's "gross criminal product" often passed the US$1 trillion mark.[5] These numbers, for drugs in particular, are the subject of considerable contestation. As R. T. Naylor, an economist who is the author of a number of books about the financial underworld, puts it, the only way that the drug "business" could be that valuable is if it included "the value of every donkey owned by every *campesino* in the Andes but priced . . . as if they cost as much as pickup trucks." He writes that a senior official of the United Nations admitted to him that these numbers are less than accurate but "were great for catching public attention."[6] Naylor does not offer an alternative figure, but his evidence strongly suggests that the scale of the illicit underworld, apart from being obviously difficult to estimate, is deliberately exaggerated to serve parochial institutional interests.

The subtext of these stories, taken together, is that there is a specter haunting globalization—the specter of international organized crime networks, coterminous with underworld mafias, snakeheads, coyotes, traffickers, and other transnational jetsam. Groups and individuals trafficking in illicit objects and substances—again, to borrow from Marx, "the dangerous class, the social scum, that passively rotting mass thrown off by the lowest layers of old society"[7]—have, we are told, taken advantage of the unprecedented ease of communication and movement offered by the new social and technical infrastructures that gird the world today to create an alternative, only partly visible, global system that exists in parallel to legitimate international transactions of corporations, individuals, and states. The dangers of this parallel system include threats to the moral, social, and natural economies of the world. The best efforts of police and border guards, domestic laws, and international conventions notwithstanding, the scale of this traffic grows daily as the sophistication of these traffickers increases apace. As Moisés Naím puts it in a recent issue of *Foreign Policy,*

> In one form or another, governments have been fighting [the illegal trade in drugs, arms, intellectual property, money, and people] for centuries. And losing. Indeed, thanks to the changes spurred by globalization over the last

decade, their losing streak has become even more pronounced. To be sure, nation-states have benefited from the information revolution, stronger political and economic linkages, and the shrinking importance of geographic distance. Unfortunately, criminal networks have benefited even more. Never fettered by the niceties of sovereignty, they are now increasingly free of geographic constraints. Moreover, globalization has not only expanded illegal markets and boosted the size and the resources of criminal networks, it has also imposed more burdens on governments: Tighter public budgets, decentralization, privatization, deregulation, and a more open environment for international trade and investment all make the task of fighting global criminals more difficult. Governments are made up of cumbersome bureaucracies that generally cooperate with difficulty, but drug traffickers, arms dealers, alien smugglers, counterfeiters, and money launderers have refined networking to a high science, entering into complex and improbable strategic alliances that span cultures and continents.[8]

Taking this further, Manuel Castells argues for the symmetry of the criminal network and the strategic business model:

> [I]nternationalization of criminal activities induces organized crime from different countries to establish strategic alliances to cooperate, rather than fight, on each other's turf, through subcontracting arrangements, and joint ventures, whose business practice closely follows the organizational logic of what I identified as "the network enterprise," characteristic of the Information Age. . . . Furthermore, the bulk of the proceedings of these activities are by definition globalized through their laundering via global financial markets.[9]

Other startling images may also be used to indicate the virulence of the problem. In an article that identifies a "greenhouse effect" in weak and transitional states that allow criminal networks to grow unhindered, Phil Williams proposes that "organized crime-corruption networks can be understood as the HIV virus of the modern state, circumventing and breaking down the natural defenses of the modern state."[10] In the present context, this kind of analysis slides easily into a description of international terrorism, a latent threat always present under the surface, equally able to mobilize the latest in technology, highly sophisticated in countering state surveillance, and, due to its very nature, impossible to stamp out or completely eliminate. And when IRA bomb-makers were discovered in cocaine-rich Colombia, the feared intersection of political terrorism and international crime indeed appeared to have come to pass.[11]

The intersection of the power of globalization with the threat of international crime appears to confirm the darkest fears of policy makers, law enforcement officials, and average citizens of industrialized countries. When globalization is taken to mean the dismantling of barriers of protection around nations and states, when it promotes, or at least fails to prevent, the free flow of disease and other threats to human security, when it appears to be the cause for the visible public presence of strangers of different races, a nationalist backlash is common and inevitable. The "End of the Cold War" becomes the temporal rallying cry marking the beginning of a new, intensified, and more dangerous phase of global transactions. To many policy makers, such deadly understandings of the contemporary world leave only one option: to develop more intrusive, authoritarian, and muscular forms of law enforcement which at their limit become forms of pre-emptive international violence. Thankfully, the alarmist interpretation is flawed.[12]

By contrast, the position taken in this volume is that we need a radically different way of conceptualizing "illegal" transnational linkages, especially if we are to understand the persistence of these flows over time and space. The dominant imagery of nation-states fighting valiantly against global criminal networks is far too simplistic and even misleading. We propose a more subtle approach to issues of legality and illegality which does not take the state as its point of departure. Instead, we build upon a distinction between what states consider to be legitimate ("legal") and what people involved in transnational networks consider to be legitimate ("licit"). Many transnational movements of people, commodities, and ideas are illegal because they defy the norms and rules of formal political authority, but they are quite acceptable, "licit," in the eyes of participants in these transactions and flows.

We argue there is a qualitative difference of scale and intent between the activities of internationally organized criminal gangs or networks and the scores of micro-practices that, while often illegal in a formal sense, are not driven by a structural logic of organization and unified purpose. While we do not seek to establish that scalar threshold, the analysis in this volume makes clear that the "armpit smugglers" or "ant traders" who cross borders all over the world with small quantities of goods may together account for huge quantities of contraband, but they do not represent global syndicates of organized crime.[13] For analytic, methodological, and policy reasons, it is necessary to rethink the core concepts currently used in analyzing transnational linkages, especially those linkages of which states do not approve.

In the absence of a global sovereign authority, it is impossible to distinguish, in an objective and timeless way, between the illegal and the legal for "criminal" flows that cross international borders. What passes for "international crime" is so closely intertwined with the domestic-legal that for analytic purposes the "criminal" and "not-criminal" systems form a coherent whole, at times legal, at times illegal. We have a vivid recent example of this intertwined legal/illegal world in the story of Dr. A. Q. Khan, the Pakistani metallurgist who was responsible for mastering the technology to enrich uranium and who then sold this technology and a bomb design to Libya. What is worth noting here is that first, Pakistan has not signed the Nuclear Non-Proliferation Treaty (NPT), which forbids the sale of international nuclear materials without safeguards and other technical precautions. This made the sale at least quasi-legal from the Pakistani point of view (Libya has signed the NPT). Second, when Khan described his activities, he noted that "the Western world never talked about their own hectic and persistent efforts to sell everything to us . . . they literally begged us to buy their equipment."[14] Determining thresholds of distinction—boundaries—between the legal and illegal will always come, in other words, by appeal either to powerful state interests or international social mores rather than by an ability to "know" in some objective fashion where the dividing line between the two lies.[15]

The contemporary social sciences are ill equipped to make sense of transnational flows due to their symbiotic history with the modern state and its interests. Most social science is expressly and unconsciously bound by state boundaries, categories that are reproduced within institutionally sanctioned academic specializations, e.g., Brazilian political science or the sociology of France. Hence, it is no surprise that the field of knowledge that seeks to understand the world beyond the state, international relations, nonetheless takes the state as its foundational unit of analysis. By highlighting the importance of movement across state boundaries in understanding transnational flows, we are alerted to the gap between our reliance on analytic categories that presuppose social fixity and the mobile practices and phenomena we are observing. For example, with new attention being paid to well-established and socially trusted forms of transnational financial exchange, the impression is sometimes given that these state-bypassing modes of exchange (known as *hawala* in South Asia) emerged solely in order to serve the interests of terrorists "with a global reach." This is far from being the case. The patterns of movement, trade, and exchange that characterize illicit traffic are often long-standing, built on ethnic and kin networks that have been in existence for centuries. For example, the *dhows* that ply the coasts between the Persian Gulf and Gujarat in India are described in Portuguese chronicles of the fifteenth century. The goods they carry may have changed, but often not by much. Traders, scholars, and religious figures from the Hadramut region of Yemen—the origin of Osama bin Laden's family—have been traveling to Southeast Asia for centuries, predating considerably the recent spread of Wahhabi ideology to Indonesia.[16] The contributions to this volume, in different ways, alert us to the limits of "seeing like a state"; adopting analytic perspectives that privilege the participants in international illicit activities leads us to very different accounts and understandings of the causes, meanings, and processes involved in the criminal life of things.

Putting this all together leads to several analytic imperatives. First is the need to rescale our visions of so-called "international crime," both spatially and temporally. Sometimes we need to scale down from the level of the nation-state (as Kyle and Siracusa do in their chapter in this volume), sometimes we need to scale up (see Smillie's chapter), and sometimes we need to scale across (see the chapters by Rivera, Wong, and Simala and Amutabi). In terms of temporality, we need to see the present as a temporary saddle point in multiple histories of efforts at regulation and authoritative control (see the chapters by van Schendel, Gootenberg, and Rivera). Without these shifts in scale we are unable to comprehend either the motivations of those participating in "illegal" activities or the systemic frame within which "international crime" takes place. The net result of differences in scale and intent, the intertwined legal and illegal, and the difficulty of studying the mobile is to propose that many of the phenomena that fall under the label of "international criminal activities" are produced by immanent contradictions of national legal, economic, social, and political forces working across international borders.

In this volume, we do not try to establish the threshold between organized crime and unorganized crime, but rather argue that "international crime" has become a residual category to mark all the practices that forces of authority do not know how to fully comprehend, identify, or stop, regardless of whether or not they are really "criminal." We argue that "international crime" appears so rampant and dangerous because of the ways in which authoritative speech and certain images and analogies are deployed to create a discourse within which the ubiquity and prevalence of international crime and criminals are taken for granted. This is notwithstanding the many contradictions of process, scale, culture, history, language, and order that contributions to this volume point to.

We begin by clarifying our methodological assumptions and elaborating our core concepts. A consideration of definitional problems associated with international crime shows how important it is to relativize the state as "just" another form of modern political authority so as to avoid using the state's own dominant categories for our analysis. We then turn to the problems of understanding movement in the social sciences and the imbrication of state practices and interests with social immobility. Finally, we outline a simple model to explore the different spatial implications that emerge when we overlay the binaries licit/illicit and legal/illegal, particularly as they allow us to distinguish between the redolently criminal sites of the "borderland" and the "underworld."

Beyond Official Discourses

Students of illicit practices need to begin by discarding the assumption that there is a clear line between illicitness and the laws of states. Of course, official rules, structures, and discourse do posit a sharp distinction between law and crime, but it is essential to understand that this claim is only one element in the nexus of practices bridging the licit/illicit divide. As Josiah Heyman and Alan Smart write in the introduction to an influential book on states and illegal practices: "Open-minded, empirical studies of state-illegality relations enable us to transcend the stultifying assumption that states always uphold the law."[17] Both law and crime emerge from historical and ongoing struggles over legitimacy, in the course of which powerful groups succeed in delegitimizing and criminalizing certain practices.[18] But their success always falls short of either winning full popular consent or fully suppressing criminalized practices. As a result, licit and illicit practices coexist in social life and are together imbricated in state processes.[19] Students of illicitness must start from the assumptions that states cannot simply be equated with law and order, and that illicit practices are necessarily part of any state.

This is true of both predatory behavior and commercial activities. The state's claim to a monopoly of regulated predation and redistribution of proceeds (i.e., taxation and state expenditure) is based on the delegitimization of other forms of predation that are constructed as robbery, piracy, fraud, warlordism, or racketeering. But historically the boundary of illicitness has shifted back and forth as bandits helped make states and states made bandits:

> Military entrepreneurs operating on both sides of the law significantly contributed to the formation of states in the modern world. . . . In situations where a central government, imperial or otherwise, was unable to impose a monopoly of violence over the means of coercion, there was a propensity for a class of men at arms whom I have called military entrepreneurs to develop. The same absence of mechanisms of control that was conducive to their appearance compelled states and social elites to employ military entrepreneurs as the legitimate security forces. This created a situation where

essentially the same groups of men were both the bandits and the police, or, in the case of pirates both the buccaneers and the navy. In-law or outlaw status was determined by the nature of the relationship of a group to the state at any specific point in time.[20]

Contemporary examples of this mechanism abound. Take an anti-outlaw campaign in Bangladesh which was directed against armed men whom the state branded as "terrorists" and who were protected by regional power holders opposed to the ruling party: "Where the presence of the ruling party is thin . . . outlaws who indicated willingness to join and work for the party were allowed to surrender [and were given jobs in the state paramilitary forces]. . . . The government . . . may be working on the strategy for next elections, where these terrorists will have a role to play."[21] For these men, legitimacy was easy to acquire, after which they continued their predatory activities by legal means and with state protection. There are, of course, many forms of state predation—or coercive appropriation of wealth by state personnel—that do not follow legal bureaucratic procedures. Such forms are known as bribery, embezzlement, extortion, and so on, and they are often bracketed under the master term "corruption." This term is problematic because it assumes a universally shared definition of licitness from which corrupt behavior deviates. But on the one hand, notions of licitness are contested within states and, on the other hand, normative codes of conduct that outsiders may consider illicit may be shared by individuals inside and outside a state system. In such situations there is

very little serious censure of corruption as long as its fruits are deemed to have been suitably and vigorously redistributed according to the logic of patronage. Condemnation is reserved for those individuals or groups (like some military cliques) who are seen to appropriate "public" resources purely out of greed and with little regard for those who would count on benefiting from such graft.[22]

What goes for predatory behavior also applies to commercial activities in which states are involved. Clearly, the two are often connected. It is not only that historically "illegal networks of armed predators played a crucial role in the spread and global triumph of capitalism," but that these networks were, and continue to be, connected to states and markets in a variety of ways.[23] As a result, state definitions of what is illicit are situational. States themselves often find it hard to pinpoint the exact cutoff point between licit and illicit state trade. They may agree that a transfer of goods is illicit if it breaks either national or international laws. But what about transfers that do not violate international embargoes but do violate international humanitarian or human rights laws? What about trade that is authorized by the receiving country but not by the sending country, or vice versa? The 2001 United Nations Small Arms Conference was unable to resolve these questions and failed to define illicit small-arms trade unambiguously. Analysts of international small-arms flows now use the distinction between legal transfers, illicit "gray-market" transfers, and illegal "black-market" transfers. Clearly, many states routinely engage in illicit trade: in 2001, at least fifty-four states were linked to shipments of small arms that were illicit because they violated international small arms embargoes. One well-publicized case was when President Carlos Menem of Argentina authorized the state arms factory, Fabricaciones Militares, to sell arms to the tune of US$100 million to Panama and Venezuela from 1991 through 1995. In reality, these arms went to Croatia (then under a UN arms embargo) and Ecuador (then fighting a border war with Peru in which Argentina was a guarantor of the peace process).[24]

It is for these reasons that studies of the production of illicitness must look beyond discourses that equate state organizations with law, order, and bureaucratic probity. Such discourses are easily recognized by their viewpoint that global order and development are advanced primarily by states and by international associations approved by states. Outside this circle, they suggest, there is only narrow self-interest which is destructive of wider social interests, and states are entitled to outlaw such activities. The result is good guys/bad guys imagery and the language of law enforcement. Many key words are reserved for the bad guys and their organizations—syndicates, cartels, gangs, triads, secret societies, mafias, guerrilla outfits, terrorist networks—and they all denote their special and separate status of being unauthorized, clandestine, underground. Such language constructs conceptual barriers between illicit bad-guy activities (trafficking, smuggling) and state-authorized good-guy activities (trade, migration) that obscure how these are often part of a single spectrum. We need to approach flows of goods and people as visible manifestations of power configurations that weave in and out of legality, in and out of states, and in and out of individuals' lives, as socially embedded, sometimes long-term processes of production, exchange, consumption, and representation.

State Effects: Borders and Social Movement

By any standard of reckoning, we can agree that these activities need to be better understood, jointly and severally. Understanding of the nature, pattern, scale, forms, and meanings of illegal transnational activities remains far from adequate. There are a variety of reasons for this, not the least of which is the difficulty of conducting research on individuals and groups who pay a premium, in cash and violence, to keep their affairs from coming to public attention.[25] There is also the problem of compartmentalization, as specialists in small arms and drugs rarely communicate, and scholars of smuggling, trafficking, and money laundering have no common forum to share their insights, all preventing a comprehensive landscape of the scale of illegal activities from being visualized.[26] The association of illegal activities with national security concerns in some cases makes a critical public discussion difficult because it touches on another shadowy world of (il)legality and official secrecy: that of the world's intelligence communities. In such cases, evidence may be kept classified because of the means by which this evidence was collected. Furthermore, some of the data produced by states, including that used in legal cases, may have been obtained by force and coercion, raising ethical questions for social science researchers.

But there is a far more fundamental reason why scholarly understanding of illicit transnational activities remains inadequate. This is a problem endemic to the social sciences, i.e., the difficulty of thinking outside the conceptual and material grasp of the modern state. One reason for these blinders is the historically close association of the social sciences with the needs and discourses of states. As is well known, for example, the field of statistics developed with the need of modern states to enumerate, categorize, and tabulate its resources, including the peoples who lived within the territories it claimed. As Alain Desrosières puts it, "the need to know a nation in order to govern it led to the organization of official bureaus of statistics, developed from the very different languages of English *political arithmetic* and German *Statistik.*"[27] The map and the census, while not historically novel techniques of data collection and representation, acquired their current forms only when drawn into alliance with the modern state and for its particular needs, especially in the colony.[28] The same goes for whole fields of knowledge production. Two fields that touch directly on the questions we have posed here, international relations and strategic studies, directly acknowledge the modern state as their *raison d'être.* Furthermore, neither structural realist studies of international relations (with their ahistorical and uncontextualized approaches to interstate relations) nor strategic studies (preoccupied with building the intellectual edifice for theories of interstate conflict) can escape the mark of having being developed in the most dominant country of their time.[29]

The weight of the state on social science takes many forms, including the historical, institutional, and definitional. What we are particularly concerned with here is the question of movement across state borders and how movement is considered in the social sciences. This as we shall see is in turn linked to the relation of states to territory, borders, and frontiers,[30] further complicating this picture. As David Ludden puts it, "Modernity consigned human mobility to the dusty dark corners of archives that document the hegemonic space of national territorialism. As a result, we imagine that mobility is border crossing, as though borders came first and mobility second."[31] In general, we would argue, movement is difficult for the social sciences to fully understand, for reasons of both evidence and conception. The evidence question has to do with the comparative weights of the archives of the sedentary and the archives of movement.[32] Where human societies have settled and lived over long periods of time, they create indelible material traces of their presence, from buildings and ecological transformations to written texts and visual images. These traces form the basis of historical and social science evidence in later years. From the days of Ibn Khaldūn, social scientists have commented on the state's urge to sedentarize mobile populations in order to tax, discipline, and count them.[33] "Combining creative powers and reconciling conflicts at intersections of mobility and territorialism preoccupy elites who produce most historical records. . . . After 1000 C.E. the force of mobility steadily increased, along with territorial conflict that provoked more mobility and made the fixing of boundaries increasingly imperative, pervasive and impossible."[34] Because of their mobility, nomadic and pastoral communities tend to leave behind little more than light traces of their passing. This relative lack of familiar and detailed evidence of presence complicates the task of social scientists and historians. But our understanding of the contemporary relation of fixity to mobility might also be quite mistaken, especially for the pre-colonial period. In Africa, as Achille Mbembe points out, "political entities were not delimited by boundaries in the classical sense of the term, but rather by an imbrication of multiple spaces constantly joined, disjoined, and recombined through wars, conquests, and the mobility of goods and persons. . . . It might be said that operating by thrusts, detachments and scissions, precolonial territoriality was an itinerant territoriality."[35]

As far as conception is concerned, moving people are typically categorized in relation to fixed social formations. The fact that mobile people are less visible to social scientists guarantees that they often appear in social theory as obscure, fleeting figures, as peripheral social actors with a lowly status in the world order, and as faceless outsiders who fit imperfectly into neat representations of social reality.[36] In general, mobile groups are of interest primarily as they move between the units that count. As such, they are often taken to be deviant, dangerous, and out of control. The classic example of the stigmatized moving group well into the present is of course the Roma, or gypsies.

The point about the pressures of staying put can be made both directly and indirectly. The great fascination in pre-modern Europe[37] with tales of intrepid travelers and explorers who face great odds and tell of bizarre encounters reinforces the point that to travel is to mark oneself off from dominant social mores and the reliable and respectable limits of place. By the very strangeness of their tales, we are reminded of how rare and dangerous journeys are. To travel was, in other words, to open oneself up to great challenges and tribulations. Only a rare few would survive them. Narratively, dangerous journeys are made safe by their structure; they are always bracketed by their domestic reception, invoking a static population waiting eagerly for stories of places and people beyond the pale.[38] It can further be argued that travel and exploration narratives of the "unknown" mark the temporal moment between the security and comfort of home and the making of modern European empires. This is evident when we consider retrospective accounts of the archetypical journeys of "heroes" like Columbus, Vasco da Gama, Pizarro, Clive, Dupleix, Raffles, Livingstone, or Lewis and Clark, journeys that for the most part are prefigured by precisely the tall tales that reinforce the symbolic and literal distance of the traveler from the point of departure.[39]

In a more direct vein, scholars of international migration have long struggled with trying to understand why people move.[40] Migration theorists begin by positing two kinds of movement, forced and voluntary, a distinction that centers on the individual and her degree of choice and helps us understand the prevalence of economic rationales underlying theories of migration. Under the varieties of forced migration, the first distinction made is between forced migration across national boundaries, the movement of refugees, and forced migration within the territory of states, the movement of internally displaced peoples. The difference between the two categories relies on the assumption of a fixed international border. Crossing international borders is materially consequential: under current international dispensation, once defined as refugees, individuals and groups may acquire access to entitlements from the international community via the offices of the UN High Commissioner For Refugees. This institution, it might be noted, is one of the few significant carryovers from the League of Nations to the present international system, a thread that ties together the anxieties of state sovereignty over two distinct periods.[41]

In noting the lack of attention paid to the state and its policies in migration theories, Aristide Zolberg criticizes social scientists for "focusing on the incoming streams [of people]" and paying "little or no attention to the fact that the streams were flowing through gates, and that these openings were surrounded by high walls." Zolberg goes on to add, *"international* migration is an inherently *political* process, which arises from the organization of the world into a congeries of mutually exclusive sovereign states, commonly referred to as the 'Westphalian system.'"[42] Zolberg's insight reinforces the taken-for-granted quality of the state in social science thinking, even where the presence or absence of the state is the fundamental condition producing distinct categories of moving people. By not considering the state and its policies directly, migration scholars can find themselves doing the work of the state, leading to an unexamined presumption that unregulated international migration is a threat to national security. Since most research on international migration focuses on south-to-north migration, it is sometimes assumed that this is the most significant form of international movement. In fact, there is greater movement of people between the countries of the South;[43] for example, the number of Bangladeshis and Nepalis entering India annually is larger than the number of Mexicans entering the United States, and the number of Yemenis entering Saudi Arabia is greater than the number of North Africans migrating to France.

Dividing the world up into two kinds of people, those who move and those who do not, is a presumption that seems hardly obvious. More effective, in our view, is to begin from the assumption that movement is an inherent quality of social bodies. Movement by itself, in other words, should not be seen as a primary marker of social distinction but needs to be relocated within an ensemble of social practices which are mobilized at different times for different reasons. The analytic demands of the study of motility thus change substantially, moving away from questions of "why move" to *how* movement takes place and what meaning is attributed to movement, especially by those who are moving.

Movement is never abstract. It always takes place somewhere; in the present world, it takes place on territory claimed by a state. Territorial control is intrinsically linked to the other normative characteristics of the modern state—its claim to a monopoly of legitimate violence and its sovereign ability to establish the law. The scope of the law and the boundaries of legitimate violence are "contained" by the territory the state lays claim to. Without territory there is no modern state; a claim to statehood must begin from the political control of land. This foundational (for the state) character of territory makes it difficult to distinguish as a separate and historically contingent aspect of political authority. As John Agnew and Stuart Corbridge point out, however, there are forms of political authority that do not rely on territorial claims, and the present-day identification of the state with a singular piece of territory is of relatively recent origin.[44] The centrality of territory to the identity and stateness of a state is most visible when there is a real or perceived loss of control over land, a factor which explains the persistence of territorial disputes even among those states that have largely eschewed violence in interstate affairs, like Japan, and even for strategically and economically worthless land like the 20,000-foot-high Saltoro Range/Siachen Glacier lying on the contested border between India and Pakistan.[45] Short of actual loss of land, the perceived loss of control over land is equally a matter of grave concern for state managers and is a perception that usually results in strong counteraction if state capacity allows it.

Loss of territory to another agent, however, may be relatively unusual in the life of the modern state, especially in the short run. Everyday state control over territory is most often expressed in the form of control over the people and goods that occupy, use, and cross over that space. Specialized and highly militarized gateways—border crossings—are created at sanctioned points of entry and exit from state territories in order to control movement. The primary activity of specialized state agencies of customs and immigration is distinguishing between the movement of permitted and disallowed goods and identifying legitimate and illegitimate, temporary and permanent residents of state territory. Hence, individuals and social groups that systematically contest or bypass state controls do not simply flout the letter of the law; with repeated transgressions over time, they bring into question the legitimacy of the state itself by questioning the state's ability to control its own territory. Of course, it is practically impossible for states to have that degree of control over people or territory even in highly regimented and technologically sophisticated city-states like Singapore. More typical states like Mexico or Bangladesh, from where large numbers of undocumented workers cross over into the United States and India respectively, are caught in a double bind. Unable to prevent this movement for reasons of sheer logistics and scale, they cannot acknowledge this condition for with every such admission comes a loss of stateness. Such a situation makes it impossible to disprove the allegation that illegal migration from Mexico/Bangladesh to the U.S./India is a matter of Mexican/Bangladeshi state *policy*.

The degree of anxiety that is expressed over the undocumented and illegal movement of people and goods across state boundaries is, in other words, also an expression of the particular political logic of modern states. With every advance of modern communication and information technologies, it becomes clearer that the modern state is ill equipped to fill the role that political theory has thrust upon it. These anxieties can only increase with time. In the meantime, conventional social science, which has internalized the mores and norms of the modern state, and the state itself look upon moving people and commodities with considerable distrust and suspicion, adding to the difficulty of distinguishing between laws that have been violated in the course of social movement and the systematic replacement of one form of political authority with another.

Commodity Chains and Regulatory Spaces

At their most general, "transnational criminal activities" are *forms of social practice* that intersect two or more *regulatory spaces* and violate at least one normative or legal rule. Rules are defined directly in relation to particular practices, usually some combination of the consumption, production, exchange, or distribution of commodities. Commodities have life cycles and are subject to various social, economic, and technological conditions under capitalism. The life cycle of the commodity may be defined through a set of linked activities captured by the image of the commodity chain.[46] The traditional commodity chain approach does not, however, consider consumption, a vital omission in the case of the transnational illicit. While in general the movement of any capitalist commodity continues until the moment of exhaustion, in the case of illicit goods, movement/consumption might also mean crossing over a key regulatory threshold. The vector of consumption, the passage of commodities from one agent to another, is also often an act of *transformation* as well as an act of exchange. Illicit-licit transformations might include legalization, as in the conversion of illegal drugs into cash through money laundering, as well as setting into motion new chains of illegality, as in the use of proceeds from one illegal substance, e.g., stolen diamonds, to purchase another, small arms, which might be used in conflict zones bypassing international embargoes. In other words, consumption cannot be separated from exchange and transformation, and movement is an inherent quality of commodity chains. Each transformation brings with it new meanings, which might convert the illegal good into something quite legal, or vice versa, depending on the regulatory space it occupies or passes through.

Production, movement, and consumption are bounded by or take place within regulatory spaces. Regulatory spaces or regimes, zones within which particular sets of norms or rules are dominant, may be either generated by states or otherwise socially produced. Regulatory regimes organize routines, make and enforce rules, enable or constrain access to resources, set and maintain borders, identify and exclude actors. Regulation affects short-term movement through the imposition of taxes, quotas, licenses, quality controls, and labor rules. Long-term movement is hindered by blockades and other restrictive conditions and is aided by the provision of infrastructure and subsidies. Regulatory spaces are always contested and are bounded by variable thresholds of trust and violence. For the last two centuries at least, the most dominant form of regulation has been the modern state.[47]

The routine practices of production, exchange, consumption and distribution of objects across regulatory spaces are well demonstrated by a brief example of the life cycle of an "illegal" commodity. In particular, we seek to highlight how illegality is a form of meaning that is produced as an *outcome* of the effect of a criminalized object moving between political, cultural, social, and economic spaces. Illegality becomes a feature of this movement and hence a product of unstable and contingent political, moral, biomedical, or other prohibitory regimes. In other words, the first casualty of approaching the criminal object from the ground up is the fixity and singularity of "crime" itself.

Qat (kat) is a plant from northeast Africa whose leaves are consumed for their qualities of keeping users awake and active, as medicine, in religious ceremonies, and for relaxation and mental stimulation.[48] Lee Cassinelli shows how qat lies at the intersection of a complex interplay of social, medicinal, cultural, historic, transnational, and prohibitory economies, creating a commodity that far exceeds any simple classification as illegal or legal, that crosses national boundaries at will, and is constantly the focus of moral and prohibitory regimes. Users cross social boundaries and include workers, farmers, religious students and judges, long-distance truck drivers, animal hunters, night watchmen, clan elders, couriers, and women. "In 1978, it was estimated that $300 million worth of qat was consumed annually within Yemen." Following the movement of qat takes us across national and transnational circuits of exchange and in and out of legal and illegal economies. Qat is trucked, flown, shipped, and carried from highland Kenya and Ethiopia using regularly scheduled flights of national airlines, ferries, and land rovers to Somalia and Yemen where it is traded for cash, watches, tape recorders, transistors, and women's clothes. Starting in the 1920s, efforts were made to prohibit the use of the plant because of its apparent association with politically subversive activities, especially its use by anti-colonial Islamic teachers and consumption during public gatherings where Somali poetry was recited. The British colonial regime tried to reduce consumption by raising prices and reducing supply. Yet by the 1940s, chewing qat "had come to symbolize refusal to accept colonial authority" and the British were still trying to prevent its use, now targeting military personnel in Kenya. Forty years later, Somalia also banned the cultivation, trade, and consumption of qat, but now for radically different reasons. Now qat chewing was seen as an individualized hobby and form of entertainment, and it led to giving "priority to personal interest rather than the general public interest." This post-colonial ban, for practically the opposite reasons invoked by the British, also passed without much success. Cassinelli concludes, "Qat has always hovered on that indistinct boundary between legality and illegality, and its official status at any one moment is the product more of political and economic considerations than of strictly medicinal and public health considerations."[49]

As this example suggests, what passes under the name of criminal activity is always both more and less than "mere" crime. What determines legality and illegality at different points of the commodity chain is the particular regulatory scale the object finds itself in. Another way of saying this is to recognize the importance of identifying the *origin of regulatory authority*. Based on this criterion, we find it useful to distinguish between political (legal and illegal) and social (licit and illicit) origins of regulatory authority.

Illegal and Illicit

In the absence of a legitimate and sovereign legal authority at the global level, the law almost always refers to the national, domestic sphere. Indeed, as R. B. J. Walker points out, this can be turned around such that the presence of the law becomes one way of distinguishing the domestic from the "not-domestic" or outside.[50] International law does exist, of course, but its scope is limited to a narrow set of issue areas, and it is especially weak in relation to interstate behavior. Most often the lack of enforcement power prevents international law from having much effect. This situation is beginning to change with the coming into force of the International Criminal Court, the revival, after fifty years, of internationally sanctioned tribunals for crimes against humanity and war crimes, and the growing number of international conventions against trafficking narcotic drugs, the use of land mines, and so on. The applicability of these international treaties to domestic law and behavior depends, however, on the procedure of adherence to international norms in each country. Some countries (Germany and the

Netherlands, for example) adhere to the doctrine of incorporation, according to which international law is automatically part of domestic law without the need for constitutional or legal ratification. Other countries (notably the United States and the United Kingdom) follow the doctrine of transformation. This requires that international law must be expressly and specifically transformed into municipal law by use of the appropriate constitutional machinery before it can have any effect in domestic jurisprudence.[51] In the last instance, however, powerful countries can decide not to respond to adverse judgments of international law with little fear of sanction, as in the case of the 1986 International Court of Justice (ICJ) judgment against the mining of Nicaraguan harbors by the United States or the studied international silence to the landmark 1996 ICJ ruling on the conditions applying to the use or threat of use of nuclear weapons. At the global scale, in other words, because of inconsistent definitions of crime across different jurisdictions and the absence of a sovereign international authority, it may not always be possible to attribute a single category of "legal" or "illegal" to practices and flows that cross national boundaries.

When we shift our nomenclature to the distinction between "licit" and "illicit," we refer less to the letter of the law than to social perceptions of activities defined as criminal. To take the example of drugs again, there is a growing agreement that the moderate consumption of some narcotic drugs, marijuana in particular, is no more dangerous than the moderate consumption of liquor and cigarettes, which are legal; moreover, the private consumption of marijuana is extremely widespread around the world. States have responded to this common-sense perception by ignoring the consumption and sale of small quantities of marijuana, by decriminalizing possession, and in a few rare cases—notably the Netherlands—by making marijuana practically a legal commodity, even taxing it. Here is a practice that, though illegal in a formal sense, is not considered illicit by the population or indeed by the law enforcement community. Decriminalizing such practices involves linguistic innovation. For example, in Dutch the special nomenclature for illegal substances is gradually and consciously being abandoned. Terms equivalent to "narcotics," "hallucinogens," "drugs," or "stimulants" are replaced by the blanket term *genotmiddelen* (pleasure goods), which refers to any pleasure-inducing substance—tea, beer, tobacco, qat, heroin, glue, crack, ya-ba, coffee, or ecstasy—without specifying whether its consumption is (il)licit or (il)legal.[52]

The social value of illegal animal products for their cultural or medicinal qualities (e.g., rhinoceros horn as material for knife handles used in coming-of-age ceremonies in Yemen or the use of rhino horn, blood, penis, and skin in East Asian medicine) offer other examples of the practical distinction between the illegal and the illicit. The demand for these products, although they are banned under the Convention on International Trade in Endangered Species of Wild Fauna and Flora (CITES) since 1977, has led to the widespread poaching and destruction of rhino herds in Asia and Africa that continues to this day. Here the distinction between the illegal and the illicit revolves around opposed cultural meanings attributed to the item in question. While killing the dwindling number of wild rhinos for their horn, skin, and organs might seem reprehensible to African mores, clearly a different standard of value is applied in Yemen and East Asia. Without a universally held norm of social value, no equivalence or translation can be found between these two conceptions of appropriate practice. For these reasons, rather than hew to the impossible distinction between the international legal and illegal, we prefer to use (il)licit parenthetically, noting the difficulty of attributing universally accepted meaning to crimes across borders.

Clearly, the mere presence of the law does not by itself produce its effect. The law, like any intersocial category, is relational, culturally inflected, and acts asymmetrically along the contours of power and social mores. Legal restrictions often come up against socially sanctioned practices, and while this may have the effect of driving these practices into the sphere of formal criminality, it does not eliminate them nor does it necessarily force them into hiding. Likewise, the absence of the law does not imply that all is permissible. Prevailing social mores can work in the opposite direction as well, to sanction practices that are not legally prevented and indeed to cause the law to be adjusted in order to reflect dominant social values.

We are interested in identifying the political spaces emergent from the interaction of formal political authority and non-formal social authority. For heuristic convenience these may be displayed on a 2x2 matrix, leading to the following categories (see Table I.1). The table can be read as follows. When the licit/legal cell (A) is contrasted against the illegal/illicit cell (D), we see two idealized forms of social dis/order in opposition to each other. The first (A) is characterized by perfect symmetry between social rules, norms, and mores and by the public legal expression of these beliefs and values. Its counterpoint is (D), a space where nothing is legal or licit, a zone of complete anarchy and self-rule. One could perhaps see these as the diametrically opposed political spaces described in the work of social contract theorists. Hobbes and others would argue that human societies seek to move from cell D to cell A through popular support given to a state. Yet no matter how much we may all want to live in cell A and stay away from cell

Table I.1. Spaces of Competing Authorities

	Legal	Illegal
Licit	(A) Ideal State	(B) Underworld/Borderland
Illicit	(C) Crony Capitalism/ Failed State	(D) Anarchy

D, these two cells represent the least interesting analytic categories due to their wholly abstract and unrealistic character. The more interesting and complex categories emerge from the cells describing the meeting of the licit and the illegal (B) and the illicit and the legal (C). Both of these cells describe the (il)licit writ large as we have described it above; however, the effects and meaning of illicit varies considerably, as we will see. The spatial product of the interaction of these categories is drawn out when one of the forces is clearly dominant over the other in each cell.

Illicit and Legal Spaces:
Crony Capitalism and Failed States

When the power of public law is used to create spaces where illicit activities are welcomed (C), we describe the money laundering havens of the Cayman Islands, Bermuda, Jersey (in the Channel Islands), and other similar sites. The same characteristic describes the principle of the "flag of convenience," where Liberia and Panama in particular generate considerable revenues by allowing owners of seagoing vessels to legally register their ships under their marine flag with a guarantee of minimal regulation. When the island of Nauru in the Pacific is used to house Afghan refugees, or when the U.S. base in Guantanamo, Cuba, is used to jail "enemy combatants," the letter of the law may not be violated, but these are examples of a situation deeply repugnant to social mores.

This space can also describe the situation characteristic of U.S. capitalism in the late twentieth and early twenty-first centuries. This development in the U.S. is in turn the latest manifestation of what was called "crony capitalism" during Southeast Asia's short-lived miracle years. What made the recent Worldcom, Enron, Arthur Andersen, and Martha Stewart/ ImClone scandals more newsworthy than everyday behavior on Wall Street and Capitol Hill was undoubtedly that laws had been broken, publics had been defrauded, and regulators bamboozled. However, when we consider the frequency of examples of corporate behavior only marginally less shady but legal, it may not be inappropriate to speak, as Vijay Prashad does, of the emergence of the "Enron Stage of Capitalism."[53] To make the point of how normalized is the relationship between the state and capital, Prashad quotes Frederick Palmer of Peabody Energy, a member of U.S. vice president Cheney's energy task force, arguing that no laws were broken in the development of an energy policy that favors energy producers: "We're all on the supply side—the electric utilities, the coal companies—and the energy plan is basically a supply side plan . . . but that's not the result of backroom deals or lobbying . . . people running the United States government now are from the energy industry, and they understand it, and believe in increasing the energy supply . . . contribution money has nothing to do with it."[54]

While money may not have "nothing to do with it," the larger point is that no laws have been broken in this close alliance between one sector of the economy and the government, ensuring the profits of the former. Public outrage at this capture of the state by sectors of capital best expresses the difference between the socially illicit and the formally legal. This process of privatizing the benefits of social assets is described by economists as rent-seeking and is bracketed with corruption when performed on a small scale.

However, when the illicit dominates the legal thoroughly, and the power of the law and enforcement agencies is inadequate to prevent or contain illicit activities, we get a situation (in cell C) that is described by Vadim Volkov. "Under the conditions in Russia in the mid-1990s, where the boundaries between public and private violence became blurred, when the de facto capacity to enforce and thereby define justice gained priority over written laws, where protection and taxation were increasingly privatized, the very existence of the 'state' as a unified entity and of the public domain itself was called into question."[55] The idea of the failed state is a subject of ongoing public policy concern these days, with Sierra Leone usually standing in as a prime example of the phenomenon. As this idea developed from a purely abstract category representing the aberrant and rare inability of a state to meet its security and welfare goals into a descriptive category of the present, the use of this term became closely related to arguments for the withdrawal of the recognition of national sovereignty by the international community. In other words, the declaration of a "failed state" has become a pre-condition for intervention by the international community or by states that are most affected by the breakdown of security.[56]

Licit and Illegal Spaces: Underworlds and Borderlands

Of particular interest for us are the tensions emergent from the interplay of the illegal and the licit (cell B). Identifying the product of the illegal and the licit in spatial terms gives us two illicit spaces that occupy distinct if unstable identities: the underground and the borderland. Politically vibrant examples of when the state's definition of illegal dominates a community's idea of the socially licit include the ongoing and multiple contestations over the use of religious symbols in public schools in France, e.g., yarmulkes, headscarves, and large crosses, the production and consumption of pornography, and, in earlier times, the circulation of *samizdat* literature in Soviet Russia.[57] Under these conditions, we suggest that a "third space"[58] becomes the site for activities that can only be called (il)licit: legally banned but socially sanctioned and protected. These third spaces might certainly include the home but also inhabit a variety of semi-private settings like social clubs, video parlors, coffee houses, bath houses, brothels, gambling dens, and, in the present, virtual spaces such as Internet chat rooms and e-mail lists. Igor Kopytoff suggests that these are sites where commoditization precedes capitalism, places "in which the consumer, in order to purchase goods and services, must first purchase access to the transaction."[59] One may see these spaces but not know how to enter them. Hence, privileged information becomes a primary distributional resource to access this space, information that might be coded in ethnic, political, religious, or class terms, producing what is often termed the "underground," sometimes but not necessarily dominated by "criminal" elements.[60]

Where the socially licit dominates the formally illegal, as for instance in the widespread availability of Indian-made film DVDs, video, and music tapes in Pakistani shops, the public spheres of commerce and media themselves become the site for a visible flouting of the letter of the law. But the everyday visibility of places with names like *Chor* (thieves) or *Kala* (black) Bazaar must be distinguished from overt political statements such as the display of a Basque flag in Spain or informal forms of dissent such as political graffiti. Participation in these illegal spheres is low-risk and widespread but involves a necessary act of volition. While the very visibility and routine character of illegal activities lends an air of normalcy to participation in them, they are never completely free of state presence and action. As a result, during moments of heightened public and civic mission, police drives might lead to illegal shops and businesses being closed down or whole areas closed to illegal traders and activities. Within a few days, or sometimes hours, and with the payment of a suitable official or unofficial fine, the black markets are back in business and life goes on as before.

For the state, everyday public violation of the boundaries of legality becomes particularly acute when we approach the political limits of the law or the geographic limits of the state.[61] If sovereignty must always imply space and control over it, as Henri Lefebvre argues, these limits are especially fraught for the modern state.[62] The absence of state order does not mean a state of disorder, as statist discourse would have us believe. The political and geographic limits of sovereignty imply the presence of competing authorities, whether other states or non-state ideological affiliations, and thereby constitute foundational crises of authority. When geography and politics coincide as described in Eric Hobsbawm's work on social banditry[63] or in the variety of political movements located on the borders between India, Bangladesh, China, and Myanmar, a full-fledged crisis might be said to exist. Such spaces formed by the intersection of multiple competing authorities are categorized as the "borderland."

For the state, the meanings of routine practices in the borderland are difficult to comprehend. Overtly political activities that threaten or question foundational precepts of the state need visibility to take public meaning, while practices that seek to use physical distance as a means of escaping state control (see Smillie's analysis of the Sierra Leone diamond business, this volume), need invisibility to succeed. This indeterminacy of vision makes the borderland only partly legible at best, producing great anxiety among state elites.[64] What cannot be seen must be imagined, and what can be seen might only be the tip of the iceberg. The state's astigmatic view of the borderland produces a paranoid field of view, reinforcing the ongoing process of securitization.[65]

The geophysical boundaries of the state bring other constraints. Neighboring states often hold different views on both the law and licitness. As a result, what is considered licit on one side of the border may be considered illegal on the other side, and this leads to much strategic mobility of goods and people. For example, cross-border shopping and cross-border gambling[66] are increasingly common as are sweatshops and brothels set up across borders to avoid labor regulations or the vice police.[67] This results in what Peter Andreas has called "border games," strategic interactions between border enforcers and unauthorized border crossers.[68] It is in such border games that contradictory definitions of (il)licitness come into sharp focus.

Definitions of what is illicit are also contradictory within each state. This can be seen clearly today as many states pursue the neo-liberal dream of a borderless economy and at the same time barricade their borders to keep out the specter of international organized crime networks, terrorist organizations, and individuals trafficking in illegal objects, substances, human beings, and ideas. The contradictions between state ideology and border praxis, between the border as a categorical divide and the border as an inter-active process, can be startling.[69] Here the state criminalizes certain forms of mobility but clashes with other state practices condoning or encouraging such border crossings. An example is the United States's spectacular sur-veillance of the Mexico border, ostensibly to throttle the supply of "illegal aliens," but without taking effective measures to dampen domestic demand for these immigrants (e.g., by penalizing employers of cheap "unauthor-ized" labor).[70] There are continual struggles, within and around the state, between political interests keen to infuse the economy with cheap labor and others concerned with showing the border to be a zone of interdiction and control. These lead to a compromise: border policing takes on features of a "ritualized spectator sport,"[71] demonstrating to a national audience the effectiveness of supply-side controls that are actually ineffectual.

> Never in history has there been a black market defeated from the supply side. From Prohibition to prostitution, from gambling to recreational drugs, the story is the same. Supply-side controls act, much like price supports in agriculture, to encourage production and increase profits. At best a few intermediaries get knocked out of business. But as long as demand persists, the market is served more or less as before. In the meantime, failure to "win the war" becomes a pretext for increasing police budgets, expanding law enforcement powers, and pouring more money into the voracious maw of the prison-industrial complex.[72]

Not surprisingly, concepts of illicitness are fluid, also throwing up con-tradictions over time. In borderland studies, this is sometimes analyzed in terms of a succession of regulatory practices, employed to initiate and control mobility and interconnections, in which states are important actors but non-state actors are also active participants and beneficiaries. Andrew Walker's exploration of successive regulatory regimes in the Thailand-Laos borderland since the early nineteenth century shows that the state has never been able to monopolize regulatory practice and that the licitness of so-cial and commodity movement is continually being renegotiated. Such historical awareness is very important in order to counter some contempo-rary claims. For example, in the case of Laos, a short period of restricted border trade (leading to increased "criminality") in the 1970s and 1980s has become to many "a powerful and timeless motif of longstanding Lao isolation." By contrast, Walker describes this brief period of criminalization of cross-border movement as "something of an anomaly in Lao history." In fact, he argues, the decriminalization of cross-border connections that followed the adoption of the Upper-Mekong Economic Quadrangle in the

1990s was less a break with the past than a re-establishment of older practices of licit cross-border mobility.[73]

Persons involved in moving objects, people, and practices across state borders may or may not share the state's categorization of their activities as criminal. If they consider their activities licit, they present us with yet another contradiction in defining (il)licitness. Borderland studies have shown how important it is to juxtapose state and non-state notions of (il)licitness if we are to understand how cross-border linkages are maintained, manipulated, and developed. Those who appear in official parlance as smugglers, criminals, traffickers, mafiosi, or illegal aliens may hold radically different views of themselves. This was the case with Buddhist monks from southern Bangladesh who, on their way back from a visit to disciples in Burma, were arrested by Bangladeshi border guards. The guards confiscated the bronze Buddha statues and Burmese money the monks were carrying. The monks protested that these were donations from their followers in Burma, but the local magistrate rejected their claim to licitness and jailed them for smuggling.[74] In other words, border games are predicated not merely on strategic interactions between border enforcers and border crossers but also on genuinely different understandings of licitness. What state officials view as illegal and therefore criminal behavior may be considered well within the bounds of the acceptable by those who display this behavior and by the communities to which they belong. We have tried to suggest that the borderland is a site of extreme anxiety for the modern state. The state's partially obscured view of borderland activities, the gap between people's understandings of what they are doing versus the state's, inconsistent notions of illegality, and the presence of other legalities across the border, all make, for the state, the borderland an area where by definition criminality is rife and sovereignty under constant threat.

Overview of the Volume

By pointing to the close relation between the interests of the modern state and the concepts used to understand social conditions, we seek to highlight the gaps and errors in our understanding of what is called "global crime" or "international criminal networks." In particular, this introduction has argued for (a) the need to rescale the frames within which we situate the events and processes we are studying, and (b) a heightened awareness of the limits of the concepts, language, and discourse used to "explain" transnational illegal flows.

The importance of dropping below the level of the nation-state is particularly evident in David Kyle and Christina Siracusa's analysis of Ecuadorian migrants to Spain. Kyle and Siracusa approach (il)licitness from the perspective of people committing a textbook case of a "victimless crime": labor migration. They ask why hundreds of thousands of otherwise non-criminals each year willingly choose to break immigration laws by contracting intermediaries—and whether they view their actions as criminal. Focusing on middle-class Ecuadorians seeking work in Spain, they show that these international migrants are well aware they break the law but that they reject the idea that this makes their venture illegal or illicit. Their argument is twofold. First, they have been let down by the Ecuadorian state elite, which they describe as a powerful mafia running a predatory state and squandering the entitlements of ordinary Ecuadorians. They feel abandoned by their country. They also point to the historical responsibility of Spain as the colonizer of Latin America. Centuries of exploitation entitle Latin Americans to forms of compensation, and getting work in Spain can be one such form. The Spanish state's refusal to countenance labor immigration is seen as hypocrisy: "when Columbus arrived in America no one asked him for papers"; moreover, "they conquered and raped us and nothing happened; today we conquer them and they get mad." This discourse of national and post-colonial citizenship is strengthened by a simultaneous discourse of justice stressing economic rights and sacrifice. Unauthorized migrants from Ecuador argue that, as world citizens, they have a right to subsistence, and if they cannot find it at home, they must go abroad. Far from being criminals, they are making important sacrifices. By emigrating, they place themselves in a vulnerable position and live "borrowed lives," but they are able to send money back home to help their relatives get by. Their remittances also are a sacrifice to Ecuador, because that state is deeply dependent on this source of income, and to Spain, because it is dependent on their labor. Finally, migrants sacrifice their own happiness to the improved life chances of their children. The importance of Kyle and Siracusa's contribution is that they reveal a crucial silence in legal and political scholars' debates about what is at stake when states attempt to control human mobility. State discourses of licitness are challenged by multiple coherent discourses of justice within sending and destination countries. Understanding these competing ways of moral reasoning is essential. As the example of Ecuadorian migration shows, "illegal" labor migrants have powerful legitimizing discourses that reject state definitions of criminal and illicit behavior.

Scaling "up" is vital to appreciate the systemic drivers and forces that are entailed in some illegal activities. Ian Smillie's article is methodologically as well as analytically important for its description and qualification of the multiple flows that go into an illegal transnational activity. By carefully analyzing the export and import figures of different African countries and Belgium, the world's largest market for uncut diamonds, Smillie is able to show first that the figures for diamonds leaving the African continent are quite different from the figures that Belgium shows entering, a discrepancy that points to the existence of a significant illegal trade in diamonds. Further, he points out that countries without diamond mines show substantial exports of diamonds, exports that temporally coincide with changing conditions in neighboring diamond-producing countries, strongly suggesting that diamonds are smuggled across porous borders to convenient havens when political conditions change. The absence of a reliable system of provenance allows legitimate diamond businesses to purchase illegally mined and smuggled diamonds without being liable for participation in an illegal activity. Or, in other words, the world diamond industry is made up of both illegal and legal elements, which coexist and are quite compatible with each other. A moment of sudden change comes when two Northern NGOs produce detailed reports showing how this opaque system works, give the illegal diamonds the media-friendly name "blood diamonds," and demonstrate that diamonds mined illegally in Sierra Leone are smuggled into Liberia (which doesn't have diamond mines), which openly exports them to Brussels, from which they travel across the globe. These are "blood" diamonds because the proceeds of the illegally mined diamonds are used to purchase weapons and other homicidal equipment to kill civilians. The outcry at these reports was also linked to the grisly practices of rebels in Sierra Leone, often young men and boys, who would horribly mutilate their victims. Smillie's terse analysis goes from the micro-practices of smuggling and purchase of single diamonds to the global scale of the South African company De Beers, which sought to combine a global monopsony of purchase with a monopoly on sales of uncut diamonds. The efforts of NGOs and friendly governments led to the Kimberley Process, an ongoing self-regulation of various actors in the world diamond industry, seeking to establish the authentic provenance of uncut diamonds, thereby creating separate categories of "conflict" and non-conflict diamonds. "Blood diamonds" mark the point where illegality and illicitness meet, where international outcries and pressures overcome the reluctance of an industry that has been built upon a regular traffic between the illicit and the illegal.

Borderlands lie across the nation-state scale, and in the following chapters we understand how different are these spaces and the limits of trying to understand them from the symbolic and material centers of power and territory. Silvia Rivera Cusicanqui explores the shifting definitions of licitness in the case of the trade and consumption of coca leaves. In the Andes region, coca consumption is an old cultural practice. Despite worldwide prohibition, this regional practice has been recognized as legal in various national laws and international conventions. But this has involved a misleading construction of coca as linked to subsistence, reciprocity, ritual, and tradition. Rivera shows how coca leaf has long been an important mercantile commodity whose production and circulation has contributed to the refashioning of social hierarchies, labor relations, and cultural connections in the Andean world. These transformations worked out differently over time and space, leading to remarkable variations in how coca was and is used and perceived. By looking at coca and its changing (il)licitness, a complex history of subaltern agency and recolonization can be reconstructed. Rivera brings these complexities to life in a rich "road ethnography." Crossing the international border between Bolivia and Argentina, she encounters contrasting national systems of dealing with coca, perceived links between coca, race and class, cross-border continuities, and negotiations over what constitutes (il)licit trade and who defines it. One remarkable finding is the emergence of coca leaf consumption in new social contexts. In Northern Argentina a modern, individualistic, and highly visible style of coca consumption had emerged among the professional middle class.

Kenneth Simala and Maurice Amutabi further develop the ways in which the licit and the legal crosscut in an African borderland, the Ilemi Triangle, lying across Kenya, Ethiopia, Uganda, and Sudan. They show how, in this ecologically fragile region, local systems of regulation based on pastoralism broke down under the impact of imperial border making, misdirected state development policies, and the emergence of military entrepreneurs. As large numbers of sophisticated small arms began to circulate in the region, cattle raiding, once a licit practice of socially controlled violence, became totally transformed. In the hands of cross-border groups of young combatants ranging from guerrilla fighters to poachers, these arms have upset the age-determined systems of regulation in which elders had dominated. With state forces almost completely ineffectual, the people of the Ilemi Triangle now reject state claims to their allegiance. Confronted with anomic violence, economic hardship, and displacement, they cling to cross-border cultural ties. The breakdown of the nation-state's legal authority is far advanced in this borderland where a bus passenger can offer a smuggled bullet as an acceptable fare.

Willem van Schendel's essay can be read as a substantial extension of the introduction, with special attention to developing the discussion of the borderland as a unique social space. In a wide-ranging comment on the current situation of border/state studies and its intersection with illegal flows, he argues that the present concern with the presumed deterritorialization of the state fails to fully comprehend the intersections and codependency of border practices with the state's political economy and national security. He begins with a critique of the fetish of arrows—a visual device that obscures more than it reveals—the threatening arrow gives the impression of grave dangers facing the heartland and helps produce the discourse of threat-from-abroad that has become a part of current understandings of globalization. By drawing attention to the metaphor of the flow, he shows how invisible fluid signs become crucial to the reinforcement of symbolic and material bulwarks against the outside, in particular the fixed and visible border. This discussion leads into analysis of the borderland, a space that is neither heartland nor periphery, a zone where illegal flows are naturalized and intersect with the licit, where the mechanism of movement is most visible. By focusing on the denizens of borderlands, van Schendel argues, it is possible to understand how borders produce new "politics of scale." He argues that three kinds of scales are most relevant: "scales we almost lost" or pre-border webs of relations, the state scale, which is most often being renegotiated or contested, and finally, border-induced scales, "cross-border webs of influence that spring up because of the border's existence." Borderland studies, he concludes, offer a way of understanding the complementary and mutual constitution of transnational flows, territorial states, and transborder arrangements; borderlands are, he argues, a vital and under-appreciated "pivot" between states and flows.

The importance of language and discourse in making "crime" is further developed in the chapters that follow. Diana Wong presents case studies of female cross-border migrants to Malaysia in order to deflate the rhetoric of human trafficking and its current deployment in the politics of migration control. She asserts that "the rhetorical production of the boundaries of the nation-state as sites of transgression—through the deployment of the trafficking discourse—rests . . . on an empirical fiction, and bears only partial resemblance to the actual contours of the economy of illicitness in contemporary mass migrations." Wong concentrates on a range of international migratory practices that are largely beyond the formal gaze of the state. Such practices are not only undocumented by states but also criminalized by them as morally and legally unacceptable. This is epitomized by a discourse of human trafficking that gained remarkable institutional support internationally after the fall of the Berlin Wall in 1989 and familiarized us with images of innocent victimhood and evil, shadowy traffickers. But this "master metaphor" for prostitution, illegal immigration, asylum seeking, and organized crime is a distortion because it ignores the agency of the migrant. Wong shows that the vast majority of international migrants in the undocumented, illegal economy of Malaysia are in active control of their own migration projects. Only where the nature of the work itself is illicit (e.g., sex work) is the agency of the migrant likely to be restricted. Reserving the term "trafficking" only for this much smaller group, Wong shows that it was employers rather than transnational organized crime groups that acted as traffickers, and that even trafficked women entered Malaysia legally and only acquired their illegal status in the country itself. These findings qualify easy assumptions about illegal migration as an imported crime of subversive border trespass by innocent victims coerced by organized crime. They also underline that what the state "does not see" belongs to the realm of the undocumented or illegal, but it is misleading to identify the illegal with the criminal.

Paul Gootenberg's contribution focuses on the intellectual dangers of uncritically adopting bureaucratic discourses on (il)licitness. He warns researchers against "talking like a state" because this envelops us in a fog of controlling words and faulty binary categories. Instead we need a language of analysis that goes "beyond the borders, and blinders, of authority." Taking drugs as his example, he shows the importance of constructing this language on the basis of a historical understanding of drugs as commodities that played a vanguard role in the creation of the modern world. In this process, the late nineteenth century stands out as a crucial moment. It was at that time that a new phase of defining illicitness commenced: certain tradable drugs became categorized as legitimate commodities and others were downgraded as illegal, dangerous pariah substances. States began to devise policies and ideologies that would culminate in a global crusade against (certain) drugs. Gootenberg takes us on a roller-coaster tour of the consequences in terms of interdiction of drugs across borders and the ways in which drugs, rather than undermining states, actually add to their capacities. He also presents a number of interpretations of the U.S. War on Drugs ("now entering its tenth decade")—from moral panics through unintended consequences to conspiracy and institutionalized collusion—and criticizes most for accepting the moral categorization of state talk. It is by revisiting how these categories of (il)licitness came about, and permutated, that we can begin to free ourselves from them.

This volume highlights the need for a reconsideration of a range of activities and processes that are now lumped together in the amorphous and politically charged term "global crime." By historicizing the rise of various forms of political order and seeing the modern state as a singular outcome of that process, and by identifying the social sciences and related knowledge conceptions as an element of the state-making project, we identify some of the limitations of conventional thinking on the subject of transnational criminal activity. The introduction and the chapters that follow point, in a variety of ways, to the imbrication of legal and illegal activities in many everyday cross-border phenomena, showing that assumed and natural-ized distinctions between the illegal and legal are often not sustainable in practice. Rather than seeking to impose new criteria for distinguishing these categories, one set of chapters and the introduction focus instead on unpacking "assumed and naturalized" distinctions, showing the extent to which such ideas uncritically rely upon state-derived conceptions of illegal and legal. By introducing the concept of social legitimacy or licitness and setting it against political legitimacy or legality, we seek to remind our readers of the politically derived nature of this distinction and its moral-in-stitutional foundations, helping to denaturalize Law as the common-sense condition of domestic national space. We demonstrate how the spatial im-plications of the binary terms legal/illicit and illegal/licit produce multiple kinds of "criminal space," and we draw attention to those spaces where legal activities that violate social norms flourish and where illegal but licit activities are commonplace. The latter arena gives us the borderland and the underground, which are conceptualized without recourse to politically loaded and analytically weak circular assumptions about the location of criminals and the meaning of crime. The value of this conceptual shift is highlighted in the chapters that tell the story of global crime from the point of view of its alleged perpetrators, showing how empirically unstable is the idea of the global criminal.

This said, it is important to recognize that this project does not seek to establish an abstract moral or other equivalence of the lawmaker and the lawbreaker nor to suggest that global criminal activities do not exist or are not consequential. What we are saying is that there is a qualitative threshold between the activities of global organized criminal groups and the scores of everyday forms of lawbreaking that are morally, politically, and economically of a wholly different order, as a number of chapters show in detail. Our concern is that analysts and policy makers are not trying hard enough—if they recognize the distinction at all—to appreciate the differences between the two levels of "crime," and as a result, thousands of "law-abiding criminals" are consigned to incarceration and worse across the globe. The relevance of these differences cannot be emphasized enough during the current phase of the "global war against terror," as it is termed in the United States, and its expression in new constraints on civil liberties that have passed into law in many countries during the past few years. In our view, the urgent need to control international terror networks associated with Osama bin Laden has led to an unwarranted expansion of the concept of the criminal, especially one who crosses international borders. In a number of countries, the sweeping provisions of anti-terrorism legislation have been used to control insurgencies, political rivals, and other non-criminal opponents who legitimately contest political power. In other countries, the wide-ranging provisions of these new laws are used to bypass reasonable due process and evidentiary conditions for establishing criminal guilt. State agents who try to control both international terrorism and global crime see these phenomena as closely related and startlingly similar in their processes and methods. But congruence of behavior does not imply identity of purpose. Understanding this distinction is essential in rethinking some of the characteristic features of the modern system of territorial political sovereignty, including the cartographic division of culturally linked communities, the criminalization of certain forms of social movement, and the emergence of non-state-dependent forms of cross-border identity. This volume seeks to make a contribution toward better understanding the social, cultural, and economic processes that follow from, and interact with, the historically particular development of the modern state system. It explores the making of illicitness—how states, borders, and language produce transnational illegal and criminal things, and how these in turn shape the modern state system.

NOTES

The authors would like to thank the other contributors to the volume, an anonymous reviewer, and especially John Agnew for their comments on earlier drafts of this chapter. Veronica Raffo read it over many times, always improving it in the process. Rebecca Tolen's comments were always insightful and helped make this chapter far more legible than it was.

1. For a valuable corrective on the nature of trafficking and its conflation with human smuggling, see Diana Wong, chapter 2, this volume, and Supang Chantavanich, "Recent Research on Human Trafficking in Mainland Southeast Asia," (review essay) *Kyoto Review*, Center for Southeast Asian Studies, Kyoto University (October 2003). http://kyotoreview.cseas.kyoto-u.ac.jp/issue/issue3/article_282.html.

2. For a recent filmic representation, see Stephen Frears (dir.), *Dirty Pretty Things*, 2002.

3. Manuel Castells, *The Information Age: Economy, Society and Culture*, vol. 3: *End of Millennium* (Oxford: Blackwell, 1998), 169.

4. Jeffrey Boutwell and Michael Klare, "A Scourge of Small Arms," *Scientific American* (June 2000): 48–53. For lower estimates around US$1 billion, see *Small Arms Survey 2001: Profiling the Problem* (Geneva: Graduate Institute of International Studies/Oxford: Oxford University Press, 2001), 166–168; and *Small Arms Survey 2002: Counting the Human Cost* (Geneva: Graduate Institute of International Studies/Oxford: Oxford University Press, 2002), 109.

5. Such estimates typically lack any methodological substantiation. According to Christian de Brie, "The annual profits from drug trafficking (cannabis, cocaine, heroin) are estimated at $300–500 billion (not to mention the rapidly mushrooming synthetic drugs), that is 8% to 10% of world trade. Computer piracy has a turnover in excess of $200 billion, counterfeit goods $100 billion, European Community budget fraud $10–15 billion, animal smuggling $20 billion, etc. In all, and counting only activities with a transnational dimension, including the white slave trade, the world's gross criminal product totals far above $1,000 billion a year, nearly 20% of world trade." Christian de Brie, "Thick as Thieves: Crime, the World's Biggest Free Enterprise," *Le Monde Diplomatique* (April 2000). http://mondediplo.com/2000/04/05debrie.

6. R. T. Naylor, *Wages of Crime: Black Markets, Illegal Finance, and the Underworld Economy* (Ithaca, N.Y.: Cornell University Press, 2002), x.

7. Karl Marx and Frederick Engels, *The Communist Manifesto* (London: Verso, [1848] 1998), 48.

8. "The Five Wars of Globalization," *Foreign Policy,* January–February 2003.

9. Castells, *End of Millennium,* 172.

10. Phil Williams, "Transnational Organized Crime and the State," in *The Emergence of Private Authority in Global Governance,* ed. R. B. Hall and T. J. Bierstecker (Cambridge: Cambridge University Press, 2003), 170, 165.

11. "Suspected IRA Trio Held in Colombia," *The Guardian,* August 14, 2001.

12. For an excellent parallel critique of the alleged dangers of globalization, focusing particularly on the work of security agencies, see Didier Bigo, "The Mobius Ribbon of Security(ies)," in *Identities, Borders, Orders: Rethinking International Relations Theory,* ed. Mathias Albert, David Jacobsen, and Yosef Lapid (Minneapolis: University of Minnesota Press, 2001).

13. The term "armpit smugglers" is used on the Ghana-Togo border. Paul Nugent, *Smugglers, Secessionists & Loyal Citizens on the Ghana-Togo Frontier: The Lie of the Borderlands since 1914* (Athens: Ohio University Press/Oxford: James Currey/Legon, Ghana: Sub-Saharan Publishers, 2002), 257. Rivera (this volume) refers to "ant" contraband on the Bolivia-Argentina border. Cf. *Small Arms Survey* (2002), 135.

14. Quoted in Peter Edidin, "Dr. Khan Got What He Wanted, and He Explains How," *New York Times* (Week in Review), Feb. 15, 2004, 7. Quotes in the article are taken from *Dr. A Q Khan Research Laboratories, 1976–2001: 25 Years of Excellence and National Service* (n.p., 2001).

15. We note a close correspondence between the arguments laid out in this volume and the research program of the group of scholars of international relations known as the "Las Cruces" group, with their emphasis on process tracing, relational analysis, and "verbing." The triad of "borders, orders and identities" is a remarkably productive schema through which to think many of the issues raised in this volume. Unfortunately, we were alerted to this important work too late to be able to engage directly with the arguments put forward by this group, though we are confident that our approach reinforces, and hopefully takes further, their theoretical and methodological critique of international relations. See Albert, Jacobsen, and Lapid, *Identities, Borders, Orders,* for a fuller statement of their views.

16. See Ulrike Freitag and William G. Clarence-Smith, eds., *Hadrami Traders, Scholars and Statesmen in the Indian Ocean, 1760s–1960s* (Leiden: Brill, 1997). The larger point is that we do not have a systematic and reliable way of distinguishing the "medium from the message."

17. Josiah McC. Heyman and Alan Smart, "States and Illegal Practices: An Over-

view," in *States and Illegal Practices*, ed. Josiah McC. Heyman (Oxford and New York: Berg, 1999), 1–24, at 1.

18. Charles Tilly, "War Making and State Making as Organized Crime," in *Bringing the State Back In*, ed. Peter Evans, Dietrich Rueschemeyer, and Theda Skocpol (Cambridge: Cambridge University Press, 1985), 169–191.

19. Alan Smart, "Predatory Rule and Illegal Economic Practices," in *States and Illegal Practices*, ed. Heyman, 99–128.

20. Thomas W. Gallant, "Brigandage, Piracy, Capitalism, and State-Formation: Transnational Crime from a Historical World-Systems Perspective," in *States and Illegal Practices*, ed. Heyman, 25–61, at 40.

21. "464 Former Outlaws to Be Recruited to Ansar Forces Today: 250 More Extremists to Surrender at Kushtia July 23," *The Independent*, July 18, 1999; cf. "'Terrorists' Now Have Legal Weapons and Legal Protection," *The New Nation*, July 19, 1999.

22. Patrick Chabal and Jean-Pascal Daloz, ed., *Africa Works: Disorder as Political Instrument* (Oxford: James Curry/Bloomington: Indiana University Press, 1999), 100.

23. Gallant, "Brigandage," 25. The ways in which privateering and *filibusterismo* cannot be separated from the overseas histories of Great Britain and the United States respectively drives this point home.

24. *Small Arms Survey* (2002): 110–111, 131–135, 148, 167. See also United Nations, Report of the Panel of Experts on the Violations of Security Council Sanctions against UNITA, S/2000/203, March 10, 2000.

25. The problems of doing such research should not, however, be exaggerated. Although we do not have a well-developed methodology for studying the interfaces between the legal/illegal and the licit/illicit, there are important new initiatives, notably the work of Carolyn Nordstrom. In a recent ethnography of war zones, Nordstrom convincingly pioneers a number of field approaches to what she defines as *shadows* (cross-state economic and political linkages that move outside formally recognized state-based channels). Carolyn Nordstrom, *Shadows of War: Violence, Power, and International Profiteering in the Twenty-First Century* (Berkeley and Los Angeles: University of California Press, 2004).

26. The journal *Global Crime* (formerly *Transnational Organized Crime*) is one of the few exceptions.

27. Emphases in original. Alain Desrosières, *The Politics of Large Numbers: A History of Statistical Reasoning*, trans. Camille Naish (Cambridge, Mass.: Harvard University Press, 1998), 16.

28. Bernard S. Cohn, "The Census, Social Structure and Objectification in South Asia," in *An Anthropologist among the Historians and Other Essays* (New York: Oxford University Press, 1987), 224–254; Benedict Anderson, "Census, Map, Museum," in *Imagined Communities*, 2nd ed. (London: Verso, 1991).

29. Richard Ashley, "The Poverty of Neo-realism," in *Realism and Its Critics*, ed. Robert Keohane (New York: Columbia University Press, 1986); Bradley Klein, *Strategic Studies and World Order: The Global Politics of Deterrence* (Cambridge: Cambridge University Press, 1994); Steve Smith, "The United States and the Discipline of International Relations: Hegemonic Country, Hegemonic Discipline?" *International Studies Perspectives* 4, no. 2 (2002): 67–86.

30. For a discussion of the historical origins of the distinction between borders and frontiers, see Jean Gottmann, *The Significance of Territory* (Charlottesville: University Press of Virginia, 1973). Thanks to John Agnew for alerting us to this reference.

31. David Ludden, "Presidential Address: Maps in the Mind and the Mobility of Asia," *Journal of Asian Studies* 62, no. 4 (November 2003): 1062.

32. David Ludden, "History Outside Civilization and the Mobility of South Asia," *South Asia* 17, no. 1 (June 1994): 1–23.

33. Ibn Khaldūn, *The* Muqaddimah: *An Introduction to History,* trans. Franz Rosenthal (London: Routledge and Kegan Paul, 1958). Cf. Michael Adas, "From Avoidance to Confrontation: Peasant Protest in Precolonial and Colonial Southeast Asia," *Comparative Studies in Society and History* 23, no. 2 (1981): 217–247; Cohn, "Census, Social Structure and Objectification," 224–254; Leo Lucassen, Wim Willems, and Annemarie Cottaar, *Gypsies and Other Itinerant Groups: A Socio-historical Approach* (Houndmills: Macmillan/New York: St. Martin's Press, 1998).

34. David Ludden, "Presidential Address," 1063.

35. Achille Mbembe, "At the Edge of the World: Boundaries, Territoriality, and Sovereignty in Africa," *Public Culture* 12, no. 1 (2000): 259–284.

36. Ranabir Samaddar, *The Marginal Nation: Transborder Migration from Bangladesh to West Bengal* (New Delhi: Sage Publications, 1999).

37. Perhaps a similar role is played by the apocalyptic narratives of Robert Kaplan today.

38. It is worth noting that these are usually stories of males and individuals, rarely of groups and women. Linda McDowell, *Gender, Identity and Place: Understanding Feminist Geographies* (Minneapolis: University of Minnesota Press, 1999); Patricia R. Poser, "The Role of Gender, Households and Social Networks in the Migration Process: A Review and an Appraisal," in *The Handbook of International Migration,* ed. Charles Hirschman, Philip Kasinitz, and Josh deWind (New York: Russell Sage Foundation, 1999), 53–70.

39. See also Mary Louise Pratt, *Imperial Eyes: Travel Writing and Acculturation* (London: Routledge, 1992), and Alison Blunt and Gillian Rose, *Writing Women and Space: Colonial and Postcolonial Geographies* (London: Guilford, 1994).

40. Douglas S. Massey, "Why Does Immigration Occur? A Theoretical Synthesis," in *Handbook of International Migration,* ed. Hirschman, Kazinitz, and deWind, 34–52.

41. Nevzat Soguk, *States and Strangers: Refugees and Displacements of Statecraft* (Minneapolis: University of Minnesota Press, 1999).

42. Aristide R. Zolberg, "Matters of State: Theorizing Immigration Policy," in *Handbook of International Migration,* ed. Hirschman, Kazinitz, and deWind, 71–93, from 73 and 81.

43. Stephen Castles, "Migration and Community Formation under Conditions of Globalization," *International Migration Review* 36, no. 4 (Winter 2002): 1147.

44. John Agnew and Stuart Corbridge, *Mastering Space: Hegemony, Territory and International Political Economy* (London and New York: Routledge, 1995), 86. See also Ludden, "Presidential Address."

45. V. R. Raghavan, *Siachen: Conflict without End* (New Delhi: Viking/Penguin, 2002).

46. See Gary Gereffi and M. Koreniewicz, ed., *Commodity Chains and Global Capitalism* (Westport, Conn.: Greenwood Press, 1994), especially the article by Terence Hopkins and Immanuel Wallerstein, "Commodity Chains: Construct and Research." For a useful comparison of commodity chains with a similar concept adopted in France called the *filière* approach, see Philip Raikes, Michael Friis Jensen, and Stefano Ponte, "Global Commodity Chain Analysis and the French Filière Approach:

Comparison and Critique," CDR Working Paper 00.3, Centre for Development Research, Copenhagen, 2000. For an anthropological perspective on "follow(ing) the commodity," see Angelique Haugerud, M. Priscilla Stone, and Peter D. Little, eds., *Commodities and Globalization: Anthropological Perspectives* (Lanham, Md.: Rowman and Littlefield, 2000).

47. See Michel Aglietta, *A Theory of Capitalist Regulation* (London: New Left Books, 1979). For the development of regulatory spaces, see also Bob Jessop, *State Theory: Putting the State in Its Place* (University Park: Pennsylvania State University Press Press, 1991), Michael Mann, *States, War and Capitalism: Studies in Political Sociology* (Oxford: Blackwell, 1988), and Anthony Giddens, *The Nation-State and Violence* (Berkeley: University of California Press, 1987)

48. Based on the discussion in Lee V. Cassinelli, "Qat: Changes in the Production and Consumption of a Quasi-Legal Commodity in Northeast Africa," in *The Social Life of Things*, ed. Arjun Appadurai (Cambridge: Cambridge University Press, 1986), 236–257.

49. Cassinelli, "Qat," 243, 253, 254.

50. R. B. J. Walker, *Inside/Outside: International Relations as Political Theory* (Cambridge: Cambridge University Press, 1993).

51. The International Court of Justice argues the "fundamental principle" that international law prevails over domestic law and notes that the inability to act under domestic law is no defense against non-compliance with international obligations (Article 27 of the Vienna Convention on the Law of Treaties, 1969). In effect, however, this indexes a political, not a legal struggle, as the ICJ has no ability to enforce these principles. Most countries follow the doctrine of incorporation for customary international law and the doctrine of transformation for treaty-based international law. Some states hold to the distinction between "self-executing" treaties, which operate automatically within the domestic sphere, and "non-self-executing" treaties, which do not. Our thanks to Veronica Raffo for clarification.

52. Annie Hubert comments on the presence of a related term in German (but not in French) and speaks of "plants of pleasure and sociability." See "Introduction," in *Opiums: Les plantes du plaisir et de la convivialité en Asie*, ed. Annie Hubert and Philippe Le Failler (Paris: L'Harmattan, 2000), 7–12. See also Wolfgang Schivelbusch, *Tastes of Paradise: A Social History of Spices, Stimulants and Intoxicants* (New York: Vintage Books/Random House, 1992)

53. Vijay Prashad, *Fat Cats and Running Dogs: The Enron Stage of Capitalism* (Monroe, Maine: Common Courage Press, 2003)

54. Prashad, *Fat Cats*, 6.

55. Vadim Volkov, *Violent Entrepreneurs: The Use of Force in the Making of Russian Capitalism* (Ithaca, N.Y.: Cornell University Press, 2002), xii.

56. Earlier discussions of the breakdown of state functions led to the term "quasi" states. Robert H. Jackson, *Quasi-States: Sovereignty, International Relations and the Third World* (Cambridge: Cambridge University Press 1990). For the link between failed states and intervention see International Commission on Intervention and State Sovereignty, "The Responsibility to Protect," Report of the International Commission on Intervention and State Sovereignty (Ottawa: Canadian Foreign Ministry, 2002).

57. Migrant-exporting schemes, described by Kyle and Siracusa in this volume, begin with the state's loss of popular legitimacy, as they offer a complex and multifac-

eted answer to the question of why so many Ecuadorian migrants are willing to ignore government laws and become "criminals."

58. Homi Bhabha, "The Commitment to Theory," in *Questions of Third Cinema*, ed. Jim Pines and Paul Willemen (London: British Film Institute, 1989).

59. Igor Kopytoff, "The Cultural Biography of Things," in *Social Life of Things*, ed. Appadurai, 73.

60. Before the 1989 "Velvet" revolution in Czechoslovakia, for example, the "underground" referred to an intellectual, artistic, and political space that was the site of multiple contestations with the state. Thanks to Petra Ticha for pointing this out. Obviously this perspective also unsettles the normality of the term "criminal."

61. David Newman, "Boundaries, Borders and Barriers: Changing Geographic Perspectives on Territorial Lines," in *Identities, Borders, Orders*, ed. Albert, Jacobsen, and Lapid, 137–151.

62. "Sovereignty implies "space," and what is more it implies a space against which violence whether latent or overt is directed—a space established and constituted by violence." Henri Lefebvre, *The Production of Space*, trans. Donald Nicholson-Smith (Oxford: Blackwell, [1974] 1991), 280.

63. Eric J. Hobsbawm, *Bandits*, 2nd ed. (New York: New Press, 2000).

64. James Scott, *Seeing Like the State: How Certain Schemes to Improve the Human Condition Have Failed* (New Haven, Conn.: Yale University Press, 1998).

65. Michael Dillon, *Politics of Security: Towards a Political Philosophy of Continental Thought* (New York: Routledge, 1996).

66. Crossing borders need not always imply moving to other countries. A number of Native American communities in the United States have used the partial sovereignty of their reservations to set up large and lucrative gambling enterprises.

67. Hastings Donnan and Thomas M. Wilson, *Borders: Frontiers of Identity, Nation and State* (Oxford and New York: Berg, 1999).

68. Peter Andreas, *Border Games: Policing the U.S.-Mexico Divide* (Ithaca, N.Y., and London: Cornell University Press, 2000), x.

69. Henk Driessen, "The 'New Immigration' and the Transformation of the European-African Frontier," in *Border Identities: Nation and State at International Frontiers*, ed. Thomas M. Wilson and Hastings Donnan (Cambridge: Cambridge University Press, 1998), 96–116, at 111.

70. Joseph Nevins, *Operation Gatekeeper: The Rise of the "Illegal Alien" and the Making of the U.S.-Mexico Boundary* (New York: Routledge, 2002).

71. Andreas, *Border Games*, x.

72. Naylor, *Wages of Crime*, 11.

73. Andrew Walker, *The Legend of the Golden Boat: Regulation, Trade and Traders in the Borderlands of Laos, Thailand, China and Burma* (Honolulu: University of Hawai'i Press, 1999).

74. *The New Nation* (Dhaka), 27 January 1999.

Spaces of Engagement

How Borderlands, Illegal Flows, and Territorial States Interlock

Willem van Schendel

A generation ago, Eric Wolf warned his fellow social scientists against study-ing the world as if it were made up of "sociocultural billiard balls, coursing on a global billiard table."[1] Today, many more scholars agree that this is a crucial problem of how we study societies, cultures, and economies. The historical background is well known. The social sciences came into being as modern territorial states were rising to unprecedented prominence in the world. No wonder social scientists stood in awe of the state: before their eyes it brought almost all of humanity and all the earth's surface under its sway. A historically unique system of states based on territorialized power and sovereignty provided social scientists with a framework within which to conceptualize societies, cultures, nations, histories, and economies. Indeed, the territorial structure of the modern interstate system came to be widely accepted as a *general* model of sociospatial organization, and most social scientists analyzed social life as if it were being played out in self-enclosed geographical units. In their work, they took the state territory as a natural starting point. In this way we have all come to think in terms of French culture, the Malaysian economy, Bolivian history, or Canadian politics.

This tendency toward "methodological territorialism" is now being challenged as never before.[2] Increasingly we realize that we have allowed our social imagination to be stifled by an "embedded statism" and that we have fallen into a "territorial trap."[3] As new forms of international connectivity present themselves and states are no longer perceived as the only protagonists on the world scene, we realize more and more that territorial states do not "contain" societies—that the notion that societies, cultures, and economies can be studied as if they were self-enclosed units that coincide spatially with the state's territory has become untenable.

Some predict the demise of states as a result of an ongoing process of "globalization" that entails the deterritorialization of economic, political, and cultural relations. Others deny this will happen but agree that a period in which political and economic power was mediated primarily by the territorial state is coming to an end; the world is being reterritorialized and reregulated, and the exceptional concentration of power that states have enjoyed for so long is being "unbundled." Whatever the outcome, we need to reconsider many of the core concepts and approaches in the social sciences: How can we overcome tendencies toward methodological territorialism? How do we study social processes in the twenty-first century? The sweeping imagery of "globalization" with its predictions of the "end of geography" and a borderless, connected, homogeneous world does not seem to provide a ready solution. Instead, we have to find more modest and more discerning ways of analyzing "processes that cross borders but are not universal, that constitute long-distance networks and social fields but not on a planetary scale."[4]

Illegal Flows and Borders

It is against this background that the study of "illegal flows"—flows of commodities, persons, and ideas that have been outlawed by one or more states—takes on particular significance. These commodities, persons, and ideas cross the borders of territorial states, and their movement is difficult to study adequately by means of a territorialist methodology or state-centered concepts. It is often asserted that we know little about illegal flows because those who are involved in them keep them secret. This is no doubt true, but our ignorance also results from our lack of tools to study these flows, an absence of concepts and approaches to describe and analyze them.

What tools do we have? A common way of dealing with the movement of objects and people that cannot be pinned down geographically is to use the image of fluidity: streams of migrants, a trickle of investments, goods flooding a market, a supply of labor that has dried up. The image is particularly appealing when discussing the cross-border movement of objects and people prohibited by states. Here fluidity becomes associated with danger: just as floodwater can undermine a building, causing it to collapse, so the uncontrolled inflow of unwanted goods or persons may subvert a state. The term "illicit flows" (actually a misnomer, as we have explained in the introduction[5]) has become very common, particularly in relation to the trade in small arms and drugs, as well as in relation to the unauthorized migration of labor.

The metaphor of illegal/illicit flows is not innocent. It calls forth the metaphor of a barrier to hold back flows, a dam thrown up against the advancing water, a fence to keep the undesirables out. This barrier is inevitably equated with the state's international border, which is seen as the prime line of defense against an assault from outside. In the discourse on illegal flows, the border is the antonym. If flows stand for the fluid, the spatially elusive, the intrusive, the underworld, then the border symbolizes the solid, the territorial, the ordered, the rule of law. The border becomes pivotal in a defensive, protectionist rhetoric that demands that states "close the floodgates against uncontrolled waves breaking in from the outside," a rhetoric that is directed "just as much at arms merchants and drug traffickers who threaten internal security as it is against the incoming floods of information, foreign capital, or labor immigration, or the waves of refugees who supposedly destroy native culture and standards of living."[6] The border stands precariously between the legitimate sovereignty of the state and a shadowy outer world of more or less organized crime. Hence the border is always vulnerable and needs to be protected and strengthened, not only against military invaders but increasingly against law evaders.[7] In a globalizing, reterritorializing world that abounds with images of transnational flows, borders are far from disappearing; they are a crucial measure of continued state control.

Contrasting Flows and Borders

The discourse on illegal flows is based on constructing multiple contrasts between flows and borders. One is the contrast between *visibility* and *invisibility*. Illegal flows thrive on being invisible for those who are not directly involved in them. The more outsiders are aware of the movement of outlawed goods and persons, the greater the risk of interference and punishment. In the case of borders, on the other hand, visibility is at a premium. At borders, states take great trouble to highlight their territorial sovereignty. Demarcation by means of highly visible symbols such as pillars, flags, fences, and signboards is commonplace. A border that is not visible for all is a border that has failed its purpose.

Another contrast is that between *fixity* and *motion*. Borders are presented as spatially rooted, solid, and durable entities, undeniable lines inscribed in the landscape, only to be moved very occasionally and in exceptional circumstances such as war or state disintegration. Illegal flows, on the other hand, are presented as highly mobile, capricious, and unpredictable, improvising new routes as they move across space. The contrast between fixity and motion is visualized in the standard map of illegal flows. It shows the earth's surface cut up into well-known state territories marked by boldly drawn borders; crosscutting these borders is an array of arrows representing objects or persons in motion. It is these arrows, rather than the borders, that are intended to convey new information.[8]

A third contrast is that between *stimulus* and *reaction*. In the discourse on illegal flows, agency rests with the flows. They are described as permeating borders, subverting border controls, penetrating state territories, seeking markets, and finding customers. Borders, on the other hand, are presented as passive, vulnerable, and reactive. Whatever changes occur at state borders are in response to proactive, indeed aggressive, attempts by proponents of illegal flows to violate them. These changes are defensive, geared toward restoring a level of national security that is in danger of being lost.

A final contrast is that between *staging post* and *target*. When illegal flows cross borders, it is suggested, their aim is not the border itself but the heartland beyond. The border is just an unavoidable staging post in an endeavor that aims to link products or laborers that have nothing to do with the border with consumers or employers who are equally unconnected with the border. The discourse on illegal flows focuses on the (ill) effects of the flows at their points of destination but has little time for possible effects at the various staging posts, including borders; it is the head of the arrow rather than its body that we are invited to concentrate on.

A Surfeit of Arrows

The cartography of illegal flows depends heavily on the persuasive value of the arrow. The arrow is a godsend for those wishing to represent illegal flows in a threatening manner because it is a discursive tool that conveys the notion of motion, stimulus, and target as perhaps no other graphic code could. The arrow purports to make visible what is essentially invisible. It perfectly suggests the velocity of objects or persons flowing illegally, their

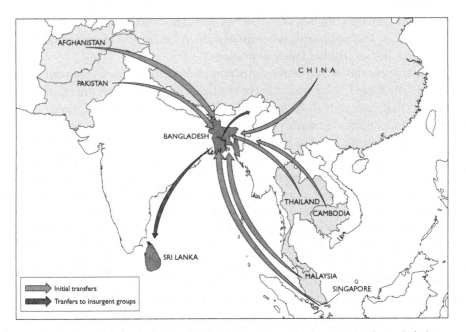

FIG. 1.1. Visualizing illicit small arms flowing through the territory of Bangladesh. Based on *Small Arms Survey 2001: Profiling the Problem* (Geneva and Oxford: Graduate Institute of International Studies/Oxford University Press, 2001), p. 182. Used by permission.

aggressive penetration of sovereign territories, their disregard for borders, and their reach deep inside the national heartland. Maps depicting illegal cross-border flows are often attempts to persuade rather than to present information accurately and even-handedly. The visual seduction of such persuasive cartography works well: the more alarming and threatening the arrow, the more effective it is—it makes policy makers sit up and pay attention. Maps filled with conspicuous arrows claiming to be scaled representations of illegal flows have been used to great effect to propagate particular ways of understanding spatial movements that lack state authorization.[9]

As tools of social analysis, however, such maps are often equivocal. When it comes to understanding illegal flows, their bold arrows hide more than they reveal. Usually they are quick stopgaps, hiding our lack of detailed knowledge, dramatizing and simplifying processes that we understand at best in outline, and forcefully pushing interpretations that need more careful consideration. They tend to close the conversation before it has begun, they suggest rather than demonstrate insights, and sometimes they actually point in the wrong direction. Clearly, arrows are highly relevant as tools to investigate cartographic discourses on the geopolitical threat of illegal

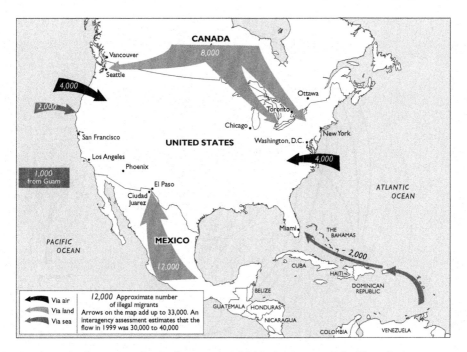

FIG. 1.2. Visualizing unauthorized migration of Chinese citizens to the United States. Based on The Terrorism Research Center, Inc., http://www.terrorism.com/documents/pub45270/752335.gif. Used by permission.

flows. For those interested in exploring the actual movements of people and objects, however, maps representing illegal flows tend to suffer from a surfeit of arrows, or "arrow disease."

Arrows are especially unhelpful in the case of borders. A recourse to arrows feeds on a misconception: that illegal flows cross borders without affecting them or being affected by them. As long as we see borders primarily from the perspective of the territorial state, as its outer skin that needs to be protected from penetration by unwanted aliens and outlawed substances, we will tend to fall prey to arrow disease and the underlying idea that borders and flows are antonyms.

Borderland Societies

For a long time, the study of borders and borderlands was deeply marked by the methodological territorialism of the social sciences. Borderlands were treated not as entities in their own right, but as the margins of states, societies, nations, economies, and cultures. The state territory was the im-

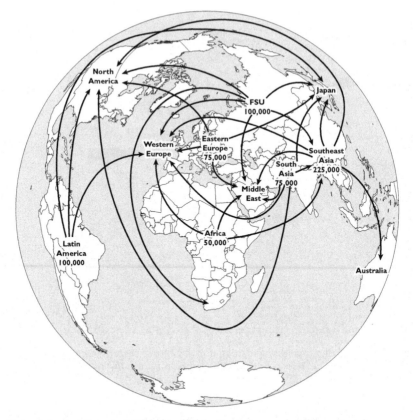

FIG. 1.3. Arrow Disease: a) Global trafficking in women and children. Based on U.S. State Department, 2000, http://secretary.state.gov/www/picw/trafficking/images/map.jpg. Used by permission.

plicit center of gravity, the point of reference, and borderlands were seen in their relationship to that territory. For this reason, we know much more about how states dealt with borderlands than how borderlands dealt with states.[10] Increasingly, however, border studies have emancipated themselves from this state-centrism, partly by elaborating the concept of "borderland." We may describe a *borderland* as a zone or region within which lies an international border, and a *borderland society* as a social and cultural system straddling that border. The reconfigured study of borderlands that is emerging takes both sides of an international border as its unit of analysis and thereby undermines "lazy assumptions" that state and society, state and nation, or state and governance are synonymous or territorially coterminous.[11] Borders not only join what is different but also divide what is similar.[12]

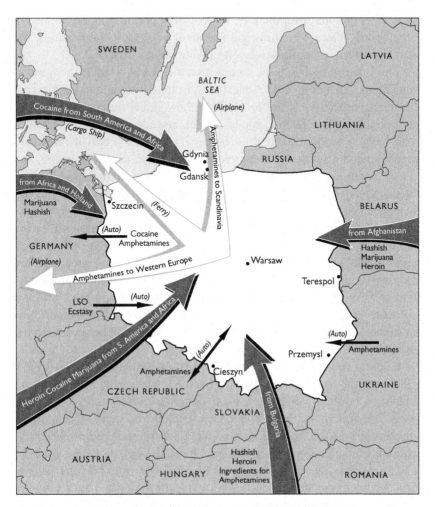

FIG. 1.4. Arrow Disease: b) Illicit drug flows in Poland. Based on *The Warsaw Voice*, http://www.warsawvoice.pl/v1433/crime.html. Used by permission.

As a result, border studies have rediscovered the historicity of social space. Borders are often seen as spatial fixtures, lines in the landscape, separators of societies—the passive and pre-given ground on which events take place.[13] But if we think of spatiality as an aspect of social relations that is continually being reconfigured, borders become much more significant. It is here that the strategy of state territoriality is dramatized and state sovereignty is paraded. It is also here that many countervailing strategies contesting state territoriality are clustered. The struggle between these strategies continually reproduces, reconstructs, or undermines borders. In other words, there is nothing passive about borders; in borderlands, the spatiality of social relations is forever taking on new shapes.

This is particularly significant now that social scientists see the world as undergoing a major process of reterritorialization. International borders are becoming crucial localities for studying how global restructuring affects territoriality. When people, goods, capital, and ideas flow across borders, what happens to them and to those borders? The contribution of borderland actors (including states) to the present round of global restructuring, and the resultant reconfigurations of social relations in borderlands, are still little understood. The rhetoric of "globalization" suggests prime movers being located in centers of production and consumption, with flows moving between them. But these flows do not move in thin air and they are not disembodied; we need to incorporate the social relations of transport and distribution, and their spatiality, in analyses of global rescaling. And although borders *may* be localities of importance when it comes to production and consumption, they are *always* localities of importance when it comes to transport and distribution—another reason to take them seriously in studies of global restructuring. In short, borders must be understood as dynamic sites of transnational reconfiguration.

It is no surprise, then, that social scientists interested in territoriality and global restructuring are now studying borders.[14] The spatial strategy of territoriality—the attempt by states to claim complete authority and control over social life in a given territory—*produces* borders and makes them crucial markers of the success and limitations of that strategy.[15] Borders need to be constantly maintained and socially reproduced through particular practices and discourses that emphasize the "other." The very extent of international borders in today's world is a testimony to the efforts devoted to this by individual states: a recent survey calculated that there are 226,000 kilometers of land border worldwide.[16] But borders are also socially reproduced by transnational actors. As students of globalization turn their attention from the "virtual" world of global financial flows to the "real" world of cross-border linkages and interterritorial economies, borders emerge as core objects of globalization research.[17]

If we accept that borders and borderland societies are continually being reproduced by an array of actors, including transnational ones, it is clear that negotiations and struggles over bordering lead to diversification—between borderlands, between segments of borderlands, between groups of actors in borderlands, and over time. And this leads to a number of questions regarding illegal flows. What conditions draw certain objects and persons to certain (segments of) borderlands? How and to what extent do illegal flows shape and reproduce borderlands? And how do changing borderlands condition and reproduce illegal flows?

Studying Flows in Borderlands

With few exceptions, the literature on illegal flows is not interested in these questions, and neither is, on the whole, the literature on borderlands. My contention is that they should be. It has always been difficult for outsiders to understand illegal flows because it is rare for insiders to make these flows visible to outsiders, to divulge the details of trade flows that are, after all, criminalized and punished by states. The circumstances under which such rare confessions are made (e.g., in prison or as part of self-glorifying memoirs) usually make the reliability of this information problematic.[18] Social scientists who have been able to get access to insiders who were willing to talk have focused largely on either upper-level trader-strategists or retailers, so we know much more about these players in "unauthorized commodity chains" than about others.[19]

Borderlands provide a site of research into illegal flows that promises a range of information and a number of perspectives that are often overlooked. As far as information is concerned, unauthorized flows may be much more visible in borderlands than in other classic sites of observation. In fact, in some borderlands it is almost impossible not to be flooded with information about unauthorized border crossings.[20] But it is more than visibility that borderlands have to offer; they also provide a number of perspectives that could enhance our analysis of illegal flows.

To begin with, studying flows in borderlands allows us to explore the perspective of the *transporters* of unauthorized goods in greater detail. The existing literature focuses on entrepreneurs, producers, retailers, and consumers, but transporters usually remain in the shadows. Borderlands provide simultaneous access to transporters at all levels, from children occasionally engaged on a daily wage, to professional truckers and supervising personnel who visit their border operations on a regular basis. This makes borderlands good sites for exploring the mechanisms and networks that actually make it possible for objects and persons to flow. In the case of human smuggling, transporters or cross-border guides go under a host of local names: African migrants on the Moroccan-Spanish border know them as wolves, Chinese illegal migrants speak of snakeheads, and on the U.S.-Mexican border they are widely known as coyotes.[21] Borderland research could reveal who are the people who fill these roles, how they are connected to wider organizations, and to what extent their roles are comparable along an entire border, or between borders. For example, according to popular images, snakeheads are tightly incorporated into long-distance networks, whereas coyotes are fairly independent entrepreneurs offering specialized cross-border travel services to all comers.[22] Would comparative research bear this out?

Second, borderlands provide an excellent site to study the *intermingling and overlapping of various legal and illegal flows*. Most studies of flows are object-oriented: they deal with one particular commodity (diamonds, arms, marijuana) or one particular category of persons (trafficked Ghanaian women, Chinese labor migrants). Although mention is often made of the fact that such flows may overlap and feed off each other, such connections have proved very hard to study. Of course, overlap may occur at any point, e.g., the point of consumption—when a Dutch drug dealer armed with a Brazilian handgun buys Liberian diamonds, or when trafficked sex workers from Nepal and Bangladesh meet in a brothel in Kolkata (India). The overlaps that occur in borderlands, however, may be uniquely complex as a result of the mix of commodities, both legal and illegal, that gravitate toward particular border locations, to be stored there for shorter or longer periods, and then to go across the border. The complexity of the overlap that occurs at borders is also a function of the fact that here transnational flows of very different size and extent meet. Thus a woman crossing the border between Angola and Congo with a cartload of tomatoes hiding an Israeli assault rifle participates not only in both legal and illegal trade but also in a short-distance trade flow and a long-distance one.[23]

A third perspective that studying unauthorized flows in borderlands opens up is the *networking around the border* that is inevitable when flows meet borders. The particularities of individual borderlands allow location-specific ways of combining (illegal) goods, labor, and capital for profit, benefiting from the advantages of two territorial systems of regulation and avoiding their disadvantages. The casinos and heroin refineries on the Thai-Burmese border, ambulant prostitution on the Czech-German border, the small-arms factories of the Pakistan-Afghanistan border, the *maquiladora* production units of the Mexico-U.S. border, and the electronic-goods assembly plants of the Bangladesh-India border are all examples of economic activities that can occur only in border regions, and only because some of their inputs (capital, labor, raw materials) and some of their markets have been defined as illegal by one of the states concerned.

Fourth, borderlands provide good sites to study *participant perspectives* on illegal flows. What motivates borderland smugglers, and how do other borderlanders perceive them? Who becomes involved and who does not?

How important is illegal trading in the lives of individuals, in terms of the time they invest in it, the income they derive from it, the identities they build around it, and the meanings they attach to it? Do they see themselves as heroes of free trade, as victims of circumstance, as traitors to their nation, as rebels against the spatial truncation of their world? When do they consider outlawed trade to be licit behavior, and why? The range of participant perceptions is likely to be wide. An aircrew consisting of various European nationals making an illegal arms delivery in eastern India considered themselves to be adventurous professionals whose assignment was purely a business deal.[24] Buyers at an illegal arms market at the tri-state point where Burma, India, and Bangladesh meet thought of themselves as freedom fighters, arming their cross-border ethnic group for a struggle of territorial independence. And inhabitants of the Belgian-Dutch borderland celebrated their historical involvement in illegal flows by erecting a "memory site" (*lieu de mémoire*) to smugglers.[25]

Finally, studying illegal flows in borderlands provides special insights into how *territoriality* and *transnationality* are negotiated in everyday practices and how people "scale" the world they live in.[27] Borderlanders, unlike "heartlanders" (and most social theorists), usually do not think of the state scale as intermediate between the local and the global (or transnational). For borderlanders, the state scale is not overarching and does not encompass the more "local" scales of community, family, the household, or the body. On the contrary, to them it is the state that, in many ways, represents the local and the confining, seeking to restrict the spatiality of borderlanders' everyday relations. Scales that most heartlanders experience as neatly nested within the state scale—face-to-face relations of production, marketing networks, or community identities—are experienced very differently by borderlanders. In their case, these scales are often less "local" than the state; they breach the confines of that scale, spill over its limits, escape its mediating pretensions, and thereby set the scene for a specific borderland politics of scale.[28] Inevitably, borderland practices are suspended between toeing the borderline and transgressing it, continually exploring and challenging the territorial pretensions of two states. The result is a variety of forms of everyday transnationality that states treat as suspect if not downright illegal practices.[29] No wonder illegal flows easily insert themselves in a border milieu: they dovetail with many of the daily routines of borderlanders.

For all these reasons, it makes sense to study illegal flows in borderlands. Around the world, borderland societies are deeply involved in the processing of unauthorized flows, and these interactions are so intense that it is fair to say that borders are as much a part of flows as they are of any territorial state.

FIG. 1.5. Celebrating a borderland society's illegal flows.
Photograph by G. Norbart, collection of Ed Ragas.
Used by permission.

It is rare to see smugglers turned into heroes for all to admire. Here we witness such a moment. Two former smugglers and a retired border guard are jointly unveiling a monument named "The Smuggler" on the border between Belgium and the Netherlands.

Before the 1960s, many inhabitants of Baarle, a small town straddling the border, had been dependent on the illegal cross-border trade in cigarettes, butter, gasoline, salt, cattle, currency, and perfume. Some of them worked for their own account, others were employees of organizations operating from European cities or, in the case of cigarette smuggling, the United States. Methods of smuggling varied from carrying sacks (as depicted on the monument) to driving armored cars through roadblocks. In Baarle, and elsewhere in the Belgian-Dutch borderland, there was a deeply rooted sense of the moral correctness of cross-border trade and outsmarting the state. Smugglers and local border guards shared a code of conduct aimed at allowing a certain amount of illegal trade while reducing the use of violence.

In the 1960s, European integration minimized price differences and removed most trade restrictions between the two countries. Illegal cross-border trade was no longer profitable and ex-smugglers had to find other means of income. In 1996, as the last generation of smugglers was reaching old age, shopkeepers in Baarle decided to commission a local sculptor to make a monument commemorating the community's history of smuggling. They donated this monument to the licitness of illegal flows and cross-border solidarity to "the people of Baarle."[26]

How Borderland Flows Are Organized

There is a vast literature on how people organize to make objects and persons move across space despite this movement's being prohibited by other groups (i.e., state personnel). Much of this literature highlights large and durable criminal organizations for which different terms have originated in different parts of the world: mafia, cartel, syndicate, tong, brotherhood, triad, secret society, and so on. Some writings even conjure up the phantasm of a Pax Mafiosa, global control by crime syndicates.[30] But there is much evidence to suggest that illegal flows are much less completely controlled by such corporations than the literature on "organized transnational crime" would have us believe. Recent studies focusing on small, flexible, and less durable alliances, as well as on individuals, argue that durable criminal corporations are actually rare and that we need a less institutional approach to understanding how illegal transnational flows cross borders.[31]

Writings on how illegal flows are organized focus mostly on their leadership and their points of production, wholesale packaging, dispatch, and retailing. Organizational studies of illegal flows rarely provide details of how people cooperate to get goods or persons to the borderland, across the border, and on to consumers (or very often yet another borderland). And yet, the organization of illegal flows is known to take on particular forms in borderlands and to adapt to local and forever changing conditions there.

Models of Organization

It may be useful to make a preliminary distinction between two models of organization at borders. The first is what Adler calls the *double-funnel pattern*, characterized by an abundance of people involved at the points of origin (growing/mining/manufacturing and packing) and disbursement (retailing and consumption) but by relatively few at the delicate and dangerous point of importation.[32] In the borderland, such an organization is at its narrowest, with only a few operatives who pass the border quickly and furtively. It has been suggested that this double-funnel or hourglass pattern may be associated in particular with large criminal syndicates and with expensive, non-bulky goods such as diamonds and upmarket drugs traveling over long distances. The arrest of Gokul Barman may be a case in point. In August 2001, Indian border authorities were astonished to discover that Gokul, who lived in a small village near the Bangladesh border, had in his possession a pouch containing 225 grams of high-grade uranium. The uranium, made in the Soviet Union in 1984, had apparently been smuggled into India from Bangladesh and was thought to be on its way to secessionist groups in Kashmir.[33]

The second model can be called the *capillary pattern*, involving many people at the points of origin and disbursement as well as at the border where the organization may actually spread out to include numerous borderlanders. It is often thought that this pattern is associated with a more fragmented trade organization, and with cheaper, more bulky goods such as agricultural produce or salt. For example, when the Thai military junta enforced an economic blockade of neighboring Laos and trade across the border river, the Mekong, was outlawed in 1976, local traders continued trading, "paddling loads of Aspirin, fish sauce and sugar across the Mekong at night to be enthusiastically and profitably received by Lao traders or officials . . . but their taste for adventure was soured when several were shot dead by Thai border police who patrolled the high river-banks."[34]

Border Diversification

How illegal flows navigate a borderland is not only determined by the type of organization or the type of object being traded. In many cases it is the characteristics of the borderland itself that exert a greater influence. For example, the hardness, or impermeability, of a border can differ along its length as a result of physical features (when a section of the border runs through water, a desert, a mountainous area, or a city), more or less intensive policing of a particular section (as in Operation Gatekeeper[35]), local cross-border agreements (e.g., between border districts or semi-autonomous border regions in neighboring countries), varying degrees of physical or linguistic difference between borderlanders on either side, or a combination of these. Unauthorized flows crossing the border at different points must adapt their organizational form to these local characteristics, even to the point of choosing to avoid certain sections.[36]

Apart from these local variations along a border's length, borders are also more or less of an obstacle to different groups of people. Citizens from one side may find it easier to cross the border than their counterparts from the other side. People with particular cultural, economic, or political characteristics may experience the border as a more formidable barrier than others. Age and gender may also play a role.[37] In order to be successful, operators of illegal flows need to exploit these differences, and this means adapting their organization.[38]

In addition to these relatively stable characteristics, the permeability of borders is forever changing. The power of neighboring states waxes and wanes, and the relationship between them is always in flux. At the border, changing interstate relations combine with the varying demands of cross-border labor and commodity markets, as well as with trade and migration policies, to produce complex patterns to which those involved in illegal flows need to be attuned.

State Attempts at Regulation

This is particularly clear when a state decides to escalate border surveillance to disrupt an illegal flow. A well-studied example is the United States's massive attempt to stop the influx of Colombian cocaine through southern Florida in the 1980s. This campaign, which involved recruiting the U.S. military into drug interdiction and classifying drugs as a "national security threat," had unexpected results.

> The Maginot Line-style strategy in south Florida did not significantly deter drug importations, but it did powerfully influence the location, methods, and organization of drug smuggling. Its most important impact was to push much of the traffic to the Southwest, making Colombian traffickers increasingly reliant on Mexican smuggling networks.[39]

Until then, Colombian cocaine exporters and their U.S. counterparts had favored light aircraft to get their product across the U.S. border. Now, the building of an "air interdiction" infrastructure forced them out of the air. As a direct result, Mexican road transporters became an integral component of the cocaine trade, and the Mexico-U.S. borderland became the hunting ground of a new type of internationally connected drug smuggler.[40] Similarly, the escalation of border controls at the Mexico-U.S. border to block unauthorized immigration into the United States disrupted traditional routes and methods of clandestine entry that had involved "either self-smuggling or limited use of a local 'coyote' [human smuggling entrepreneur]," making room for the emergence of professional smuggling agencies that elbowed out smaller operators.[41]

Such state regulation turns borderland societies into landscapes of control and fear without necessarily achieving its goal of blocking illegal entry. If measures are draconian enough, they can stop cross-border flows, at least for a while, but few states have been able or willing to go to such lengths. Although the Mexico-U.S. border is routinely described as being under the most intense and high-tech surveillance in the world, it is instructive to compare it with, for example, the German Democratic Republic's achievement in this respect. After a period of considerable permeability

(1945–1952), it closed its border with the Federal Republic of Germany by means of an accumulation of measures that were unusually effective: Thousands of border residents were deported and the border was protected by a five-kilometer-deep exclusion zone, a five-hundred-meter protection strip, and a ten-meter sand-covered control strip that was constantly being patrolled and in which you could see every footprint. Barbed-wire fences, towers, guard dogs, trip wires, land mines, curfews, and checkpoints completed the picture.[42]

Where the state does not develop into a true "gatekeeper state" that can enforce complete closure, illegal flows adapt to higher levels of surveillance by strengthening their own organizational and technological prowess in order to retain the border porosity that is being threatened by the new state policy.[43] Often, this means not only the emergence of more complex, better armed, and more violent organizations—as well as their deeper entrenchment in borderland society on either side of the border—but also much more mimicry: goods and persons whose entry is not authorized are hidden among shipments of "legal" goods for which the border is more porous.[44] Thus state attempts at regulating illegal cross-border flows may have the effect of replacing the capillary pattern of organization by the double-funnel one, with related organizational adaptations well beyond the borderland.

How Borderlanders Domesticate Illegal Flows

Inhabitants of borderlands share with people involved in illegal flows an uneasiness about dominant conceptions of spatial reality. Their lived experience makes it impossible for them to accept as given, and unproblematic, the contemporary organization of the world as defined by state elites.[45] For them, the world of states is problematic, and so is the idea that the interests of a "national community of citizens" should take precedence over all others. They cannot restrict their imagination to the territory of a single state, and they see those who do so as imprisoned in a delusion. In short, they have always been acutely aware of the distortions of what social scientists have begun to refer to as "embedded statism" and the "territorial trap."

In their endeavors to rethink state-centrism, social scientists could therefore do worse than take a leaf out of the borderlanders' book. Around the globe, inhabitants of border regions have devised practices and worldviews that take account of the state but never as an undisputed, overarching entity. In borderlands, two projects of national scalar structuration meet, complementing and strengthening each other. The material consequences, mediated through a host of bureaucratic, military, logistic, and symbolic practices, establish the border as an undeniable physical and political reality. But the hegemony of the national scale is never complete because states fail as "gatekeeper states" and cannot eliminate unauthorized cross-border practices.

As a result, state elites' attempts to use the border as a tool of statecraft to maintain political and economic inequalities based on territoriality are constantly being challenged. A vibrant borderland society, a social and cultural system straddling the border, becomes the engine for quite different projects of scalar structuration. Unauthorized cross-border trade, illegal migration, cross-border manufacturing systems, and regional autonomy movements—all these can be seen as practices intended to counter the inequalities across space that result from state territoriality. How these pan out in certain localities and at certain times determines the changing geographies of a borderland. The outcome is always highly complex, and all along the borderland competing forms of territoriality exist simultaneously in diverging social practices.[46]

Clearly, then, illegal flows are not external forces that, arrow-like, fly past supine borderland societies. On the contrary, they are actively domesticated and incorporated into borderland projects of scalar structuration. One way of understanding how illegal flows can become imbricated in borderland societies is by looking at the ways borderlanders and those who are involved in illegal flows map their environment. If we want to understand how they "scale" the world, we must start from their cognitive maps—their organized representations of their spatial environment and their own place in it.[47] Since these maps are rarely stored externally (in the form of a physical map), an essential part of studying the changing geographies of borderlands is to access cognitive "maps in minds."[48]

Everyday Transnationality

Although borderlanders' scaling practices have rarely been studied in a systematic way, there is considerable evidence to show that many borderlanders comfortably accommodate multiple cognitive maps. Let me give a few examples from the India-Bangladesh borderland. When an arms smuggler uses the pronoun "we" to refer not only to a group of citizens (Indians) but also to a cross-border trade organization (arms smugglers) and a regional religious category (Muslims in West Bengal [India] and Bangladesh), he demonstrates a capacity to position himself simultaneously in a variety of scales, only one of which is national. When a dozen insurgent groups in northeast India in a joint statement call for a boycott of India's Independence Day, arguing that "the northeast was never a part of India and so the question of celebrating Independence Day does not arise," they reject the national scale altogether.[49] When people from both sides of the border come together to enjoy an open-air opera (*jatragan*), to pray together, or to sell their produce in a border market, they defy the restrictions imposed by the national scale and insist on a cognitive map that includes the world beyond the state border.[50] When an old revolutionary from the India-Bangladesh borderland reminisces about how Zhou Enlai, the Chinese minister of foreign affairs, used to fête him in Beijing in 1970, he invokes a transnational brotherhood of revolutionary socialists.[51] And when an Indian man takes three months' leave from his government job to accompany his pregnant wife to her parents' house in Bangladesh for the birth of their first child, they may flout the citizenship laws and visa regulations of both states, but they affirm the scale of borderland kinship that links individuals and family groups across the border. In the partitioned geography of a borderland, cognitive maps will never overlap completely because individuals must frame their conceptions of spatial reality in non-consonant ways, some accepting the border, others not.[52]

Inevitably, the politics of scale in borderlands will focus on the issue of bordering. Often, state practices are ignored by borderlanders who continue to scale their world in ways that do not coincide with state borders. Their scales spill over the spatial limits set by the state's territory even at periods of extreme tension between states. Despite a long history of state formation in borderlands, the state scale has rarely won the cognitive war. It certainly has established itself as a most important scale among borderlanders, but it has seldom attained hegemony. Overt defiance is visible in pitched battles between smugglers and border guards (a regular feature in Bangladesh), in borderland insurrections (e.g., in Kashmir) and in the unauthorized cross-border movement of populations (e.g., in the Sahel). And covert defiance is expressed in smuggling, assistance given to illegal immigrants, and unauthorized transborder production and marketing systems. The politics of borderland scaling certainly use the state scale—when borderlanders hide behind the border, when citizenship claims are made, when national holidays are celebrated, when attempts are made to pull border guards into local conflicts and so elevate these to the status of international border incidents—but the limits of this scale are frequently dissonant with borderlanders' other, and sometimes more powerful, conceptions of spatial reality.

Three types of scale appear to be especially relevant for people in borderlands. The first type is formed by *scales-we-almost-lost*, pre-border webs of relations that have weakened under the onslaught of state formation but have not quite vanished. The second is the *state scale*, the web of relations that comes with the border and is confined to the national territory. And the third is made up of *border-induced scales*, cross-border webs of relations that spring up because of the border's existence. These three types of scale originate at different times and can therefore be distinguished as pre- and post-border phenomena. Although borderlanders can readily make such distinctions, they are rarely interested in the historicity of these scales. Rather it is the various interlinkages between these scales that inform borderlanders' representations of their spatial environment and their own place in it. In an intensive practice of scaling and rescaling, they have long since reworked these three types of webs of relations, and the outcomes are diverse.

As we have seen, borderlanders do not experience the state scale as encompassing more "local" scales or as intermediate between the local and the global (or transnational); rather, it is the state that represents the local and confining, seeking to restrict the spatiality of borderlanders' everyday relations. It is the persistence of highly meaningful pre-border scales that provides inhabitants of many borderlands with a sense of stability. They are actively involved in maintaining cross-border family networks, religious communities, marketing regions, trade routes, political connections, and webs of sociability.[53] Not only are such scales not obliterated by the state, they actually form the foundation on which new border-induced scales emerge. These new scales may be tolerated by the state and hence be "legal," as in the case of authorized cross-border commuting, schooling, or shopping.[54] But they may also be frowned upon by the state and hence be "illegal." Knowledge of old trade routes may lie at the basis of smuggling, a border-induced activity *par excellence*. Some borderlanders may be involved in illegal trade networks as smugglers, illegal migrants, traffickers of humans, or receivers of migrants' remittances. Other borderlanders may not be directly involved in smuggling, but they are well aware of how it rescales the borderland, and their cognitive maps also include the topographies of everyday transnationality.

At any border, the politics of scale revolve around competing forms of territoriality, expressed in diverging social practices. In a borderland, scale redefinitions and scale "jumping" frequently alter the geometry of social power by strengthening some people while disempowering others.[55] For this reason, the political geography of a borderland is never static. These struggles become especially visible when the state attempts to impose its version of territoriality and rein in more expansive transnational scales. Much of the defiance and violence that makes borderlands so suspect and vulnerable in the eyes of state elites can be read as clashes between state agents' localizing politics of scale and borderlanders' attempts to organize their lives according to less territorially confining scales. The outcome of these clashes is unpredictable because state agents are often drawn into cross-border politics of scale, and borderlanders' politics of scale can entail infiltrating a porous state structure.[56] For this reason, a heavily guarded segment of the border can easily be a segment where border guards are heavily involved in private gain from cross-border trade.[57] Their uniforms and other visible trappings of territorial discipline do not necessarily match the spatiality of their everyday relations or how they scale their environment and their place in it. If the evidence is to be believed, the very sentinels of the state are often highly susceptible to the lure of the borderland and become active agents in forms of scalar structuration that weaken state territoriality and strengthen illegal flows.

Beyond State-Centrism

We have seen that the social sciences are struggling to free themselves from the dominance of the nation-state as an overarching scale. "Postmodern cracks in the Great Westphalian Dam" have opened up, and we are increasingly aware of the limitations of the "territorialist epistemology" that has so long held sway in the social sciences.[58] The inherited model of state-defined societies, economies, and cultures looks increasingly contrived, and so do studies that treat states as the conceptual starting point for their investigations.

As the social sciences are moving beyond this paradigm, which is based on how state elites define the organization of the world, the question is what to put in its place. The deterritorialization thesis (which prophesies a borderless world of flows and an end to geography, territory, and distance) is hardly convincing. It takes insufficient account of the fact that global flows must always be premised upon various forms of spatial fixity and localization.[59] It also pays too little heed to the political backlash of global scalar restructuring and the cognitive dissonance it produces; those who feel that disorder and insecurity are growing around them demand that their state grow stronger to protect them from threatening transnational flows by creating a safe territory behind impermeable borders.

The relationships between localities and flows are clearly changing, and forms of enforcement that involve the active use of geographic space to control people are changing with them. As state strategies of territoriality and governance are becoming less central and transstate entities and regulatory systems are pushing ahead, we are faced with the fact that our conventional political map of the world is fraying and becoming undone.[60]

The state's concern with controlling the movement of objects and human beings across space is a recent development in human history. It is characteristic of modern states to claim the exclusive right to authorize and regulate movement—to monopolize the legitimate means of movement[61]—but it is only in recent times that many states actually have acquired the technological and bureaucratic capacity to effectuate that claim. Movement across borders, now conceived of as sharply defined lines in the landscape indicating the precise limits of state sovereignty, became an important yardstick of a state's sovereign power, and borders came to exert extraordinary power over how we view the world and how we divide human beings into distinct groups. In order to prepare ourselves for a new world of post-Westphalian territorialities, we need to question our broad acceptance of the often violent border practices of states and the attendant definitions of what (and who) is legal or illegal, included or excluded.

The study of transborder flows, the movement of objects and people across international borders, may help us break out of our state-centered chrysalis. How do various forms of trade and migration negotiate space? How do they relate to competing forms of territoriality in borderlands? How do they beat, circumvent, and shape regulatory systems, entities, and alliances? I have argued that extra-territorial flows of goods and people do not stand in simple opposition to territorial organizations but in a relationship of mutual constitution. For example, states that challenge flows by defining them as "illegal" create more barricaded and violent borders as well as more sophisticated, albeit outlawed, organizations to keep flows going. In this way, policies of state intervention ("interdiction") and surveillance produce new transborder arrangements that may turn out to be a bigger challenge to state territoriality. The image of states as simply reactive, responding to the growth of clandestine transnational flows, is misleading because it understates the degree to which states actually structure, condition, produce, and enable clandestine border crossings.[62]

However, the study of transborder flows itself is often state-centric. Discourses on unauthorized transborder flows are usually one-sided in the following ways. First, they focus attention on what enters the state territory but not on what leaves it. The Bangladesh discourse on international migration exemplifies this. It is vocal about unauthorized entry (e.g., Rohingya refugees from Burma) but silent about the much larger flow of Bangladeshi migrants to India, whose departure from the territory of Bangladesh is unauthorized and about whom complaints from India are very audible.[63]

Similarly, U.S. discourses on unauthorized flows highlight the flows into
U.S. territory (mainly of drugs and migrants) but ignore the fact that the
United States is probably the world's single largest exporter of smuggled
goods as well.[64]

Second, these discourses tend to ignore the fact that it is consumer demand within the state territory that fuels unauthorized transborder flows.
Thus goods and services the local economy cannot provide, and that the
state deems undesirable (or admissible only if heavily taxed), become contraband as a result of state action. There is often a striking gap between
state pronouncements about the need to stamp out unauthorized transborder trade and state policies to stop it. For example, in both India and
the United States, vibrant discourses on unauthorized immigration project
images of borders as being subverted by infiltrating and unwanted aliens,
and inspire state policies of border interdiction, fencing, and expulsion. In
neither country, however, does the state effectively target or penalize domestic employers of "illegal aliens," thereby ensuring that the demand for
the immigrants' cheap labor, and thus incentives for further unauthorized
immigration, continue to exist.[65]

Third, state-centric discourses on unauthorized transborder flows are
usually one-sided in that they ignore how states facilitate these flows and
benefit from them. To stick to the example of labor emigration, states may
come to rely on it as a safety valve for their problems of unemployment.
Emigration allows them to implement economic policies that aim at
growth and structural adjustment rather than at creating jobs, and so en-
courage workers to look for employment abroad.[66] Such states take no steps
to curb unauthorized emigration, but they are keen to tax the remittances
that migrants send back home. To this end they try to make sure that these
remittances flow through official banking channels. Bangladesh is a good
example of a labor-exporting country that is continually and unsuccessfully
struggling to stamp out privatized forms of remitting money (here known
as *hundi* or *hawala*).

States benefit from unauthorized transborder flows in other ways as well.
For example, if national industries can get their products to foreign consumers cheaply by evading import duties in the countries of destination, the
home state may benefit by taxing these industries. Many Indian companies
access the Bangladesh market in this way,[67] and this is also how products
from countless industrialized countries around the world clandestinely find
their way to millions of consumers in India.[68] The link between the state
and unauthorized transborder flows is even closer when the state is involved
in the production and trade of goods (e.g., drugs, arms) that are banned

in the markets of destination. Power holders in Burma, Afghanistan, and Colombia have been accused of running "narco-states"—states that are dependent on income from the trade in outlawed drugs—but many governments denouncing this practice are themselves involved in "gray-market" transfers of arms.

In analyzing unauthorized and poorly documented extra-territorial flows of goods and people, then, it makes little sense to construct a sharp opposition between these flows and territorial organizations such as states. States may strive for territorial control, a monopoly of the legitimate means of movement, or secure borders—but in reality borders are semi-porous and state action devised to interdict clandestine border crossings actually rescales and sometimes enables these crossings. Conversely, unauthorized flows can rescale states. The challenge is to look at territorial states, transborder territorial arrangements, and transnational flows as *complementary* elements in processes of global reterritorialization. The current drift of these processes appears to be toward making institutions at the national level less central and toward strengthening direct links between localized arenas (e.g., borderland networks) and supranational ones.

In this game of unequal power and unpredictable outcomes, state elites hold some important cards: access to state institutions with their rich pickings from tax, their legitimizing authority, their access to other states and supranational organizations, and their superior military clout. But "unauthorized" entrepreneurs hold other important cards: the power to operate profitably while remaining largely illegible to states,[69] a high degree of organizational and regulatory flexibility, the capacity to be spatially mobile, and the skill to redirect state institutions, undermine state territoriality, and rescale states. Transnational entrepreneurs and state elites can form alliances that simultaneously prop up state structures and allow these to serve the interests of "unauthorized" transnational flows. In this process, which is sometimes described as the criminalization of the state, those who routinely undermine the state's territoriality emerge as its kingmakers and office bearers.[70]

But borderlanders also hold important cards. Their power is based on a detailed knowledge of topography, social fields, and overlapping scales that allows objects and persons to navigate the border safely. Borderlanders incorporate illegal flows into their transborder projects of scalar structuration, and these are not easily manipulated by either states or transnational entrepreneurs. The three-cornered ambivalence is expressed in a mixture of trust, rewards, threats, violence, avoidance, and subterfuge. When states attempt to interdict clandestine border crossings and unauthorized access to markets beyond the border, they highlight that they are waging war against transnational crime lords. But what is often forgotten is that they are also joining battle with borderland societies, their projects of scalar structuration, and their sense of social justice.

In other words, global reterritorialization is best approached by looking simultaneously at states, transborder arrangements, and transnational flows because these are overlapping, interlocking arenas of power and profit—or spaces of engagement[71]—and they are far more difficult to separate than "billiard ball" theorists have assumed. It is often only states and flows that figure in analyses of reterritorialization. Transborder arrangements are usually overlooked—or considered to be derivative, marginal, or insignificant. In this chapter, I suggest that this is a serious misjudgment. In reterritorialization (or globalization) studies, borderland societies form a "missing link" because they act as pivots between territorial states and transnational flows (as well as between separate flows), and the transborder arrangements worked out in the world's myriad borderlands have a direct impact on the shape, legitimacy, and organization of both states and flows.

NOTES

1. Eric R. Wolf, *Europe and the People Without History* (Berkeley: University of California Press, 1982), 17. Wolf criticized an approach to society and culture that has strong links with the conventional model of international relations and international law, for instance, "the world . . . consists of nation-states regarded as independent actors within an anarchic environment, who make more or less rational decisions in pursuit of the preservation and expansion of their own power." Jürgen Habermas, *The Postnational Constellation: Political Essays* (Cambridge: Polity Press, 2001), 69.

2. Neil Brenner, "Beyond State-Centrism? Space, Territoriality, and Geographical Scale in Globalization Studies," *Theory and Society* 28 (1999): 45–46, 48.

3. Peter Taylor, "Embedded Statism and the Social Sciences: Opening Up to New Spaces," *Environment and Planning A* 28, no. 11 (1996): 1917–1928; John Agnew, "The Territorial Trap: The Geographical Assumptions of International Relations Theory," *Review of International Political Economy* 1, no. 1 (1994): 53–80.

4. Frederick Cooper, "What Is the Concept of Globalization Good For? An African Historian's Perspective," *African Affairs* 100, no. 399 (2001): 189.

5. The conceptual distinction between "illicit" and "illegal," which we highlight in the introduction to this book, is rarely encountered in the discourse on cross-border flows. Many cross-border flows are illegal because they defy formal political authority, but they are only illicit if they defy informal social authority as well.

6. Habermas, *The Postnational Constellation*, 81.

7. Peter Andreas, *Border Games: Policing the U.S.-Mexico Divide* (Ithaca, N.Y., and London: Cornell University Press, 2000), 140.

8. This does not always work as intended. The lack of fixity of many contemporary borders may lead to strange cartographic effects that draw attention away from

the arrows. For example, some observers may find it hard to put a name to the small state wedged in between Pakistan and China in figure 1. In fact, this is no state at all but a part of Kashmir that both China and India claim and whose borders have never been settled.

9. Jeremy Black warns that although subjectivity is of course central to the production of all maps, we should not jump too easily to the conclusion that maps are "conspiratorial devices of the powerful. Some maps may indeed serve such ends but maps are a medium, not a message." Jeremy Black, *Maps and Politics* (Chicago: University of Chicago Press, 1997), 168. For a general treatment of propaganda maps, see John Pickles, "Texts, Hermeneutics and Propaganda Maps," in *Writing Worlds: Discourse, Text and Metaphor in the Representation of Landscape*, ed. Trevor J. Barnes and James S. Duncan (London and New York: Routledge, 1992), 193–230. The term "persuasive cartography," coined by J. A. Tyner, is cited on p. 197. The theme is developed with particular regard to historical maps and geopolitics in Claude Raffestin, Dario Lopreno, and Yvan Pasteur, *Géopolitique et histoire* (Lausanne: Éditions Payot, 1995). For an English translation of the most relevant chapter, see Claude Raffestin, "From Text to Image," in *From Geopolitics to Global Politics: A French Connection*, ed. Jacques Lévy (London and Portland, Ore.: Frank Cass, 2001), 7–34. On the historical intersection of European mapmaking, European colonialism, and the cartographic rationalization of space, see Ricardo Padrón, "Mapping Plus Ultra: Cartography, Space and Hispanic Modernity," *Representations* 79 (2002): 28–60.

10. For a fuller treatment, see Michiel Baud and Willem van Schendel, "Toward a Comparative History of Borderlands," *Journal of World History* 8, no. 2 (1997): 211–242; and Willem van Schendel, *The Bengal Borderland: Beyond State and Nation in South Asia* (London: Anthem Press, 2005).

11. James Anderson and Liam O'Dowd, "Borders, Border Regions and Territoriality: Contradictory Meanings, Changing Significance," *Regional Studies* 33, no. 7 (1999): 602–603.

12. Tobias Wendl and Michael Rösler, "Introduction: Frontiers and Borderlands: The Rise and Relevance of an Anthropological Research Genre," in *Frontiers and Borderlands: Anthropological Perspectives*, ed. Michael Rösler and Tobias Wendl (Frankfurt am Main: Peter Lang, 1999), 2.

13. Neil Smith, "Contours of a Spatialized Politics: Homeless Vehicles and the Production of Geographical Scale," *Social Text* 33 (1992): 66.

14. In their excellent overview of border studies, Donnan and Wilson speak of a "burgeoning literature on borders." Hastings Donnan and Thomas M. Wilson, *Borders: Frontiers of Identity, Nation and State* (Oxford and New York: Berg, 1999), xiii. Cf. Rösler and Wendl, eds., *Frontiers and Borderlands*.

15. In his survey of the world's international borders, Foucher speaks of the cutting up of the world as a result of a process of "planetary geodesy." Michel Foucher, *Fronts et frontières: Un tour du monde géopolitique* (Fronts and Borders: A Tour of the Geopolitical World) (Paris: Fayard, 1991).

16. If this figure, calculated by Foucher, is correct, and if we take the depth of the borderland to be an arbitrary 10 km on either side, the world's borderlands cover an area of 4,500,000 square km. Foucher, *Fronts et frontières*, 15.

17. Anderson and O'Dowd, "Borders, Border Regions," 600. This provides a healthy counterbalance to much recent writing on globalization that focuses on connections between urban, even metropolitan, centers and has abandoned the image of the Global

Village for that of the Global City, resuscitating modernist images of social change emanating from city to countryside that appear particularly at odds with assertions of universal connectedness and an end to geography.

18. E.g., *Chaktow: het verhaal van een drugsdealer* (Chaktow: A Drug Dealer's Story) (Utrecht: Het Spectrum, 1995); Christopher Seymour, *Yakuza Diary: Doing Time in the Japanese Underworld* (New York: Atlantic Monthly Press, 1996); Bart Middelburg, *De Godmother: De criminele carrière van Thea Moear, medeoprichter van de Bruinsma-groep* (The Godmother: The Criminal Career of Thea Moear, Co-Founder of the Bruinsma Group) (Amsterdam/Antwerpen: L.J. Veen, 2000).

19. E.g., Patricia A. Adler, *Wheeling and Dealing: An Ethnography of an Upper-Level Drug Dealing and Smuggling Community* (New York: Columbia University Press, 1985); Frank Bovenkerk, *La Bella Bettien* (Amsterdam: J. M. Meulenhoff, 1995); Edwin van der Torre, *Drugstoeristen en kooplieden: onderzoek naar Franse drugstoeristen, Marokkaanse drugsrunners en het beheer van dealpanden in Rotterdam* (Drug Tourists and Traders: A Study of French Drug Tourists, Moroccan Drug Runners and the Management of Safe Houses in Rotterdam) (Deventer: Kluwer, 1996); Damián Zaitch, "Traquetos: Colombians Involved in the Cocaine Business in the Netherlands" (Ph.D. diss., University of Amsterdam, Amsterdam School of Social Science Research, 2001).

20. As I found out when doing research on another topic, the history of a rural industry that happened to be located in the India-Bangladesh borderland. Villagers and smugglers in two small villages facing each other across the Ganges were eager to discuss and show the importance of illegal trade. Willem van Schendel, "Easy Come, Easy Go: Smugglers on the Ganges," *Journal of Contemporary Asia* 23, no. 2 (1993): 189–213.

21. The term "snakehead" is more encompassing and also refers to entrepreneurs in unauthorized migration. On the use of animal categories for human smugglers and illegal migrants, see Henk Driessen, "The 'New Immigration' and the Transformation of the European-African Frontier," in *Border Identities: Nation and State at International Frontiers*, ed. Thomas M. Wilson and Hastings Donnan (Cambridge: Cambridge University Press, 1998), 96; Donnan and Wilson, *Borders*, 134–136.

22. Zai Liang and Wenzhen Ye, "From Fujian to New York: Understanding the New Chinese Immigration," in *Global Human Smuggling: Comparative Perspectives*, ed. David Kyle and Rey Koslowski (Baltimore and London: Johns Hopkins University Press, 2001), 203–204.

23. I owe this image to examples given by Carolyn Nordstrom.

24. One of the arms-trading companies involved in this case (which became known as the Purulia Arms Drop case) was aptly named Border Technology and Innovations Ltd. Some of the international flavor of this case is brought out in the following quotation: "An athletic-looking Dane, with blond hair, blue eyes and an arrest warrant for armed robbery, hires a British arms dealer with a colorful resume. In Latvia, they buy a Russian cargo plane and have it flown to Bulgaria where it is loaded with 77 cases of weapons, including 300 assault rifles, ammunition, pistols, hand grenades and rocket launchers. The plane then heads east to India. When it gets over the village of Purulia, near Calcutta, the weapons are shoved out, drifting down under parachute rigging purchased in South Africa. The deal is financed out of Hong Kong. The intended recipient is a violent religious sect." Raymond Bonner, "Murky Life of an International Gun Dealer," *The New York Times*, July 14, 1998. Cf. Suhrid Sankar Chattopadhyay, "Waiting to Go Home," *Frontline* 18, no. 10 (May 12–25, 2001): 10.

25. Pierre Nora and his collaborators stress the need to give priority to the study of "sites of memory," i.e., monuments, museums, archives, events, texts, ideas, and so on, that support the notion of the nation. These are reminders of the nation; studying them may help us in understanding the relationship between individual memories and public memory, and between both of these and power. But memory sites may be reminders of other scales as well, as in this case which proudly supports the notion of a borderland identity that is inseparable from illegal cross-border flows. Such celebrations are not uncommon in borderland cultures, but usually they are frowned upon or suppressed by states—e.g., the *narcocorridos*, songs lionizing drug smugglers in the northwestern Mexico-U.S. borderland that became popular in the wake of U.S. drug interdiction campaigns. Cf. Pierre Nora, ed., *Les lieux de mémoire* (Sites of Memory), 3 vols. (Paris: Éditions Gallimard, 1997); Elijah Wald, *Narcocorrido: A Journey into the Music of Drugs, Guns, and Guerrillas* (New York: Rayo/Harper Collins, 2001).

26. Ed Ragas, *Baarle op de grens van twee eeuwen: Enclavedorpen in beeld* (Baarle on the Brink of Two Centuries: Images of Enclave Villages) (Baarle: Bruna, 1999), 54. The photograph shows a Belgian border guard and two ex-smugglers, one Belgian and one Dutch.

27. Scales are spatial representations, ways in which we frame conceptions of spatial reality. People with different conceptions of spatial reality may engage in struggles over these ("politics of scale"), and these struggles result in webs of relations and other material outcomes. For introductions to this concept, see Smith, "Contours"; Erik Swyngedouw, "Excluding the Other: The Production of Scale and Scaled Politics," in *Geographies of Economies*, ed. Roger Lee and Jane Wills (London: Arnold, 1997), 169; Richard Howitt, "Scale as Relation: Musical Metaphors of Geographical Space," *Area* 30, no. 1 (1998): 49–58; Katherine T. Jones, "Scale as Epistemology," *Political Geography* 17, no. 1 (1998): 25–28; Brenner, "Beyond State-Centrism?"; Sallie A. Marston, "The Social Construction of Scale," *Progress in Human Geography* 24, no. 2 (2000): 219–242.

28. On the politics of scale, see Smith, "Contours" and Swyngedouw, "Excluding the Other." In a more recent contribution, Brenner suggests two other terms: the "politics of scaling" and the "politics of scalar structuration." Neil Brenner, "The Limits to Scale? Methodological Reflections on Scalar Structuration," *Progress in Human Geography* 25, no. 4 (2001): 591–614.

29. For an extreme case of such everyday transnationality, see Willem van Schendel, "Stateless in South Asia: The Making of the India-Bangladesh Enclaves," *The Journal of Asian Studies*, 61, no. 1 (2002): 115–147.

30. E.g., Claire Sterling, *Crime without Frontiers: The Worldwide Expansion of Organised Crime and the Pax Mafiosa* (London: Little, Brown and Co, 1994).

31. E.g., Frank Bovenkerk, *Misdaadprofielen* (Profiles of Crime) (Amsterdam: J. M. Meulenhoff, 2001). The literature emphasizes the more durable forms of transnational criminal organization but does not provide an assessment of the relative importance of these forms vis-à-vis *ad hoc* alliances, small family operations, one-person operations (e.g., a Belgian woman smuggling her Kurdish lover into Italy in her suitcase), or people sneaking across a border on their own, in an act of "self-smuggling." "Kurdish lover sent packing," *Kurdistan Observer*, 13 July 2002, http://home.cogeco.ca/~kurdistanobserver/14–7-02-reu-kurdish-lover-packed.html.

32. Adler, *Wheeling and Dealing*, 33.

33. "Uranium Seized from Villager in W. Bengal," *The Times of India*, August 27,

2001; and "India to Seek Bangla Help in Uranium Case." *The Times of India*, August 27, 2001.

34. Andrew Walker, *The Legend of the Golden Boat: Regulation, Trade and Traders in the Borderlands of Laos, Thailand, China and Burma* (Honolulu: University of Hawai'i Press, 1999), 58.

35. This immigration interdiction campaign was restricted to the California section of the Mexico-U.S. border. Joseph Nevins, *Operation Gatekeeper: The Rise of the "Illegal Alien" and the Making of the U.S.-Mexico Boundary* (New York: Routledge Press, 2002).

36. Such spatial diversification is analyzed for unauthorized migration across the Mexico-U.S. border in Audrey Singer and Douglas S. Massey, "The Social Process of Undocumented Border Crossing among Mexican Migrants," *International Migration Review* 32, no. 3 (1998): 581.

37. See, e.g., A. P. Cheater, "Transcending the State? Gender and Borderline Constructions of Citizenship in Zimbabwe," in *Border Identities*, ed. Wilson and Donnan (1998), 191–214; Elizabeth Jelin, "Epílogo II: Fronteras, naciones, género: Un comentario" (Epilogue II: Borders, Nations and Gender: A Comment), in *Fronteras, naciones e identidades*, ed. Alejandro Grimson (Buenos Aires: Ediciones Ciccus, 2000), 333–342.

38. An example of the adaptive skills of borderlanders is given by a woman from Fuzhou in China who was smuggled into the United States via Mexico. "Several Mexicans worked as guides. They were very nice to women. They gave us plenty of food. They instructed us to 'be quiet' in Mandarin, and to 'lie low' and 'kneel down' in the Fuzhou dialect." Quoted in Ko-lin Chin, *Smuggled Chinese: Clandestine Immigration to the United States* (Philadelphia: Temple University Press, 1999), 79.

39. Andreas, *Border Games*, 44.

40. Andreas, *Border Games*, 52–53.

41. Andreas, *Border Games*, 95. Cf. Singer and Massey, "The Social Process"; Peter Andreas, "The Transformation of Migrant Smuggling across the U.S.-Mexican Border," in *Global Human Smuggling*, ed. Kyle and Koslowski (2001), 107–125; David Kyle and John Dale, "Smuggling the State Back In: Agents of Human Smuggling Reconsidered," in *Global Human Smuggling*, ed. Kyle and Koslowski (2001), 29–57.

42. "Die Todesgrenze der Deutschen" (The Germans' Border of Death), *Der Spiegel*, 24 June 1991, 58–83; 1 July 1991, 52–71; 8 July 1991, 102–116; and Daphne Berdahl, *Where the World Ended: Re-unification and Identity in the German Borderland* (Berkeley: University of California Press, 1999).

43. Here I use the term "gatekeeper state" in the sense of a state that can open or close the border at will. This is a more restrictive use than the one proposed by Nevins, from whom I derive the term. According to Nevins, the gatekeeper state is a state "the task of which is to provide extraterritorial opportunities for national territory-based capital (thus intensifying the process of globalization) while, somewhat paradoxically, providing security against the perceived social costs unleashed by globalization—especially immigration." Nevins, *Operation Gatekeeper*, 178.

44. On the Mexico-U.S. border, this became a growing dilemma with the creation of the North American Free Trade Agreement (NAFTA) that made that border much more permeable for many goods from Mexico, allowing illegal trade to piggy-back on them. Nevins, *Operation Gatekeeper*, 134–138, 178.

45. Cf. Nevins, *Operation Gatekeeper*, 186.

46. Cf. Ansi Paasi, "Boundaries as Social Processes: Territoriality in the World of Flows," *Geopolitics* 3, no. 1 (1999): 669–680.

47. Cf. Roger M. Downs and David Stea, *Maps in Minds: Reflections on Cognitive Mapping* (New York: Harper & Row, 1977), 6. On scale and cognitive maps, see also Peter Orleans, "Differential Cognition of Urban Residents: Effects of Social Scale on Mapping," in *Image and Environment: Cognitive Mapping and Spatial Behavior*, ed. Roger M. Downs and David Stea (Chicago: Aldine Publishing Company, 1973), 115–130.

48. For the interactive nature of these representations and their content, selectivity, and organization, see Downs and Stea, *Maps in Minds*, esp. 99–145.

49. "Rebel Groups Call for Independence Day Boycott," *The Times of India*, July 31, 2001; cf. "Mixed Response to 'Black Day,'" *The Telegraph*, October 17, 2002.

50. "BSF Free 13 Bangladeshis," *The Daily Star*, December 13, 2000; Probir Pramanik. "Tragedy on Border over Prayer," *The Telegraph*, December 29, 2000.

51. Sourin Bose was a leader of the Maoist uprising in Naxalbari in 1967 and an emissary of the Communist Party of India (Marxist-Leninist)—also known as the Naxalites—to China in 1970. Sourin Bose, interview by Shahriar Kabir and Willem van Schendel, video recording, Siliguri, West Bengal, India, 1999 (available at the International Institute of Social History, Amsterdam).

52. Cf. Alejandro Grimson, "Introducción ¿Fronteras políticas versus fronteras culturales?" (Introduction: Political Borders vs. Cultural Borders?) in *Fronteras, naciones e identidades* ed. Grimson, 9–40.

53. On the persistence of such networks in the China-Thailand-Burma borderland, see Chiranan Prasertkul, *Yunnan Trade in the Nineteenth Century: Southwest China's Cross-Boundaries Functional System* (Bangkok: Institute of Asian Studies, Chulalongkorn University, 1989).

54. On "shopping the border" in Ireland, see Donnan and Wilson, *Borders*, 117–122.

55. Swyngedouw, "Excluding the Other," 169. According to Smith's original formulation, "jumping scale" means to organize the production and reproduction of daily life and to resist oppression and exploitation at a higher scale. This has been nuanced by Cox, who showed that such resistance can also be expressed at a more local scale. As we have seen, however, in a borderland situation the architectural imagery of higher and lower scales (or more local and more global ones) breaks down, and the direction of scale jumping is in the eye of the beholder. See Smith, "Contours," 60; Kevin Cox, "Spaces of Dependence, Spaces of Engagement and the Politics of Scale, Or: Looking for Local Politics," *Political Geography* 17, no. 1 (1998): 1–23.

56. Van Schendel, "Easy Come, Easy Go," 204–205.

57. For a discussion of the "disjuncture between official threats and the reality in which state officials were actually aiding and abetting smuggling" on the Ghana-Togo border, see Paul Nugent, "Power Versus Knowledge: Smugglers and the State along Ghana's Eastern Frontier, 1920–1992," in *Frontiers and Borderlands*, ed. Rösler and Wendl, 94.

58. Scott Relyea, "Trans-State Entities: Postmodern Cracks in the Great Westphalian Dam," *Geopolitics* 3, no. 2 (1998): 30–61. According to Neil Brenner, the territorialist epistemology entailed a "transposition of the historically unique territorial

structure of the modern interstate system into a generalized model of sociospatial organization, whether with reference to political, societal, economic, or cultural processes." Brenner, "Beyond State-Centrism?" 48.

59. Brenner, "Beyond State-Centrism?" 62.

60. Timothy W. Luke and Gearóid Ó Tuathail, "The Fraying Modern Map: Failed States and Contraband Capitalism," *Geopolitics* 3, no. 3 (1999): 14–33.

61. John Torpey, *The Invention of the Passport: Surveillance, Citizenship and the State* (Cambridge: Cambridge University Press, 2000), 6–10.

62. Andreas, *Border Games*, 7; Nicholas P. De Genova, "Migrant 'Illegality' and Deportation in Everyday Life," *Annual Review of Anthropology* 31 (2002): 419–447.

63. In terms of numbers, the inflow of unauthorized Rohingya refugees from Burma runs into several hundreds of thousands, whereas the number of unauthorized Bangladeshis in India is estimated at between 12 and 20 million, with 5 million living in the Indian state of West Bengal. If these figures are correct, the number of unauthorized Bangladeshi immigrants in West Bengal alone equals that of *all* unauthorized immigrants in the entire United States of America. According to calculations by the U.S. Immigration and Naturalization Service (INS), 5 million illegal immigrants were residing in the U.S. in 1997, of whom 2.7 million were from Mexico. Andreas, *Border Games*, 4n.

64. Andreas, *Border Games*, 16–17.

65. On India, see Ranabir Samaddar, *The Marginal Nation: Transborder Migration from Bangladesh to West Bengal* (New Delhi: Sage Publications, 1999), 120–121. On the United States, see Andreas, *Border Games*, 32–39; Nevins, *Operation Gatekeeper*.

66. On Mexico, see Andreas, *Border Games*, 37–38.

67. E.g., Indian companies producing phensidyl, a cough syrup that is extremely popular in Bangladesh, although it is banned there as a narcotic because of its high codeine content. Other well-known Indian products are woolen shawls from Kashmir, silk *saris* from South India, table fans, cosmetics, razor blades, medicines, and components of trucks and buses.

68. A bewildering variety of commodities enter Bangladesh largely to be traded illegally across the border to India, e.g., Japanese, Korean, and Taiwanese electronics; Danish, Dutch, and Australian milk powder; Russian, Chinese, and Israeli assault rifles; American cigarettes and cosmetics; French perfumes; Thai concrete and fertilizers; and Swiss watches.

69. On (il)legibility, see James C. Scott, *Seeing Like a State: How Certain Schemes to Improve the Human Condition Have Failed* (New Haven, Conn., and London: Yale University Press, 1998).

70. Jean-François Bayart, Stephen Ellis, and Béatrice Hibou, *The Criminalization of the State in Africa* (Oxford/Bloomington: Currey/Indiana University Press, 1999).

71. Cf. Cox, "Spaces of Dependence."

The Rumor of Trafficking

Border Controls, Illegal Migration, and
the Sovereignty of the Nation-State

Diana Wong

It is in a sense about the way objects move, but it is more decisively about the way in which
moving objects and people are identified, assimilated, marginalized or rejected.
—Jonathan Friedmann, *Cultural Identity and Global Process*

Furtive flows of human cargo slipped through the border controls of
otherwise sovereign nation-states—this dramatic image has emerged in
the last decade as the visible embodiment of a menacing "dark side of
globalization."[1] Illicit movements of other flows—of drugs, weapons, and
money—bloating that underbelly of globalization which "threatens to damage our societies and our economies,"[2] do not lend themselves as easily to
arresting media images as do multitudes of huddled masses left stranded
at lonely border outposts. Spectacular scenes of rickety boats filled to the
brim with swarming men, women, and children hovering off the shores
of Europe, the United States, and Australia have imprinted themselves
on the public imagination. No less spectacular has been the public policy
response. From a poorly funded, NGO women's issue in the early 1980s,
"human trafficking" has entered the global agenda of high politics, elicit-
ing in recent years significant legislative and other action from the U.S.
Congress, the European Union, and the United Nations.

This chapter is about the power of the trafficking discourse and its deployment in the politics of migration control in the Western industrialized
states of the post–Berlin Wall era. In his magisterial study of the conditions
of possibility for the establishment of the free market in the nation-states of

nineteenth-century Europe, Karl Polanyi famously referred to the necessary intervention of the state: "The road to the free market was opened and kept open by an enormous increase in continuous, centrally organized and controlled interventionism. To make Adam Smith's 'simple and natural liberty' compatible with the needs of human society was a most complicated affair."[3] I shall argue that a century later, with the creation of a global free market at stake, the corollary is just as true: an enormous amount of transnational state interventionism has been necessary to hinder the emergence of the free mobility of labor, that "simple and natural liberty" compatible if not with the needs then with the dynamics of a global economic order predicated on the free mobility of capital and goods.

I should note at the outset that the use of the term "rumor" in the title of this chapter is not in the least intended to suggest the absence of trafficking as a criminal practice. Rumor here is meant to refer to its use in a political field of meaning as "a rhetoric, a project, or a contested topos." The project, as suggested above, is one of political and social boundary-maintenance; the language of trafficking derives its power to moralize and criminalize from its semantic proximity to terms such as prostitution, smuggling, and slavery, and its present currency is reminiscent of an earlier instance of "moral panic," i.e., the "white slave trade," in the first decades of the twentieth century (see below).

The reality which the rhetoric purports to describe is more difficult to ascertain. Empirical evidence from Malaysia, where undocumented migration has been an issue since the early 1970s, will be adduced to indicate the relatively minor role of trafficking by transnational organized crime in the actual cross-border movement of migrants, as against the smuggling and overstaying measures undertaken by the migrants themselves. In making this point, I shall be introducing a distinction between trafficking and smuggling which departs from the definitions established by the United Nations Vienna Convention, and I shall be arguing for a necessary distinction between sociological (analytical) conceptualizations of empirical processes on the one hand and administrative and juridical categories on the other. In migration research, there is the unfortunate tendency to unthinkingly adopt the latter as conceptual and categorical givens.[4]

Based on the Malaysian data, it would appear that the deployment of the trafficking discourse—in the rhetorical production of the boundaries of the nation-state as sites of transgression—rests on an empirical fiction and bears only partial resemblance to the actual contours of the economy of illicitness in contemporary mass migrations. The trope deployed therein of illegal crossings subverting endangered boundaries and eroding state sovereignty rests, I would argue, on a questionable conceptual identity between national boundaries, territoriality, and sovereignty.[5] Undocumented, "illicit" border crossings of people have actually been much more common in the history of the nation-state than has been generally assumed. Borders have been important to the modern nation-state in real terms as much for the establishment of internal sovereignty and for the control of movement of goods as for the control of people movements. The current obsession with immigration and border control as the basis of a state's sovereignty and as intrinsic to its logic of being—for which the discourse on trafficking is a *chiffre*—is specific, I suggest, to a historical era which acquired a consciousness of itself with the fall of the Berlin Wall in 1989.

One final issue will be raised in this essay, namely, the conceptualization of illicitness itself. The trafficking discourse works in a double register of the moral and the legal, criminalizing, in both senses of the word, practices of cross-border irregularities. These practices, as research on contemporary migrations indicate, are extremely far-flung and widespread, as well as deeply embedded in various formal state and market structures. Indeed, individual migrant lives constantly weave their way in and out of intersecting spheres of legality and illegality.[6] The criminalization of these practices through the moral power and legal force of the trafficking discourse occludes their quotidian and "normal" occurrence.

Illicitness, I suggest, should be used to draw attention to the broad range of practices located in that space which is beyond the formal data-collecting gaze of the state. This space of the undocumented or the illicit is not so much illegal as extra-legal. It is in and from this space of the undocumented, and hence illicit, that the "new forms of territoriality and unexpected forms of locality"[7] which are reconfiguring the nineteenth-century landscape of bounded and contiguous nation-states are arising. Casting this space into the shadow of the criminal dark forces of globalization keeps the fecundity of its everyday practices from view.

The chapter falls into three parts. The first centers on an account of the elaborate discursive and institutional machinery at the international level which has been developed around the question of trafficking and smuggling. It attempts to historicize the power of this contemporary trafficking discourse by looking at earlier antecedents (the white slavery campaign), as well as by locating its emergence in the historical conjuncture marked by the 1989 fall of the Berlin Wall. Underlying the account is the conceptual premise that in this discursive economy, trafficking works as a master metaphor for the illicit as the criminal, assigning prostitution, asylum, and migration in equal measure to the undesirable underside of globalization.

The next section looks at the empirical contours of the economy of trafficking and smuggling in Malaysia, a country which has experienced extraordinarily high levels of illegal migration since the mid-1970s.[8] Exemplified by two case studies, but based on a larger study of illegal migrants in Malaysia conducted in 2000, this account of the economy of illicit migration deploys a conceptual distinction between trafficking and smuggling which departs from the definitions, now widely accepted in the literature, established by the UN Convention Against Transnational Organized Crime. The distinction introduced here is based on the agency (which is, it should be noted, never absolute) of the migrant and the conditions under which the migration project is undertaken. The findings on the Malaysian experience presented here qualify easy assumptions ("rumors") about illicit migration as an imported crime of subversive border trespass by innocent victims coerced by transnational organized crime.

In the final part of the chapter, the conceptual homology between sovereignty, territoriality, and border policing, constituting the political logic which underpins the rhetorical power of the trafficking discourse, will be questioned. Notwithstanding a state discourse in which all three are seen to be ontologically merged, the politics of sovereignty in post-colonial states has generally been agnostic with respect to the border and negligent with practices of border control. At the borderlands of these states, a societal logic, rather than a border logic, of ethnic affinity or historical consociationality governs the traffic of goods and people, a flow to which the notion of border trespass is immaterial. The trafficking discourse, with its metaphor of the materiality of the border and the criminality of border trespass, misrepresents not merely the reality of such borderlands but the nature of such post-colonial nation-states as well.

The Power of the Trafficking Discourse

The New Migration and the "White Slavery" Scare, 1910–1913

The trafficking discourse is not new. It has an eminent precursor in the "white slavery scare" which raged in Britain and the United States at the turn of the last century, peaking between 1910 and 1913 and vanishing by 1917.[9] The white slavery discourse centered around prostitution and came to mean "the procurement, by force, deceit, or drugs, of a white woman or girl against her will, for prostitution."[10] As against earlier pre-Victorian depictions of the prostitute as a "fallen woman," the white slavery narratives constructed the prostitute as a youthful, innocent victim, trapped into the trade through force or deceit, and unable to escape from the subsequent depths of moral depravity on account of debt peonage. The youth of the victim was often stressed, and the white slavery issue became closely linked to that of child prostitution.

The counterfoil to the figure of the victim was that of the villain-trafficker. In the United States in particular, as Keire's study points out, "urban reformers intertwined the story of the sexually coerced maiden with a heated condemnation of the business of vice."[11] Indeed, in the course of the campaign, as the abolitionists gained the upper hand over the regulationists, it was the white slave traffic which came to hold center stage over the white slave victim, both on the legislative agenda as well as in the media representations. Silent movie titles such as *Traffic in Souls*,[12] *The Inside of The White Slave Traffic*,[13] and *Smashing the Vice Trust*,[14] testify to the focus on the criminal and commercial critique.

The success of the campaign was extraordinary. The theme of innocent victim/evil trafficker was played out in numerous novels, plays, and silent movies of the period, besides receiving extensive coverage in the world's press. With public opinion galvanized and several organizations devoted to its cause, the campaign culminated in the passage of new national laws (the Criminal Law Amendment Bill of 1921 in Great Britain and the Mann Act of 1910 in the United States) as well as a series of international agreements.

Notwithstanding all that sound and fury, contemporary historical research has since debunked the material basis of that campaign. The historical evidence is that "the actual number of cases of white slavery, as defined above, are very few."[15] Of note is that the "scare" arose at the time of the "new" transatlantic migrations, which drew into its vortex migrants from "non-traditional" eastern and southern European countries of origin, as well as larger numbers of women migrants, and that it faded away as this wave of migration came to an end with the outbreak of the First World War.

Toward the end of the century, some six decades later, a new trafficking discourse made itself heard, this time involving the trafficking of third-world women and children to the Western industrialized world. In her analysis of this discourse, Doezema[16] draws the parallel to its predecessor as another instance of "moral panic." Both discourses were centered around the issue of prostitution and female migration. Both shared the motif of innocent victimhood, as well as a similar absence of material basis to the enraged claims of the virulence and scale of the phenomena.[17]

The new discourse had originated in the early 1980s from the social activism of progressive feminists on behalf of trafficked and stranded third-world women in the West, who had continued to respect their right to work while championing their right to protection. Doezema argues that this discourse was then taken over by a conservative abolitionist agenda which magnified and dramatized the "sex slavery" issue, an agenda which met with increasing success as growing female migration in the 1980s generated male anxieties and "boundary crises." By the end of the 1990s, it was clear to the "progressive" feminists that the trafficking discourse was one capable of raising public attention and funding (now going mostly to the "other" camp),[18] but also "the spectre of regressive approaches to sexuality, race and gender."[19]

Illegal Immigration and European Asylum Policy, 1989–1993

Doezema's account of this re-emergent trafficking is of one initiated by, and confined to, women NGO circles. In contrast to its predecessor, relatively little attention appears to have been given to the trafficker. The villain of the piece was to be found in Western development policies and Western sex tourism, or in third-world villagers who sold their daughters to "traffickers."[20] In the following, I shall suggest that the career—and power—of the trafficking discourse took another remarkable turn in the late 1990s when it was hijacked and reframed from its initial context of imported third-world prostitution into the larger one of illegal immigration and European asylum policy. Indeed, it is striking how central the issue of illegal migration has become to migration research in Europe and the United States.[21]

According to Morrison and Crosland,[22] the conjunction of trafficking and illegal immigration materialized into the political consciousness of Europe at the 11th International Organization for Migration (IOM) Seminar, devoted to the theme of "Global Human Trafficking" in 1994. In an influential paper presented to that conference by a leading European scholar on international migration, the emergent model of the new unholy trinity threatening the borders of Europe—trafficking, illegal immigration, and organized crime—was introduced and authoritatively quantified.

> Trafficking brings annual incomes to gangster syndicates in the magnitude of at least US$5 to US$7 billion a year. Other official data on illegal immigration to various countries is by definition not available. However, various estimates can be made. Thus, the number of aliens who in 1993 managed to illegally trespass the borders of Western European states, for the sake of illegal employment or residence, could be estimated to have been in the magnitude of 250,000 to 350,000. This estimate is established on the basis of extrapolations on how many illegals finally reached their intended goal,

as a reflection of the known number of migrants who were apprehended when seeking to transit through the green [i.e., land] borders of intermediate countries on their way to the stated final goal.[23]

The political consciousness of Europe in the early 1990s was haunted by the new migration frontier on its eastern flank created by the fall of the Berlin Wall in 1989. Following the 1974 recession, European countries such as Germany and the Netherlands had scrapped their "guest worker" policy of recruitment of foreign workers into their post-war, labor-scarce economies. All subsequent legal entry into these countries had to fall under restrictive conditions for residence and employment (such as student visas and temporary employment passes) or family reunion provisions for foreigners already granted rights of residence. Virtually the only other channel for acquiring a legal status (aside from that of marriage to a citizen or permanent resident) was through the procedures established for the asylum regime. It is not coincidental that following the halt of the labor importation program in 1974, a steady increase in the number of asylum applications from Turkey, an important source country for earlier labor migrants to Germany, was observed.

This steady trickle, initiated in the mid-1970s and augmented in the 1980s by third-world migrants fleeing from a variety of conflicts fueled by the closing convulsions of the Cold War, such as the wars in Afghanistan, Iran, and the horn of Africa, grew into a tide with the end of the Cold War and the ignominious collapse of the Soviet Union. Military conflicts and the flights of population they are wont to generate, previously contained in distant peripheries, now flared up in direct proximity to Europe's own frontier. The brutal breakup of Yugoslavia was particularly damaging. For the European Union as a whole, this resulted in a tenfold jump in the number of asylum applications: from 66,900 in 1983 to 675,460 in 1992, with Germany alone receiving 438,190 applications.[24] This was the situation in which the IOM Seminar referred to above, at which the trafficking discourse was introduced to the "European political consciousness," was held.

1992 was the year asylum applications peaked (the statistics of course are only released in the following year). By 1994, the number of asylum claims filed had halved to 309,710. It fell further to 233,460—its lowest in the decade—in 1996. Thereafter, a slower but steady increase was again registered until 2000, when its rise was capped at 391,460. In 2001, the figure fell again to 384,530. A similar curve, though delayed in time, can be observed for asylum claims in the United States. There, the figures rose from 150,740 in 1992 to peak at 216,150 in 1996 before falling to a low of 46,020 in 1999. In 2001, the figure had again risen, to 86,170.[25]

These statistics lend themselves to a simple interpretation: actions undertaken by the European Union, and somewhat later by the United States, have been successful, although not entirely so, in reducing the number of asylum seekers in their territories. Indeed, the decade of the 1990s can be seen as one marked by the massive rise and subsequent containment of the phenomenon of "asylum migration" in the West. The containment policy has been largely based on techniques developed to "export" migration and border controls,[26] underpinned by legislative and administrative amendments.[27]

It is primarily within the context of the asylum system that the issue of illegal immigration has gained its critical edge. A foreigner who has managed to file a claim to asylum discards the status of an illegal immigrant and acquires that of an asylum applicant. However, given the formidable obstacles to legal entry for foreigners seeking protection or employment in the European Union in place since 1993, access to the asylum system is often impossible without the assistance of "traffickers and smugglers." Asylum seekers generally have to enter the country illegally. Hence it is that asylum, illegal immigration, and trafficking has assumed its functional and rhetorical unity.

With this new asylum and immigration context came a reconfiguration of the motifs familiar from the earlier discourse. Unverified statistics, such as the figure of US$5 billion to US$7 billion a year in commercial profit, have remained a standard feature. There is however a notable shift in focus from the victim to the trafficker, and more specifically to the involvement of criminal "gangster syndicates." Similarly highlighted is the physical transgression of the border or the metaphor of illegal trespass. And clearly "trafficking" has become a metaphor under which the smuggling of illegal migrants "for the sake of illegal employment or residence" is subsumed and indeed mainly understood.

The Great Trafficking Consensus, Post-1994

Framed by this "dominant paradigm,"[28] which to a lesser degree would also hold in the United States, the international career of the trafficking discourse has been nothing short of phenomenal. Following upon that influential 11th IOM Seminar in 1994, the IOM, which had been established in 1951 as the ICEM (Intergovernmental Committee for European Migration) to handle resettlement problems posed by the widespread presence of internally displaced peoples in Europe, as against the refugee mandate of the United Nations High Command for Refugees (UNHCR), found a new *raison d'être*. Renamed the IOM in 1989 as the impending end of the

Indochinese refugee crisis appeared to signal the end of the necessity for resettlement activity in the international system (and the possibility of institutional obsolescence), the IOM Council endorsed in 1994 the adoption of a new IOM objective: "to curtail migrant traffic and to protect the rights of migrants caught up in its practice."[29] Since then, as the lead international agency on migration and trafficking, it has, through its research funding, publications, and countertrafficking programs, succeeded in putting the issue of migrant trafficking at the center and forefront of today's international migration research agenda.

The IOM today is only one of more than thirty intergovernmental fora, in Europe alone, addressing the issue of trafficking.[30] NGOs devoted to this issue also mushroomed and formed anti-trafficking coalitions at around the same time, including the Coalition of Trafficking Against Women (CATW) in 1993 and the Global Alliance Against Traffic in Women (GAATW) in 1994. Their growth has also been impressive; from one secretariat in 1993, the CATW, for example, grew to six in 1996. Various UN agencies are also devoting resources to anti-trafficking programs. They include the UNHCR, OHCHR, UNICEF, UNIFEM, UNESCO, and the ILO. An ESCAP document recorded, as of March 2001, the existence of sixty projects in the ESCAP region devoted to the trafficking of women and children, involving the following UN agencies: ESCAP, ILO, IOM, UNDCP, UNIAP, UNESCO, UNHCR, UNICEF, and UNIFEM and their respective NGO, national government, and university research partners.[31] Major research programs on "human trafficking" are located in several universities and research institutes, such as UNICRI, Johns Hopkins, and the University of Hawai'i.

Media attention has also not been wanting, and it is in the media reporting that the new rhetorical figure of trafficking as a master metaphor for prostitution, illegal immigration, and organized crime is most clearly crystallized:

> The way the traffic in human beings is reported nearly always obscures the international aspects of the trade, evades criticism of European laws which victimize whole communities and conflates "ethnic" gangs with "ethnic" victims. Such stereotyping invariably serves a political purpose. As 100,000 Albanians attempted to flee to Italy across the Adriatic, on fishing boats and old ferries, the Italian press focused almost entirely on Albanian criminality, thereby justifying the state of emergency brought in by the government and the refusal to take in any more refugees. As Portugal began preparations to hand over Macau colony to China in 1999, the press reports focused on the Macaunese criminal triads involved in human smuggling and the trade in fake identity papers.[32]

Similarly, in conjunction with the trafficking of women, "we continue to see 'trafficking' used interchangeably with talk about the sex industry, prostitution, and sex slavery in the media."[33] This criminalizing tendency has remained the predominant thrust in the media coverage, notwithstanding the enrichment of the trafficking discourse with the issues of human rights and safe migration by other civil society and international organizations, in particular the OHCHR, from where the attempt to contest its repressive power from the "inside" has been undertaken.[34]

Indeed, much of the subsequent institutionalization of the trafficking discourse through the passage of two key pieces of legislation in the year 2000 has occurred under the rubric of transnational crime. In December 1998, the United Nations General Assembly established an intergovernmental *ad hoc* committee charged with developing a new international legal regime to fight transnational organized crime. The result is the UN Convention Against Transnational Organized Crime, supplemented by three additional treaties (protocols) dealing respectively with Smuggling of Migrants, Trafficking in Persons—Especially Women and Children, and Trafficking in Firearms, adopted by the General Assembly in November 2000. In her incisive analysis of the background to this convention, Gallagher notes,

> The significance of these developments should not be underestimated. The Vienna process, as it has come to be known, represents the first serious attempt by the international community to invoke the weapon of international law in its battle against transnational organized crime. Perhaps even more notable is the selection of trafficking and migrant smuggling as the subjects of additional agreements. Both issues are now high on the international political agenda. While human rights concerns may have provided some impetus (or cover) for collective action, it is the sovereignty/security issues surrounding trafficking and migrant smuggling which are the true driving force behind such efforts.[35]

In the same year, the Victims of Trafficking and Violence Prevention Act of 2000 was signed into law in the United States. The act sets minimum standards for the elimination of trafficking, which are applicable to "the government of a country of origin, transit or destination."[36] Non-compliant states, beginning in 2003, shall lose access to non-humanitarian, non–trade-related U.S. assistance. In addition, such countries will also face U.S. opposition to their seeking and obtaining funds from multilateral financial institutions including the World Bank and the IMF. This extremely powerful act (its only precedent is the Human Rights legislation passed under the Carter administration) calls for the production of annual reports by the State Department on all UN countries. It is clear from the first two reports since presented that notwithstanding the rhetoric of morality and the abolitionist thrust of the trafficking discourse in the United States Congress, they have been "heavily biased in favour of strong law enforcement responses"[37] against transnational organized crime and its perceived threat to border controls.

An elaborate trafficking discourse, indeed a moralizing and criminalizing anti-trafficking consensus, of global reach and institutional depth, encompassing states, international organizations, and NGOs—and academic institutions—has been established in a relatively short span of time. In charting its breathtaking journey from a feminist-based third-world NGO issue to the agenda of global high politics, I have referred to its rhetorical and metaphorical functionality. It is time now to give the discourse its due and to examine the claims it makes about the nature of illicit cross-border flows of people in the contemporary world.

Trafficking and Smuggling in the Economy of Illegal Migration

The Traffic in Figures

Three empirical claims are made by this trafficking discourse to justify the need for public funds and legislative action: claims related to the scale, the victimization, and the criminal organization of contemporary "trafficking in human beings." Central to these claims should be the legal distinction between trafficking and smuggling established by the UN smuggling and trafficking protocols, under which

> [s]muggling of migrants shall mean the procurement, in order to obtain, directly or indirectly, a financial or other material benefit, of the illegal entry of a person into a State Party of which the person is not a national or a permanent resident.
>
> Trafficking in persons shall mean the recruitment, transportation, transfer, harbouring or receipt of persons, by means of the threat or use of force or other forms of coercion, of abduction, of fraud, of deception, of the abuse of power or of a position of vulnerability or of the giving or receiving of payments or benefits to achieve the consent of a person having control over another person, for the purpose of exploitation. Exploitation shall include, at a minimum, the exploitation of the prostitution of others or other forms of sexual exploitation, forced labour or services, slavery or practices similar to slavery, servitude or the removal of organs.[38]

As figures are trafficked, however, the distinctions established above are ignored. Much of the traffic in numbers departs, as did IOM itself earlier, from "definitions tendered [which] commonly include both a formulation that provides the basis for a criminal offence as well as a more descriptive, often non-exhaustive account of the types of situations and activities commonly understood by the term."[39] As figures are trafficked between research and media reports, however, "trafficking" is generally taken to refer to more inclusive definitions, allowing for numbers to be magnified and inflated.

The thicket of statistical confusion which prevails, even in serious research literature, and with the IOM as the source of reference, can be seen in the following. In a recent journal article on trafficking in people, the scale of the phenomenon was suggested by two sets of figures: "estimated current global figures for people held in various contemporary forms of slavery run as high as 200 million people" and "the IOM estimates the number of people trafficked globally today at some four million."[40] The IOM deputy director was quoted in a March 7, 2003, press release giving a figure of "2 million women and children [who] were trafficked across borders in 2001."[41] On its official home page, however, IOM refers to the figure of "700,000 women and children trafficked yearly" out of an estimated total of fifteen to thirty million irregular migrants worldwide, a figure it appears to have adopted from the U.S. Department of Justice (see below).[42]

As recent research has been cautioning, all these widely invoked figures are highly dubious. UNICRI itself notes that "reliable data on smuggling in migrants and trafficking in persons . . . are scarce,"[43] and another recently completed Australian study notes that "in Australia, as in most countries of the world, limited evidence is available about the incidence and nature of human trafficking."[44] The most authoritative study done thus far, commissioned by the CIA, comes to the conclusion that "an estimated 45,000 to 50,000 women and children are trafficked annually to the United States."[45] It is likely that the current U.S. Department of Justice figure of 700,000 worldwide rests on methodological assumptions used in this study.

Trafficking versus Smuggling: The Economy of
Illegal Migration in Malaysia

Beyond the question of the scale or magnitude of trafficking and/or smuggling is the question of its nature and its organization. As argued above, the trafficking discourse and the conflations and distinctions it has spawned have arisen largely out of the European and North American context of public debate over illegal immigration and the vice industry. Within that context, the issue of illegal migration has been reduced to one of migrant trafficking and smuggling, treated as conceptually identical under the rubric of "human smuggling," and this singular entity in turn has been reduced to the nefarious business of transnational crime.

I turn now to another regional context of extensive illegal migration to call these reductions into question. In Southeast Asian countries such as Malaysia and Thailand, the stock of illegal immigrants is estimated to equal if not exceed the large numbers of legal labor migrants circulating within the region.[46] For the year 1997, the total stock of foreign migrants, legal and illegal, in these two mid-sized Southeast Asian nations, estimated at around three million, would have equaled if not exceeded the total number of illegal immigrants then found in the European Union.[47]

Malaysia, with an estimated one and a half to two million foreign migrants in 1997, has been experiencing large-scale illegal immigration, in particular from the neighboring islands of Indonesia, since the mid-1970s.[48] Foreign labor presently constitutes almost 20 percent of the total labor force. Since 1989, there have been more or less concerted attempts by the state to crack down on illegal migration and to replace illegal migrant recruitment with a regulated "guest worker" system of recruitment.[49]

Notable since the mid-1980s, and in tandem with state campaigns against illegal immigration, has been the emergence of a hostile anti-immigrant public discourse, prominently featured in the mass media, laced with derogatory terms such as "illegals" and "aliens."[50] Interestingly, this discourse is focused almost entirely on the migrants themselves, with scant though occasional attention paid to the traffickers or "syndicates" which bring them in. With the exception of NGOs working against the trafficking of women into the vice industry in the country, this national anti-immigrant discourse has not linked up with nor utilized the prevailing international trafficking discourse.[51] The metaphor of border trespass, central to the trafficking discourse, is clearly not at issue in the local, national political context (as I shall argue below, border trespass is not necessarily synonymous with the undermining of state sovereignty), even where strong anti-migrant sentiments can be discerned. The national imaginary is troubled, it would appear, by the moral liminality of the migrants themselves, not of the traffickers.

Apart from the absence of political valence in the Malaysian context, the lack of resonance of the international trafficking discourse is also due, I would suggest, to the overwhelming preponderance of smuggling versus trafficking in the economy of illegal migration in Malaysia. In making this argument, however, the distinction between smuggling and trafficking, so often smudged through the careless use of statistics as well as of terminology, is critical. A strict application of the definitions of the two provided in the UN Convention protocols (see above) would already point to a clear preponderance of smuggling over trafficking in the practice of illegal immigration to Malaysia.[52] However, drawing on the empirical contours of

Malaysia's illegal migrant economy as described below, I would like to introduce a distinction between the two which differs from that of the UN Convention, a distinction which departs from the perspective of the migrant rather than from that of the smuggler/trafficker (as in the definition contained in the UN Convention). The key criterion would be the degree of relative autonomy and control over the migrant project. From this migrant perspective, the organization of the "local" illicit migrant economy as described below may be indeed more paradigmatic of "global human smuggling" than that suggested by the metaphor of trafficking.

This account draws upon the findings of two recent studies of the organization of illegal immigration into Malaysia, one on the trafficking of Filipino women into the sex industry in Sabah, East Malaysia,[53] the other on illegal migrants (in the construction, plantation, domestic, and petty trading sectors of the economy) in West Malaysia.[54] Two case studies will be presented, followed by a further discussion on the distinction between trafficking and smuggling.

Trafficking into the Vice Industry

The story of Laniah (see Appendix 2.1) provides clear evidence of the existence of trafficking into the vice industry in the frontier state of Sabah, which shares a porous maritime border with the southern Philippines.[55] At the center of this economy of vice are entertainment centers (used as a generic term here to refer to pubs, discotheques, and karaoke lounges), which are serviced by the trafficked women. In the particular case studied here, the company ran two entertainment centers, a pub which opened from 2 P.M. to midnight and a discotheque which closed at 5:30 A.M. At any one time, the company has about thirty women in its employ.

The majority of the women were trafficked by the company itself. The company depended on agents in the source country, which in the case of the Philippines are invariably employment agencies operating in metropolitan Manila, as well as in provincial cities such as Cebu, Davao, and Zamboanga. The women were channeled to the employment agencies directly, via media advertisements, or through neighbors, former employees of the company, and other "recruiters" who receive a commission for sending women to the agencies. Potential recruits were accosted in places such as supermarkets, shops, restaurants, and entertainments premises. When an agency had collected a sufficient number of women, the company was notified and the boss then flew to Manila to interview the women, not all of whom were selected.

The women were told that they were being interviewed for jobs in

Malaysia as housemaids or as sales assistants. None of the women were informed that they were destined for vice activities, although some may have had their suspicions. No upfront payments were required as the employer advanced the cost of travel and job brokerage. In addition, the company used its contacts in the Philippines to arrange for the women to be provided with Filipino international passports (with false names) and Malaysian social visit passes valid for one month. This was arranged within three days of the confirmation of the contract. This mode of recruitment is highly attractive to the recruit as no initial outlays are required for the migration enterprise. Later, however, the women discovered that the company imposed a fee of RM 4,500 (US$1,184) to cover these expenses, a clearly inflated sum.

The girls (in this case, it was a group of eight) were then flown, in the accompaniment of an employee of the employment agency, from Manila to Zamboanga, a town in the southern Philippines which is a ferry ride away from the town of Sandakan, on the east coast of Sabah. In Zamboanga, they received the ferry ticket from the agency and crossed the border from Zamboanga to Sandakan on their own, entering Sandakan as tourists. In Sandakan, they were met at the ferry terminal by an employee of the company, whose photograph had already been shown to them in Zamboanga. He provided them with the RM 450 in cash necessary to secure their entry as tourists at the immigration control counter. From Sandakan, the girls were flown to Kota Kinabalu, the capital of Sabah, and from there to Labuan. It was in Labuan that they were turned into illegal migrant workers in the vice trade, forced into the job in large part out of the necessity to pay off the debt of RM 4,500 incurred in making the legal entry into Sabah.

In Labuan, they were housed together in company quarters and brought to and from the quarters to the place of work by the company driver. In addition, there was a security guard at the quarters and another at the center. There was a manager at each center who further oversaw the movements of the women. In principle, however, the women were not subject to restrictions on their movements outside of their working hours. What in practice restricted their mobility was that their passports were held by the company as ransom for the debt (RM 4,500) owed to the company for expenses incurred for the passage to Sabah. This sum included the cost of the passport as well as of transportation. As long as the women were in debt to the company, they had to work to pay off the debt and redeem their passports. And without their passports, they could not move freely within Sabah for fear of police detention, nor could they return to the Philippines. The women were thus subject to three forms of control over their mobility:

the physical control of the male supervisors, the economic control of debt, and the police control of unlawful presence.

Given the earnings potential of the women, it should have been theoretically possible to clear the debt in six months. Once the debt was cleared, the contract could then be renewed on a voluntary basis. This, however, seldom happened. Most of the women remained in debt to the company for more than a year. For example, eighteen women who were detained and deported after eleven months in Labuan were found to owe RM 80,000 to the company. The reason for this was not so much a low level of income as a high level of expenses, which forced the women to contract new debts with the company and thus remain in a continuous state of debt bondage.

Apart from regular expenses such as accommodation, food, transportation, and medical expenses, as well as remittances to the families (usually once every three months), there were some other heavy items of expenditure which were peculiar to the trade. One important item was extortions by lower level police personnel, allegedly to the tune of RM 1,000 every other month or so. The other was the heavy consumption and high cost of drugs such as ecstasy pills, *syabu* (the local name for a popular drug), and amphetamines, encouraged by the company. Furthermore, the women were made to pay the company RM 350 every month for the renewal of their social visit passes (which the company never did). The net result was a constant postponement of debt redemption.

Notwithstanding all this, within eleven months the company would lose the girls it had recruited. Some were caught by the authorities and deported as illegal migrants, some left after their debt was covered, and some ran away or were taken (bought) over by men who kept them as mistresses. This means there is a constant need for fresh recruitment, and the market demand for women in Labuan far exceeds the current supply. "Without the girls, no business." The key to the business is the supply and control over women.

It is noteworthy, however, that the bulk of the procurement is effected by the entertainment companies themselves. Apart from trafficking women for deployment in its own entertainment center, the company also "sells" the women it recruits in this fashion to other entertainment centers in Limbang and Kota Kinabalu. There are also small-time "retailer" recruiter-suppliers who specialize in the recruitment and smuggling of women into Sabah for supply to the vice businesses. On the whole, however, direct recruitment by the vice industry itself appears to be the predominant trafficking practice. Apart from small "retailer" recruiters, there is no evidence of an independent trafficking industry in the bustling vice trade in Sabah.

Smuggling into the Market of Casual Labor

Outside of the vice sector, however, the recruitment of illegal migrant labor is organized along quite different lines. The story of Maimunah (see Appendix 2.2) exemplifies migrant smuggling into the casual labor market in West Malaysia. For Maimunah, also a female illegal migrant, the experience of illegal immigration could not be more different than that of Laniah.

She entered the country with no identity documents whatsoever, not even a forged passport from her country of origin, Indonesia. Maimunah comes from Flores, an island in the far east of Indonesia, 1300 kilometers from Jakarta, the administrative capital. In those parts, documents of any kind, even forged ones, are prohibitively rare. Her husband, himself an illegal migrant in Malaysia, had sent for her in a letter delivered by a fellow villager back on a home visit. She was to follow this villager back to Malaysia.

Maimunah, who had been tending the small family farm in her husband's absence, raised the RM 1,000 necessary for the long journey in part from her own savings, in part from her in-laws. Together with her husband's friend and fellow villager, who organized the entire journey, she first traveled westwards by ship to Surabaya in Java and from there to Dumai on the east coast of Sumatra. From Dumai, they paid a boatman for navigating the short, illegal entry across the Straits of Malacca onto the coast of Malaysia. Once dropped off by the boatman, they continued their journey by bus, reaching their final destination, a squatter settlement in Kuala Lumpur, in five hours. Her husband found her a job immediately as a street cleaner. She subsequently worked on a construction site for a while before landing her present job as a helper in a small restaurant.

In Malaysia, she dodges the authorities with the assistance of forged Malaysian identity papers. She lives with her husband in rented accommodations and plans to return to Flores in a year's time to visit her children, who are still there.

Maimunah's entry into the illegal migrant economy in Malaysia is fairly typical, although it is only one mode of entry from a range of available options. Of the 100 migrants surveyed, 54 percent entered Malaysia without any documentation whatsoever, not even a passport. Another 41 percent entered the country legally on a tourist visa, 9 percent by air, and 30 percent by ferry. The remaining 5 percent had entered the country via its official labor market—as legally recruited foreign workers—and had subsequently "migrated" from the legal to the illegal sector.

Which mode of entry is chosen, legal or illegal, directly into the underground economy or via the official one, depends on a number of other factors, one of the most important being the kinds of intermediaries available for the organization of the migration enterprise. Here again, the range of discernible options is striking. In 16 percent of the cases, a *taikong* (broker) from the home village, who either on his own or in conjunction with larger syndicates, arranged the entire journey from the village of origin to the worksite in Malaysia for the migrant. The payment made to the *taikong* in this case included the cost of job brokerage as well as the cost of safe passage. In 4 percent of the cases, the *taikong* did not take immediate payment from the migrant, "selling" the migrant to an employer who would deduct the cost of the loan from the future wages of the migrant.[56]

More often, however, the *taikong* was the boatman who was necessary only for the boat passage across the straits, with the rest of the passage, and entry into the labor market in Malaysia, actually being organized or facilitated by the father (1 percent), husband (4 percent), friends (25 percent), and relatives (22 percent). The story of Maimunah, as narrated above, is typical in this regard. It is interesting to note that in 11 percent of the cases, the migration venture was an entirely individual enterprise, with the migrant himself organizing his journey across the straits and finding a job in Malaysia on his own (3 percent) or through information provided by fellow travelers met along the way (8 percent).[57]

It is in this context of irregularity in Malaysia itself that another "immigration industry" has developed to serve the needs of the migrants. "*Imigresen Chow Kit*" was the term used by Indonesians to refer to the trade in forged documents, run mostly by Indonesians in possession of permanent residence in the country, located in Chow Kit, a neighborhood in Kuala Lumpur associated with the presence of Indonesian foreign workers. Various forged documents could be obtained, both (supposedly) of Malaysian and Indonesian provenance. Apart from major documents such as work permits, identity cards, etc., other documents specific to the needs of irregular migrants were also issued, such as forged Indonesian marriage certificates. The cost was relatively low; forged work permits could be acquired for between RM 600 and RM 800, a forged red identity card for RM 200–300, while a forged passport or social visit pass only cost between RM 40–80.

Clearly, the assistance of the immigration industry (in this case, an immigration industry which services illegal migrants already in the country, as distinguished from the one specialized in providing illegal entry into the country) was indispensable to the lives of illegal migrants. Often, however, it was the employer whose help was sought, especially when there was trouble with the police or a need for a place to stay.

Apart from professional intermediaries and the employer, it was above all friends and relatives who continued to play a key role in the provision of help and protection. Of the migrants, 58 percent had friends and relatives in Malaysia, of whom 13 were in possession of work permits, i.e., were in the country legally. Of even greater significance is that another 16 percent of these friends and relatives were in possession of permanent resident status in Malaysia. Many of them had become entrepreneurs in the construction industry as subcontractors and in petty trading as owners of stalls and shops. Many had also established homes in squatter settlements throughout the city. These ethnic businesses and settlements were an important focal point for fresh migrants in search of work, residence, and knowledge of survival skills. The availability of these informal networks with a legal status in the country were as indispensable to the lives of the illegal migrants as was the immigration industry.

THE VICTIM, THE CRIMINALS, AND THE BORDER-CROSSING IN THE ILLICIT ECONOMY

Not all illicit traffic across Malaysian borders thus involves victims. Laniah, who was trafficked into the vice industry, was clearly a victim of deception, and then was subject to the coercion of debt peonage for the cost of the passage which had been organized and pre-financed by her future employer in Malaysia. Maimunah, on the other hand, came to join her husband who was already in Malaysia. The cost of the journey, including payment for the boatman who took her across the straits to Malaysia, was raised from her savings and those of her in-laws. Once in Malaysia, she sought employment in different sectors of the labor market. Her sense of victimization derived from her vulnerability to police raids ("rush") on illegal migrants in the area where she lived.

The key distinction to be made here, I would suggest, is one based on the agency of the migrant and the conditions under which the migration project is undertaken, a distinction, I suggest, which could serve as a more salient sociological distinction between smuggling and trafficking than the one established in the UN Convention. This is the distinction between the service of those intermediaries or *taikong* who primarily execute the border crossing (e.g., as boatmen for that one leg of the journey which involves evasion of border patrols, both into and out of the country) for migrants who are in active control of their own migration project[58] (either alone or with the help of friends and relatives), and those intermediaries who recruit the migrant, organize the transport, and "sell" him to an employer in Malaysia, or are the employers themselves.

The vast majority of migrants in the illicit economy in Malaysia belong to the first category. Their tenuous subterranean existence would not be possible without the existence of an extensive "immigration industry." In the main, however, this immigration industry appears to be much like that of any other service provider—in this case, it is primarily a transport and document-delivery service.[59] Migrants outside the official legal recruitment system[60] take advantage of and pay for these services as and when the need arises. A number of migrants fall into the second category. Here, recruitment, initial transaction cost, transport, and employment are all arranged by a single source. The level of self-control over the migration project is correspondingly low. The key factor here appears to be the nature of the labor market in which the migrant ends up working. Where the nature of the work itself is illicit, as in the vice sector, there appears to be a far greater likelihood for the second pattern to prevail.

While the entire immigration industry works beyond the pale of the law, the role of sinister "transnational organized crime" groups in the organization of the above regional cross-border movements is likely to be exaggerated.[61] The CIA study of the international trafficking of women to the United States found that trafficking was dominated by "mom and pop" type operations: "perpetrators tended to be smaller crime groups, smuggling rings, gangs, loosely linked criminal networks, and corrupt individuals who tend to victimize their own nationals. None of the traffickers' names were found in the International Police Organization's database, indicating that these traffickers were not under investigation for trafficking or other illicit activities in other countries."[62] Similarly, in the case of trafficking into the vice industry in Sabah, the trafficker involved was a licensed discotheque owner who acted as direct recruiter of his foreign staff. In the broader field of illicit services provided to those smuggled but not trafficked, as defined above, there appears to be a robust, decentralized retailer market with a fair amount of competition.

One final empirical note should be made at this point: All the women who were trafficked into the establishment in Sabah in the case study above crossed the border legally. Their illegal status was acquired within the country when they overstayed their visas. Similarly, 46 percent of the illegal migrants in the sample had entered the country legally and overstayed. Legal entry preceding illegal status appears to be of significance to the phenomenon of illegal immigration in the European Union, the U.S., and Australia as well.[63]

The illicit, at least as it takes human form, is hence not merely a commodity to be kept without; it becomes so from within. Neither is the world of the illicit one solely of victims terrorized by criminals. Yet the rhetorical production of the trope of the nation's borders as endangered by illegal immigration abetted by the machinations of organized crime has been highly successful. In Europe, as Gallagher notes,

> illegal migration is now being construed as an imported crime, so that commercial assistance for refugees is accordingly categorized as "organized crime." In line with this scenario, risks to internal security are to be met by addressing "criminal geography" and by identifying socially adjusted "control filters" . . . ultimately, an "overall European security zone" will be constructed based on the "organised crime" scenario and on the criminalisation of migration . . . using a criminological redefinition of offenders (smugglers and traffickers) and victims (penniless refugees, women forced into prostitution), police forces and public authorities are trying to use human rights to justify and legitimise their actions.[64]

Border Controls and Nation-State Sovereignty

The metaphor of the materiality of the border and of border trespass —and its identification with the territorial body and sovereignty of the nation-state—constitutes the unquestioned political logic underlying the power of the trafficking discourse. Another reduction is at work here; nation-state sovereignty is equated with border inviolability, the border in turn is conceived as a fencing mechanism for the control of population movements or flows. The work of the border of a sovereign nation-state—so the assumption goes—is that of keeping unwanted outsiders out, this function having been the immutable principle of its being since the emergence of the modern nation-state.

This assumption is based on the standard narrative of the development of the nineteenth-century Westphalian state, as in the following account:

> But what happened in the 19th Century was new, although it was the almost inevitable outcome of the Westphalian state. The broad acceptance of the doctrine of national sovereignty implied a particular kind of frontier and border control. After the appearance of the modern nation state in its mature form, from the time of the French Revolution, the coincidence of the military and security border, with the frontier of tax regimes, ecclesiastical boundaries, limits of provision of public assistance, public health services, licensed professions, education and economic regulatory regimes was completed. It became taken for granted that states had not only the right but the legitimate authority to control all activities on their territory and to

do this they needed, in principle, absolute control of passage across their borders.[65]

In this standard narrative, "these ideas of state sovereignty and territoriality were diffused from Europe to the rest of the world" in the late nineteenth and early twentieth centuries and have since been in practice with the extension of the Westphalian nation-state system to the entire globe.[66]

It should be borne in mind, however, that although "these ideas of state sovereignty and territoriality" found institutional expression in the European states in the nineteenth century, state practices of border control came to full maturity only in the following century. The two world wars of 1914–1918 and 1939–1945 were critical in this respect. Up until the outbreak of World War I in 1914, possession of an identity-control document such as a passport was not necessary for the great transatlantic passage,[67] nor, need it be said, for the other vast population movements spawned by imperial expansion in Asia and Africa in the nineteenth and early twentieth centuries. World War II had, in its turn, a further profound effect on border control regimes in Europe. "The changes in border controls across Europe since the end of the Second World War are both radical and without genuine precedent," Roger Dion wrote, and continued: "the war of 1939–45 conferred on political frontiers an efficacy, equaling or surpassing that of natural phenomena. A frontier as artificial as the Franco-Belgian separates economic regimes so different that we question a traveler coming from Belgium with as much curiosity as ten years ago one coming from Australia; and the line separating a democratic country from a totalitarian one can be in 1940 more difficult to cross than a formidable mountain barrier. Whether or not corresponding with natural frontiers, the linear frontiers of Europe have become terrible realities."[68]

The novelty of political borders was even more apparent for many of the new nation-states which were established in the aftermath of World War II. And yet, artificial as these borders were, the inherited colonial boundaries, as Mbembe astutely observes, have remained "essentially unaltered" and "the sacrosanct character of the boundaries inherited from colonization" have not been challenged by state action.[69] In respecting the "sacrosanct" nature of state boundaries, what appears to have been of primary concern to states is the internal sovereignty—to discipline, command, and extract—delimited by their territorial borders. It was the power of enforcement over the space enclosed within borders that occupied the energies of the new nation-states. "As soon as independence was won," Mbembe notes, "Africa began a vast enterprise of remodeling internal territorial entities even as it accepted the principle of the inviolability of boundaries among states. Almost everywhere, the redefinition of internal boundaries was carried out under cover of creating new administrative districts, provinces, and municipalities."[70]

This preoccupation with internal reterritorialization which Mbembe observes for Africa would also hold for state behavior in Southeast Asia. But to the degree that the existing territorial boundaries were accepted by the new nation-states, I would argue that these external boundaries were also neglected. One could perhaps speak of state indifference to these often extensive and remote borders. Frontier borderlands remained largely peripheral to the interest of nation-state elites located in the center, whose nation- and state-building projects often took no account of those more than a day's journey away. The social and economic life of these border-lands, straddling in many cases artificial if not arbitrary borders, remained robust, even if out of view of the national governments, and in defiance of the overriding and ineluctable political logic that governed the border in post–World War II Europe.[71]

In the post–World War II world of new post-colonial states, borders thus retained their porosity without states relinquishing their sovereignty. Indeed, the large movements of population which continued to move across many of these territorial boundaries is striking. This became particularly visible in the course of the many refugee crises in Asia and Africa in the decade of the eighties.[72] Such clear instances of dramatic "distress migration" spilling across borders may, however, obscure the more mundane existence of substantial transgressive cross-border movements, often along pathways stretching back to pre-colonial times, occurring under conditions of covert state sanction. In Malaysia, Indonesians who entered the country illegally often managed to acquire permanent residence status within a few months of their arrival, a state practice that ended only in 1989. Control of its extensive maritime and land border with Indonesia hardly existed until the outbreak of military hostility between the two countries in 1963. Cross-border ethnic and cultural affinities thus continued to impact the evolving border-control regimes of newly established pluralistic nation-states. For such states, the touchy question of sovereignty was not necessarily, or not yet, identical to that of immigration control at the border.

In *Seeing Like a State*, Scott documents the state's drive to reorder society through improved techniques of surveillance and control such as the mapping of territory and the documentation of personal identity through the insistence on surnames.[73] Notwithstanding these "attempts at legibility and simplification," the high modernist state's social engineering projects ultimately failed, Scott argues, thanks in part to the hubris of the planners and the authoritarian state, but in no small measure thanks also to the very success of this enterprise of administrative ordering and documentation itself.

The success of this enterprise should not be overestimated. As the various chapters in this volume show, large commodity chains—of labor, drugs, weapons, diamonds, and ideas, among others—continue to circulate tirelessly—and undocumented—across the established and accepted borders of today's nation-states. The economy of the illicit, I would argue, is homologous with the space of the undocumented, that which continues to remain hidden from the administrative order of the modernist state, that which the state does not see. Much of this space is topographically located in the borderlands, at border intersections which, contrary to state discourse, have often been of little interest to the sovereign power of the new post-colonial state. Whether the space occupied is merely of a residual character, or whether more is at stake, such as "new forms of territoriality and unexpected forms of locality," as in the formulation by Mbembe, are questions beyond the scope of the chapter. I have tried to show, however, that in the continuing historical contestations over emerging forms of territoriality, the nation-state remains one of the most important actors.

Its power derives in part from its ability to set the terms and conditions of the national and international research agenda. Hence the institutionalization, and the seductive power, of the trafficking discourse. The state's power to define—and distort—remains central to its enterprise of administrative ordering and documentation, within and at the border. It is for the conceptual policing of the border that its administrative and juridical categories have been developed. Their unquestioning adoption as sociological tools of the trade by the research community lies behind much of the conceptual penury in the study of migration and of other borderline issues in the economy of the illicit.

The deflation of the trafficking discourse attempted here is not a denial of the existence of trafficking and the very real questions of human rights and human security which are at issue. Neither should a rejection of the imputed nexus between migrant smuggling and transnational organized crime imply the inefficacy or illegitimacy of state practices of border control. The recourse to the empirical in this chapter has been deliberate. What the state does not see is also not available as processed data. Seeing like the state in research practice on border issues hence has often translated into empirical as well as conceptual penury. Even as we begin to pay attention to the transformative outcomes of illicit flows across borders, it is the careful and critical attention to detail with which research practice will have to begin.

APPENDIX 2.1. The Story of Laniah

After a long silence, she resumes talking, carefully, firmly. In Filipino English: "I am from Santa Mesa, Metro Manila. It is a big city, many entertainment places there like Harrison's Club. But in Manila I am still a good girl. My family is also good . . . all my neighbors respect my family."

She continues, "I came here not for this kind of job. I came here for a good job. Boss Tong cheated my friends and me. During the interview, he said we would be working here in a supermarket.

"In Manila I had worked in three supermarkets. The first and the second one not so long, about six months each. At the last one, I worked for about two years. My salary in that supermarket was about 5,000 pesos per month.

"I lived with my parents . . . although I lived in Metro Manila, I was not free to go anywhere . . . because my mother didn't like me to be involved in bad activities . . . if I went shopping, my sister was always with me. . . ." And she adds, "I know in Manila many many discos and karaoke. Harrison Club in Mabini close to Makati City is one of the bigger entertainment place in Manila, there, there are many young girls from Bisaya . . . many of their customers are Americans, but I didn't like this kind of place. . . ."

That was her past. "I already had a good job in Manila. But this company promised me a good salary here and many facilities would be provided free such as housing, medical expenses and transportation."

Her life changed, she says, when ". . . I was approached by an old woman while my friend and I were eating during happy hours. This woman asked me where I was working. I said, here at the supermarket. She ask me again, how much is your salary? I said 5,000 pesos. She said, oh! If you work in Malaysia, your salary would be double. I said, where in Malaysia? She replied, in Kuala Lumpur! I said to her, yah it is good, but I have no money to go to Malaysia. In my mind it must need much money, because when my friend went to Japan to work she needed 75,000 pesos. But this old woman said, no! If you really want to work in Malaysia, you need not have any money. I said, how can? She explained to me that I need not pay any money. All my expenses until in Malaysia will be advanced by the company. I only had to pay the credit through a monthly deduction from my salary, until the credit is finished. When your credit already finished, then all your monthly salary belongs to you."

The old woman left after saying to Laniah, ". . . this is the best opportunity for you to go and work in Malaysia, without paying even one cent of money . . . if I were you, for sure I would not let it go. . . ." She told Laniah to "think about it. . . . If you decide to accept it, then please contact me. . . ." The old woman gave her contact address and telephone number to Laniah.

After thinking it over for about three weeks, Laniah contacted the old woman. They met at a Jollibee restaurant close to her place of work. The old woman said she would arrange an interview with the representative of the company in Malaysia and would get back to Laniah as soon as possible to tell her the date and the place of the interview. Three days later, the interview was arranged.

On that day, at about 2 P.M., Laniah took a taxi with the old woman from her place of work to the place where the interview was to be held. While waiting for her interview, she was thinking about the questions which the interviewer would raise. Hardly any were raised. She was asked what her present work was and whether she really wanted to follow the company to work in Malaysia. That was all. But to Laniah's big surprise, the Chinese man asked her to take off her dress, down to her underwear. Laniah strongly objected to the request and asked for an explanation. The man said it was necessary because there was a lot of competition among the supermarkets in Malaysia and they had to attract customers with attractive workers, which is why he came to Manila to recruit suitable workers. Laniah still refused, and finally the interviewer agreed to drop his demand and the session ended. Laniah was still not satisfied with this matter of undressing for the interview, and outside the hotel, she continuously questioned the old woman, who gave her a similar reply.

A week later, Laniah got the news that only eight girls out of the fifteen had been successful in the interview. She thought to herself that she was one of the unsuccessful ones, as she had refused to undress during the interview. But she was not regretful, as her parents were against her working in Malaysia. She had told her mother about her encounter with the old woman in the restaurant, and her mother had expressed strong objections to the idea. She had gone for the interview without the knowledge of her mother.

But soon after, the old woman came to see her at her place of work and told her that she was among the fortunate few who were selected. The old woman encouraged her to grab the opportunity as, she said, it was not easy for girls like her to get good jobs in Malaysia without having to pay even a single cent. The old woman left by saying she hoped Laniah would accept the offer.

It took Laniah three months to finally decide to accept the offer. Once again she tried to get her mother's blessings to work in Malaysia. But her mother's stand remained unchangeable: ". . . I don't want. . . . I don't want. . . . I don't want. . . ." Laniah finally decided to disregard her mother's objection to her decision, and she notified the old woman of her decision.

The next day Laniah met with the man from the company. He told her that all the passport matters would be arranged by the company. Laniah only needed to provide the passport photos and duplicates of her birth certificate and identity card. A week later, the passport was ready. She was then told that the journey to Malaysia would be via Zamboanga City. Eight girls had been collected, and she should prepare herself for departure very soon.

Given her mother's objections, Laniah had to run away from home and stay with a friend for three nights before meeting with the group that was to leave for Malaysia. Transport had been arranged for them to be taken to Manila airport, and they were accompanied to Zamboanga by Madam Lh. They stayed in a hotel, four to a room, in Zamboanga City for five days while waiting for the ferry to Sandakan, Sabah.

That first night in the hotel room, Laniah thought of her mother and cried. She said, "When I left my home that evening, I felt very sad at separating from my parents, my sisters and brothers. When I stepped out of the house, I prayed to God. . . . 'Oh my God! Please don't be angry with me . . . please forgive me. . . . I did not tell the truth to my mother.'" When her friends asked her why she cried, "I replied to them that I remember my mother. I come here to go to Malaysia without the knowledge of parents. My mother had not allowed me but I cheated her. I had run away from home."

On January 18, 2001, the girls boarded the ferry to Sandakan. Madam Lh. sent them to the ferry and explained to the girls that a man would pick up them at the Sandakan ferry terminal. She gave the photo of the man to Laniah. The man, she told Laniah, had long hair and a small body. "When you arrive, look up at the right side of the terminal, the man will be there."

When they arrived, Laniah saw the man immediately. "I looked at the photo again and recognized the man. He also guessed who we were. He gave a signal with his right hand. I approached him. He said, 'How many of you? Eight persons. Where are they? There! Call them here.'" The man gave each of them RM 500 to show to the immigration officer. If asked how many were traveling together, they were to say only one.

The man who met them in Sandakan was K, the manager of the disco in Labuan where she was to work. He brought them from Sandakan to Labuan. There she again met the man who had interviewed her in Manila. He was the boss of the company, Boss LT. She was also introduced to Mami O, guest relations officer of the disco and a senior worker in the company. Mami O was about fifty years old. She was a Filipina from Zamboanga. As a Mami, she controlled all the women workers of the disco. She organized the bookings of all the girls.

When Laniah was briefed by K and Mami O on the work she was to do, she felt her heart would explode and she would die. Her heart said, "Please what I hear is just a dream, not the truth." When she heard the truth, her mind returned to her hometown. She remembered her mother, father, sisters, and brothers. She kept thinking of escape. She kept thinking of the future she had wanted with a husband and children.

Four days after arriving in Labuan, she called her mother. "She was crying . . . angry with me. 'Why are you so thick-headed?' she said. . . . I knew the job here; I am crying . . . my mother said, 'you talk to your boss that you want to go back to Manila.' But I said to my mother, 'no lah ma I got job here.'" Laniah said, "Until now my parents don't know my job here. My mother asked me what my job is and I only say that my job is good."

For more than two weeks, Laniah locked herself in her quarters. Although the boss pressed her every day to start working, she refused. Many women also approached Laniah to offer advice. Most told her to start work as soon as possible. Among the advice given by the friends: "Keep in mind that here nothing is free. Everything must be paid for. Quarters rental has to paid each month. Credit due to the company must be paid. Passport's cost must be paid to the company every month. The everyday necessities like food and cosmetics must be bought with your own money. So if you don't work, how can you get the money to cover all the fixed expenses? And then how can you talk about going back to Philippines?"

But she was also told, "Why you come here if you have never done this work! The people here knew well the work they had to do before follow the company here! . . . we had husband before and divorced . . . we had children at home who are growing and need education . . . we are here because we want money! You have never had a relationship . . . ? No husband and not yet married . . . still no baby! So why you come here?"

Laniah had brought 7,000 pesos from Manila, the savings from three months of work in Manila. Every week she exchanged 1,500 pesos with the moneychanger. After three weeks, when she ran out of pesos, Laniah agreed to commence work.

(My thanks to Gusni Saat for permission to use this story.)

APPENDIX 2.2. THE STORY OF MAIMUNAH

Maimunah is a married woman of thirty-seven from a rural district in Flores who lives in a rented house in a squatter settlement in Subang Jaya.[74] She has completed elementary school and was engaged in farming before coming to Malaysia a year and a half ago.

In Subang, she lives with her husband, who came to Malaysia several years ago and is now in possession of a forged red identity card.[75] Their eldest son is also in Malaysia, but he works in another state, while their three younger children, who are still in school, are still in Flores.

She entered Malaysia together with her husband's friend, who is from the same village of origin and who works in Malaysia as a lorry driver and also lives in the same residential area as they do now in Malaysia. On a visit home to the village, this friend had brought a letter from her husband asking her to join him in Malaysia. They entered without any travel documents, traveling from Ende in Flores to Surabaya by ship (a three-day, two-night journey, with three days transit stay in Surabaya), from Surabaya to Dumai by bus (five days and five nights with two days of transit in Dumai).

From Dumai on the Sumatran coast, they used the services of a *taikong* (a boatman broker) to cross over to Tg. Sepat on the Malaysian coast by boat, an eight-hour crossing. From Tg. Sepat, they made their way to their destination in Kuala Lumpur by bus, a journey of another five hours. The entire journey, including finding the services of the *taikong* for the Dumai–Tg. Sepat crossing, was organized by the husband's friend. The cost of RM 1,000 came in part from her own savings, in part from her in-laws.

When she first arrived, she found a job as a street cleaner with a Chinese contractor and was paid RM 20 per day. After three months she left, as the pay was low and always slow in coming. Two weeks later, she found a job as a *kongsikong* (general laborer) for a Chinese contractor at a construction site for which she was paid RM 30 a day, but she left after four months because the work was too tough. After a week, she found her present job, at which she has been working for eight months now, as a restaurant helper. She earns RM 700 monthly.

Illegal status is troublesome. She is fearful of roadblocks, and in particular of "rush" (police raids) on the housing area. If there is news of an impending "rush," the migrants don't sleep and prepare to run away if necessary. The other disadvantage of not having a permit is difficulty in getting work, and the lower wages.

She hopes to return to Flores in a year, as the children are still there. She will use the services of a *taikong* to return, at a cost of RM 400.

NOTES

1. Invoked in the Communiqué of the Ministerial Conference of the G8 Countries on *Combating Transnational Organized Crime*, Moscow, October 19–20, 1999. The G8 countries comprise Canada, France, Germany, Italy, Japan, Russia, the United Kingdom, and the United States. The European Union also participates and is represented by the president of the European Council and the president of the European Commission.

2. Communiqué of the Ministerial Conference of the G8 Countries.

3. Karl Polanyi, *The Great Transformation* (Boston: Beacon Press, 1944), 140.

4. Diana Wong, "The Semantics of Migration," *Sojourn* 4, no. 2 (1989): 275–285.

5. See Achille Mbembe's critique of this "simplistic" notion of boundaries constituting territoriality and sovereignty in the history of the African state in "At the Edge of the World: Boundaries, Territoriality and Sovereignty in Africa," *Public Culture* 12, no. 1 (2000): 259–284.

6. See David Kyle and Christina A. Siracusa, chapter 5, this volume.

7. Mbembe, "At the Edge of the World."

8. It has been estimated that in 1997, on the eve of the Asian financial crisis, the estimated number of foreign workers in Malaysia and Thailand alone, two mid-sized countries in Southeast Asia, was close to the estimated number of all foreign workers in Europe, i.e., between three and three and a half million. See Chris Manning and Pradip Bhatnagar, "The Movement of Natural Persons in Southeast Asia: How Natural?" http://rspas.anu.edu.au/economics/publish/papers/wp2004/wp-econ-2004-02.pdf.

9. See Jo Doezema, "Loose Women or Lost Women: The Re-emergence of the Myth of 'White Slavery' in Contemporary Discourses of 'Trafficking in Women,'" *Gender Issues* 18, no. 1 (Winter 2000): 23–50; and Mara L. Keire, "The Vice Trust: A Reinterpretation of the White Slavery Scare in the United States, 1907–1917," *Journal of Social History* 35, no. 1 (2001): 5–41, from which the following account is largely derived.

10. Doezema, "Loose Women or Lost Women," 25.

11. Keire, "The Vice Trust," 6.

12. *Traffic in Souls*, directed by George Loane Tucker, 1913.

13. *The Inside of The White Slave Traffic*, directed by Frank Beal, 1913.

14. *Smashing the Vice Trust*, directed by unknown, 1914.

15. Doezema, "Loose Women or Lost Women," 26.

16. Doezema, "Loose Women or Lost Women."

17. Drawing largely on the 1997 report by the Global Alliance Against Trafficking in Women (GAATW), authored by M. Weijers and L. Lap-Chew, Doezema notes that much of the "evidence" was based on unrevealed or unverifiable sources, that statistics, where documented, tended to refer to the total number of illegal migrants or domestic sex workers, and that in fact the evidence seemed to suggest a preponderance of sex workers rather than "coerced victims" in this "traffic." See M. Weijers and L. Lap-Chew, "Trafficking in Women, Forced Labour and Slavery-Like Practices," in *Marriage, Domestic Labour and Prostitution* (Utrecht and Bangkok: The Foundation Against Trafficking in Women [STV]/The Global Alliance Against Trafficking in Women [GAATW], 1997).

18. See Gallagher for an account of the bruising debates between these two "camps" in the negotiations around the Vienna Process. Anne Gallagher, "Human Rights and the New UN Protocols on Trafficking and Migrant Smuggling: A Preliminary Analysis," *Human Rights Quarterly* 23, no. 4 (2001).

19. Fiona David, "New Threats or Old Stereotypes? The Revival of 'Trafficking' as a Discourse," paper presented at the History of Crime, Policing and Punishment Conference, Canberra, December 9–10, 1999. Available at http://www.aic.gov.au/conferences/hcpp/david/pdf.

20. Doezema, "Loose Women or Lost Women," 38.

21. Michael Samers, "An emerging geopolitics of 'illegal' immigration in the Euro-

pean Union," European Journal of Migration and Law, 6: 23–41; and David Kyle and Rey Koslowski, eds., *Global Human Smuggling: Comparative Perspectives* (Baltimore: Johns Hopkins University Press, 2001).

22. John Morrison and Beth Crosland, "The Trafficking and Smuggling of Refugees: The End Game in European Asylum Policy?" *New Issues in Refugee Research*, Working Paper no. 39, UNHCR, 2001.

23. Jonas Widgren, "Multinational Co-operation to Combat Trafficking in Migrants and the Role of International Organisations," paper presented to the 11th IOM Seminar on International Responses to Trafficking in Migrants and Safeguarding of Migrant Rights, Geneva. October 26–28, 1994. http://www.oefm.org/documents/TraffickingUndok.pdf.

24. UNHCR, Statistics, http://www.unhcr.org, accessed January 28, 2003.

25. All figures are from UNHCR 2003.

26. L. Morris, "Globalization, Migration and the Nation-State," *British Journal of Sociology* 48, no. 2 (1997): 192–209.

27. For an account of the measures undertaken, seen as signaling the "endgame" of the asylum system in Europe, see Morrison and Crosland, "Trafficking and Smuggling."

28. Morrison and Crosland, "Trafficking and Smuggling."

29. International Organisation for Migration (IOM). http://www.iom.int/en/who/main_policies_trafficking.shtml#chap0, accessed April 4, 2003.

30. These include the Budapest Process, the Council of Europe, the European Parliament and Commission etc. Cf. Morrison and Crosland, "Trafficking and Smuggling."

31. http://www.unescap.org/wid/04widresources/03traffick/trafficking-directory-updated.pdf.

32. Liz Fekete and Frances Webber, "The Human Trade," *Race and Class* 39, no. 1 (1997): 67–74.

33. David, "New Threats or Old Stereotypes."

34. "I do not know if it is possible to use the discourse of trafficking to the benefit of workers in the sex industry, migrant or otherwise. But I do know that extensive negotiations are going ahead on this issue in the UN at the moment and that it may be more productive to be on the inside of these discussions, rather than altogether on the outside." David, "New Threats or Old Stereotypes," 7.

35. Gallagher, "Human Rights and the New UN Protocols," 975.

36. In brief, these standards require governments to: (1) prohibit and appropriately punish severe forms of trafficking and (2) make serious and sustained efforts to eliminate such trafficking.

37. Anne Gallagher and Susu Thatun, "The US Government Report—A Critique," *Step by Step*, newsletter of the UN Inter-Agency Project on Trafficking in Women And Children in the Mekong Sub-Region, Third Quarter, 2001, 4.

38. "The consent of a victim of trafficking in persons to the intended exploitation shall be irrelevant where any of the means set forth (in the definition) have been used. Furthermore, the recruitment, transportation, transfer, harboring or receipt of a child for the purpose of exploitation shall be considered 'trafficking in persons' even if this does not involve any of the means set forth in the definition." Protocol against the Smuggling of Migrants by Land, Sea and Air, Supplementing the United Nations Convention Against Transnational Organized Crime, November 15, 2000, and Protocol to Prevent, Suppress and Punish Trafficking in Persons, Especially Women

and Children, November 15, 2000, available at http:www.unescobkk.org/culture/trafficking/definitions.htm.

39. Patrick Twomey, "Europe's Other Market: Trafficking in People," *European Journal of Migration and Law* 2 (2000): 7.

40. Twomey, "Europe's Other Market," 8.

41. UNIFEM press release, March 7, 2003. http://www.unifem.org/newsroom/press/pr_030307_IOM_MOU.html.

42. http://www.iom.int/en/who/main_service_areas_counter.shtml#traffdef, accessed April 4, 2003.

43. http://www.unicri.it/project_document.htm.

44. Adam Graycar, "Human Smuggling," paper presented at the Centre for Criminology, the University of Hong Kong, February 19, 2000. Available at http//www.hku.hk/crime/humansmuggling.html.

45. Amy O'Neill Richard, *International Trafficking in Women to the United States: A Contemporary Manifestation of Slavery and Organized Crime* (Washington, D.C.: Center for the Study of Intelligence, 1999), 13. Available at http://www.cia.gov/esi/monograph/women/trafficking.pdf.

46. Graziano Battistella and Maruja M. B. Asis, "Southeast Asia and the Specter of Unauthorized Migration," in *Unauthorized Migration in Southeast Asia*, ed. Graziano Batistella and Maruja M. B. Asis (Manila: Scalabrini Migration Center, 2003), 169–227.

47. Manning and Bhatnagar, "Movement of Natural Persons," 4.

48. Diana Wong and Teuku Afrizal Teuku Anwar, "*Migran Gelap*: Irregular Migrants in Malaysia's Shadow Economy," in *Unauthorized Migration in Southeast Asia*, ed. Batistella and Asis, 169ff.

49. Diana Wong, "The Recruitment of Foreign Labour in Malaysia: From Migration System to Guest-worker Regime," paper presented at the conference on Migrant Labour in Southeast Asia: Needed Not Wanted, Armidale, December 1–3, 2003.

50. Wong and Afrizal, *Migran Gelap*, 170.

51. Notable among the few NGOs in the country working on behalf of foreign migrants in the country is Tenaganita. Tenaganita has drawn attention to the increasing number of women trafficked from countries such as Indonesia, the Philippines, China, Vietnam, as well as former states of the Soviet Union, such as Uzbekistan.

52. See Arif Nasution, "Aliran Pekerja Indonesia Malaysia: Kes Tentang Pekerja Indonesia dalam Sektor Pembinaan di Kuala Lumpur, Malaysia" (Ph.D. dissertation, Universiti Kebangsaan Malaysia, 1997); and Ernst Spaan, "*Taikongs* and *Calos*: The Roles of Middlemen and Brokers in Javanese International Migration," *International Migration Review* 28, no. 1 (1994): 93–113.

53. Diana Wong and Gusni Saat, "Trafficking of Persons from the Philippines into Malaysia," unpublished report submitted to United Nations Interregional Crime and Justice Research Institute, 2002.

54. Wong and Afrizal, *Migran Gelap*, 169–227.

55. A fact often denied, even by immigration officers in the state. Wong and Saat, "Trafficking of Persons from the Philippines into Malaysia," 30. As the story above indicates, Laniah is a victim of trafficking as defined by the United Nations Protocol on Trafficking in Persons by virtue of the deception which her employer used to recruit her into the economy of vice.

56. This would approximate most closely the definition of "trafficking" as introduced in this essay.

57. It may be pertinent here to note the tremendous improvements in public transportation in Indonesia over the past decade, which have simplified long-distance travel by bus and ferry considerably.

58. Obviously, given the constraints of illicit entry into the country as well as its labor market, this control can only be relative in nature.

59. The industry also encompasses an extensive recruitment sector based in Indonesia. See Sidney Jones, *Making Money Off Migrants: The Indonesian Exodus to Malaysia* (Hong Kong: Asia 2002 Ltd., and Centre for Asia-Pacific Transformation Studies, University of Wollongong, 2000).

60. For an account of the parallel systems of foreign labor recruitment in Malaysia, see Wong, "The Recruitment of Foreign Labour in Malaysia."

61. "Organized crime is generally defined by US law enforcement agencies as criminal acts committed by self-perpetuating, structured, and disciplined associations of individuals or groups combined together in a hierarchical or coordinated manner. These activities are generally conspiratorial and tend to insulate their leadership from direct involvement. Their primary goal is economic gain from illegal activities." Richard, *International Trafficking*, vii.

62. Richard, *International Trafficking*, vii.

63. David, "New Threats Or Old Stereotypes," 6.

64. Gallagher, "Human Rights and the New UN Protocols," 59.

65. Malcolm Anderson, "The Transformation of Border Controls. A European Precedent?" in *The Wall around the West: State Borders and Immigration Controls in North America and Europe*, ed. Peter Andreas and T. Snyder (Lanham, Md.: Rowman & Littlefield, 2001), 15–29.

66. Anderson, "Transformation of Border Controls," 18.

67. John Torpey, *The Invention of the Passport: Surveillance, Citizenship and the State* (Cambridge: Cambridge University Press, 2000).

68. Anderson, "Transformation of Border Controls," 16.

69. Mbembe, "At the Edge of the World," 271.

70. Mbembe, "At the Edge of the World," 267.

71. See Willem van Schendel, chapter 1, this volume.

72. The asylum seekers from exotic third-world countries from the horn of Africa such as Ethiopia and Eritrea, or from central Asia such as Afghanistan, who made their way into the asylum regime of countries in the European Union represented but the tip of the iceberg. Hundreds of thousands of Eritreans fleeing the fighting in the horn fled—and settled—in the Sudan, as did similar numbers of Afghan refugees in Pakistan and Iran. By 1984, according to the UNHCR, there were some 500,000 Ethiopians, most of whom were Eritreans, in Sudan, and 2,500,000 Afghans in Pakistan. Although animosity and ill feeling at the local level has not been absent, these large intakes of population streaming across the border—and remaining within—did not generate "boundary crises" and "moral panics" of the sort which emerged in the final decade of the twentieth century in Western Europe and the United States.

73. James Scott, *Seeing like a State: How Certain Schemes to Improve the Human Condition Have Failed* (New Haven, Conn., and London: Yale University Press, 1998).

74. This is a middle-class neighborhood in the capital city of Malaysia.

75. A red identity card is a personal identity document issued to foreigners with permanent resident status in the country.

three

Talking Like a State

Drugs, Borders, and the Language of Control

Paul Gootenberg

This chapter explores the relationships between illicit drug flows and state borders. The larger theme, for other objects-in-flow, is how languages of "control" underlie their construction and maintenance as *illicit* and criminalized flows. Researchers might usefully make state discourses about such flows an explicit object of study. But in doing so they should also beware of the possible intellectual and political pitfalls of "talking like a state"—that is, of adopting the categories or characterizations of the illicit deployed by policing and regulatory agencies—for thinking productively about flows. The chapter winds its way to these ideas by addressing three topics: first, the relation of drugs to "commodity studies" writ large (how drugs were differentiated from other goods during the historical rise of commercial and industrial capitalism); second, the relation of drugs to the building of borders and states; and third, the role of bureaucratic control language in marking and naturalizing the thin line between "controlled substances" and freer commodities.

A critical definition: "drugs"—which are actually tricky to define—are psychoactive substances and commodities which for a variety of reasons since 1900 have been construed as health or societal "dangers" by modern states, medical authorities, and regulatory cultures, and which are now globally prohibited in production, use, and sale.[1] In commonsense terms we know exactly what they are—heroin, cocaine, marijuana, ecstasy, quaaludes, methamphetamines, LSD, etc.—but they are often difficult to disentangle from other legal and popular mind-altering commodities (such as coffee, tea, alcohol, tobacco, kola nut) or valorized "traditional" ones (such as magic mushrooms, yage, kava, qat, coca leaf, peyote cactus) or legal and commercial scientific-medicinal drugs (ether, morphine, Demerol, steroids, Prozac, Viagra). There is no hard-and-fast alkaloidal or natural distinction between illicit drugs and other drug-like goods. Indeed, the "set and setting" of commodities in general (for example, the associations generated by advertising or by the power of money itself) may well induce mind-altering effects or addictive attraction in their consumers. Hence the need to secure legal and discursive borders between illicit drugs and analogous commodities, pleasures, and medicines, and the need for now-huge international bureaucracies (from the DEA to INTERPOL) devoted to the day-to-day dirty work of fighting drug flows. The global trade in illicit drugs—worth about US$300–500 billion in "street sales" annually—is among the world's largest commodity trades, everywhere in tandem with other flows and institutions, despite these massive efforts at control.

Drugs Are/Are Not Like Other Global Commodities

The economic forces driving cocaine's production and generating hostility towards it are no different today from what they were three centuries ago when the rising commerce in tea, coffee, sugar and tobacco linked Western Europe to its tropical colonies and revolutionized world consumption.[2]
—Sidney W. Mintz, "The Forefathers of Crack"

Heroin is emerging as the ideal product for a global [narcotics] industry that is streamlining for the post 9/11 age—slashing payrolls, flattening hierarchies, marketing aggressively and keeping a low profile.[3]
—Matthew Brzezinski

A useful starting point is to simply consider drugs as just like "other commodities," susceptible to the same approaches customarily used in interdisciplinary commodity studies. This is a good start because economic or structural perspectives help to cool down some of the passionate rhetoric (or state talk) that distorts much of the inner workings of modern drug flows.

Thus, to take some working examples, the booming world heroin trade can be seen as comprising shifting patterns of supply and demand, profit-seeking and risk-taking entrepreneurs, rationalized labor and schedules for flexible production, extensive networks of middlemen and retailers, transport and outsourcing dilemmas, product testing and product substitution, and a crunching global competition. In this, drugs are the consummate "free-market" activity—attracting businessmen as voracious or heroic as any multinational CEO, with tens of thousands of employees and dynamic spin-off effects. Or the Andean-U.S. cocaine flow can be approached as a "political economy" problem, where rival states and rent-seeking interest groups (entrenched lobbies, syndicates, political factions, bureaucracies) struggle over the profits and perils of the trade, frustrating along the way the dominant state strategies of control.[4] Drugs are also essential flows in globalization theory; now clearly a "global habit," illicit drugs were among the first global goods to supersede borders and regulatory states in the quest for profit by, for example, forging new markets in Eastern European postcommunist regimes (with their decadent consumerism) or establishing flexible production sites and transshipment routes across neo-liberal Latin America and fourth-world sub-Saharan Africa—ahead of statist international cops and drug repression. Globalization and its inequalities make a mockery of hard-line ideas of drug-war "victory." Drug trades are both the underside and product of trade liberalization; pressures for enhanced commerce and for shrinking states collide with the dictates of tighter control over unwanted trades. Nowhere is this tension clearer than with NAFTA and intensified smuggling and militarization along the U.S.-Mexico border during the 1990s. Another example is that the location and typology of distinctive layers of drug flows (street dealing, wholesale "kingpin" distribution rings) can be modeled by economic geographers. The "crack" dealers of East Harlem are ripe for class and ethnographic analysis—of how displaced Caribbean peasants and ex–factory workers find occupational "respect," much like the coca-growing peasants of eastern Peru and Bolivia, thousands of kilometers away.[5] Example: from trade theory, drug prohibition/interdiction acts as protective tariff walls. The early 1970s U.S. crackdown on imported Mexican marijuana traffic in turn gave a huge boost to the domestic "home-grown" grass industry, which, making striking productivity strides, has emerged as rural America's number one "cash crop." Or the World-Systems model of "commodity chains" is suggestive for taking us beyond the bifurcated idea of drugs as driven by supply and demand. Such sociological ideas foreground the linkages between power-laden geographies of consumption and production. This approach might help explain how lucrative world drug economies, where the value of drug commodities multiplies hundreds of times from producers to consumers, involve such desperate actors (dirt-poor poppy farmers in Myanmar; homeless Mexican street gangs in L.A.) at its extremes.[6] All these are highly useful and legitimate commodity approaches to drug flows.

Seeing drugs as commodities is also *historically* deeper; it helps question how illicit drugs were "made" during the dual process of forming early modern world capitalism and modern national states. Historians of commodities know that key stimulants—foreign spices, coffee, tobacco, chocolate—played defining roles in consumption and class styles in the construction of European capitalism. The proliferating eighteenth-century London coffeehouse, following the rich interpretation of historian Wolfgang Schivelbusch, brought with it a new mentality, and institutions, for bourgeois politics and enterprise—including the insurance empire of Lloyds. Starting in the late sixteenth century, European colonialism jump-started on the networks and revenue windfalls made possible by new staples such as American tobacco—arguably the first modern "world commodity." Habit-forming captive "drug-foods" developed taxable "cultures of dependence" like those of tobacco, rum, and tea in Anglo North America. Subsequent British imperialism conquered much of Asia using the weapons of tea plantations and smoking-opium commerce, forcibly foisted upon India and China during the nineteenth-century colonial "opium wars." The rise of the world sugar industry, captured in the holistic anthropological optic of Sidney Mintz, connects the expulsion and enslavement of millions of Africans to Brazil and the Caribbean to the transformation of sucrose from a Mediterranean medicinal luxury into the defining article of the modern English industrial working-class lifestyle.[7] The sugar plantation was a precursor to the factory industrial revolution, and as a quick non-nutritional fix, sugar even anticipates the post-industrial American urban crack boom of the 1980s.

One prominent historian of drugs dubs these broad cultural shifts as capitalism's "Psychoactive Revolution." Not all of these new substances gained an easy acceptance in the West, though these early modern transformations (often in the uses, forms, and cultures of stimulants) occurred before the post-1900 emergence of the global movement for drug prohibitions. The central question raised by this burgeoning historical literature, now explicit in David Courtwright's recent *Forces of Habit: Drugs and the Making of the Modern World*, is how and why certain tradable drugs become legitimate commodities of European taste while others become downgraded by the late nineteenth century into undesired pariah substances.[8] The classical dilemma of early states was how to tax the flush revenues afforded by drug-foods, tobacco, sugar, tea, alcohol, opium, which contributed to a weighty early state and colonial interest in their fiscal demarcation and control. There were other commodity sets too: indigenous drug substances and knowledge that was not readily or culturally exportable (in the native American drug cornucopia alone, Andean coca leaf, Amazonian yage, Mexican peyote, Oaxacan mushrooms, Aztec morning glories, Colombian daturas, Paraguayan mate). Only today can these be sampled as goods in the global village of Queens, N.Y., shaman guide services included. Another group of drug commodities were powerful derived alkaloids of late-nineteenth-century modern chemistry and medicine such as cocaine, purified caffeine, and heroin, "heroic" new drug commodities (hence the Bayer brand name "Heroin") that precipitously rose and fell in medical and social prestige. In the mid-twentieth century, certain synthetics (famously, LSD in the 1960s) actually escaped from secret government labs (involving CIA experiments in "mind control") and became swiftly and purposefully transformed into mass-media commodities to fulfill the mind-expanding (hence "psychedelic") crusades of its proponents.[9] In the 1990s, this cycle of medical promotion–recreational disrepute assumed post-modern velocity, with new corporate synthetic painkillers like Oxycontin, in the unlikely setting of rural Appalachia.

In sum, commodity perspectives can be used to produce a clearer and more relational portrait of the economic interests and structures behind global drug flows that is more objective than the mobilizing anti-drug *mis*-information and forced interpretations of governments and of allied "drug control" professionals (such as medical addiction specialists). They are historically richer too: prior to the last century, drugs were not generally divided into illicit and licit classes, and as border-crossing commodities they actually played vanguard economic and cultural roles in the construction of the modern world. For some economists—odd bedfellows such as Milton Friedman and Lester Thurow—this artificial divide generates a radical critique of the perverse price theory behind drug prohibitions policy. The field of "commodity studies," itself in renaissance, is rich with implications for understanding drugs, informed by the anthropological foundations and global constructionism of Arjun Appadurai's "social life of things."[10] But where commodity and structural perspectives fall short is in deciphering the mysteries of how certain substances became classed as "good" and "bad" in the first place (for our bodies, minds, and societies) and the often wildly irrational rhetoric (racial or gender panics) that accompanied the establishment and maintenance of anti-drug prohibitions. Why do mind- or culture-altering drugs stir up such intensely ambivalent passions, what pioneer drug researcher Sigmund Freud, in the last of his famous 1880s "cocaine papers," dubbed a "craving for and dread" of drugs?[11] Not to mention the gross irrationalities that keep this global dysfunctional system going after more than a century of failures.

PAUL GOOTENBERG

Drugs on the Borders of the State

What crosses the blood-brain barrier is now open to the same surveillance as what crosses international borders. There is a customs in the cranium, a Checkpoint Consciousness.[12]
—David Lenson

Before moving beyond borders, we need to look at the junction of drugs with the border and "the state." Why do illicit drugs exhibit such a known propensity for border crossings and what are their larger intersections with statist regulatory spaces? How does "talking like a state" help stake out these official (or artificial) licit and illicit drug spaces? These are questions rife with paradox.

A short answer to the question of drugs-across-borders is that ecological conditions and local knowledge govern the distance that drugs travel, and necessarily across many borders. Most alkaloidal plants, the original natural plant drugs like tea, opiates, kola, cannabis, and coca, were semi-tropical ones, whereas most modern consumers of stimulant plants emerged in northern industrial countries (historically poor in drug resources or drug cultures, drowned out by centuries of alcohol use).[13] Thus, border crossing was initially an economic question of "natural" or comparative advantage, especially given the low production cost of raw materials like poppy in central Asia. This argument served well into the late nineteenth century and was even adopted by colonial authorities (British, Dutch, German, French), who experimented in imperial botanical gardens with new psychotropic plants and command labor as colonial staples. Oftentimes, going back, local peasant communities were the only ones who harbored the technical agrarian lore for these drug plants, as well as of their medicinal or spiritual-sensory qualities, just as today multinational pharmaceutical firms seek controversial botanic patenting pacts with rain forest tribes. An opium trail existed, run by Greek, Jewish, and Armenian merchants, across the middle-eastern Golden Crescent. Regional hashish circuits flowed before nineteenth-century colonialism divvied up South Asia and North Africa into separate spheres, piquing the interest of both concerned colonial officials and intrigued anti-establishment Parisian intellectuals and bohemians. A three-century interregional Spanish colonial coca leaf trail traversed what is now Peru, Bolivia, Chile, and northern Argentina, largely for mine workers and other hard laborers. It predated the creation of a global taste and market for coca, which only started with the French luxury commodity drink *Vin Mariani* in 1863, and later industrialized during the German medicinal *kocain* boom of 1884–1887.[14]

106

Drug trades may also arise out of long-standing legal long-distance or related contraband trades. Colombia's 1970s "drug lords" began with prime intermediary location and the experience of smuggling cigarettes in the 1950s and marijuana in "the 60s"; they also exploited a new trail of undocumented Colombian émigré workers in Miami and New York. Amphetamine ("speed") is obvious in following trucking routes almost everywhere. Drugs are specially suited to long-distance trade, for beginning life as luxuries, they are exemplary high value-to-weight items that more than pay for freight costs. Only jewels such as diamonds travel with such universal ease.

From this view, the original drug flow is born autonomously, with borders an obstacle later superimposed with the rise of modern states and later evolving into an obstacle course as drugs became categorized, outlawed, and tracked by expanding Western power during the twentieth century. During the same post-1900 era, borders have generally become better defined and less permeable. Given the notoriously high price "elasticity of demand" for habit-forming products, once illegal to sell, drugs easily take care of the extra "risk premium" demanded by smuggling operations. Moreover, highly concentrated refined modern drugs (like cocaine or heroin) are physically simple to conceal, unlike, say, bulky cigarettes or silks. Artificial illicitness premiums compensate the risk that a portion of shipments (some 10 to 30 percent in official guesses) is bound to be seized. Once this illicitness cycle accelerated during chase-'em-down drug wars, first with post-war Middle Eastern heroin, then with 1970s Andean cocaine, the amount of these drugs produced skyrocketed and their prices plummeted, making them dramatically available for the masses (as in the infamous downward price cycle of cocaine—crack of the mid-1980s). As a related rule, "harder" drugs become more profitable to market than softer drugs. Only the DEA acts oblivious to this perverse price cycle by premising drug wars on the pipe dream that interdiction drives *up* drug prices and discourages their use. The amounts seized to actually do this would need to be unrealistically high (above 80 percent of drugs produced). And historical data show the opposite; they show, after an initial bump up with the creation of black markets, secularly falling prices for illegal drugs.

Of course, with technological revolutions and galloping global integration, strict geographic factors no longer prevail. Even earlier, colonialism swept indigenous coca to East Asia (Dutch Java) for a spectacular commercial boomlet of the 1920s and 1930s; Paraguayan yerba-mate became a useful habit of itinerant Syrian workers from Buenos Aires; airlifted Andean drugs now cross through African cities with little prior expertise in the global logistics of drugs. In the mid-1990s, pressurized illiterate Colombian peasants quickly learned the age-old secrets of quality opiates cultivation and processing (reputedly tutored by imported Asian specialists), becoming North America's high-end heroin supplier in less than a decade.[15] Fast-expanding synthetics, "ATSs," ecstasy (MDMA), and the ultimate yuppie "designer" drugs (sometimes designed to temporarily evade chemically defined UN bans) can all be profitably produced "at home," but still drift across borders for safe haven. For example, global ecstasy now slips into the United States from Holland by way of Israeli know-how and the Internet. A strong possibility—more likely after expanded 9/11 militarized border surveillance—is genetic engineering of high-alkaloid hybrid plants, for example, an Iowa corn stalk that could actually produce perfectly good cocaine. We have previewed this border substitution with marijuana since the 1960s. Once imported and branded from Colombia, Panama, Jamaica, and Mexico (Colombian "Gold," "Oaxaqueño"), marijuana is now basically a domestic cottage industry in the United States, grown hydroponically (an indoor "sea of green") and fueling the blighted rural economies of Georgia, Tennessee, and northern California. This is mainly thanks to Richard Nixon's early 1970s "Operation Intercept" (bulky grass was easy to smell out and catch at borders), especially the toxic spraying of Mexican weed, and thanks to an army of homegrown geneticists (some going Dutch), who planted the seeds of this new American industry. Buying American has also meant that the old-fashioned "nickel bag" of wild import weed or hash has been shunted aside by pricey high-THC dope, "Sinsemilla" hybrids with scary names like "White Avalanche," that many veterans of the 1960s can barely tolerate.[16] With high-tech possibilities, the older comparative advantage of drugs are no longer a given.

The second level of explanation for drugs-across-borders is forced dispersion. Once certain drugs became restricted or banned—starting with a long line of international opiates conventions since 1912—they fast escaped to scattered zones where production could be safely concealed and pursued. Commerce became smuggling, and the newly defined crime of "narcotics peddling" became tainted in the West as an arch-evil crime. Yet until the 1950s, with the exception of tightly governed colonies, most of the globe was not effectively enveloped by this paper prohibitions system, which was not consolidated until today's still-hegemonic 1961 UN Single Convention on Narcotic Drugs. This treaty enshrined the American ideal, articulated since 1912, of tracking drugs to their "source" and progressively eradicating their raw materials where they are grown abroad. So, after 1960, no legal cross-border safe havens for drugs remained, though weak enforcement capacities or incentives (or a degree of cultural tolerance) remained a factor in uneven drug regulatory spaces. Moreover, drug cops were historically slow to cross borders and share information and tactics—the international-ization of drug agents (from the United States, UN, or INTERPOL) was a gradual affair, not achieved on any significant scale until the 1970s.[17] Since then, we have a familiar pattern: a greater policing squeeze at borders or across them to chase down couriers, refiners, or peasants leads to a wider dispersion of illicit activities into even more inaccessible intractable drug territories—deserts, jungles, mountains. Drug suppression radically elevates illicit profits, but combines with geopolitical factors in shaping where drugs end up flowing.

Thus the typical global hot zone of drug production, whether remote from or close to final markets, is a zone of refuge, with a displaced, alien-ated, or ethnically segregated peasantry (for working drug plantations) and an especially weak state or ill-defined borders. A history of disintegrating warfare helps, or so it seems. The "Golden Triangle," "the Golden Cres-cent," the uncharted danger-ridden Afghani-Pakistani mountain border, the Andean sub-tropical Huallaga Valley or Chaparé Amazonian frontiers, the northern Mexican Sierra Madre badlands of Sinaloa and Chihua-hua, devastated peasant Guatemala, Lebanon's Bekaa Valley, southern Colombia's war-torn Putumayo and Caqueta forests—most of these areas host flourishing "borderlands" cultures, often antagonistic to national po-litical centers, where multiple borders converge, weakly policed (in part because so easily broached by smugglers), and where drug production finds not only security but a committed material or even ideological base among destitute, refugee, or colonizing peasants and regional middlemen. The armed "hill tribes" of the Golden Triangle are a classic example. (A similar illicit geography of drug entrepôt cities—say, Rotterdam, Tijuana, Marseille, Shanghai—would make a great book.) I am stressing these so-cial-spatial geographies over commonly held ideas that essentialize the illicit commodities themselves, such as former World Banker Paul Collier's well-known notion of "conflict"-inspiring or "grievance" "goods," in which drugs notably figure. And if global political institutions push drug making into such forbidding zones, they have been exiled to the proverbial "briar patch"—perfect areas for thriving drug cultures.

Another factor is the particular nature of the state. Economist Fran-cisco Thoumi has rigorously surveyed competing theories of Colombia's true advantage in the drugs trade, and he highlights its "weak state," one that was easily infiltrated or bypassed by rapidly enriched drug lords of the 1970s and 1980s.[18] Peru's Huallaga Valley became an irresistible illicit coca haven in the early 1970s when the strong-state leftist experiment of the Velasco era collapsed, leaving thousands of colonized farmers there bereft of public services and control. Attempts to artificially "strengthen" illegitimate or low-institutionalized drug-producing states, such as militarizing American aid to Peru and Bolivia during the 1990s, have usually led to intensified violence and repression on the ground, and even if successful (since many local authorities and generals work with drug traders) has led to the "exit" of the industry to even wilder territories—such as the dramatic concentration in the late 1990s of coca-cocaine, vertically integrated, in guerrilla-run, stateless borderlands of southern Colombia. "Narco" states, Banzer's Bolivia of the 1970s or Noriega's Panama of the 1980s, are typically tottering or non-institutional ones. Paradoxically, "neo-liberalism" has meant a proliferation of such sites by bringing on third-world state collapse, a phenomenon that also worries anti-terrorist specialists. Now, drug platforms quickly shift locales, jumping across borders with the greatest of ease, a behavior commonly dubbed the "ballooning effect" from the enforcement perspective. In current memory, the sheer tonnage of illicit drugs placed on world markets never "ratchets *down*," but it does constantly shift provenance and product mix.

There are some cardinal paradoxes of drugs-across-borders—beyond the central one that exporting and upping drug repression usually spawns conditions and incentives that worsen "the problem."[19] The other major related fallacy is seeing borders as static given "things"—instead of fluid spatial relationships under constant construction and renovation, mainly from fuzzy or contested frontiers, over most of the last century. The border controls that exist today (information gathering, physical barriers, surveillance, intricate fiscal and legal operations) were barely in place fifty years ago, and before that not even the individual passport was universal. One wonders what the drug trade itself (along with stigmatization and control of undocumented migrants) has meant for the hardening of borders, say, on the southern U.S. rim. Across the globe in Chinese history, scholars now talk of "opium regimes," a suggestive approach that drugs, rather than undermining states, subtly and progressively added to their novel capacities and controls during the nineteenth century.[20] Borders are never sealed to drugs. It is post-9/11 public knowledge that less than 2 percent of all freight into North America is physically inspected in any fashion, high- or low-tech, no matter how motivated the state is. Borders will remain permeable and now exist metaphysically in every airport, pleasure boat, computer, and banking terminal.

A second related paradox is how the border traffic of drugs into the United States and Europe is rarely seen as a two-way street. Certain items in the exchange are lost from view, like most of the laundered cash profits (often via "legitimate businesses" or respectable barter goods like upscale cars), the small-arms flow, or chemical inputs into drug territories. Borders, for political reasons, also seem to mask the end of any "visibility" of murky trafficking organizations. We rarely will see how the borderlander Arrellano-Félix or García-Abrego gangs operated on "the other side" of the Mexican-U.S. divide, though profits are astronomical in domestic distribution, whereas the media exaggerate the vigor and organization of "cartels" on the third-world side. (This was one compelling aspect of the simulacra Hollywood blockbuster *Traffic*, originally made about the flow of Asian opiates to Britain: it reveled in these border imbrications, if still coloring its Mexican landscapes in ominous sepia tones.) The frequent complaint of Latin Americans about drug discourse is just this: North American "demand"-driven, the drugs trail mysteriously "stops" at the border, where the drugs are apparently dumped, with no one of note ever implicated in the domestic political economy. Needless to say, the drug-intensified border region also becomes an area of heightened risk opportunity, services, and interchange, even for coveted information about the flows.

States erect the borders, circling themselves protectively, so it is worth pondering the basic relations of states and illicit drugs—bearing in mind the world of differing state styles (at their stark simplest, American, European, and third-world) and discourses. The relation looks more "symbiotic" than the zero-sum *oficilista* idea that governments ban and fight bad drugs and that sinister narcotics dealers subvert states and rules. Much is written on this theme since drug literatures are characteristically "state-centric." Much of this analysis centers on the U.S. state—the lead polity, historically, in setting world patterns and norms of drug control.[21]

To begin, the relation is structurally "ambivalent"—analogous to the love-hate relationship of drugs (as remedy and scourge) that Dr. David Musto has diagnosed as "the American Disease," a deep, almost Freudian tension behind the original move to drug prohibitions from 1900 to 1920. Denial continues to rule drug policies, starting with political denial that there is much endgame in zero-sum warring on substances. The core dynamic functions under institutional denial: that the harder we ban them, the harder we press against existing drug trades, the more lucrative they become, resulting in ever more extended and socially injurious drugs. This equation is sometimes critically analyzed as a variety of permanent unquestionable "drug-war politics," analogous to the permanent "National Security" state and military-industrial complex that dominated the Cold War.[22] Ideological and symbolic obfuscation, or a generalized suspended public belief, loom central to state-declared drug wars.

So other interpretations arise, of hidden purposes behind the stated objectives and speech of governmental and international anti-drug forces. Some are frankly conspiratorial and unfortunately have their grains of truth. For instance, that intelligence services and their allies profit from drug trades is well-documented. They sometimes have, since the covert wars the CIA launched throughout the Cold War and now beyond were fought out in many of the same third-world refuge zones, which offer underground contacts, organization, expertise, and invisible funding. (As businessmen, some drug traders have been concerted anti-communists, especially as Marxist states proved to be the only ones effective at stamping out drugs). The anti-communist mafia of southern Europe, protagonists of the "French Connection" of the 1950s and 1960s, were no strangers to Allied spies and covert-ops, some financed by untraceable drug profits. Alfred McCoy long ago richly exposed the roles assumed by drug-running CIA surrogate armies in Cold War Southeast Asia, even as U.S. troops and returning vets became hooked on their Asian heroin. A similar episode and charge surfaced with Reagan's "Iran-Contra" pirates of the 1980s (recently revived in controversial urban legends that ascribe the spread of crack in African American communities to CIA plots) and will no doubt rise again in the current al-Qaeda wars, since our friends and peasants in Afghanistan have begun quickly sowing the poppies strictly scorned by the Taliban.[23] A problem with these popular theories from the left is that they share the reflexive anti-drug moralism of the right: rather than evil cartels, evil CIA drugs are behind American moral decay. But such imperial political alliances and entanglements can, at best, only partially explain drug empires.

Others propose, with equal seriousness, the idea that swelling drug bureaucracies serve ulterior purposes—concrete ones, as in Edward Jay Epstein's classic *Agency of Fear: Opiates and Political Power in America*, which portrayed the birth of the DEA in 1972 as the linchpin of Richard Nixon's larger project of a repressive central state in the U.S., the one that stumbled into Watergate. For sure, the DEA (and drug law enforcement generally) work to the detriment of civil liberties, especially of poor people of color, who since the 1980s have made the United States (disgracefully) the world's leading country in terms of citizens incarcerated. Politicians routinely cultivate drug menaces as classic sociological "moral panics" to divert attention from root causes in urban social distress. The Reagan-Bush cocaine drug war of the 1980s, with its racially encoded hysteria about "crack babies," was embedded in sharply worsening social inequality in the United States and the bipartisan abandonment of the urban underclass. It hardly mattered that "crack babies" were another urban legend; the image institutionalized "blame the victim" and linked it to the threat of faraway dark-hued Bolivian peasants to boot.[24] Still, official motives of political control and structural racism also make partial accounts of state drug interest.

Other scholars present less frightening "bureaucratic" models. Government agencies are not very good at fighting elusive non-state networks, learning from the past, or at grasping wide-ranging Mertonian "unintended consequences of social action." Or that in political cycles, or within top-heavy organizations, the long run is difficult to conceive, allowing the political dominance of contradictory short-term solutions like greater drug repression. Interestingly, some agencies, such as the CIA, appear less invested than others in the drug war and thus continue to produce (unheeded) intelligence reports that warn of its futile or dire consequences abroad.[25] Some point to material vested interests created by drug warring—larger, skyrocketing "war" budgets in a war without end. Local U.S. police forces, with diminishing federal aid, can live off proceeds of confiscated "dealers" property, with scant concern for constitutional due process for the policy's victims. In the brief 1990s interlude between the Cold War and the global war on terrorism, many analysts saw growing military interest in drug wars as mission-enhancing budgetary politics. In policing politics, the pyramidal cell structure of drug trades ensures that higher-ups garner far more "protection" and immunity than exposed foot soldiers or users on the street, who institutionally swell prison facilities and state budgets. Mediating financial institutions, such as Anglo banks in Miami or Houston, are relatively immune from prosecution. All these ideas suggest that drug traders and anti-drug warriors are actually in institutionalized collusion. They need one another to prosper.

"Narco-diplomacy," Richard Friman's term for state-to-state drug relations, has long pitted a focused monomaniacal American state interest (exporting drug prohibitions, "winning" the drug battle abroad) against far more variegated overseas ministries, agendas, or states.[26] On the ground —say in the U.S.-sponsored UMOPAR anti-coca strike force and eradication program in Bolivia's Chaparé—these bureaucratic relations fuel a number of permanently defeatist paradoxes that sustain rather than curtail illicit production. The flow of aid depends on the flow of drugs, as Peruvian generals also learned with the spigot of the Huallaga Valley. Given these dynamics, some drug-making states have spawned rent-seeking states-within-states, replete with services and mini-monopolies of protective violence, local armies, or social movements labeled with the 1980s

Reaganite misnomer of "narco-terrorism." Some leftist guerrilla groups too, such as Peru's *Sendero Luminoso* and now the Colombian FARC, have in fact taken advantage of drug money and the unpopularity of drug policies among peasants to sustain themselves. During the 1950s and beyond, U.S. narcotics officials routinely equated drug peddling with "Communism," overriding reality, in order to impress budget-producing lawmakers. The United States vents frustration at such complicated drug war "allies," who indeed must still pass through the annual congressional ritual of certifying entire governments as "dirty" or "clean."

"Corruption" is the key word in these relationships—of drugs to states, and the United States to allies across borders. Corruption can be a blinding phrase to the violence and graft opportunity that exported policies have wrought on neighboring states and peoples, for example, those of Colombia, who suffered the terrorism spawned by the late-1980s U.S. campaign for the forced extradition of national drug figures.[27] In a straight political science sense, systemic corruption seems to undermine the very state institutions and legitimacy, such as the enhanced "rule of law," needed to combat illicit activities in the long run. But bribery and like practices also serve as adaptive responses to bad laws or to the perceived gap between imperatives and realities—as in the colonial Spanish-American bureaucratic adage, apparently still alive, of "we listen but do not obey." Corruption may be the sole method available for states to surreptitiously tax, as it were, the illicit economies of drugs: to appease low-paid disgruntled bureaucrats, float a weak national currency, or even to pay off the IMF. Drug money in the third world sometimes (not always) has redistributive effects that are just—symbolically at least taking from L.A. yuppies and giving to the *comunero* slum dwellers of Medellín, where the poor instinctively appreciated the economic populism and public services (like lighted neighborhood soccer fields) of drug lords like Escobar. The unavoidable facts are that underpaid civil servants and officers in most of the world have every incentive to work with local drug trades rather than fulfill external agendas—or better yet, to work for both. The mobilizing force of easy export dollars is legendary. For example, the Mexican state, with graft and secrecy oiled by six decades of PRI one-party rule, entered a final stage of "kleptocracy" in the 1990s, fueled by the proximity of the U.S. drugs market and the squeeze put on the Miami cocaine corridor of the 1980s. Mexican transshipment grew swiftly to fill the void and blurred the thin line separating criminal and state activities: the neo-liberal president's entrepreneurial brother looted the state in cahoots with illicit empires, as was a faction of his increasingly fratricidal political party; the ministry of transport and communications built faster cocaine routes to the north; the modernizing drug czar (General Guttiérez Rebollo), a U.S. intelligence partner, embarrassingly turned out to be on the payroll of northern mafias (also dramatized in the movie *Traffic*); popular singers heralded gun-toting drug runners as new folk *desperados*. Corruption, fanned by American drug and trade policies, became so institutional as to preclude serious U.S. efforts to use the imploding Mexican state against drugs.[28] Yet systemic graft can sometimes prove functional too. The long reign of Fujimori-Montesinos in Peru (1990–2001), though a more "corrupt" regime than anyone imagined (outside its CIA handlers and videotapers), was also a quite good one for dealing with the U.S. foreign policy objective of halting terrorist-inspired state disintegration and the Huallaga cocaine trades, both of which were reversed by a strong mix of Fujimori insider deals and repression. So it is hard to say *a priori* whom "corruption" serves: freer markets, a dysfunctional state, drug lords, the people, the DEA. But overall, the licit states system and illicit drug flows look far from mutually exclusive.

Languages of Control

The significance of drugs is distended with veiled social meanings; it is their status as Other that permits this overloading.[29]
—Marek Kohn

By training and inclination, I am not one to slip into the discursive or linguistic "turn"—the wildly popular idea among 1990s academics (under the influence of cross-border flows of French theory) that social realities are "constructed" by the language, categories, or representations used to depict them, and hence that *everything* is intrinsically functional to "social control."[30] But the subject of drugs, or other illicit flows, is particularly tempting for discourse analysis because of drugs' social invisibility (which allows much myth making) and because of the cloud of passionate official rhetoric around them. With their power on imagination, drugs invite a slew of gender and racial fascinations, notions of the domesticated and the alien, of good/bad substances, and elaborate fantasies about human loss of control—or inversely, fantasies about the state's possible "control" of the psychoactive realm.

States have a special purpose promoting such discourses of control, which we might call (after James Scott) "thinking like a state" or at least *talking* like one—though clearly mass anxieties about drugs (and media sensationalism) enable this kind of drug talk to succeed. States must mystify illicit drugs in order to fight them. For, as seen, the border between licit commodity drugs (cigarettes, Valium) and illicit ones (coke, grass) is a tenuous one, undermined daily by the borderline involvements of most states in illicit spheres. States are also often targeting a substantial part of their own citizenry who enjoy or make illicit substances (for example, a quarter of European adults smoke cannabis), who must be convinced of this drastic cure. The paradox is not that crusading states talk a lot, but that they fall victim to their own speech acts and believe in their chimera of control. "Weberian" Western states may have begun with rationalizing regulatory discourses about the illicit, but in the course of carving their monopoly on the licit, they entered into a byzantine cycle of political and discursive irrationality.

Discourses of control are hard to categorize or catalogue. Some relate peculiarly to drugs or to particular drugs while others are more general to modern governance of borders or the construction of modern disciplined subjects (to adopt the non-statist, bodily concern of discursive theorists). Representations of "drugs" (the bad kind) are rife with essentialism, puritanical morality, and individualized languages of self-control. Historically, medical debates long raged about drugs and their effects on body, mind, and society, and even on attempts to ban or regulate some. But only in the late nineteenth century did such discourses emerge systematically, representing the anxiety-prone Victorian moment of the modernization of everyday life. The professionalization of medical and pharmacy trades contributed to these languages of control, as advancing scientific "allopathic" medicine established stricter boundaries, in league with the regulatory state, of legitimate cures and national public health. In the urbanizing United States and Europe, relatively harmless and familiar users or "habitués" of drugs like opiates or cocaine became transformed, in this process of medicalization, into wild and violent drug "fiends." These men and women would end up transformed, by medical representation, into pathetic victims of an uncontrollable but well-defined pathology of "addiction." By the 1920s, drug addiction was diagnosed as a disease, socially infectious, with specific etiology and vectors (restless young male populations, parasitic or invasive traffickers). A good historical literature traces the evolution of this Western "addiction paradigm." Long contested, addiction remains of doubtful objectivity or therapeutic value today, even with "twelve-step" mantras or MRI scans of cocaine brains routinely passed off as "addiction science."[31] Of late, addiction talk (and its weaker form, dependency and "co"dependency talk) has spilled over promiscuously from alcohol and drugs to everything from sex to Krispy Kreme doughnuts, thus undermining its own scientific specificity. This addiction ideology always held an uneasy yet reinforcing alliance with police-driven criminalizing or "punitive" models of drug control.

Addiction and the drug-control discourses that go with it have two chief sources. One is scientific reductionism: the idea that "drugs" are the thing—brain-altering alkaloids to be exact—that work overpowering effects on people. In this trope, the drugs themselves take over and "control" minds; users, lacking will power, then crave them obsessively, which leads down the familiar path of abandoned self-control and rationality. Addicts are sickened victims of external forces. "This is your brain on drugs" was only the latest televised version of this twentieth-century notion. This bio-reductionism helps draw the separation between "drugs" and other freely available pleasure commodities. Since drug (ab)use amounts to personal enslavement, drugs no longer belong to the legitimate realm of free and desirable consumer choices. As dangerous drugs became thus defined and categorized early in the century, they became undifferentiated "narcotics"—the word exudes deadening menace—a label that misrepresents both the pleasurable sensations and specific perils of the majority of illicit substances. Like the related medical addiction paradigm, this "pharmaco-centric fallacy" has drawn sharp rebuttals. It abstracts from the relational social context and actual plasticity of drug effects, so-called drug "set and setting," and dehumanizes the agency or choices of actual drug users.[32]

The second source of drug discourses are obsessions with "control" and the transgression of behavioral or social boundaries. There are historical roots to the corny personal boundary marking that sounded in Nancy Reagan's late-1980s "Just say No!" anti-drug campaign. A person "on drugs" is assumed to be "out of control"—which may or may not be true—a notion that taps into deep-seated social anxieties about self-control, which were particularly acute in the Victorian societies where these anti-drug ideas first blossomed in the 1890s. Like the medically diagnosed sexual "nymphomaniac" (or the era's self-destructive masturbator), the newfangled "narco-maniac" or "dope fiend" was a visibly uncontrolled person who was swiftly descending into the lower orders or already privy to the urban underclass and its criminal culture. In an era of great social flux and of potent new industrialized drugs like morphine and cocaine, these fantasies rang true—as brilliantly depicted in Marek Kohn's *Dope Girls* for early-twentieth-century London. Drugs attracted spiraling social and cultural anxieties about proper gender, sexual, racial, and class boundaries (as drug users and their incipient drug cultures seemed to promiscuously cross borders of respectability) and became signifiers of unstable identities and threatening social spaces. Like coeval American alcohol prohibition, drugs sparked a powerful "symbolic crusade," one drawing upon the rich earlier liberation-ist vocabulary of anti-slavery (i.e., addiction as enslavement).

Such control and otherness discourses swiftly became part of the basic vocabulary of even the most respectable drug reformers. Prohibitionists whipped up "moral panics" with racial overtones: blaming uppity "negroes" and prostitutes for spreading cocaine pleasures in the Jim Crow south; tar-geting Chinese immigrants for "opium dens" that "enslaved" others (mainly white women) in Britain, the United States, Australia, or across Latin America; blaming Mexicans and black jazz musicians for the "killer weed" marijuana during the American Great Depression. Uncouth and rootless Jews and greasy Italian mobsters became the ideal sinister archetypes for early drug dealers and controlling "combinations" long before the fearsome Dominican "gangs," Jamaican "posses," or Chinese "triads" and Colombian "cartels" of our times. It is tempting to read these episodes—which surely helped consolidate drug-control regimes with an international WASP civilizing class of Col. Hobson, Hamilton Wright, and Bishop Brent—as antecedents to the media-orchestrated "crackhead"-"crackwhore" frenzies of the 1980s. Yet despite the exaggeration of race (white folks historically consume drugs at socially representative rates), there is also a reality to the marginal ethnic composition of nascent drug cultures and smuggling net-works.[33] Early depictions of narcotics, for example in widespread editorial cartooning of the 1910s and 1920s, reveled in the deathly imagery of "for-eign dope" infestations, plagues, or, as frequently, in strangling orientalist predators such as vipers and snakes. Vulnerable youth—i.e., civilization's future—were the visually obvious victims of their Eastern venom.

The thrust of racialized drug archetypes was and is to locate the epi-center of drugs on the "outside." Drugs were/are an alien pollutant to the European body—a mortal danger to its purity, to pose it in symbolic an-thropological terms. Mind-altering drugs transgress symbolic boundaries, such as race, along with real borders, an understandable conflation from this the height of European colonialism. Certain states of consciousness became criminalized, declared outside of the nation and its white body politic. The particularly American ideal of hermetically sealing out these undesirable substances—closing them off at the borders, or crossing borders to hunt them down at their threatening third-world haunts, was actually a long-standing policy and political fantasy of early drug reformers and diplomats, who did not have to deal with many of these messy or profitable colonies themselves. It originates in the 1910s with the Shanghai Conven-tion, though American zeal in this crusade only won international approval a half-century later with the UN Single Convention of 1961. Along with this "alterity" of illicit drugs, their formal bureaucratic categorization (according to the fascinating federal classificatory system, "Schedule I" drugs—like marijuana—are the most dangerous because they possess no "legitimate" medical usage), advancing externalist vocabularies, and institutions of global "drug control" came a systematic cultural denial about them. The British buried their long-standing domestic cultures of opium usage and pretended as if someone else had introduced the drug to China. To invoke a longer historical example, in 1900, nothing seemed more "all-American" than imported Andean coca leaf—the active ingredient in the rising national beverage Coca-Cola and a hugely popular herbal cure for neurasthenia or "American nervousness." Thirty years later, coca leaf was deemed a nasty base "addiction" of remote Peruvian Indians and no one remembered its domesticated phase, and by the 1980s, coca leaf, made into illicit cocaine, was depicted by the Reagan-Bush regimes as an aggressive organized foreign security threat to the United States, with crack a kind of African primitivist invasion of once civilized American cities.[34]

Initial "rationalizing" FDA-type drug regulation and medicalized "drug control" thus escalated, at least in the U.S., into demonization of users, of foreign substances and peoples, into a grand-scale demonology which by the mid-twentieth century infused the global crusade against drugs. Most European states, if passing through similar discursive stages, have managed somehow after World War II to keep the original hygienic medical model alive despite pressures to conform, avoiding some of the extremes of punitive American drug talk, and eventually allowing some of the de-escalation experiments of the Dutch, British, or Swiss governments. These differing possibilities had to do with the relative weight of immigrant or minority populations (which perhaps underlie demonization of drugs), their long tolerance of profitable colonial drug trades in Asia, as well as the more vigorous social democratic regulatory regimes and relative health of urban life in Europe. In the United States proper, generalized drug fears were blatantly manipulated by Harry J. Anslinger, the famously dedicated "drug czar" of the long middle era 1930–1962 (or infamous for his "reefer madness" campaign to banish marijuana in the 1930s), who raised anti-drug discourse to the shrill tone of Dr. Strangelove's anti-communist phobia of "bodily fluids." Although its genealogy has not been rigorously researched, the contemporary metaphoric idea of a "war on drugs" followed: a socially rooted hard-nosed Cold War ideology (akin to "containment") informed the U.S. version of the 1950s through the 1970s, before the pure Reagan-esque total victory fantasy took off with the "Star Wars" version of the 1980s and beyond. Whichever, the promise of drug policy is always extermina-tionist. Drug evils will be "wiped out" or at least radically "controlled"; we must, we can, we will achieve a "drug-free" America, starting with all those (allegedly) drug-free schoolyards. American extremism in recent years at least has spawned a small but purposeful peace camp, groups, and now a few countries raising the white flag of "harm reduction" or relegitimized "medical" usage (as in surprisingly successful state-level medical marijuana campaigns).

I belabor this obvious point about the "essentialist" and "externalist" mooring of anti-drug discourse because, by whatever means, these ideas enjoy great historical staying power, a powerful "genealogy," if periodically invigorated by novel drug scares and a refurbished imagery of fear. This vocabulary goes a long way to discursively explain the survival and legiti-macy of this hopeless U.S. War on Drugs, now entering its tenth decade. On a speculative level, these resolute anti-drug passions, besides politically driven, are the psychological inversion of popular cravings for drugs—as exotic, libidinal, enchanting, and ultimately forbidden fruit. The more they are prohibited, the greater their symbolic worth, to both users and the abhorred. In this sense, illicit drugs are clearly not banal everyday com-modities like apples or microchips.

Once etched into state policy and mass culture, control discourses around drugs merge with "governance-speak" that spans the whole range of criminalized modern commerce. This is to telescope a possibly much broader discussion on the reifications (to use a big word) and silences (to use a hip word) that inform official cosmologies of the illicit. There are plenty of official silences: on the connections and complicity of mainstream institutions and home markets to illicit drug flows, on the chicken-and-egg problem of prohibition and reactions to it. There are curiously centraliz-ing demonologies: concentrated "cartels" and corruptive "narco-states" are easier shooting targets than invisible impersonal market signals or much looser networks involving thousands of faceless peasants and dollar-loving entrepreneurs. Aping the early-nineteenth-century anti-slavery movement that legitimized emerging market individualism and free wages, anti-drug discourse of the global age adopts a dramatically atavistic vocabulary of "feudal" barbarism. Drugs are cast as the antithesis of borderless free-trade capitalism, as a warring medieval black-and-white spectacle of evil "drug lords," "drug czars," and "drug bazaars." If today's drug discourse were actu-ally a Hollywood movie, it would run like a blend of *Mad Max* and *Lord of the Rings*, rather than the cool realist footage of *Traffic*.[35]

In many producing areas, NGOs and international aid agencies introduce instead a neutralist or technical vocabulary of "alternative develop-ment," which offers few uncoerced alternatives to commodity-hungry grow-ers who are usually pursuing the sole existing developmental option left after the anti-developmental neo-liberal 1980s. Paradoxically, drugs often offer the best in grassroots alternative development, something grasped by smart market liberals like Hernando de Soto in Peru. NGO talk serves as the velvet-fisted side of exterminationist drug "eradication" policies, with all its scorched-earth and dislocating grassroots violence. To these modern-day missionaries, peasants can be relocated, converted, re-educated, or civilized in "good" market behavior. Generalized smokescreens of "drug-related" violence obscure exactly what those "relations" are: institutional, economic, and judicial violence against minority populations at home, and violence displaced across distant borders. "Drug-related" (as in crime) systemati-cally obscures whether all this disorder and mayhem is prompted by drugs or drug laws themselves. Once all this rhetoric gets off the ground, the question of which causes greater harm, laws or drugs, legal or illicit drugs, becomes moot.

What can researchers do about the pervasive discourses of control around drugs and other illicit flows? There is no pat formula to reconcile approach-es that cut through fogs of controlling words—objectifying or commodity lenses—and approaches that grapple head-on with the irrational representa-tions and discourses that help constitute illicit drugs. One must take both seriously. There is also a staggering practical dilemma of biased or faulty research sources: drug agency, policing, and criminal records are usually the only available "data" on illicit trades, past and present, infused with the day-to-day suspicion-laden languages and categories of control. Polic-ing statistics are notoriously contaminated, pumped up, or even fabricated to suit political ends. The secrecy and invisibility of the flow leaves few alternative documents and subjectivities for neutral researchers to build upon, hence the seeming safe ground of the rationalist commodities ap-proach. Some scholars try to address these dilemmas of talking like a state. There is the ironic "deconstructionist" (resi)stance to drug discourses, as in recent literary-critical works like Avital Ronell's *Crack Wars* and David Lenson's *On Drugs*. Others focus on the genealogy of drug representation, over the story of the flow itself, as cultural writer Marek Kohn achieves with *Narcomania*—a history of control-laden British fear and loathing of heroin, a social fear larger than the drug itself. Mexican drug sociologist Luis Astorga combines the heroic and demonizing regional "mythology" of northern Narcos with insider research on their working networks and tie-ins with the Mexican state. Cocaine historian Joseph Spillane compares the "construction" of the early American "cocaine fiend" to the actual social profile of the era's drug users and follows how this representational gap impacts drug-control crusades.[36] What many of these new scholars suggest, at the least, is that critical or semiotic techniques may go beyond "economistic" models (long assimilated to the realists in drug agencies) in demystifying drug control. Academic drug-control rhetoric, whether the political science "wonking" kind or by sincere drug policy reformists, accepts at its peril the binary categories and contours of the problem: foreign cartels, local addicts, illicit and licit drugs, supply and demand strategies, dangerous and softer drugs that are all in fact conceptual weapons of this unjust, futile, and harmful war. Critical approaches can begin by working to free us from those demons of control.

Guns and Money and Lawyers?

Because of their concentrated mind power, drugs epitomize other stateless flowing objects, including undocumented workers, subversive persons and refugees, hot laundered money, kiddie porn, blood diamonds, guns of every caliber, hazmats and endangered species (both "drug-related" in Amazonia), and other junked, stolen, contraband, or coveted goods. Indeed drug flows, which may well constitute 8 percent of all current international trade, elicit and underwrite a number of allied spheres of informal activities, including underground wars and violence and all the mundane above-ground rice and beans to feed the illicit flow passing the other way. At the risk of a terrible pun, illicit drug flows are a "gateway drug" to other risky businesses.[37]

What lessons are there for other out-of-control objects, other interstitial sites? The three-pronged analysis attempted here—looking at historical differentiation during modern commodity-making processes, its relation to state building and border making, and the discourses that accompany, naturalize, and blur these constructions—could presumably apply to other flows. The study of illicit flows calls for a mix of "structural" and "discursive" approaches, one that understands the cool hidden realities of flows along with their overtly heated representations. One can assume that other objects and their discourses of control will vary according to cultural and national origins, the nature and force of the non-state flow, and the conjuncture of its emergence, and that no iron law governs their grammatical code, vocabulary, or thematic core. But what may ultimately distinguish the new "beyond borders" approach to global flows, besides its wide-angled and mobile optic, is the effort to develop a language of analysis that goes beyond existing borders, and blinders, of authority. That stops talking like a state.

NOTES

Thanks to Laura for taking over Danyal in the dog days of writing and to all "BB" participants in beautiful beyond-the-border Vancouver.

1. For some common (or political) conundrums of defining "drugs," see, e.g., Introduction to United Nations International Drug Control Programme (UNIDCP), *World Drug Report* (Oxford: Oxford University Press, 1997); Erich Goode, *Drugs in American Society*, 2nd ed. (New York: Knopf, 1984), 14–18; Andrew Weil and Winifred Rosen, "What Is a Drug?" chapter 2 in *From Chocolate to Morphine* (Boston: Houghton Mifflin, 1994).

2. Sidney W. Mintz, "The Forefathers of Crack," *NACLA Report on the Americas* 22, no. 6 (March 1989).

3. Matthew Brzezinski, "Re-engineering the Drug Business," *New York Times Magazine*, June 24, 2002.

4. A recent journalistic example is Brzezinski, "Re-engineering the Drug Business"; the think-tank genre of Patrick Clawson and Rensselaer W. Lee III, *The Andean Cocaine Industry* (New York: St. Martin's Press, 1996); or economist Francisco Thoumi, *Economía Política y Narcotráfico* (Bogotá: Tercer Mundo Editores, 1994); Mario De Franco and Ricardo Godoy, "The Economic Consequences of Cocaine in Bolivia: Historical, Local and Macro-Economic Consequences," *Journal of Latin American Studies* 24, no. 2 (1992): 375–406. The "commodity" perspective is not alien to anti-drug organizations; see "The illicit drug industry: production, trafficking and distribution," part 4 of the 1997 UNIDCP *World Drug Report*.

5. Paul B. Stares, *Global Habit: The Drug Problem in a Borderless World* (Washington, D.C.: Brookings Institution, 1996); Jean-Claude Grimal, *Drogue: L'autre mondialisation* (Paris: Gallimard, 2000); Peter Andreas, "When Policies Collide: Market Reform, Market Prohibition, and the Narcotization of the Mexican Economy," chapter 5 in *Illicit Global Economy and State Power*, ed. H. Richard Friman and Peter Andreas (Lanham, Md.: Rowman & Littlefield, 1999); on "similarities and differences" of drugs to "legal commodities," see George Rengert, *The Geography of Illegal Drugs* (Boulder, Colo.: Westview Press, 1996); Philippe Bourgois, *In Search of Respect: Selling Crack in "El Barrio"* (Cambridge: Cambridge University Press, 1995); Edmundo Morales, *Cocaine: White Gold Rush in Peru* (Tucson: University of Arizona Press, 1989).

6. Suzanne Wilson and Marta Zambrano, "Cocaine, Commodity Chains, and Drug Politics: A Transnational Approach," in *Commodity Chains and Global Capitalism*, ed. Gary Gereffi and Miguel Korzeniewitz (Westport, Conn.: Greenwood Press, 1994); similarly, Amy Bellone, "The Cocaine Commodity Chain and Development Paths in Peru and Bolivia, in *Latin America in the World-Economy*, ed. Roberto Patricio Korzeniewicz and William C. Smith (Westport, Conn.: Greenwood Press, 1996). See two of my works on cocaine and commodity chains: Paul Gootenberg, "Cocaine in Chains: The Rise and Demise of Global Commodity, 1860–1950," in *Latin America and The World Trade*, ed. S. Topik, C. Marichal, and Z. Frank (Durham, N.C.: Duke University Press, forthcoming) and Paul Gootenberg, ed., *Cocaine: Global Histories* (New York: Routledge, 1999), a comparative volume organized around cocaine chains.

7. Wolfgang Schivelbusch, *Tastes of Paradise: A Social History of Spices, Stimulants and Intoxicants* (New York: Vintage Books/Random House, 1993); Jordan Goodman, *Tobacco in History: The Cultures of Dependence* (New York: Routledge, 1993), espe-

cially chapter 1; Sidney Mintz, *Sweetness and Power: The Place of Sugar in Modern History* (New York: Penguin Books, 1985); Jordan Goodman, "Excitantia: Or, How Enlightenment Europe Took to Soft Drugs," chapter 6 in *Consuming Habits: Drugs in History and Anthropology*, ed. Jordan Goodman, Paul E. Lovejoy, and Andrew Sherratt (New York: Routledge, 1995); Rudi Matthe, "Exotic Substances: The Introduction and Global Spread of Tobacco, Coffee, Cocoa, Tea, and Distilled Liquor, 16th–18th Centuries," chapter 2 in *Drugs and Narcotics in History*, ed. Roy Porter and Mikulas Teich (Cambridge: Cambridge University Press, 1995).

8. David T. Courtwright, *Forces of Habit: Drugs and the Making of the Modern World* (Cambridge, Mass.: Harvard University Press, 2001). One might compare Courtwright's interesting effort to "commodity" histories that broadly include drugs, for example, Kenneth Pomeranz and Steven Topik, *The World That Trade Created: Society, Culture, and the World Economy, 1400–The Present* (Armonk, N.Y.: M.E. Sharpe, 1999), chapter 3; and critical histories of commodities (such as Eric R. Wolf, *Europe and the People without History* [Berkeley: University of California Press, 1982] and Sidney W. Mintz, "The Forefathers of Crack").

9. LSD has a fascinating "historiography": see Jay Stevens, *Storming Heaven: LSD and the American Dream* (New York: Atlantic Monthly Press, 1987); Martin A. Lee and Bruce Shlain, *Acid Dreams: The CIA, LSD and the Sixties Rebellion* (New York: Grove Press, 1985); or even (more conspiratorial) David Black, *ACID: A New Secret History of LSD* (London: Vision Paperbacks, 1998). Ecstasy was different, as adoring psychologists tried fruitlessly to keep its secret powers (as therapy) under wrap; Bruce Eisner, *Ecstasy: The MDMA Story* (Berkeley, Calif.: Ronin Publishing, 1994).

10. Arjun Appadurai, ed., *The Social Life of Things: Commodities in Cultural Perspective* (Cambridge: Cambridge University Press, 1986), optics globally "post-modernized" in his *Modernity at Large: Cultural Dimensions of Globalization* (Minneapolis: University of Minnesota Press, 1998).

11. Sigmund Freud, "Craving for and Fear of Cocaine" (July 1887), chapter 15 in *Cocaine Papers*, ed. Robert Byck (New York: Stonehill Press, 1974); David C. Musto, *The American Disease: Origins of Narcotic Control*, expanded ed. (New York: Oxford University Press, 1987), links such cultural ambivalence to the American drive for drug "control."

12. David Lenson, *On Drugs* (Minneapolis: University of Minnesota Press, 1995), 191.

13. Schivelbusch, *Tastes of Paradise*; Courtwright, *Forces of Habit*; Richard Rudgley, *Essential Substances: A Cultural History of Intoxicants in Society* (New York: Kodansha International, 1994), part of a rehabilitation of northern "drug cultures"; Piero Camporesi, *Bread of Dreams: Food and Fantasy in Early Modern Europe* (Chicago: University of Chicago Press, 1989); Richard Evans Schultes and Albert Hoffman, *Plants of the Gods: Their Sacred, Healing and Hallucinogenic Powers* (Rochester: Healing Arts Press, 1992) on wealth of the (non-commodified) American drug complex.

14. Gootenberg, *Cocaine: Global Histories*; Silvia Rivera Cusicanqui's recent video *Las fronteras de la coca* (ADEPCOCA, 2002) traces some still-existing networks in questioning the duality of "traditional/modern" coca usage.

15. For illustration of some of these phenomena, see Paul Gootenberg, "Between Coca and Cocaine: A Century or More of U.S.-Peruvian Drug Paradoxes, 1860–1980," *Hispanic American Historical Review* 83, no. 1 (February 2003): 123–53; Eva Bertram

et al., *Drug War Politics: The Price of Denial* (Berkeley: University of California Press, 1996), for comprehensive analysis.

16. Brian Preston, *Pot Planet: Adventures in Global Marijuana Culture* (New York: Grove Press, 2002); Michael Pollan, *The Botany of Desire* (New York: Random House, 2001), chapter 3; on high-tech drugs trades, see Paula Kaihla, "The Technological Secrets of Cocaine Inc." *Business*, July 20, 2002.

17. William B. McAllister, *Drug Diplomacy in the Twentieth Century: An International History* (London: Routledge, 2000), especially chapter 7 on the Single Convention; Ethan Nadelmann, *Cops across Borders: The Internationalization of U.S. Criminal Law Enforcement* (University Park: Pennsylvania State University Press, 1993), chapters 4–5 on DEA.

18. Francisco E. Thoumi, "Why the Illegal Psycho-Active Drugs Industry Grew in Colombia," *Journal of Inter-American Studies and World Affairs* 34 (Fall 1992): 37–63; Alfred E. McCoy, "Heroin as a Global Commodity: A History of Southeast Asia's Opium Trade," in *War on Drugs: Studies in the Failure of U.S. Narcotics Policy*, ed. Alfred McCoy and Alan A. Block (Boulder, Colo.: Westview Press, 1992), 237–255; Michael L. Smith et al., *Why People Grow Drugs: Narcotics and Development in the Third World* (London: Panos Institute, 1992).

19. Ethan Nadelmann, "U.S. Drug Policy: A Bad Export," *Foreign Policy* 70 (1988): 97–108, and "Global Prohibition Regimes: The Evolution of Norms in International Society," *International Organization* 44, no. 4 (1990): 479–526; for paradoxes on ground (Bolivia), see Jaime Malamud-Goti, *Smoke and Mirrors: The Paradox of the Drug Wars* (Boulder, Colo.: Westview Press, 1992).

20. Timothy Brook and Bob Tadashi Wakabayashi, "Introduction: Opium's History in China," in *Opium Regimes: China, Britain, and Japan, 1839–1952*, ed. Timothy Brook and Bob Tadashi Wakabayashi (Berkeley: University of California Press, 2000). See also Louis R. Sadler, "The Historical Dynamics of Smuggling on the U.S.-Mexican Border Region, 1550–1998: Reflections on Markets, Cultures and Bureaucracies," chapter 7 in *Organized Crime and Democratic Governability: Mexico and the U.S.-Mexican Borderlands*, ed. John Baily and Roy Godson (Pittsburgh: University of Pittsburgh Press, 2000).

21. See H. Richard Friman and Peter Andreas, ed., *The Illicit Global Economy and State Power* (Lanham, Md.: Rowman & Littlefield, 1999), which focuses on a similar set of issues with a more "statist" optic.

22. Musto, *American Disease*; there is no shortage of books analyzing/criticizing U.S. Drug War politics; e.g., Mike Gray, *Drug Crazy* (New York: Random House, 1998); Steven B. Duke and Albert C. Gross, *America's Longest War* (New York: Putnam's Sons, 1993); Michael Massing, *The Fix* (New York: Simon & Schuster, 1998), save for his apologetics to Nixon.

23. Alfred W. McCoy, *The Politics of Heroin: CIA Complicity in the Global Drug Trade*, rev. ed. (Chicago: Lawrence Hill Books, 2003); Peter Dale Scott and Jonathan Marshall, *Cocaine Politics: Drugs, Armies and the CIA in Central America* (Berkeley: University of California Press, 1991); Kenneth C. Bucchi, *C.I.A.: Cocaine in America? A Veteran of the C.I.A. Drug Wars Tells All* (New York: Spi Books, 1994), etc.—conspiracy issues fruitlessly "debated" on the left in *The Nation* by Alexander Cockburn and JoAnn Kawell.

24. Edward Jay Epstein, *Agency of Fear: Opiates and Political Power in America*,

rev. ed. (New York: Verso, 1990); Elliott Currie, *Reckoning: Drugs, the Cities, and the American Future* (New York: Hill and Wang, 1993); Bourgois, *In Search of Respect.*

25. Jeremy Bigwood, "Plan Colombia's Potential Impact on the Andean Cocaine Trade: An Examination of Two Scenarios" (CIA Intelligence Report, DCI Crime and Narcotics Center, September 19, 2000), available at http://jeremybigwood.net/FOIAs/2Scenarios-Colombia/CIA-2scenarios-Colombian_coca-2000.htm. Bureaucratic politics model is Bertram et al., *Drug War Politics* or historically, William Walker III, ed., *Drug Control Policy: Essays in Historical and Comparative Perspective* (University Park: Pennsylvania State University Press, 1992) or McAllister, *Drug Diplomacy.*

26. H. Richard Friman, *NarcoDiplomacy: Exporting the U.S. War on Drugs* (Ithaca, N.Y.: Cornell University Press, 1996); Malamud-Goti, *Smoke and Mirrors* (on Bolivia); certification process in U.S. Department of State, *International Narcotics Control Strategy Report* (Washington, D.C., March 2000).

27. Alma Guillermoprieto, *The Heart That Bleeds* (New York: Knopf, 1994), chapters 1, 5 on Bogotá and Medellín; on drugs corruption, see essay by Nobel laureate Amartya Sen, "On Corruption and Organized Crime," in UNIDCP, *World Drug Report*, 150–53; Nadelmann, *Cops across Borders*, chapter 5; Baily and Godson, *Organized Crime and Democratic Governability*; or innovative historical essays in Claudio Lomnitz, ed., *Vicios públicos, virtudes privadas: La corrupción en México* (Mexico City: CIESAS, 2000), especially Luis Astorga, "Traficantes de drogas, políticas y policías en el siglo XX mexicano," 167–93.

28. Mary Roldan, "Colombia: Cocaine and the 'Miracle' of Modernity in Medellín," chapter 8 in Gootenberg, *Cocaine: Global Histories*; Julio Cotler, *Drogas y política en el Perú* (Lima: IEP, 1999); for the latest on Mexico's transborder culture of drugs, see Elijah Wald, *Narcocorrido: A Journey into the Music of Drugs, Guns, and Guerrillas* (New York: Rayo/HarperCollins, 2001).

29. Marek Kohn, *Narcomania: On Heroin* (Boston: Faber and Faber, 1987), 167.

30. We call this 1990s phenomena "grad-student Foucauldianism." For a "po-mo" manifesto on drugs, see Desmond Manderson, "Metamorphosis: Clashing Symbols in the Social Construction of Drugs," *Journal of Drug Issues* 23, no. 4 (1995): 799–816; or David Lenson, *On Drugs*; Erich Goode, *Between Politics and Reason: The Drug Legalization Debate* (New York: St. Martin's Press, 1997), argues that the drug debate is inherently irrationally discursive; limits to "constructionism" are explored by Ian Hacking, *The Social Construction of What?* (Cambridge, Mass.: Harvard University Press, 1999).

31. For addiction paradigm, see Marek Kohn, *Narcomania*, chapter 4; or Geoffrey Harding, *Opiate Addiction, Morality and Medicine: From Moral Illness to Pathological Disease* (Houndmills, Basingstoke, Hampshire: Macmillan, 1988); Herbert Fingarette, *Heavy Drinking: The Myth of Alcoholism as a Disease* (Berkeley: University of California Press, 1989).

32. Norman Zinberg, *Drug, Set and Setting* (New Haven, Conn.: Yale University Press, 1984); Andrew Weil, *The Natural Mind: An Investigation of Drugs and the Higher Consciousness* (Boston: Houghton-Mifflin, 1972); Dan Waldorf, Craig Reinarman, and Sheila Murphy, *Cocaine Changes: The Experience of Using and Quitting* (Philadelphia: Temple University Press, 1991); John Morgan, M.D. (a critical pharmacologist), coined "Pharmaco-centric fallacy" in John P. Morgan and Lynn Zimmer, "The Social Pharmacology of Smokeable Cocaine: Not All It's Cracked Up to Be," chapter 7 in *Crack in America: Demon Drugs and Social Justice*, ed. Craig Reinarman and Harry G.

Levine (Berkeley: University of California Press, 1997). This literature focuses on the plasticity of drug experience, relating to its social setting (heroin, the most "addictive drug," addicted few U.S. soldiers in Vietnam, who used it situationally).

33. Marek Kohn, *Dope Girls: The Birth of the British Drugs Underground* (London: Lawrence & Wishart, 1992); Musto, *American Disease*, chapter 2, on use of race; Joseph R. Gusfield, *Contested Meanings: The Construction of Alcohol Problems* (Madison: University of Wisconsin Press, 1996); for typical imagery, see illustrations (e.g., 172) in Courtwright, *Forces of Habit*; on recent drug "demonology," see Reinarman and Levine, eds., *Crack in America*, especially Introduction and editors' chapter 16, "The Cultural Contradictions of Punitive Prohibitions."

34. Mary Douglas, *Purity and Danger: An Analysis of the Concepts of Pollution and Taboo* (London, Routledge & Kegan Paul, 1966); on genesis of U.S. concepts, see Arnold H. Taylor, *American Diplomacy and the Narcotics Traffic, 1900–1939* (Durham, N.C.: Duke University Press, 1969); Virginia Berridge and Griffith Edwards, *Opium and the People: Opiate Use in Nineteenth-Century England* (New Haven, Conn.: Yale University Press, 1987); Mark Pendergrast, *For God, Country and Coca-Cola: The Unauthorized History of the Great American Soft-Drink and the Company That Makes It* (New York: Scribner's, 1993), especially chapter 2 on coca culture; or Paul Gootenberg, "Secret Ingredients: The Politics of Coca in U.S.-Peruvian Relations, 1915–65," *Journal of Latin American Studies* 36, no. 2 (2004): 233–265.

35. I am indebted to coffee man Steve Topik for this insight about "feudal" discourse; for analogy of slavery and markets, see Eric Foner, *Free Soil, Free Labor, Free Men* (Oxford: Oxford University Press, 1970) or David Bryan Davis, *The Problem of Slavery in the Age of Revolution* (Ithaca, N.Y.: Cornell University Press, 1975).

36. Avital Ronell, *Crack Wars: Literature, Addiction, Mania* (Lincoln: University of Nebraska Press, 1992); Lenson, *On Drugs*; Kohn, *Narcomania*; Joseph F. Spillane, *Cocaine: From Medical Marvel to Modern Menace in the United States, 1884–1920* (Baltimore: Johns Hopkins University Press, 2000), chapter 6; Luis A. Astorga, *Mitología del "Narcotraficante" en México* (Mexico City: Plaza y Valdés, 1995) and his *El siglo de las drogas: Usos, percepciones y personalidades* (Mexico City: Espasa Hoy, 1996). For critical analysis of media constructions, see Jimmie L. Reeves and Richard Campbell, *Cracked Coverage: Television News, the Anti-Cocaine Crusade, and the Reagan Legacy* (Durham, N.C.: Duke University Press, 1994).

On the other hand, there are dozens of books and proposals sporting titular keywords "drug control" and "drug policy," e.g., William Walker III, *Drug Control in the Americas*, rev. ed. (Albuquerque: University of New Mexico Press New Mexico, 1989), though a thaw is coming even here; see Baily and Godson, Introduction to *Organized Crime & Democratic Governability*, for political scientists grappling with problems of "representation" of the illicit.

37. Alain Labrousse, *La droga, el dinero y las armas* (Siglo Veintiuno, 1993; originally published in Paris, 1991); his now-defunct "OGN—Observatoire Geopolitique des Drogues" was devoted to factually uncovering these worldly connections. See UNIDCP, *World Drug Report*, 124, for 8 percent guess.

four

"Here, Even Legislators Chew Them"

Coca Leaves and Identity Politics in Northern Argentina

Silvia Rivera Cusicanqui

In La Quiaca there aren't any Argentine or Bolivian Indians. There are, simply, Indians.
—Jaime Molins, 1916

Chewing coca leaves is an ancient habit in the Andes that is currently spreading among Westernized urban consumers in northern Argentina. In this chapter I take you on a journey through this region. You will meet journalists, doctors, members of parliament, mine workers, billiard players, and government officials who chew coca leaves much as others around the world consume coffee or tea. They do so openly in the course of their daily work or when socializing at night. To them, chewing coca is an enjoyable habit and an expression of regional identity.

There is something unusual about this. Coca leaves do not grow locally but have to be imported from Bolivia. Coca chewing came to northern Argentina with Bolivian labor migrants, a low-status group. Their practice became incorporated into the cultural repertoires of contemporary Argentines who had no previous involvement in Andean culture, turning an "exotic" practice into an emblem of local identity.

But there is more that is unusual about coca chewing in northern Argentina. It is a habit with a checkered legal record. Up to the mid-twentieth century it was perfectly legal to import coca leaves from Bolivia, but after the publication of a United Nations report condemning coca chewing in 1950, Argentina imposed increasingly strict quotas on coca leaf imports until a total prohibition was enforced in 1977. Coca chewing was now strictly prohibited in Argentina. In 1989, however, the chewing of coca leaves was legalized, but importing the leaves from Bolivia remained illegal. As a result, the Argentine state considers the current boom in consumption as legal but the large imports on which it is based as illegal.

The absurdity of this situation of illicitness is not lost on the traders who supply coca leaves to Argentina, nor on the consumers there who have to pay high prices. This absurdity is brought out particularly clearly at the Bolivia-Argentina border, and this is where our journey through the region will start. We begin in the Bolivian border town of Villazón, then we cross the river to the Argentine border town of La Quiaca, and then we travel to several cities in northern Argentina. Throughout this journey, the tensions between two types of authority will be inescapable. In northern Argentina, the formal authority of the Buenos Aires–centered state is continually being questioned. Within the Argentine state itself, the legal status of coca chewing is part of politico-legal struggles between the central and provincial levels. In addition, the state's legal authority is continually being challenged by large numbers of citizens for whom coca chewing, and all it entails, is a highly meaningful and respectable cultural practice. This distinction between what is socially approved (licit) and what is legally allowed is essential in analyzing the consumption of coca leaves in northern Argentina.

From Tolerance to Prohibition, and Back Again

In 1989, after a twelve-year period of strict prohibition, Argentina legalized coca leaf chewing (known locally as *akhulliku, coqueo,* or *akusi*). This was a remarkable occurrence because 1989 was also the year in which all signatories to the Single Convention on Narcotic Drugs (1961) were to eradicate the cultivation and consumption of coca. In Argentina, the act legalizing coca chewing was popularly known as the "Snopek Act" after a senator from Jujuy who promoted it and who is known to have been a habitual coca chewer himself. The act allowed the consumption and possession of coca leaves but prohibited their import. This was striking because the only way to obtain coca leaves is by importing them from neighboring Bolivia. This legal paradox led to sharply increased prices for coca leaves and high profits and risks for illegal importers. In practice, state personnel at the border undermined the law because they allowed individuals to cross the border with up to half a kilogram of coca leaves, generating an illegal but tolerated "ant trade" across the bridges linking Bolivia with Argentina at places like Villazón–La Quiaca, the starting point of our journey.

The size of the Argentine coca market is unknown. Rural labor migrants from highland Bolivia, who have been migrating seasonally to Argentina since the nineteenth century, invariably carried coca leaves. A traveler from Buenos Aires described coca consumption among this work force employed in the agro-industry of northern Argentina as follows:

> Local traffic [through the border town of La Quiaca] is restricted to cloth-ing, some tools and staple goods. Coca leaf is a transit item. It goes to the sugar mills in Jujuy, Salta and Tucumán, to be retailed to the workers (*peonadas*). It is usually acquired in Villazón and it comes from the North [Bolivia], from Cochabamba and La Paz.[1]

According to Molins, annual imports were about 265 metric tons. Coca leaves crossed the border without any restriction and generated substantial tax incomes for both governments. The demand for Bolivian coca leaves grew quickly, and in 1948 Argentina and Bolivia signed an agreement where-by Bolivia would supply Argentina 500 tons annually.[2] In addition to this of-ficial trade, an unknown volume of coca leaves reached Argentina through traditional networks of reciprocity and barter, and through "ant trade."

In 1950 the United Nations Commission of Inquiry on the Coca Leaf published a report that would have a devastating effect on these commer-cial relations. Suddenly, the Buenos Aires media were full of medical and psychiatric opinion condemning coca chewing as backward, and in 1951 the Ministry of Public Health classified coca leaf as a narcotic or "stupefy-ing" drug.[3] This was followed by the Argentine government's decision to gradually decrease the import quota and impose a total ban in twenty-five years' time (1977): whoever sold, possessed, or consumed coca leaves could be sentenced to up to fifteen years to jail.[4]

Despite official discouragement, coca leaf consumption in Argentina appears to have increased during the 1960s and 1970s, reaching a peak of about 900 tons just before prohibition was imposed.[5] It is impossible to estimate the volume of coca leaf imported after 1977 because it is no longer mentioned in the official record. Criminalized, it surfaced occasionally only in police records and press reports. Observers agree, however, that the demand increased rather than decreased and that coca chewing con-tinued more or less openly and defiantly. The prevalent attitude was one of pragmatic tolerance.[6]

Argentina's decision to decriminalize coca chewing in 1989 gave an impetus to Bolivia's coca leaf crop, in particular for "selected" leaves from the Yungas, near La Paz.[7] In 2000, an official survey in the province of Jujuy concluded that the annual demand for dried coca leaves among male chewers aged between eighteen and fifty was 117 tons. This figure excluded women, adolescents, and the elderly (all consumers) and omitted eight out of fifteen departments of the province.[8] Coca chewing was also spreading in the provinces of Salta (with almost twice the population of Jujuy), Tucumán, Catamarca, Córdoba, and Rosario, as well as in the suburbs and night spots in Buenos Aires. Raúl Noro, Jujuy correspondent of the national newspaper *La Nación*, estimated that the value of the trade in three provinces (Jujuy, Salta, and Tucumán) alone was about US$50 million.[9] According to another estimate, Bolivia exported about 1,100 tons of coca leaves to Argentina.[10]

Coca Consumption and Modernity

Consumers in Argentina chewed the leaves, but they also drank coca leaf tea, took coca as a medicine, or used it in rituals. According to Ricardo Abduca's unpublished research, modern forms of consumption came up in the 1920s, a result of the urban elite's romantic rediscovery of the *gaucho*. Coca leaves began to be sold in drugstores around 1924, a tradition that was interrupted during prohibition (1977–1989).[11] But during this time, coca chewing did not disappear. On the contrary, it was popular

> a) among peasants of indigenous background, b) among Andean wage-work-ers in big enterprises, such as mines or rural plantations; and c) among the popular sectors of [the cities of Jujuy and Salta]. . . . Since in these provinces the members of the elite chew coca leaves, the habit does not function as a marker of ethnic or class affiliation: in northwestern Argentina it has be-come a symbol of regional belonging.[12]

In fact, during prohibition, coca chewing became a form of cultural resistance to the hegemony of Buenos Aires, an act of self-identification and a challenge to the law. It implied a rejection of the Eurocentric norms dictated by Buenos Aires that northerners considered to be "absurd, not in force"[13] and created a sense of pride among the provincial elite who would openly chew coca in clubs, *peñas* (restaurants where folk music groups per-form), and family gatherings. Even members of the provincial parliaments in Jujuy and Salta chewed coca in public during legislative sessions in an act of civil disobedience.

Rabey's study shows how the provincial elite's social etiquette affirms a northern identity linked with regional customs and the landscape of northern Argentina.[14] Syrian-Lebanese settlers were instrumental in spreading coca chewing among the higher strata. These so-called "Turks"—a misnomer for migrants from Syria, Lebanon, and Palestine who settled in large numbers in northern Argentina and southern Bolivia—adopted the habit first, as a substitute for a similar habit in their countries of origin. In 1927, Fausto Burgos, an author of *costumbrista* literature, portrayed the Syrian-Lebanese as merchants who obtained coca leaves from muleteers who imported them from Bolivia. In Burgos's short stories, coca chewers are mostly peasants of Andean origin, herdsmen, muleteers, weavers, and—occasionally—European travelers and Syrian-Lebanese settlers. The habit may have spread out from Syrian-Lebanese saloons in northern Argentina and southern Bolivia, horizontally among petty merchants, gamblers, bohemians, and liberal professionals, and vertically to reach the urban elite.[15]

Unlike in Bolivia, where coca chewing remained confined to the world of game houses and bars and was widely condemned as backward, dirty, and intemperate, in northern Argentina it became popular in other social contexts. Here students, musicians, and union leaders all chewed, and it was a popular habit at soccer games, political meetings, and festive gatherings. According to Rabey, chewing coca leaves was "a symbol of maturity, and the acquisition of rights and social recognition. It is for these reasons that adolescents and women (those 'others' of modern civilization) have adopted the habit as a symbol of their full rights."[16] Argentines did not stigmatize Bolivian labor migrants because of their coca habit, which was remarkable because Bolivians were perhaps the most discriminated-against group of migrants in Argentina. The link between coca consumption and northern identity provided the only horizontal connection between Argentines and Bolivians in a context that was otherwise marked by racism and violence against Bolivian immigrants.

The social acceptance of coca chewing among the middle classes of northern Argentina was driven home to me in 1998 when I traveled there and met a tall, blond young man with a huge wad of coca leaves (*jach'u* or *akusi*) in his cheek. He was a physician from Salta on his way to Tartagal Hospital to work the night shift. He was chewing coca leaves to stay awake during the long working night when he would have to cope with pregnant women, workers with tuberculosis, and *chagas* disease. This "pragmatic" consumption of coca leaves is based on a recognition of their stimulating effect, their capacity to enhance work performance and keep sleep and hunger at bay.[17]

Crossing the Border: People and Coca from Bolivia

As soon as we came off the train at Villazón, a town on the Bolivia-Argentina border, my travel companion Félix Barra and I were accosted by a Qhichwa-speaking *mestizo* youth. He worked for an Argentine bus company, La Veloz del Norte, offered to help us with our luggage, and tried to sell us tickets almost by force. We decided to follow his advice, and we felt La Quiaca deserved its poor reputation as a border post where Bolivian travelers are ripped off. There were other bus companies with offices in Villazón, selling tickets to destinations in Argentina such as Buenos Aires, Escobar, Zárate, Villa Madero, Lomas de Zamora, and other small towns that are well known in Bolivia. The companies hoped to attract migrants to those places by offering special services to assist them in bypassing the obstacles put up by the Argentine border police, the *Gendarmería*.[18] Although Félix, who was the permanent secretary of ADEPCOCA (Departmental Association of Coca Leaf Producers of La Paz), and I were hardly typical migrants trying to get into Argentina, we also experienced mistreatment by the Argentine *gendarmes*, perhaps in a milder form than our compatriots, specially if they were illiterate, uneducated, poor laborers.

The bus company offered to sell us a one-way ticket and "lend" us the return ticket, which we had to show at the border. They said they did not charge anything for this service, but later we found out that they had actually charged an extra dollar per ticket for the La Quiaca–Jujuy route, which cost US$15. But worse was to come. It turned out that La Veloz del Norte, a bus company with a good reputation for comfortable, new, and fast two-storied buses, actually did not operate from La Quiaca but was merely a front for the Jama company.[19] Jama's fleet of buses was old and uncomfortable.

We were also offered a "loan" in cash because as tourists we had to show money at the border to prove our status. Afterwards we discovered the cost of the "loan": US$300 per US$1,000. We declined the deal because we thought we had enough money to risk crossing on our own. But how much money would we need? At Villazón, the owner of the Palace Hotel had told us we needed US$50–100 per day. We decided to cross the border for an exploratory visit to confirm the requirements. Anyone could enter La Quiaca from Bolivia just by presenting an identity card and receiving a numbered badge, which was given with no questions asked. We realized, however, that a hidden video camera was recording our faces and movements from a window of the *Gendarmería*. After finding out about the requirements for tourists, we returned to the Bolivian side to arrange for the necessary

FIG. 4.1. Bolivia-Argentina border, South America. Map by Bill Nelson.

paperwork by fax: a recent salary slip, a work certificate, a social security card. These were needed to enter Argentina, besides a passport, round-trip tickets, and "enough money to pay for each day of the trip." That amount we could only guess, since various people had suggested different amounts of money required per day in Argentina.

By ten o'clock the next morning we were lining up in front of the *Gendarmería*, with all the necessary papers and faxes, to get a tourist visa. But the head officer had gone to Villazón, and he kept us waiting for more than an hour. Finally we entered his office. The video camera's images were displayed on a computer screen, and we could follow events on the border bridge in full color. The officer asked us all kinds of questions, made rude remarks ("You can't believe anything a Bolivian says"), and doubted the authenticity of our documents. When he asked us to show the money to "prove" our solvency as tourists, Félix showed him US$500 and asked for a seven-day visa, and I showed him US$800 and asked for a ten-day visa. He accepted with some reluctance; we guessed he had established the adequacy of the amount by means of some "racial arithmetics" between our skin color and our social façade.

Later, at Salta, a Ph.D. student working on identity formation in the Argentina-Bolivia borderland confirmed our impression that border crossers provide a flourishing illegal business for many enterprises involved in smuggling, unequal exchange, and various techniques for fleecing migrants, especially those from Bolivia and Peru. The moneylenders provide the migrant with about US$1,000 (ostensibly for a ten-day tourist visit at US$100 per day) to show to the cops. Once through and inside the bus taking them to the interior of Argentina, the moneylender's agent collects the money from them, but instead of US$1,000 they have to return US$1,300. In a little over an hour, the migrants have incurred interest on their loan of 30 percent! Ricardo Abduca has called this system of border exploitation a "border rent," a kind of colonial rent demanded from migrants on account of the existence of an international border as well as specific power-knowledge relations based on racial and economic stereotyping. The peculiarities of the border regime create economic opportunities for actors with access to formal power, such as *gendarmes*, to exploit migrants and traders informally as well.[20]

As we crossed the border, we each showed that we were carrying half a kilogram of fresh coca leaves. This was the amount we had calculated to be permissible based on information gathered in Villazón and La Quiaca. The coca leaf merchants in Villazón and Tupiza had stated that the most one could carry through the border was a quarter of a kilo. The owner of the Palace Hotel, however, had asserted that the limit was half a kilo, and the "Indio King," a Bolivian miner resident in La Quiaca, told us that they let you cross with one kilogram. We averaged these suggestions and crossed without problems, each with half a kilogram of the best "selected" coca leaves we had been able to get at the Villa Victoria market of ADEP-COCA. We had brought more but had to sell the rest in Villazón for fear of its being confiscated.

During a previous trip I had thought La Quiaca to be a lively town, full of people and stores with all kinds of goods ready to be smuggled into Bolivia. This time, it was like a ghost town, with empty buildings and closed stores, locked-up doors, and few passers-by. In contrast, Villazón was full of people and boasted a lively high street where many commodities were being sold: electric appliances, clothes, foodstuffs, coca leaves, alcohol, sodium bicarbonate, *lejía*, and cigarettes. Waiting at the border, we had observed that the "ant trade" here was a line of porters, men and women, going in one direction and carrying big packs on their backs. They were bringing into Bolivia the few articles that were still profitable. We saw soft drinks and flour, vegetables, and citrus fruits. We also saw a truck crossing the border with a load of peppers, tomatoes, and fruit. A row of stationary trucks with Argentine license plates were waiting in line with who knows what products under their covers. Nothing like this was happening on the other side of the border. There could not have been a greater contrast in the appearance of these two border town facing each other across the river: somnolent La Quiaca in Argentina and bustling Villazón in Bolivia, the two connected by a very visible one-way "ant traffic" across the border bridge. These "ants" were Bolivian men and women, Qhichwa-speaking peasants from local communities, who carried their goods across the border and through the Bolivian customs into Villazón.

This invisibility was particularly striking in the case of coca leaves. We had seen huge loads of coca bundles (*takis*) in the Villazón bus terminal. But at the border no bundles were in sight; the cross-border coca leaf trade from Bolivia to Argentina remained invisible to us. As we traveled from the border into Argentina, however, descending the high-altitude mountains and down the Quebrada de Humahuaca toward the provincial capitals of Jujuy and Salta, coca leaves came into view again. We saw them being offered for sale and the illegal and secret trajectories that had brought them across the border faded against this illusion of a free and open market.

"Here Even Legislators Chew Coca Leaves"

We arrived in Jujuy on the evening of July 27 and found a modest hotel near the bus terminal. After a short rest, we went out to explore the lively atmosphere in the town center. We stopped at a large well-lit billiard saloon full of people, mostly men. They were chewing coca openly as they were playing on a dozen billiard tables. The atmosphere drew us in because, to Félix's total surprise and in sharp contrast with the situation in Bolivia, public coca chewing did not seem to carry any prejudice or social censure here.

The saloon was quite large, with high ceilings and billiard tables arranged in two adjacent neon-lit rooms. Playing in groups of two to five, these *jujeño* night owls concentrated intensely on their game, meanwhile chewing coca leaves as if it were the most natural thing in the world. We noted that consumption was strictly an individual affair; nobody offered coca to anybody else. Every once in a while they would take a little *bica* (sodium bicarbonate) from special containers and add it to their wad to improve the leaves' flavor and effect. Nobody actually "chewed" the coca leaves; instead, they kept their wad (*bolo* or *akusi*) tucked away in their cheek for hours on end, gently turning it around and sucking it, adding a bit of *llipta* (*quinoa* ash, or ash of another plant) or *bica* now and then. Some billiard players were smoking cigarettes, as were most people seated at the surrounding tables; they were also drinking local alcoholic beverages such as gin, beer, and wine, or imported ones such as whisky. The style of chewing, the concentration on the game, and the individualized way of consumption all pointed clearly to the modern nature of these consumers. They all belonged to a *mestizo* urban middle class that, perhaps unconsciously, shared some habits and cultural traits with the Andean tradition.

Around midnight, Félix, who had been drinking the local brew (*ginebra*), enthusiastically offered coca leaves to three middle-aged men sitting at a nearby table. This was clearly an unusual gesture, but the men invited us to join them and we struck up a lively conversation, sharing *ginebra* and coca leaves. Soon the waiter joined us. Félix offered generous shares of "selected" leaves from Coripata and was delighted to share them with these people who as consumers were so distant, both socially and geographically, from the producers. For them it was also a novelty to get to know a representative of the producers of the leaf. One of our new friends happened to be a journalist with *El Pregón*, the province's most prestigious and widely read newspaper. He told us that in his circle, *taki* leaves, small leaves from the Yungas region of La Paz (Bolivia), were the preferred variety. He and the other men were also acquainted with the "selected" variety of coca leaf from the Yungas region and regretted that its price was so high here that it was restricted to elite circles. "Here even legislators chew coca leaves," they said, an expression that became a *Leitmotiv* for the entire trip.

> Félix Barra, pointing to a one-ounce bag of green plastic: "How much does this bag of coca leaves cost?"
> Man: "Two pesos" [equivalent to US$2 at the time].
> Félix Barra: "And roughly how much do you consume per week?"
> Man: "Ouf . . . I chew two of these bags every day . . . "
> Félix Barra: "That means you spend four pesos daily."
> Man: "Every day. . . . So you better hurry bringing your coca leaves over here . . . !"[21]

The journalist invited us for an interview at his newspaper the next morning and Félix was thrilled by the success of our first night's venture. He gave everybody a copy of the ADEPCOCA calendar with its motto "Coca Is Not Cocaine" (*la coca no es cocaína*) and with photographs of Chicaloma, his hometown. He also gave a copy to the bartender so he could hang it on the wall as a souvenir of our visit. Gazing at the walls of the saloon covered in huge red-and-white Coca-Cola posters, I saw the irony of putting the calendar of an organization of coca leaf producers (*cocaleros*) on these same walls. Their product is forbidden at the border, considered illegal contraband, unlike the beverage patented by the *gringos*. It was past two in the morning when we finally left. By then, the atmosphere had become even livelier. No doubt many customers would stay up till sunrise.

Our meeting with the journalists of *El Pregón* underlined that coca leaf chewing was common in northern Argentina. In the newspaper office, men and women were chewing coca leaves while they were working. A woman interviewed us (the paper published the interview prominently the following day).[22] A photographer took the coca leaves that Félix offered him by putting his hands together as a cup, as is often done in Bolivia. "Do you usually receive coca leaves like this?" I asked. "Yes, of course. It is a matter of respect," he replied. As Félix passed around leaves, the journalists took out their coca leaf bags and cases. One had an old aluminum tobacco box lined with a plastic bag to keep his leaves fresh. "These are really good. Are they from the Yungas?" he asked Félix.

A few days later we were invited to a party. The Association of Bolivian Residents of Jujuy (*Asociación de Residentes Bolivianos en Jujuy*) celebrated Bolivia's national holiday, August 6. During this all-night occasion, I saw people drinking alcoholic beverages and Coca Cola. After a big meal consisting of a national dish, *picante mixto* (mixed cooked meats in hot sauces), people began to dance and drink heavily, but very few indeed were chewing coca leaves. It presented a striking contrast. Jujuy's middle classes had adopted an indigenous habit but Jujuy's elite Bolivian immigrants had not. These Bolivians had come from the country that was the source of the coca leaves *and* they were living in a center of modern coca chewing. And yet they rejected the habit, setting themselves apart. Later that night these Jujuy Bolivians performed what they thought was the *Saya* dance (actually it was not a *Saya* but a stylized version of the *Caporales* dance). Ironically, the *Saya* dance is the signature dance of Bolivia's *afro-yungueño* people who produce the coca leaves that are exported to Argentina.

The public nature of coca chewing in northern Argentina was illustrated by our experiences in the next city we visited, Salta. Here we visited a folkloristic restaurant (*peña*) where customers were chewing coca leaves in connoisseur style. Nobody actually chewed the leaves; they sucked them.

You could see the big wads of coca leaf pushing out people's cheeks and being moved around slowly and deliberately. Occasionally, people would add alkaline substances and new leaves to promote the effects of the leaves' fourteen alkaloids. A blonde *salteña* woman was sitting at one table; she happened to be a high official of the Bureau for the Prevention of Addictions (*Dirección de Prevención de Adicciones*), chewing coca before having a cup of wine with a friend. She mentioned the law decriminalizing coca chewing and pointed to the irony that physicians were currently using coca leaves in the treatment of addictions, to wean addicts from cocaine and other "hard drugs."

One image symbolized the new type of consumer market well. A very good-looking woman in her thirties had put her cell phone, the keys to her car, and her bag of coca leaves on the table. There was also a glass of wine and a dish with sodium bicarbonate. As she drank the wine and chewed the leaves, she seemed the perfect modern consumer, an independent professional or upscale bureaucrat who was enjoying herself alone and visibly at ease during this night of partying and music.

The next day we were off to the "Concert of the Mountain" in an amphitheater naturally carved into a huge red rock on the way to the town of Cafayate. The scenery was magnificent and the rock served as the acoustic shell for an extraordinary concert of both folk and classical music, performed by various groups. All over the place, people were chewing coca. The audience seemed particularly fond of Bolivian musical genres such as the *waynu*, the *kacharpaya*, and carnival dances of Oruro. This "appropriation" of Bolivian music by Argentines would have bothered more than a few chauvinists and purists among the Bolivian elite. To me, a group from Buenos Aires playing *Señora Chichera*, *La Diablada*, or *Ojos Azules*, emblematic Bolivian pieces, did not appear as "cultural theft" but rather as evidence of Andean culture's potential for expansion and hybridization in a crisis-ridden country which insisted on its Western metropolitan culture. Coca leaves were being consumed as a matter of course by everybody in the audience, from hippie artisans to university professors. Among them were many survivors of the Argentine military dictatorship that had caused so many disappearances and deaths. In this culturally and politically heterogeneous environment, the chewing of quasi-legal coca leaves had become a symbol. To share coca leaves with our friends in the magnificent amphitheater of Cafayate was to be part of a cultural and commercial reality full of emotional and political paradoxes. It connected modern coca leaf markets with old memories and practices.

All these impressions suggested that, in northern Argentina, coca leaf consumption is as general and normal as the coffee break in other urban and modern contexts. It is characterized by individual chewing, unlike the more "traditional" practice of sharing the leaves. People from all walks of life and different age groups indulge in it. We asked all taxi drivers who took us around Jujuy and Salta whether they chewed coca leaves and they all confirmed that they did. We observed our long-distance bus drivers chewing coca during every trip. When we asked various users how and why they had first taken up the habit, some mentioned a physical or psychological ailment such as gastritis or tobacco addiction. The neutral term "habit" seems to be well-suited to describe both the useful and the pleasurable aspects of coca chewing. What may have begun as a way of staying awake during a night shift or a means to alleviate the pain of, say, a peptic ulcer, ended up becoming a pleasure, not just in terms of consuming alkaloid substances, but also as a symbol of a certain status, an expression of personhood in the polymorphous modernity of neo-liberal capitalism. As such, the habit of coca chewing symbolizes practices and tastes that are produced locally but also are part of ever-widening circuits of communication and meaning.

The Licitness of Selling Coca

It may be illegal to trade in coca leaves, but selling and buying them is clearly acceptable in the cities of northern Argentina. In the center of Salta, we saw many signs and posters advertising coca. One read: "Don't Tell a Soul! Export-Quality Coca." The sign also advertised candy, beverages, and cigarettes. Another store, Ke Koka, offered coca leaves at various prices, in packages from one ounce to a quarter kilo, twenty-four hours a day. In its logo, the letters E, O, and A were coca leaves. Another sign read: "Selected Coca Leaves. Bolivian Bica." Down the road, the San Silvestre store (which has branches in several other cities) sported a neon sign with green coca leaves on a blue background. In all these stores the product was sold in sealed bags embellished with the store's logo, and sometimes a little package of sodium bicarbonate or *llipta* came with the bag. Ke Koka and Secus had stickers with their logos and a green coca leaf design. San Silvestre had plastic bags with its logo, a big coca leaf in the upper corner, and the addresses of its various branches. This store acted as a wholesale outlet, supplying other retailers. Without a doubt it had its own arrangements for importing leaves from across the border, only eight hours away.

Customers of these various stores would stop by in their cars. There was a continual bustle of men and women leaving the stores with bags of coca.[23] Many did not even bother to ask for the leaves. They just put some coins or bills on the counter and the store assistant would immediately bring the required amount of coca. Store assistants told us that their clientele consisted of lawyers, judges, physicians, and all types of professionals and public employees. They would stop by daily to get fresh coca leaves. It was as if the other merchandise being displayed in the stores was of secondary importance compared to the turnover in coca leaves. At a small store I saw a car come to a halt. A young lad, dressed in loose-fitting jeans and a cap worn backwards, asked for a one-ounce bag and paid two pesos for it. Showing him my own bag of coca leaves, I asked him, "You also chew coca leaves?" He replied, "Coca leaves are not chewed, lady. You take the leaves and gently suck them, you don't chew them." Then, taking me for a tourist, he showed me how it was done.

Far from Salta's town center we discovered a less self-confident form of marketing coca leaves. Here Bolivian *caseras* (street vendors), sitting precariously on stools in a marketplace, displayed their goods on wooden boxes. All goods were from Bolivia: coca, alcohol, and a variety of *lliptas*. The coca leaves were pre-packaged in green plastic bags of various sizes. We noticed only lower-class customers here, migrant workers of both sexes who usually chose one-ounce bags. No doubt this clientele was attracted by the low prices: the *menuda* or *taki* varieties sold at just one peso (US$1.00) per ounce. In the big stores in the center of town, the *taki* variety sold for two and a half pesos and the selected variety for three pesos per ounce. Selected leaves, with their stalks removed (*despalillada*), reached as much as four pesos per ounce and usually included *llipta* or sodium bicarbonate. At this top price, a kilo of leaves cost 130 pesos, or US$130, that is to say, thirteen times as much as the best selected leaves sold at the Villa Fátima market in La Paz.

The licitness and acceptability of these quasi-legal leaves to the general public also reverberated in the two live radio interviews Félix and I gave at Radio FM Noticias 88.1 and Radio Universidad. In both cases we had a phone-in. Members of the audience generally supported our viewpoints and contributed more information and analysis. One person read Article 15 of Act 23.737 on drugs, arguing that the trade in coca leaves actually was not prohibited but merely omitted from the act. He mentioned the lack of regulatory instruments to complement the act. This same person calculated the number of coca leaf chewers in northern Argentina (Salta, Jujuy, Tucumán, and Catamarca) at half a million, i.e., half the size of the entire Bolivian market as calculated in the 1970s.[24] Various people phoned in to suggest that the issue of coca leaves should be resolved by "whitening" (legalizing) the "black economy" of coca leaf smuggling. To us Bolivians, the term "white" sounded contradictory because in Bolivia it is associated with the "white powder," cocaine. Pushing these color metaphors a bit further, we agreed that the border was a "gray area" of ambiguity which produced official behavior varying from tolerance to repression, and that it was a fertile breeding ground for illegal trade, corruption, and discrimination.

Legal Puzzles and a Dead Baby

One journalist we met summarized the tensions between the law and common practice in Argentina well:

> There is an article somewhere, I don't know in what law, that allows coca leaf chewing, no problem. But what happens? In reality it is allowed only in Salta and Jujuy, not in the rest of the country. My brother-in-law travels a lot, he goes to Buenos Aires and elsewhere. He feels like dying when he leaves the province because if they catch him with half a kilo of coca leaves elsewhere in Argentina he will go to jail. He can go to jail for just carrying leaves—because down there they don't know that there is this little passage, this article, in the law that allows coca leaf chewing.[25]

This ignorance explains why coca leaf prices skyrocket as one moves south. A kiosk owner in a busy street in Jujuy said that in Catamarca and Córdoba (cities further south, halfway to Buenos Aires) coca leaves cost US$70 per kilo and that in Buenos Aires they can reach as high as US$20 per ounce. This is many dozens of times the price in Bolivia, even for the most expensive leaves.

Some tried to fight ignorance about the law. Journalist Raúl Noro gave us a postcard showing the text of Article 15 of Federal Act 23.737 of 1989 which deals with the status of coca leaves as a "drug":

> Art. 15: The possession and consumption of coca leaves in natural form, as a habitual practice of *coqueo* or chewing, or as coca-leaf tea, will not be regarded as possession or consumption of drugs.

The postcard also stated:

> Federal Act 23.737 was sanctioned on September 21, 1989, approved on October 10, 1989 according to Art. 70 of the National Constitution, and published in the Official Bulletin on October 11, 1989.

This postcard had been printed by the National Congress in August 1994 for use by consumers who wished to travel outside the provinces where coca chewing was a widespread habit. These travelers could use it to support their legal rights as coca leaf consumers in case the police would try to arrest them, as the *El Pregón* journalist's brother-in-law feared.

The legal paradox was bizarre. Possession and consumption of coca leaf was allowed because it was not considered a drug. And yet it was illegal to import coca leaf or trade in it. Consequently, supplying the Argentine market was dangerous, and Bolivian wholesalers and retailers were criminalized. The press in northern Argentina carried many stories of traders being abused. Many people told us that *gendarmes* stationed at the border receive bribes to let the leaves pass, and that they privately sell the leaves they confiscate. Sometimes the media also showed public burnings of confiscated coca leaves near the border at La Quiaca, official demonstrations that the authorities were enforcing the law.[26] Crossing the border with coca leaves can be dangerous, however, in particular for stigmatized populations. For example, Argentine *gendarmes* had stabbed a baby to death in her mother's backpack because they thought the bundle was a stash of coca leaves.[27]

Ceremonial Consumption of Coca Leaves

The licit nature of coca consumption in northern Argentina was linked to modern urban lifestyles. It was also linked to ritual contexts that united the two sides of the borderland. On the night of July 31 we were invited to Manos Jujeñas in Jujuy, a restaurant whose owner, "Negra" Cabanas, was a middle-aged woman from La Quiaca whose mother was Bolivian. Manos Jujeñas is one of the best "typical" restaurants in Jujuy. It serves hot stews such as *picante de lengua* (cow tongue in hot sauce) and *sajita de pollo* (chicken in hot sauce) while well-known musicians from the region perform folk music. That night was special because it was the eve of the *Pachamama* (Earth Mother) festivities, and a ceremony had to be performed. Such ceremonies in honor of *Pachamama* are held throughout Jujuy and Salta during the month of August. This ceremony consisted in burying a dish of *t'iltincha* (steamed meat), tubers, and grains in a huge earthen pot (*berque*) full of earth. After the meal the sponsors invited all guests to form a long queue and offer coca leaves, cigarettes, and alcoholic beverages to the earth in the pot. It was a ceremonial libation that joined people from various social and cultural backgrounds. The place was full and most customers were women. At one table, three very attractive young women were chewing coca leaves, drinking wine, and smoking cigarettes. When it was time to dance to the nice deep voice of Tomás Lipán, the girls danced the *chacareras* and *zambas* together, with a sensual cadence. In their tight leather jeans, long blonde hair, and silver jewelry, they were a most conspicuous example of modern nightlife in northern Argentina, a mix of invented traditions, vague memories of a pre-capitalist past, and a host of debts to rural Andean cultures on both sides of the border.

At 11 A.M. the next morning a bigger ritual was held in the gardens behind Jujuy's old railway station. It was a *ch'alla* to *Pachamama*. This time the offerings consisted of lots of food and *chicha* (maize beer), libations of alcohol, and offerings of coca leaves. Musicians such as Tomás Lipán stayed past noon, playing all kinds of rhythms from the region and from Bolivia. That afternoon we went to Maymara, an hour toward La Quiaca. Here I left Félix Barra at the bus terminal because he had to return to La Quiaca and from there by train to Oruro and La Paz. I headed for the house of Mercedes Costa, an anthropologist friend from Buenos Aires who had been living in the area for many years, researching the impact of tourism and Bolivian migration on the cultural paradoxes of northern Argentina. Mercedes has opened a restaurant, El Patio, in Tilcara, eight kilometers north of Maymara. She told me many stories about *Gendarmería* abuses she had witnessed in the borderland community of Santa Victoria, one of her research sites. This community's territory lies on both sides of the border and its people have been famous muleteers for centuries. Of course, they are also well-respected small-scale smugglers.

The next morning on her patio, Mercedes made an offering to *Pachamama*. I had brought her a *misa dulce* from Villazón, quite a generous one by *jujeño* standards. We performed a hybrid ceremony, combining the burning of coca leaves and alcohol (as is done in La Paz) with the burial of food and offerings in a hole dug into the earth (as is done in Jujuy). The fumes of our *misa* mingled with the scent of incense and *q'uwa* that wafted over the plaza as our offering joined countless others that were being performed in Tilcara that day. *Sahumerio*[28] or *mesa dulce*[29] seems to have been included only recently in *Pachamama* ceremonies in northern Argentina; the burial of food is probably linked to local rituals dating from early colonial times. At the Jujuy market it was quite impressive to see how many small "tables" sold for one to ten pesos. It was as if the big offerings that one buys in La Paz or Villazón were split into several small pieces, each containing the complete set of sweets and mysteries, *pacha mixtura* and *q'uwa*, *untu* and animal figures, houses, cars, good-luck symbols (prominent among them the snake and the frog), and lots of colored wool and coca leaves. A lively trade in *sahumerios* and other ritual items always springs up in the days prior to traditional festivities. This trade has been expanding as a result of the general revival of rituals and cultural expressions in the towns and villages of the region. It is linked to the revitalization of Bolivian migrants' rituals, including the celebration of patron saint days and the *Alasitas* fair. When I briefly lived in Jujuy thirty years ago, I was not aware of *Pachamama* rituals, even though I stayed from August to December, because then they were not as public as they are today. Nevertheless, coca chewing was a general habit back then and I was able to earn some cash by buying leaves wholesale and repacking them in one-ounce plastic bags that I sold, together with sodium bicarbonate, cigarettes, and alcohol, before soccer matches at the local stadium.

The Indio King

It is quite possible that Bolivian mine workers, who migrated in several waves from the 1950s and found work in mines at Pirquita, El Aguilar, and Santa Victoria in northern Argentina, were instrumental in the expansion of Andean rituals and Bolivian-style *ch'alla* ceremonies. The same may be true for seasonal migrants to sugar mills and other agro-industries in Salta and Tucumán. Today these rituals, practiced by all strata, have become a shared "invented tradition."[30] This connection between cross-border culture, migration to dangerous industrial surroundings, and ritual innovation was demonstrated to me by the "Indio King."

On my way back to Bolivia I stopped in La Quiaca to look for Zacarías Gutiérrez, founder-director of a Devil's Dance group, Los Mercenarios, that had provoked a public scandal and even a diplomatic incident between the Argentine consul in Villazón and his Bolivian counterpart in La Quiaca in the mid-1990s. Anthropologist Gabriela Karasik explored the conflict and the double rejection that expressions of Bolivian folklore suffer at the border.[31] During a carnival at La Quiaca (the Argentine border town), dancers of Bolivian descent perform a particularly faithful and grandiose version of the Devil's Dance from Oruro. Native Argentines (including earlier migrants) usually view this as a foreign cultural intrusion that distorts the identity of northern Argentina. Bolivians on the other side of the border, however, view it as a form of cultural robbery, illegal exportation, and the expropriation of genuinely Bolivian folklore. Paradoxically, now that the carnival of Oruro has been recognized internationally as "Cultural Patrimony of Humanity," the Bolivian elite will be strengthened in its nationalist proprietary attitude toward the cultural expressions of (dominated) indigenous or *cholo* Bolivians.

That the Devil's Dance group is stigmatized on both sides of the border, but for different reasons, shows that ethnicity, class, and nationality are entangled in a contradictory fashion. Zacarías Gutiérrez testified to this when talking with Gabriela Karasik. Curious to see how his experiences might be connected with other Andean customs and habits, such as coca chewing, I went to look for him. Unfortunately he was away on a long-distance trip, so I asked to speak with his father, also named Zacarías, the legendary "Indio King," a well-known character in the local cultural scene. There are many stories about his deeds in the mines, and local folklorists and writers have even recorded some of these in writing. He was born in rural Toledo in the department of Oruro (Bolivia) and his mother was a Qhichwa-speaking Indian. As a youth working in the mines, he soon gained the nickname of Indio King for his skills as an explorer who could find minerals in the deepest and most difficult mine shafts. He worked for twelve years in the mines of Huanuni, Siglo XX, and San José. Then, gun in hand, he took part in the Bolivian Revolution of 1952. Afterwards, he could not find work anywhere and, enraged by the indifference shown by the revolutionary cadres to grassroots insurgents such as himself, he and other miners took the road south to the Argentine border in 1953.

As a famous and infallible ore-finder, the Indio King was wrapped in an atmosphere of myth and legend. He was said to drink much alcohol and to practice strange rituals to the Devil. Perhaps that is why people thought of him as their last resort to save the Pirquita mine, which had been given up because of low productivity. Pirquita, a mining town in northern Argentina, had been almost dismantled, but the Bolivian miners, desperate to prevent their source of livelihood from going bankrupt, pushed the mine managers to call upon the Indio King. He happened to be on a drinking binge at the time. "Alcohol is powerful," he told me when he showed me his altar with seven huge Devil's masks, arranged among desiccated animals, dressed in dance costume. Two big photographs of statues in the mines stood in the middle. They showed *Ukako* or *Tío* (uncle) of the Pirquita mine and the *Usqulla* of the Santa Victoria mine.

The Indio King gave a detailed account of his first entry into the Pirkita mine shaft. A Protestant miner who had converted during the emergency took him to the mine gallery, but the Indio King entered the chilling water of the flooded shaft alone. Beforehand he had fortified himself with coca leaves and alcohol. To perform his task he took along basic tools and, above all, he was carrying all kinds of ritual elements: alcohol, coca leaves, and other offerings. He went all the way to the end of the tunnel, secured with huge logs. Here he performed his task in a deep trance, chewing coca leaves and offering alcohol libations. He prayed, invoking the spirits of the mine, sometimes whispering softly and at other times shouting angrily. Then he became intoxicated and was overcome by sleep. At last he began to tap the mine walls and to taste and smell bits of ore, until finally he found a huge deposit of tin casiterite, which extended the mine's life with twenty-seven years of renewed productivity and employment.

The Indio King is also a legendary trickster and cheater of women. He has forty-one children by sixteen different women. Today he repents for all the suffering he has inflicted on them: "So many riches have passed through my hands . . . and I have nothing now. . . . The *Ukako* is like that, he gives, but he also takes away." These remarks take us to the heart of Andean beliefs about the transgression of conjugal fidelity as a precondition for a mine worker to have "luck." A pagan version of the "pact with the Devil" emerges here, associated with the *Ukako* (*Tío* or uncle) and the chaotic fertility of the underworld, the earth's entrails that the mine worker penetrates. In this endeavor he risks his blood (in a mine accident), so he hopes to appease the deities of the mine shaft by animal sacrifices, ritual libations, and *ch'allas* that take the place of his blood. This Andean ideology of "luck" has its basis in the powers of the coca leaf, which the Indio King consumed in such an intense, ritualized manner. In this he differed from the ways of indigenous shamans (*yatiris*), who consult or "read" the leaves. Coca leaves are key to the rituals for entering the mine, for searching for ore, and for celebrating its discovery (the so-called "*ch'alla* of the new-found ore"). The owners and managers of the Pirkita mine could not believe the quantity of ore that the Indio King had found. The next day he made a mud model of the *Ukako* around a nucleus of tin and silver, and he inaugurated a tradition of ritual coca chewing (*akhulliku*) and performing *ch'allaku* and *wilancha* ceremonies to the *Ukako* that continued to take place at fixed dates during the ritual calendar until the mine ceased to operate.

The Indio King's discovery ushered in not only a long cycle of mining productivity, but also the regular provision of coca leaves to the mine's 700-odd workers. The company itself used to buy these leaves; this was at a time when import restrictions began to be enforced. The Indio King and other heads of work teams would distribute the leaves to the mine workers as advance payment for their work as well as for their daily chewing and their ritual consumption. The collective ceremonies performed during the ritual calendar (mainly Carnival Friday and August 1) were followed by smaller rituals performed individually or in small groups, according to the habits and customs of the migrant mine worker's place of origin—mostly Bolivia or the Jujuy mountain range. Libations with the blood of ritually killed animals (*wilancha*) were performed in the main mine shaft every August 1. On one occasion the Indio King asked for a live calf to be brought from Salta, and the *ch'alla* reached gigantic proportions. He adorned the calf with tin and silver, with Andean textiles and silver coins, and threw it alive into the depths of the mine shaft.

Beliefs regarding "good luck" in the mine, as well as invocations and prayers for *Ukako's* protection (done each Tuesday and Friday), reveal the old culture's force in this new capitalist context. They demonstrate how coca chewing was an inseparable part of the labor process. It connected the performance of a dangerous, skilled job with cosmic dispositions and intuitions. Mine workers perceived the mine as a living organism with moods, whims, and gestures of benevolence or anger. Therefore it was essential to seek its cooperation, or avoid its punishment, by means of proper ritual invocations and by generously sharing alcohol and coca leaves with the other members of the work team, and with the earth itself.

The Indio King told me he had forced the president of the mining company to share the ritual with the miners. The president was a *gringo* who usually lived in Buenos Aires but who could not ignore the magical explanation given by the Indio King to account for his sudden riches. Avelino Bazán (a union leader from El Aguilar and author of a book of testimonial folk stories of northern Argentina) portrayed the Indio King, in a short story entitled "El Ukako," as a blend of a work-team chief and a moral authority who would stimulate and organize cooperative work teams by improving work discipline, unleashing a collective energy to produce, and making it possible for mine workers to face the risks and technical challenges of mine-shaft work.[32] This inversion of the Protestant ethic highlights the peculiarities of mine-shaft labor and its sacred and cosmic implications. Andean cosmology associates the hidden forces of the underworld (*manqhapacha*) with the domain of the Devil or *Ukako* (*Tío* or uncle).[33]

Since it was early August when I visited, the Indio King had served the *Pachamama* food on her altar in La Quiaca. This food, in various dishes and cups, had been lying there since the previous Friday. He had to bury the food soon in order to close the ritual cycle of the "open mouth of the Earth" (*lakapacha*, as the month of August is known in Aymara). No doubt the ritual performed by the Indio King differed from the rituals we had observed in Salta and Jujuy. But no doubt there were mixed ingredients in his ritual, too, as in all invented traditions. For example, the Tío was invoked as "Momo God," and among the images on his altar were two tiny Buddha statuettes. The motley heterogeneity of the Indio King's altar is but one example of the type of cultural mélange that is produced at this border where Andean labor migrants articulate deep, long-standing beliefs with new incorporations and assimilations. These new incorporations often act as cultural masks, protecting and covering traces of older memories and symbols. What struck me most in all this was that in the middle of the altar there was a tiny silver figurine of the Devil and that it had received lavish offerings of confetti, coca leaves, and flowers. "That one is growing," said the Indio King. "Each year he grows a little." In the Indio King's cosmology of the Devil, there is a living entity: the mineral that grows and changes within the earth and follows hidden paths, waiting for the "lucky" mine worker but evading a negligent or non-believing one.

"The Devil Knows No Borders"

The interview with the Indio King, a Bolivian mine worker who had lived in Argentina for five decades, provides an appropriate closure to my essay. It shows that the revitalization of the *Pachamama* cults and the August offerings are linked to rituals for the mine-shaft deity. This is an old root, perhaps reaching back into the colonial period, which has generated a series of recent cultural transformations in the whole border region.

One of the more recent developments in this field was the establishment of Los Mercenarios, the Devil's Dance group. During the carnival the group performs the *Relato*, a play (*auto sacramental*) dating back to the eighteenth century and a specialty of the Devil's Dance groups of Oruro (Bolivia). This new development at the border was possible thanks to the efforts of Zacarías Gutiérrez Jr., who got in touch with Oruro and recognized in the texts some aspects of his father's mining stories. Speaking with Gabriela Karasik, Zacarías explained why he felt it was legitimate to cross the border with the costumes, music, text, and choreography of the Devil's Dance. "The Devil knows no borders," he said. In this way he inadvertently synthesized for us the social representations involved in the Devil's Dance, as well as in other cultural and ritual practices.

The same could be said of coca leaves. They show the permeability and flexibility of Andean cultural practices. They also demonstrate the hegemonic potential of these practices in modern scenarios of industrial capitalism and globalized urban cultures. The current coca leaf "boom" in northern Argentina is predicated on a dense texture of beliefs and traditions, halfway modern and halfway archaic (or at least constructed as archaic). These beliefs and traditions permeate labor relations in mining companies and agro-industrial enterprises as much as urban nightlife and the daily habits of large numbers of Westernized middle- and upper-class Argentines.

In addition, the coca leaf "boom" in northern Argentina is also predicated on ritual renewal. Wherever rural and urban people mingle with *gringo* tourists and Bolivian labor migrants, local actors of many social and economic backgrounds are actively involved in inventing ceremonies and rituals to *Pachamama*. Such "invented traditions" sustain a large cross-border trade in coca leaves which is at once illegal and licit, outlawed and respected. Coca leaves in northern Argentina attest to the extraordinary vitality of Andean diasporic culture in new social contexts. They contribute to new meanings, new poetics of identity, and new identity politics among a multiethnic population. They are key to explaining the peculiarities of this borderland, not just as a space of commodity circulation, but also as a space of cultural circulation, with repercussions at both the national and the international levels.

NOTES

1. Jaime W. Molins, *Bolivia. Crónicas Americanas* (Buenos Aires: Libro Primero, 1916), 17.

2. This contract was negotiated between the Argentine Institute for the Promotion of Exchange (*Instituto Argentino de Promoción del Intercambio*) and the Bolivian Corporation of Coca-Leaf Producers (*Corporación Boliviana de Productores de Coca*). See Mario Rabey, "Legalidad e ilegalidad del coqueo en Argentina," in *La coca . . . tradición, rito, identidad,* Instituto Indigenista Interamericano (México: Instituto Indigenista Interamericano, 1989), 58.

3. Rabey, "Legalidad e ilegalidad del coqueo en Argentina," 59–60.

4. Rabey, "Legalidad e ilegalidad del coqueo en Argentina," 65.

5. Carter and Mamani have found documents concerning imports of Bolivian coca leaves between 1968 and 1976 (one year before total prohibition was enforced). The figures show an increase from 671 tons in 1968 to 938 tons in 1974, with a slight decrease to 868 tons in 1976. See William E. Carter and Mauricio Mamani, *Multidisciplinary Study: Traditional Use of the Coca Leaf in Bolivia* (La Paz: Museo Nacional de Etnografía y Folklore, 1978).

6. Ricardo Abduca, "De los yungas paceños al noroeste argentino: Nuevo enfoque sobre la producción de coca para consumo tradicional" (unpublished manuscript, ca. 1994), 23. The author thanks Ricardo Abduca for access to this unpublished manuscript; Rabey, "Legalidad e ilegalidad del coqueo en Argentina."

7. Abduca, "De los yungas paceños al noroeste argentino," 37.

8. In Argentina, a "province" is equivalent to a "department" in Bolivia, and vice versa. The survey was conducted on behalf of the secretary of health of the provincial government of Jujuy. See Secretaría de Salud del Gobierno de la Provincia de Jujuy, *Encuesta sobre el consumo de hoja de coca en la Provincia de Jujuy* (San Salvador del Jujuy: Secretaría de Salud, 2000).

9. Raúl Noro, personal communication.

10. Abduca, "De los yungas paceños al noroeste argentino," 35.

11. Drugstore sales contributed to a restriction of consumption to the elite and to the proliferation of clandestine retail networks. Moreover, in the drugstores the usual reactive *llipta* or *lejía* (vegetable ashes) were substituted by sodium bicarbonate, which continues to be the favorite reactive for coca chewing in urban northern Argentina. Cf. Abduca, "De los yungas paceños al noroeste argentino," 26–35.

12. Rabey, "Legalidad e ilegalidad del coqueo en Argentina," 42, 50.

13. Rabey, "Legalidad e ilegalidad del coqueo en Argentina," 68.

14. Rabey identifies three causes: "a) the regional elite's need to differentiate itself from the Buenos Aires elite; b) the presence of an important contingent of ethnic Syrian-Lebanese settlers, and c) the need to exhibit a social conduct that is beyond the law." Rabey, "Legalidad e ilegalidad del coqueo en Argentina," 50.

15. Abduca suggests that all these factors contributed to the formation and consolidation of a "quasi-legal" market for coca leaves, similar to the transnational market for qat leaves. Qat is another stimulant which is chewed as fresh leaves. Its market has expanded from Yemen to neighboring countries such as Ethiopia and Somalia and to diasporic communities from this region in the West. Abduca, "De los yungas paceños al noroeste argentino." (Also see editor's introduction).

16. Rabey, "Legalidad e ilegalidad del coqueo en Argentina," 55.

17. It is ironic that in 1949 doctors on the United Nations Commission of Inquiry on the Coca Leaf dismissed as a superstition the "general belief that coca leaves suppress hunger, thirst and drowsiness" and that now other doctors, equally white and Western-minded, bear witness to the emptiness of their older colleagues' claim by using coca leaves themselves.

18. These small towns in the agricultural belt surrounding Buenos Aires were witnessing a most intense process of land transfer and the leasing of land to Bolivian immigrants and, at the same time, terrible violence against these immigrants, including armed aggression and murder, in a kind of low-intensity "ethnic cleansing." *La Prensa*, May 3 and 25, 2000, and June 9, 2000.

19. A suggestive name. In Aymara, *jama* means "shit."

20. Abduca, "De los yungas paceños al noroeste argentino," 9–10.

21. Interview by author, videotape, Jujuy, July 27, 2001. See *Las fronteras de la coca*, directed by Silvia Rivera Cusicanqui, 29 min. videocassette, 2001.

22. "Cocaleros de Bolivia miran con esperanza a Jujuy" (Coca producers from Bolivia look hopefully to Jujuy), *El Pregón*, July 30, 2001.

23. Everywhere we noticed that at least 30 percent of the customers were women.

24. Carter and Mamani, *Multidisciplinary Study*; William E. Carter and Mauricio Mamani, "Patrones del uso de la coca en Bolivia," *América indígena* 38, no. 4 (1978).

25. Group interview, *El Pregón*, Jujuy, July 30, 2001; see Rivera Cusicanqui, *Las fronteras de la coca*.

26. Zacarías Gutiérrez, interview by author, La Quiaca, August 7, 2001.

27. Mercedes Costa, interview by author, Maymara, August 2, 2001.

28. *Sahumerio* (from the Spanish verb *sahumar*) is an offering that is to be burnt, as its fumes carry the scents of herbs, sweets, *untu* or llama lard, and many symbolic items to the heights of the regional mountain gods. This ethereal aspect is combined with libations and the burying of offerings to the Earth Mother (*Pachamama*). The fact that the two motions—toward the earth (low, flat, and deep) and towards the mountains (high, steep, and elevated)—are complementary seems crucial in the perception of "wholeness" inherent to the Andean worldview.

29. *Misa* and *mesa* are interchangeable in Aymara or Qhichwa, which know only three vowels (a, i, u). It means both a mass (*misa*), the main ceremony of the Catholic Church, and a table (*mesa*), the place where a ritual meal is to be eaten.

30. Eric Hobsbawm and Terence Ranger, *The Invention of Tradition* (Cambridge: Cambridge University Press, 1983).

31. Gabriela Karasik, *Formas de sociabilidad de un grupo de migrantes andinos en*

el Gran Buenos Aires (Buenos Aires: Consejo de Investigaciones Cientificas y Tecnicas (CONICET), 1987); Gabriela Karasik, "Trabajadoras bolivianas en el conurbano bonaerense. Pequeño comercio y conflicto social," in *Inmigración limítrofe: Los bolivianos en Buenos Aires,* ed. Roberto Benencia and Gabriela Karasik (Buenos Aires: Centro Editor de América Latina, 1995); Gabriela Karasik, "Tras la genealogía del diablo. Discusiones sobre la nación y el Estado en la frontera argentino-boliviana," in *Fronteras, naciones e identidades. La periferia como centro,* ed. Alejandro Grimson, (Buenos Aires: La Crujia, 2000).

32. Avelino Bazán, *Voces del socavón: Relatos, vivencias y sucesos en El Aguilar* (Jujuy, 1986).

33. The meaning and cultural roots of the names of this particular *Tío* (uncle), *Ukako,* and of the female deity of Santa Victoria, *Usqulla,* are still to be explored. The first name could be a variant of *iqaku* or *ekeko* (a small deity who represents the mercantile prosperity that people seek to achieve during the *Alasitas* fair). The second name is the feminine form of *usqullu,* a small Andes jaguar.

Seeing the State Like a Migrant

Why So Many Non-criminals Break Immigration Laws

David Kyle and Christina A. Siracusa

The Human Smuggling Problem through
the Eyes of Destination States

James Scott pondered the question of why "the state" seems to be the enemy of people who move around, though this question led him to write a much broader book regarding the failure of state planning due to how states "see like a state."[1] In short, states seek to radically simplify and reduce social reality to fit management schemes imposed from above. We turn the lens around to ask the opposite question: How do migrants see states? We argue that the answer to this question is critical for understanding why so many non-criminals around the world are breaking states' immigration and labor laws.

When states began focusing their vision in the 1900s on managing and controlling migrants *en masse*, assigning a variety of legal statuses with or without the right to work, they created "illegal aliens."[2] Thus, illegal populations increase when states retract the legal means of entry and work for foreigners. The hallmark of such periods of retraction, typically during economic downturns, is the assertion that—at least for now—migrants' costs outweigh their benefits to receiving states. Yet the lobbying efforts of employers of immigrant labor, and above all the fact that immigration policy is also a foreign policy concern, mitigate "immigration reforms" during even the peaks of anti-immigrant periods. Thus, the resulting strategic complexities of the muddled and ever-changing laws and enforcement strategies related to immigration provide sufficient profitable ambiguities for major employers of immigrant labor and, consequently, endless hope for potential migrant workers and asylum seekers.[3] The domestic and foreign political challenges and ethical questions raised by these ever-changing migrant management calculations represent a topic of intense debate among economic, legal, philosophical, and political theorists.[4]

Yet during the past decade, a new actor shaping migration patterns has become the focus of mostly negative attention of those across the political spectrum concerned with immigration issues—the migrant smuggler, or trafficker, who aids the unauthorized migrant or asylum seeker into a foreign country for profit (with prices ranging from US$50 to US$50,000).[5] The migrant smuggler, since the mid-1990s, has been the primary target of novel border security policies and legislation for reducing illegal immigration, including the recent "Victims of Trafficking and Violence Protection Act of 2000" in the United States. The successful smuggling operations aiding migrants and asylum seekers in their clandestine or falsely documented entry into Western states has produced a growing number of government and multilateral programs around the world to combat smugglers and traffickers. These programs, for the most part, construct migrants who contract smugglers as passive victims of "organized crime," which may be distinguished, as James Finkenauer has pointed out, from "crime that is organized."[6] They are able to do so in part by focusing primarily on the most egregious cases of smuggling abuses, including enslavement. Similarly, migrant smuggling is now estimated to be the fastest growing type of "transnational crime," with analogies to other criminal networks moving drugs, arms, and other illegal commodities across borders.[7]

For example, a series of articles appearing in the *Arizona Republic* in late May 2001, reporting the deaths of fourteen migrants, represent the starkly divergent discourses of who is to blame for immigrant deaths and organized immigration lawbreaking. The first article blames the smuggler who led the migrants to an area named "Devil's Path" in which they baked in the scorching Arizona desert and were then allegedly left to die.[8] It quotes Attorney General John Ashcroft: "They are to be condemned for putting profits before people." A second article, after realizing that one of the dead, found crouched under a cactus, was in fact a smuggler, leads,

"Suddenly the smuggler isn't a very bad guy anymore."[9] A few months later, the newspaper, in an all too rare investigation, examined a town in Mexico in which nearly everyone is involved in the illegal migration business as a normalized activity.[10] This story took a much more sociological perspective on the illegal migration business, including the role of mutual trust between migrant and smuggler. Far from being an isolated incident, these deaths and the debate surrounding them demonstrate the complex ethical dimensions at play once we move beyond simplistic arguments either blaming the criminal smuggler, the migrant, or the unintended consequences of state actions.

Rather than enter into a normative debate regarding the foundational and evolving rights of states and immigrants, for the sake of our argument we will assume that states have legitimate interests in controlling who enters their territory, though this has not always been a high priority for states. Instead, the growing global business of migration services raises some empirical sociological questions that need to be examined along with more deductive economic, political, and criminological theorizing.

What has been lacking from most public debates and news reporting on migrant smuggling and human trafficking is the empirical reality of how migrants themselves view their actions and the often orderly, contractual nature by which they enter into a diverse range of "migrant-exporting schemes" (see following section). By understanding the political and moral reasoning of undocumented workers and those who aid them, we gain a better understanding of why so many non-criminals are choosing to selectively disregard some states' immigration laws prohibiting unauthorized entry and work. During a period in which clandestine border crossings are not nearly as simple as they used to be just five years ago, we ask what may be posed as the "human smuggling question": Why do hundreds of thousands of otherwise non-criminals each year willingly choose to break immigration laws by contracting intermediaries? In other words, do migrants and their abettors (who are now subject to lengthy prison sentences in some destination countries—but in few sending or transit countries) view their actions as "criminal"?

While simplification is necessary to all analytical frameworks, the simplistic notions of "trade in human cargo" carried out by "human smugglers" is much too inadequate to the task. A more useful concept would attempt to overcome the complex relationships among various apparent dichotomies such as micro/macro; legal/illegal; state/non-state. To this end we develop the concept of "migrant-exporting schemes."[11]

Migrant-Exporting Schemes: The Orderly
Business of Disorderly Migration

Migrant smuggling is best understood as a strategic set of "migrant-exporting schemes" embedded in historical social relationships involving both private and public actors. The concept of a scheme implies both its strategically opportunistic (legal and illegal) and visionary meanings. This concept also provides a better conceptual grasp of the organization and logic of "human smuggling," which narrowly limits its field of vision to one small, albeit important, part of a wider field of social action. The label of "migrant smuggling" fails to capture the mix of legal and illegal strategies (often blurring the lines) used by those who are attempting to gain work abroad for a price.

The primary goal of a migrant-exporting scheme is to provide a limited or "package" migration service to a specific country, and often a specific locale or employer. Typically, migrants are driven to professional smugglers by blocked social mobility, pre-existing corruption, and uneven development—not absolute poverty. Many would be considered middle-class within their home communities. Ethnic persecution and sexism are also common reasons for perceived ceilings in mobility.

Most of the organizational activity takes place on the sending side; the contract is terminated once the migrant has arrived at the destination. In some cases, however, financial loans for the smuggling fees also become an important source of income after arrival, but there is great variety in the terms of interest and payment and the division of labor; the smuggler is not necessarily the loan shark. It is quite common for family members already abroad to lend the smuggling fee for a reduced rate. Such migrant-exporting schemes are often characterized by highly irregular, often short-lived criminality, much of it opportunistic and therefore shaped by one's social networks. And since many "migration merchants" are part-timers, halting organized illegal migration is not simply a matter of breaking up a stable criminal organization.

In many parts of the world, the business of migration as a form of exportable commodified labor has been developed by economically debilitated and politically weak states, which view their own citizens as their most valuable comparative advantage. Formal government programs, as well as tacit acceptance of illegal migration of its citizens, as in the case of the Philippines, form part of an export-led strategy that conveniently resolves two of the most challenging problems for weakened state regimes that have adopted export-led development and International Monetary Fund (IMF) "stabilization and structural adjustment programs." First, emigration provides a safety valve for some of the country's most ambitious but frustrated citizens who may cause political instability.[12] At the same time, exporting labor provides a source of hard currency, which in many countries has now overtaken some of the traditional natural resource and commodity exports of migrant-exporting countries. After all, developed states with declining birth rates have experienced shortages in specific occupational areas, ranging from unskilled agricultural labor to relatively high-skilled medical occupations. Several countries that have developed this labor export strategy have erected government bureaucracies with overseas outposts, thus institutionalizing the orderly export of their citizens abroad, championing the rights of illegal residents, and offering dual citizenship to those who are assimilating politically.

When migrant-exporting schemes develop as a sort of grassroots development project without government authorization, which typically involves some level of corruption of state officials, sending states generally find little political will to disrupt such schemes. This is due to both a lack of criminal law for related "smuggling" activities in most sending and transit states and, especially, due to the large sums of migrant remittances outpacing earnings from other major state exports. Like state regimes that turn to export-led strategies for political as well as economic reasons, would-be illegal migrants have moral claims based on notions of social, economic, and political (in)justice which help shape their decision to override the various legal routes to work abroad. Migrants make particularistic claims to certain immigration rights to enter and work in states using a historical logic. Illegal migrants often view themselves as a type of economic citizen of the political economic empire Western states and transnational corporations have created. This idea is relentlessly reinforced in the popular discourse of "globalization" as a naturalized social reality promoted in a myriad of institutions, and it has led to the real blurring of state claims to sovereignty.[13]

The methods by which migrants break immigration laws, far from being a completely underground criminal activity, is typically done in an orderly, businesslike manner using legal contracts to borrow smuggling fees. In most sending regions those public officials and private citizens involved in migration services are well known, and they quite often publicly, though discreetly, advertise their services. The intermediaries who help migrants cross borders, obtain false identities, or find work in the underground labor market—many of whom are return migrants—also commonly believe that their actions are justified and, in many cases, humanitarian. While this may be dismissed by law enforcement as the common self-serving rhetoric of criminals, we must consider that even legal scholars argue that immigration lawbreaking is the textbook case of a "victimless crime."[14] Hence, illegal migration and work has become not only a means to an end but itself a profitable business for entrepreneurial non-migrants and especially return migrants willing to risk the initial investment period of a few years of indebtedness (not unlike many college students).

The purpose of this description of "migrant-exporting schemes" as an ideal type is not to gloss over its very real dangers, including the regular malfeasance of the intermediaries (migration merchants) and corrupt state officials, as well as the bad luck of soaring temperatures or sudden storms at sea. Hundreds each year in various parts of the world die *en route* due to the risky conditions under which they undertake their journeys, sometimes simply due to unforeseen conditions as they cross oceans and deserts, and other times due to the negligence and human error of the migrant smugglers.[15] These dangers grow exponentially when *slave-importing operations* take advantage of immigrants' precarious illegal status by opportunistically enslaving a substantial minority of unsuspecting migrants who thought they were simply part of a victimless migrant-exporting scheme. Migrant-exporting schemes provide the opportunities for organized crime to operate slave-importing operations, which unlike a migrant-exporting scheme, makes most of its profits from unpaid labor in the destination state.[16] However, once again, both the enslavement of illegal migrants by opportunistic criminal organizations and the deaths of migrants *en route* can only be understood against the backdrop of the ubiquitous businesslike migrant-exporting schemes and their relation to a wider set of local, national, and foreign institutions of power.

Research Design and Methods

This chapter is part of a larger study to illuminate the commodification of migration services in many regions of the world, with Ecuador as our most in-depth case study. How does one study illegal migrants who have been part of a migrant-exporting system? Obviously random-sample surveys are precluded for interviewing actual smugglers or "migration merchants," but they can be used in sending communities. In this study we conduct most of our interviews in destination countries. This chapter is based on primary interviews with illegal aliens, brokers, immigrant political organizers, and political representatives, along with secondary data collected from government and news sources and Internet sites dedicated to transnational immigrant communities. In several cases, immigrants without legal documents permitting them to work in Spain allowed us not only to interview them but videotape them and their places of recreation. That we can easily and readily discuss with migrants their various strategies, both in Ecuador and in the destination countries, tells us a lot about how migrants view their own actions as justified. Unlike many accounts of human smuggling or other systematic transnational lawbreaking, "transnational criminals" in the traditional sense do not figure in the migrant-exporting schemes of Ecuadorians working illegally in Spain. This is also a telling difference between the smuggling, including self-smuggling, of humans and other illicit commodities crisscrossing the planet—transnational criminal organizations may be present in some networks but are not a *necessary* condition.

The rest of this chapter is organized into three sections: First, an overview of the Ecuadorian mass migration; second, the political and economic realities faced by Ecuadorians at home and in Spain and their testimonies characterizing Ecuador as a predatory state. The level of destitution and generalized loss of hope by Ecuadorians as a result of the predatory state leads to the rationalization, "If we can't beat 'em, join 'em," which brings us to testimonies describing the decision to enter migrant-exporting schemes. The final section discusses migrants' claims that illegal work is not a real "crime."

We turn to a case that has many features of migrant-exporting schemes as an ideal type. Ecuadorians represent a new wave of long-distance illegal emigration, built not simply on long-standing social networks but on local economies emboldened by the increasing involvement of sending and receiving states and employers seeking to profit from their cheap labor. Migrants' remittances back to Ecuador are the second largest source of hard currency behind oil exports. To understand why Ecuadorian migrants have been leaving in large numbers in just the past three years, we must first examine the magnitude of the failure of the Ecuadorian state and, most importantly, the general perceptions by Ecuadorians of its causes.

Ecuadorian Migration to the U.S. and Spain: An Overview

Throughout most of the 1980s and 1990s, international migration from Ecuador was highly concentrated in the southern provinces of Azuay and Cañar, from which most made their way to New York City.[17] They typically entered and worked illegally, using local migrant-exporting schemes; most "coyotes" came from the same communities as the migrants and were often related by kinship. Mass emigration from this original sending region is still continuing unabated; however, international emigration is now widespread throughout the country and at all socioeconomic levels. While any illegal population is difficult to estimate, the Ecuadorian diaspora is calculated to include more than two million people, approximately half of whom live in the U.S.[18] Between 1999 and 2000 alone, 400,000 Ecuadorians joined their one million compatriots already in the United States.

Departures to Spain escalated from 5,000 people in all of 1994 to more than 7,000 per month in 2000.[19] Before April 2003, Ecuadorians entered Spain legally as tourists without visas, but generally almost immediately sought employment rather than tourism, thus making their status illegal. Though this is not "migrant smuggling," Ecuadorians do make use of migrant-exporting schemes, with the price set at roughly half that of the U.S. destination (US$8,000 to US$10,000). The price includes transportation and the initial funds needed to show the Spanish authorities upon entry (approximately US$2,000) that they bring a "tourist" budget. Because Spanish authorities are now much more likely to question the intentions of Ecuadorians, migrant-exporting schemes also include a variety of routes and strategies for entering a European Union state as a believable tourist. Once at work, the income earned can be astounding to some: "With the salary of one or two days I cover the month's expenses; the rest is savings,"[20] says Rocio, an Ecuadorian emigrant working in Murcia. Tens of thousands have followed Rocio. Ecuadorians have contributed mightily to Spain's rapid transition from labor exporter to labor importer, making them the largest immigrant community in Spain after Moroccans.[21]

So what prompted this mass exodus of Ecuadorians from their country? In the last decade, Ecuadorians have witnessed one of the more dramatic economic and political downturns in the country's history. Beginning with the undeclared border war with Peru in 1995 and the political instability generated by the populist presidency of Abdala Bucaram (1996–1997), Ecuador then suffered the collapse of its coastal agro-export sector due to the climatological effects of El Niño, resulting in a loss of US$2.8 billion, all of this exacerbated by an international financial crisis rippling through Latin America. The deepening economic crisis reached a peak when small- and medium-scale savings accounts were indefinitely frozen in 1998 (some for more than two years). In 1999, the GDP fell more than 7 percent, along with the greater part of the country's financial system, when President Jamil Mahuad eliminated the national currency, the sucre, to replace it with the U.S. dollar, unleashing what could rightly be called total chaos in the short term.

Near-complete state collapse in the late 1990s has brought a dubious success: it has caused the rapid development of mass migration to the United States and Europe of broad sectors of Ecuadorian society, producing more than US$1 billion per year to the Ecuadorian economy in remittances.[22] Migrants' remittances exceed revenues from banana and shrimp exports and are second only to the country's oil revenues.

But the rise of illegal migration and human smuggling can also be linked to the processes of democratization and economic liberalization in Latin America in the 1980s as well as to failed development projects. When economies went sour and unfulfilled expectations were primed by the successes of previous small-scale migrations, established social networks were quickly revitalized. In this sense, migrant-exporting schemes can be viewed as a "successful" large-scale strategy of integration into the global marketplace rather than a criminal fringe activity.

Ecuadorians are increasingly blocked by both U.S. and Mexican border authorities and navies as Mexico makes a bid to cut a deal for its own illegal aliens in exchange for blocking Central and South Americans.[23] The U.S. Coast Guard now regularly transfers hundreds of Ecuadorian migrants off the Mexican waters to detention centers in Mexico.[24] As a result, Spain has become a refuge, particularly for women and the middle class. Even the wealthiest and most productive regions of Ecuador are sending thousands of workers abroad,[25] who in Spain work for as little as half the minimum wage paid a Spaniard. Many of them are professionals with children who lost their jobs, their savings, and generally their quality of life prior to the great monetary devaluation of 2000. This rapid depreciation of their savings—while inflating their debts by about 400 percent[26]—precipitated the collapse of banks, businesses, and several government regimes. Even Ecuadorian sailors attempted to transform a navy ship into a smuggling vessel for their own escape, creating the image of a stampede out of the country. "We can't detain the wave of emigration. . . . If things continue like this, the country could lose half of its inhabitants in the next decade,"[27] said Fernando Vega, a priest and director of the non-governmental organization Movilidad Humana ("Human Mobility").

If, however, such a truly mass migration from Ecuador comes to pass, emptying the country of its working-age population, two common themes of current migrants' perceptions will have to persist and even deepen. First, that Ecuador is an incorrigible predatory state, and second, that breaking immigration and labor laws is not a *real* crime in destination countries willing to hire them, a perception that is exacerbated by the mixed messages and ever-changing immigration and labor laws governing their tenuous legal status and economic survival.

Theme One: Ecuador as a Predatory State

This section weaves political and economic realities faced by Ecuadorians in Ecuador and Spain with their views on the Ecuadorian and Spanish states, regardless of the views' empirical validity. It is the result of interviews carried out in Spain in December 2001 and July/August 2002, and rich Internet testimonies of migration through various Ecuadorian websites. An overwhelming theme of these testimonies is the view of Ecuador as a predatory state in which crimes of the elite have completely debilitated the economy. The elite is defined as interlocking public and private officials who use the state apparatus to pilfer funds from the middle class and write legislation for the outright pillaging of state funds and foreign aid or loans. In short, the impression that laws are written for lawmakers is widespread. There is a corollary theme: corruption is possible only by the powerful. And insofar as Spain is the former imperial power in Ecuador, the Spanish state, or at least its policies, is seen by many as an extension of the predatory state—willing to speak the language of globalization and transparency for its economic and political convenience but to the detriment of the migrant laborer.

In Riobamba, Ecuador, as a schoolteacher for twelve years, Eduardo made US$50 a month and drove a taxi to supplement his salary. He has been in Spain five years and has several jobs including his own business in Bilbao running a *locutorio*, which specializes in long-distance phone calls back home for a variety of immigrants. He explains how as the head of a household with two children, "I was always paying debts, at the end of every month, more debts. Do you know what a teacher is there? A teacher is he who most gives of himself, because you always give, and then you still have debts. The end of the month would come and I would pay debts, every month, debts."

By leaving their country, migrants incur debts, but they are debts with a possible future for escaping debt, as Eduardo saw it. In Ecuador, he had lost all hope of being able to support his family and provide them a prosperous future.

> In light of this, a professional with children who wants to give the best to his children, I realized that there in my country they weren't giving me a chance. Five years ago I resigned from my work. I've been here in Bilbao four years. Every year in Ecuador got worse. Instead of improving, things got worse, getting deeper into debt. The state was in greater debt always. It was normal for the state to pay us with two months delay. It was "normal"—the super famous burglaries of the state treasury by a congressperson who would steal three billion sucres and another who would steal five billion sucres.

The time comes when you feel an impotence to act. And everyone knows it. The news stories were that so and so had stolen $5 million and was now in the United States. And f——! There I am, killing myself to make $50. And to see my children go hungry? The crisis got worse and the moment came when I realized there was nothing to be done. There was no hope for tomorrow. It was a terminal cancer—there was no hope. Here I have nothing to do. I'm leaving. I went to Bolivia. I didn't like it. I went to Caracas. There was more poverty, Latin American insecurity. At least in Ecuador there was peace. But in Caracas it was terrible. I'm better off in my country. A friend told me Spain was good to work. Let's go to Spain! he said. I bought my ticket and sold everything I had to buy my ticket for Spain. I gathered my money and traveled by myself. I didn't know anyone here but I couldn't back out. I had resigned my job and gone into debt to travel. My brother acted as guarantor. . . . I came November 4, 1998. I arrived in Madrid. I went to El Retiro [Park] and by chance I ran into a guy who had been my student years before. He told me that in Bilbao there were few foreigners and there was work there.

Eduardo opened up his own *locutorio* with a Spanish partner in Bilbao's Old City. He has already bought some land in Quito. Now he wants to buy a truck to transport vegetables from Riobamba to Guayaquil and pick up banana refuse in Guayaquil to take to a pig farm he wants to start in Riobamba. He will leave a chauffeur in charge and return to Bilbao. If the business in Ecuador goes well, he will stay in Ecuador.

I want to stay a maximum of two (more) years (in Spain). I have my two boys there in Riobamba. When I talk to them they call for me. They say their friends ask them why their father doesn't go to the school meetings, if they even have a father. One gets depressed here. Until when? This is a borrowed life.[28]

Buttressing Eduardo's claims and frustration, Ecuador received the title of the most corrupt country in Latin America by Transparency International for the year 2000, only to become Transparency International's second most corrupt country in 2001. This is not to lessen the historic structural limitations on the Ecuadorian economy that could be argued are reason enough for failed economic and political "development." But as many Ecuadorian observers assess the situation, responsibility for the Ecuadorian economic crisis rests with the neo-liberal economic policies of the successive governments of Jamil Mahuad and Gustavo Noboa, which advocated policies in lockstep with IMF and World Bank prescriptions[29]—policies which, unwittingly or not, were geared to the specific interests of a less-than-"transparent" oligarchic banking sector protected by the state and fattened by a captive national market.[30]

Ultimately, the dramatic social costs of the dollarization of the economy led to a *coup d'état* by an odd and short-lived junta of military and indigenous ("Indian") leaders that cost Jamil Mahuad his presidency on January 21, 2000. But the economic "adjustment" program was assured with the succession to power of Gustavo Noboa, Mahuad's former vice-president and Ecuador's sixth president in five years,[31] in the return to a semblance of a democratically elected regime. Despite the inaugural US$2 billion IMF credit and a welcome increase in oil exports, President Noboa and the mobilized peasant–indigenous masses confronted each other over IMF-prescribed and government-implemented price hikes on gasoline and domestic gas consumption, a necessary condition for continued IMF credits despite pacts with the mobilized popular sectors.[32] IMF structural readjustment measures imposed in December 2000 led to a series of mass mobilizations, particularly among Ecuador's indigenous and rural populations, more than 75 percent of which lived in poverty and lacked basic housing, health, education, and employment.[33] One hundred percent yearly inflation, out-of-control budget deficits since the 1980s, rampant government corruption,[34] and a complete lack of faith in Ecuador's banking system only served to undermine Ecuadorians' faith in their government, which came to be seen as a shadow regime of the military. The armed forces constitutionally receive ten percent of all oil revenues, and its own investments have made it the dominant economic and political institution in Ecuador.[35] After the peaceful sit-in of a university in Quito by 5,000 indigenous Ecuadorians, the state decreed a national state of emergency and lifted basic constitutional rights[36] in January 2001. As one emigrant said, "corrupt politicians have a safe-conduct to political exile. . . . Corruption has its nurturing mother in the marriage of politics and economic power. Can we be hopeful of a divorce? I believe that this marriage in Ecuador will be more long lasting than the war against terrorism."[37] In fact, the Ecuadorian state is sometimes referred to by Ecuadorian immigrants and journalists alike as an organized and powerful mafia. One Ecuadorian émigré, albeit to New Jersey, wrote in to *Vistazo*, Ecuador's premier news periodical, prior to the 2002 presidential election: "Despite where I may live, today I am here, another day perhaps not; the only thing I can tell you is that I am a combatant of corruption and opportunism and I am in the know with how Creole-Enrons [reference to the Enron scandal] operate; in Ecuador I will never give my vote to Ecuadorian politicians."[38]

Recognizing the impending implosion of the Ecuadorian state and economy, many Ecuadorians started to leave the country in what would develop into a mass migration by the late 1990s. This migration erupted onto the political agendas of both Spain and Ecuador with the tragic accident of January 3, 2001, when twelve undocumented Ecuadorian workers were hit by a train in Lorca, Murcia, while being transported in a van at dusk to pick crops. This tragic incident symbolized the significant informal labor market for illegal immigrant labor; most importantly, it launched a relatively unknown immigrant group onto center stage of Spanish immigration politics. In Spain, the surrounding drama of investigating the accident, the high-level diplomatic coterie attending the funerals, and the ensuing diplomatic negotiations involved in compensating the victims' families and returning the bodies to Ecuador proved to be, symbolically and politically, seminal events.

On January 23, 2001, just days after the accident at Lorca, Spain's revised immigration law, or *Ley de Extranjería*, came into effect, albeit with several aspects being challenged in Spain's constitutional courts. The government's foremost concern in redrafting the law, as diplomatically stated by Spanish president and then president of the European Union Jose Maria Aznar, was in instituting a rigorous "law and order" procedure and a clear distinction between what is legal and what is illegal—a real challenge given the way migrant-exporting schemes operate and of serious concern to institutionally developed social systems like that of the European Union.[39] President Aznar put immigration on the European Community's agenda, framing it in the language of global order beneficial to European needs: "We wish for legal migration, an immigration that we can integrate, that is beneficial and that helps the country develop. Illegal immigration, with the blurring of legality and illegality, only allows for marginalization, for the creation of an underclass, and can only lead to, unfortunately, phenomena of insecurity."

It is within this context that Ecuadorian migrant labor began to see the Spanish state as egotistical and hypocritical, particularly given the historic prism of colonial exploitation: "They conquered and raped us and nothing happened; today we conquer them and they get mad."[40] What is even more aggravating to many Ecuadorian immigrants is that after complying with Spanish labor laws, with work permits in hand, businesses refuse to contract them because many businesspeople are not willing to pay workers' social security quota as the law requires. "If the money for enrollment in the social security system comes from your pocket, the vacancy is yours. We have no options. If we don't pay it, we don't get our visas renewed." Another migrant laborer explains that work contracts are consummated in a matter of seconds. "No questions asked, no answers given; without signing a contract in some occasions and with doubts over payment at the end of the day's work."[41] The "*pistolero*," as the construction middleman who subcontracts foreigners is called, "takes us in his car and from there nobody knows where to. If we are lucky, he will not get away without paying us."[42]

The practices of "powerful" economic interests and the Spanish state are not immediately associated with each other for many. But for Ecuadorians, accustomed to the marriage of economic power and corrupt political influence, the seeming dissociation between Spanish laws and practices is all too familiar. On the one hand, this nurtures the profitable ambiguities that continue to lure more migrants to Spain. But on the other, it could embolden migrants to react against Spain as they associate the state's policies with that of the corrupt state they have fled, and worse, as they consider Spain a negligent warden of its former colonial child.

For other Ecuadorian migrants, their state's corruption spills over onto larger supranational organizations such as the IMF. From Switzerland one émigré writes:

> The national budget . . . is earmarked to pay off the debts of the unscrupulous state leaders and their allies . . . (leaders) who in addition have channeled funds to also pay key sources to maintain themselves in power, like the police and the armed forces, who have become participants in this true crime against the economy and the development of our country and people. . . . I implore you that this is our opportunity to turn around the development of the country . . . without bending to the IMF, but rather putting the cards on the table to win this battle against poverty and also against this voracious and merciless neo-liberalism that has done nothing more than make the middle class poor and the poor wretched, and that cannot continue to be.[43]

But to return to the connection that some migrants make between corruption at home and corruption/hypocrisy of the state in Spain, we must look at the fallout of the Lorca accident for labor migrants in Spain and the various permutations of Spain's oft-revised *Ley de Extranjería*. Thousands of undocumented workers throughout Spain found themselves unemployed and unemployable for months after the Lorca accident, with employers fearing government sanctions for hiring illegals. Migrants' financial resources were particularly depleted after the Lorca accident, which caused hundreds of undocumented Ecuadorian immigrants to depend on food handouts, live in cars, be taken in by friends after being evicted, or be sheltered by churches and other non-governmental organizations.[44] Before Spain's revisions of the 2001 *Ley de Extranjería*, undocumented migrants simply faced fines. As of 2001, they have no right of assembly, no right to protest, unionize, strike, or work.

The perception by both legal and illegal migrants is that the underlying cause of their economic degradation rests squarely with those in control of the Ecuadorian state and their collaborators. While this is not surprising, the more important question in light of this observation is: Why would so many essentially choose to enter corrupt networks underlying a myriad of migrant-exporting schemes? That is, strongly disagreeing with the policies of a corrupt state doesn't necessarily lead to risky lawbreaking in foreign countries. Thus, the second dominant theme of illegal migrants is of key importance to answering our main research question.

Theme Two: Illegal Labor Migration Is Not a Real Crime

From the perspective of Ecuadorian migrants, the compounded circumstances of a predatory state, the lure of Spanish laws and businesses offering work and hope for a future, and the commodification of migration through migration merchants at home and abroad congealed in 2001 with enforcement of illegal labor hiring freezes, a result of the Lorca accident. This policy tightened the noose around the necks of those who had risked their futures entering into migrant-exporting schemes. Labor migrants in Europe today are caught in the as yet unresolved tangle of evolving immigration laws and state security concerns. But Ecuadorian migrants' historical interpretations and analyses of their situation within the larger global economic picture clearly shape their political actions and demands on the Spanish state. Rather than seeing themselves as criminals, they view themselves as victims of historical and present-day injustices.

On the heels of the accident and massive layoffs of illegal laborers, 1,000 migrants set out on the seventy-kilometer "March for Life" (Caminata por la Vida) to demand government work permits for immigrant labor. Three hundred protestors completed the march to ask Spain for "solidarity" and were met by some 1,500 immigrants at the end, beginning a dramatic nineteen-hour rally. The march began and ended with the Ecuadorian anthem, recalling past centuries of Spanish colonialism: "Indignant your children for the yoke the audacious Iberia imposed on you / Indignant about the just and horrendous tragedy / that weighed heavily on you / holy voice to the heavens lifted / noble voice of unequaled promise / to avenge us of the bloody monster / to break that servile yoke."[45] Some of the signs marchers carried read: "Because we don't have papers, we work your fields"; "We don't come to beg but to demand papers"; and "When Columbus arrived in America no one asked him for papers." In addition, in Spain, Ecuadorians dramatize their historical colonial ties by drawing blood from their arms to demonstrate the common blood of Spanish ancestry and the historical obligations that that implies.[46]

Echoing Ecuadorians' historical argument, Jaime Mayor, minister of interior of the governing conservative Popular Party, explains: "Spain has historical obligations with those countries that form with us a common culture. And in that sense a special treatment can be given to citizens of those countries. It is not about giving priority to those who speak a particular language or profess a particular religion, but that society knows it must fulfill particular historical obligations."[47] In coordination with Spanish unions eager to eliminate clandestine labor hiring practices, the Spanish government brokered a deal with Spanish businesses in need of laborers by which all illegal Ecuadorian migrants in Spain, having previously obtained a pre-contract to work, were required to return to Ecuador to process their visas. Although the agreement privileged Ecuador with the first bilateral agreement,[48] upon the signing of the agreement, Ecuador's estimated 150,000 labor migrants already in Spain were now threatened with harsher penalties and a reduction in civil rights unless they complied with the repatriation agreement for obtaining a work visa.

Auter Solano, a twenty-eight-year-old Ecuadorian, was among the first immigrants to take the Spanish government up on its offer to regularize his status by returning to Quito to obtain a work visa with a Spanish pre-contract in hand. His diary of the journey back home to Ecuador and to the fields of Murcia again reveals much about the normalization of migrant-exporting schemes:

> If they don't give me the papers, in any case, I will return to Spain. There is no doubt. I will get there through Italy or Holland. If I entered undocumented to Newark [U.S.] at age 17, why not Murcia? . . . the first time I emigrated from Ecuador was 1991. My father was the first to go to the United States. Then, came his children's turn. When it was my turn, I was 17 years old and I was already married. I remember the factory in which I worked for five and a half years. . . . My decision to go to Spain was easy. I was advised to go to Murcia where the Ecuadorians were, and to look for a man who had an apartment. There was work. . . . Tomorrow I return to Spain. I am an immigrant. But I hope my children will not be. I've sworn to myself to not stay more than three years. Then I will return to Ecuador to never leave again. . . . [In Spain this time], I know I will earn less than in other places because I have to work for the person who offered me the pre-contract at 600 pesetas an hour [about US$2.75/hour]. In construction they pay 1,000 pesetas an hour. Let's see if I can work three or four months for this gentleman and then I'll look for something better.[49]

The families of "stranded" and unemployable Ecuadorian labor migrants in Spain anguished over accepting Spain's work visa repatriation requirements. Fearful of the likelihood of actually returning to Spain once the visa was obtained and incurring even more debt, family members in Ecuador testified, "I don't know what to do. The interest of the debt my husband contracted now totals some 8,000 dollars and the land we mortgaged to a *chulquero* [loan shark] isn't even ours." She added that she preferred that her husband stay and work as an illegal so that he may send at least some money.[50] Another woman said, "I don't want my husband to return. We are in debt for more than 3,500 dollars and we haven't made two payments. If he returns, they will put him in prison." Another woman said, "In the name of mothers I want to ask that the Ecuadorians abroad not return. My son is undocumented over there and because he isn't sending money I know he doesn't have work. The debt is asphyxiating us." Another woman said, "The *chulqueros* are pressuring us too much because we are behind on our payments. The loan we took out is at 20 percent monthly interest and if my son returns, where are we going to get the money to pay them?" Amidst this anguish, Ecuadorians "lament" their repudiation, as they see it, by the "*madre patria*" or "mother homeland" of Spain: "The motherland asks us for papers," but "the papers were paid for when Columbus discovered America—for this life and the next!"[51]

Ironically, at the same time that Spain is getting tough on both legal and illegal immigrants—driven primarily by a fear of African immigration—Spain needs laborers in both traditional sectors and to meet the growing demand for domestic labor. And like the rest of the developed world, as the economy of Spain has been transformed into a more information-based service economy with a relatively highly educated workforce, and as a critically low birth rate threatens Spain's armed forces[52] and social welfare system, the need for immigrant labor to fill the lower strata of Spain's productive and service sectors has risen.

Infuriated at the implications of his government's signing of the labor and repatriation agreement, one Ecuadorian academic pleaded with Heinz Moeller, Ecuador's minister of foreign affairs and chief negotiator of the agreement with Spain, not to sign: "A quota system that includes some and excludes others is an extremely dangerous thesis for the sending country. . . . All of us who have the privilege to carry the Ecuadorian passport abroad, and we who carry it with honor and pride, with love, and knowing or imagining, or wishing that it were so, that behind that cordovan colored notebook is not only a people, a history, many cultures, a geography, a flag, but a Government that protects us. . . . Ours is a passport of work, of tenacity, of effort. We do not steal nor take anything from anyone."[53]

Speaking on behalf of those migrants who might not be able to obtain a pre-contract in time and might therefore face deportation, Juan Carlos Manzanilla, spokesperson of the Hispano-Ecuadorian migrant association

Ruminahui, threatened, "If repatriation of Ecuadorians is carried out in accordance with the Spain-Ecuador bilateral agreement, we will file suit against both states in international courts for approving a law that goes against human rights."[54] Foreign minister Heinz Moeller's signing of the agreement was called a "betrayal" of Ecuadorians by migrant association leaders.[55] In the end, the Spain-Ecuador labor agreement remains an empty law given the absence of labor contracts from Spanish companies who, as it turns out, prefer to hire labor from eastern Europe, namely Poland and Romania, where transportation costs are significantly lower and wage demands are competitive for Spanish businesses—though illegal migrant labor is likely still preferred when they can get it.[56]

While many migrants' testimonies are focused on personal circumstances, by contrast "Eduardo" clearly links his situation as a migrant victim to larger state structures:

> the government isn't interested in knowing, quantifying or qualifying people. The only thing the government is interested in is that there be good labor and that it be cheap. The state and businesspeople like it that way. It's that it is so plain, it is so simple. The people know that the state needs people to work, and there is work, lots of work. The only thing is that the government puts obstacles. I'm talking about here, in Spain; I don't know how it is in other parts but it must be the same. There is a demand for labor. There are countries that have workers but no demand for work. Here 70 percent of immigrants work without papers. Why? Because the very government doesn't want to issue papers . . .but it is so simple. With just one law they could do it. It seems to be the government's policy. I've thought about this and with my *companeros* we've analyzed this. But shit! It's so simple! Issue working papers and get to work legally! There's work. . . . It's so easy to finish with the problem of migration but in this case, I don't know . . . they don't want to see the problem and they don't want to fix the problem because it would be so simple with one law.[57]

Eduardo sees his crime as simply a crime of legal status—something temporary, particularly given the ever-evolving regularization laws of Spain and the European Community.

Similarly, along with the attempts to formalize migration channels and enforce immigration controls, clandestine immigration into Spain and anti-immigrant attacks are continuing unabated, further increasing the perception and reality among Ecuadorian immigrants of opportunity and victimization by states.[58] The unintended consequence of these high-profile government regularization/criminalization strategies has been to effectively advertise labor opportunities in Spain, further legitimizing migrants' actions within migrant-exporting schemes. Not only do many immigrants see their migration as a necessary risk, but they see it as morally justified in that their remittances allow for the sustenance of their immediate families. But the discourse of many migrants also reflects their moral justification for their possible illegal migrant status on the political/patriotic basis of the "larger" family or Fatherland. As one Ecuadorian migrant put it: "I hope they hear this strong cry for Ecuadorians from those of us who are in the north, begging that our country remember us, since we have every right to make demands because we are the first power in generating income to maintain so many lazy and corrupt politicians."[59] Another immigrant wrote in to the immigrant website of Ecuador's leading newspaper: "I am Ecuadorian and I feel abandoned by my country and by everyone."[60] Another asserted:

> We have been victims of everything, from being humiliated, forced to work, many times we've been swindled or they pay us very little for what we do. We all have a story to tell, but I think they all have the same ending, and that is how much we miss our country and our families. With all of this that has happened to us, we begin to wonder if we return and see what condition our country is in, I feel like working even more and continuing with this since it pains us to see what is happening in our country.[61]

The profits, both legal and illegal, to be made from migrant-exporting schemes are illustrated in the aggressive move by Spanish and U.S. companies as well as by their governments to capitalize on the profits of Ecuadorian migration. The Ecuadorian state is now offering would-be migrants financing to buy out travel agency loans, while the IMF is recommending that Ecuador use remittances for "development." The hypocrisy of international banks and development agencies, however, which, having failed in their prescriptions for Ecuador, now try to balance their accounts with migrant remittances, shows the ease with which papers can be shuffled, and it shows a political callousness not lost on Ecuador's migrant population and struggling middle class.[62] "If we were birds," explains author Oscar Jara, "we would be protected; but we are a species, not threatened with extinction but with expulsion thanks to the *Ley de Extranjería*."[63] And in the case of Ecuadorians, expulsion or condemnation to eternal illegal status quite literally could spell economic and social extinction.

While political and legal scholars debate what is just for states and their control over human mobility and work, what is lacking is an understanding of how multiple voices within sending and destination countries, foremost those of the migrants themselves, have developed a fairly coherent discourse of justice. It is a discourse most analogous to a type of "economic citizenship" transcending national citizenship. After all, some states have already been willing to give up parts of their sovereignty by allowing migrants to be citizens of more than one country through dual citizenship (most frequently migrant-origin states). Migrants are further motivated by their perception of the reality that it is they who are making a sacrifice not only for their families, but for both the sending state dependent on remittances and for the destination state dependent on their labor.

Many observers have pointed out the unsustainable discrepancy between the opening of our "economic borders" and political sovereignties through common regional and multilateral institutions and, in stark contrast, the *ad hoc* retraction of our political borders (national labor markets) to economic labor migrants, buttressed by physical barriers, an enormous increase in border enforcement personnel, and various technologies of control. However, more than a simple discrepancy, the dilemma of facing chronic economic and political crises at home on the one hand, and the attraction of employment opportunities and social mobility in developed countries on the other, has real negative consequences for many caught in the cross-currents of these opposing global trends. People are choosing to break immigration laws and risk death, rape, detention, xenophobic attacks, and enslavement, while developed states take measures to diffuse the political and economic risks of an actual reduction in immigrant labor through bilateral negotiations (e.g., with Mexico) for the strategic legalization of "illegal aliens" on which some U.S. industries depend.[64]

With these mixed messages, more and more migrants are turning to a growing migration industry of legal and illegal services to help them either enter destination states illicitly or "regularize" their illegal immigration status. Though many state agents and media place the blame for rising levels of "human smuggling" at the feet of "organized crime," this conveniently ignores the other agents involved, namely the voluntary migrants themselves who enter into migrant-exporting schemes and their own moral and economic reasoning. Migrant-exporting schemes will remain resistant to even the harshest border controls, not due to the sophistication of their strategies, but due to a much more fundamental reality—the conviction that they are justified in crossing borders illegally to obtain work or in helping others to do so. Wilson Montenegro, twenty-one, who was caught by the U.S. and Mexican navies in February 2002 in one of three fishing vessels attempting a clandestine passage to the U.S., sums up the legitimizing discourse of illegal migrants who place their actions in the context of their personal and national relation to the global political economy. When asked why he paid thousands of dollars to board a rickety boat crammed with 150 to 200 would-be illegal migrants, he replied, "Shrimp is a major product of my country [its third largest export] and I never get to eat it. . . . I want a job that pays me a man's salary. I want my sons to have pencils and notebooks for school. I want them to eat shrimp."[65] The migrant-smuggling question is a very real one faced by millions each year who must ask whether they should trust the promises of local and national politicians more than the promise of work abroad with an illegal status that will likely be temporary. For many in countries like Ecuador, in which "export-led development" has been the cornerstone of IMF and World Bank policies, both staying put and leaving carry grave risks.

NOTES

1. James Scott, *Seeing Like a State: How Certain Schemes to Improve the Human Condition Have Failed* (New Haven, Conn., and London: Yale University Press, 1999).

2. For understanding the evolution of state control over its citizens by regulating who may enter its territory, see John Torpey, *The Invention of the Passport* (Cambridge: Cambridge University Press, 2000).

3. Several researchers have recently analyzed the inconsistencies and unintended hypocrisies of U.S. immigration law and its uneven enforcement by the U.S. Immigration and Naturalization Service. See Douglas S. Massey, Jorge Durand, and Nolan J. Malone, *Beyond Smoke and Mirrors: Mexican Immigration in an Era of Economic Integration* (New York: Russell Sage Foundation, 2002); Peter Andreas, *Border Games: Policing the U.S.-Mexico Divide* (Ithaca, N.Y., and London: Cornell University Press, 2000); Joseph Nevins, *Operation Gatekeeper: The Rise of the "Illegal Alien" and the Making of the U.S.–Mexico Boundary* (New York and London: Routledge, 2002); Peter Andreas and Timothy Snyder, *The Wall around the West: State Borders and Immigration Controls in North America and Europe* (Oxford: Rowman & Littlefield, 2000); Wayne A. Cornelius, Philip L. Martin, and James F. Hollifield, eds., *Controlling Immigration: A Global Perspective* (Stanford, Calif.: Stanford University Press, 1994); and Timothy J. Dunn, *The Militarization of the U.S.–Mexico Border, 1978–1992: Low-Intensity Conflict Doctrine Comes Home* (Austin: Center for Mexican American Studies, University of Texas at Austin, 1996).

4. See, for example, the recent works of two eminent philosophers: Michael Dummett, *On Immigration and Refugees* (London: Routledge, 2001), and Jacques Derrida, *On Cosmopolitanism and Forgiveness* (London: Routledge, 2001).

5. See Diana Wong, chapter 2, this volume.

6. James Finkenauer, "Russian Transnational Organized Crime and Human Trafficking," in *Global Human Smuggling: Comparative Perspectives*, ed. David Kyle and Rey Koslowski (Baltimore: Johns Hopkins University Press, 2001), pp. 166–186.

7. Moisés Naím, "Five Wars of Globalization," *Foreign Policy* (January/February 2003): 28–36.

8. *The Arizona Republic*, May 25, 2001 (online version).

9. *The Arizona Republic*, May 30, 2001 (online version).

10. *The Arizona Republic*, October 14, 2001 (online version).

11. See David Kyle and John Dale, "Smuggling the State Back In: Agents of Human Smuggling Reconsidered," in *Global Human Smuggling*, ed. Kyle and Koslowski, pp. 29–57.

12. For a systematic analysis of the effects of IMF and World Bank policies in the promotion of free markets, including a series of "IMF food riots" in every region of the world, see John Walton and David Seddon, *Free Markets and Food Riots: The Politics of Global Adjustment* (Oxford: Blackwell Press, 1994).

13. See Saskia Sassen, *Losing Control: Sovereignty in an Age of Globalization* (New York: Columbia University Press, 1996).

14. Peter Schuck, for example, argues that typically it is the victim who first learns of the crime; in this area of immigration criminality, tellingly, it is the employer who first becomes aware of "the crime." See "Law and the Study of Migration," in Caroline B. Brettell and James F. Hollifield, eds., *Migration Theory: Talking across Disciplines* (New York: Routledge, 2000), 187–204.

15. Karl Eschbach, Jacqueline Hagan, Néstor Rodríguez, Rubén Hernández, and Stanley Bailey, "Death at the Border." *International Migration Review* 33, no. 2 (1999).

16. See Kyle and Dale, "Smuggling the State Back In," for a discussion of the distinctions between migrant-exporting schemes and slave-importing operations.

17. David Kyle, *Transnational Peasants: Migrations, Networks, and Ethnicity from Andean Ecuador* (Baltimore: Johns Hopkins University Press, 2000).

18. Sanjuana Martinez, "Psicosis por la Ley de Extranjería. Espana-Ecuador: La guerra migratoria," *Proceso*, no. 1267 (February 11, 2001).

19. See Brad Jokisch and Jason Pribilsky, "The Panic to Leave: Economic Crisis and the 'New Emigration' from Ecuador," *International Migration* 40, no. 4 (2002).

20. Marcia Cevallos, "Ecuador, un país en estampida," *El País*, January 7, 2001.

21. See Wayne A. Cornelius, "Spain: The Uneasy Transition from Labor Exporter to Labor Importer," in *Controlling Immigration: A Global Perspective*, 2nd ed., ed. Wayne A. Cornelius et al. (Stanford, Calif.: Stanford University Press, 2004).

22. Sebastian Rotella, "As Crises Converge on Ecuador, an Exodus," *Los Angeles Times*, July 13, 2000, p. A1.

23. Mary Jordan and Kevin Sullivan, "Mexico Plans a Tighter Grip on Its Border to the South," *The Washington Post*, June 18, 2001, p. A01.

24. "Los 250 migrantes presos estan en Puerto Madero," *El Comercio*, May 20, 2002; "Mexico: interceptan a indocumentados, la mayoria ecuatorianos," *El Comercio*, May 17, 2002.

25. "Los Rios: inmigrantes al exterior aumentan," *El Comercio*, May 17, 2002.

26. Marcia Cevallos, "Ecuador, un país en estampida," *El País*, January 7, 2001.

27. Marcia Cevallos, "Ecuador, un país en estampida," *El País*, January 7, 2001.

28. "Eduardo," interview in Bilbao, Spain, August 9, 2002.

29. See Wilma Salgado, "La crisis en el Ecuador en el contexto de las reformas financieras," *Ecuador Debate* 51 (2000): 7–22.

30. Victor Breton Solo de Zaldivar, *Cooperacion al desarrollo y demandas etnicas en los Andes ecuatorianos* (Quito: FLACSO and Universitat de Lleida, 2001).

31. "Postrado Ecuador," *El País*, February 6, 2001.

32. "Postrado Ecuador," *El País*, February 6, 2001.

33. "Sobre el Estado de Ecuador," *El País*, February 13, 2001.

34. In June 2002, Ecuador's finance minister, Carlos Julio Emanuel, resigned after it emerged that he had run a ministry-level scam taking bribes of up to 38 percent of

unbudgeted funds handed over to local governments, with congressmen and other ministries also grabbing payoffs. While Noboa has denied any wrongdoing, Noboa and Emanuel are not the first senior officials to be accused of corruption in Ecuador. President Abdala Bucaram was ousted by Congress after corruption allegations and fled to Panama. His replacement, Fabian Alarcon, was jailed in 1999 for fraud. And his elected successor, Jamil Mahuad, who was ousted by a coup in January 2000, accepted campaign contributions from a corrupt banker. Corruption, in the form of bribes, pervade the administrative, political, and judicial systems of Ecuador, from policemen to justices. See "Taken for a Ride," *The Economist*, August 3, 2002, p. 31.

35. "De que huyen los ecuatorianos," *El País*, January 23, 2001. In 1992, democratically elected left-of-center statesman Rodrigo Borja ended his five-year term, handing the presidency over to Sixto Duran Ballen, a senior politician and neo-liberal proponent, and his Harvard-trained neo-liberal vice-president Jamil Mahuad, later to be the deposed president of the dollarization plan.

36. Indigenous peasant mobilizations in Ecuador are carried out with a repertoire of road blockades, long marches, and peaceful occupations of official buildings and parks in Quito and Amazonian oil fields.

37. Jorge Vivanco Mendieta, "Carta del emigrante," http://vistazo.com, October 25, 2001.

38. "Los que se van," http://vistazo.com, November 14, 2002.

39. Jose Antonio Alonso, "Europa frente a las mafias," http://elpais.es, April 15, 2002.

40. "'Esperanza' in Testimonios de inmigrantes," http://www.elcomercio.com, October 17, 2002.

41. Patricia Villarruel, "Espana: la lucha es por un dia de trabajo," elcomercio.com, December 16, 2002.

42. Patricia Villarruel, "Espana: la lucha es por un dia de trabajo," elcomercio.com, December 16, 2002.

43. Angel Sion, "Saludo a mi pueblo ecuatoriano," http://www.elcomercio.com, January 4, 2003.

44. "400 ecuatorianos en Murcia necesitan comida urgentemente," *El País*, February 27, 2001.

45. Maria J. Lopez Diaz, "300 inmigrantes caminan 70 kilometros en Murcia en demanda de permisos," *El País*, January 11, 2001.

46. Javier Fresneda, vice president of the Ecuadorian migrant association Ruminahui, personal communication, Madrid, December 2001.

47. "Elecciones en el País Vasco. 'Lo prioritario es la legalidad,'" *El País*, May 8, 2001.

48. Signed on May 29, 2001, between the Spanish and Ecuadorian foreign ministers, this was Spain's first bilateral "Labor and Repatriation Agreement." The agreement makes government-issued work permits the only avenue for non–European Community labor migrants to enter Spain. According to the agreement, 40,000 Ecuadorian migrants would be recruited *in* Ecuador and granted work permits in the construction, domestic service, and seasonal agricultural labor sectors.

49. M. J. Lopez Diaz and M. Cevallos, "El diario de un inmigrante de ida y vuelta," *El País*, March 12, 2001.

50. "Angustia por emigrantes," *El Universo*. April 22, 2001, http://www.eluniverso.com/informab.

51. T. Constenla and M. Cevallos, "El Ecuador pasa por Lorca," *El País*, January 29, 2001.

52. "IU propone que se incorporen inmigrantes a la policía," *El País*, May 23, 2002. Apart from proposals to incorporate immigrants into the Spanish police force, as of December 2002, Ibero-American immigrants are being recruited into the Spanish armed forces in order to fill the deficit of candidates to the ranks. See "Defensa necesita 2,000 inmigrantes al ano para paliar el deficit de tropa," *El País*, March 20, 2001; Patricia Villarruel, "Ecuatorianos al Ejército de Espana," http://www.elcomercio.com, December 16, 2002; "625 ecuatorianos quieren ir al Ejército espanol," http://www.elcomercio.com, January 27, 2003.

53. Cesar Montúfar, "El pasaporte ecuatoriano," *El Comercio*, August 1, 2001.

54. "Mayor Oreja no escucho protestas," *El Universo*, April 22, 2001.

55. "Políticos y académicos cuestionan en Ecuador el pacto de inmigración firmado con Espana," *El País*, February 26, 2001.

56. "Gobierno y sindicatos culpan a los empresarios de no cubrir el cupo," *El País*, June 11, 2002.

57. "Eduardo," interview in Bilbao, Spain, August 9, 2002.

58. See Pilar Marcos, "Aznar asegura que la inseguridad disminuye y se concentra en los extranjeros," http://www.elpais.es, April 25, 2002.

59. Mario Rolando Paredes, "Desde New Jersey," http://www.elcomercio.com, December 24, 2002.

60. "Saludos," http://www.elcomercio.com, January 7, 2003.

61. In "Testimonios de inmigrantes," see "Nos hace madurar," elcomercio.com, January 7, 2003.

62. See "El BID acuerda se abarate el envío de dinero al exterior," elcomercio.com, January 25, 2003.

63. Oscar Jara writes this in *Ecuador en Espana. La realidad de la migración*, cited in "El fiasco del paraíso," http://elcorreodigital.com, September 23, 2002.

64. For example, a U.S. Department of Labor Report found that approximately 40 percent of California's agricultural workers are undocumented (or falsely documented) migrants, *Migrant Farmworkers: Pursuing Security in an Unstable Labor Market*, Research Report 5, May 1994.

65. Ginger Thompson, "Migrants from Afar See Mexico as Steppingstone to U.S.," *New York Times* (online version), March 1, 2002.

Criminality and the Global Diamond Trade

A Methodological Case Study

Ian Smillie

This chapter was written when the "blood diamond" phenomenon it describes was at its height and when international efforts to control the trade in illicit gem diamonds were still in their infancy. Since then, a great deal has changed. The chapter, therefore, is a snapshot of a work in progress. It has been left unchanged to underscore the challenges that were faced in halting illicit diamond flows. An epilogue updates the story to 2005.

Three Scenarios[1]

Diamonds represent one of the most difficult of illicit objects to study, both because of their small size and easy conversion into cash, and also because they are part of an extremely secretive and profitable industry that has taken enormous amounts of trouble over the past century to prevent unauthorized outsiders from getting to know its inner workings. Diamonds represent one of the best examples of the gray areas between "licit" and "illicit," and they demonstrate how "illicit"—left to its own devices—can become more clearly "illegal," with direct connections to theft, murder, human rights abuse, and terrorism. Diamonds also extend the discussion of "borderlands." Illicit and illegal behavior in the diamond trade begins with cross-border smuggling in Africa—between Sierra Leone and Liberia, between Angola and its neighbors, between Kinshasa on one side of the River Congo and Brazzaville on the other. But there are other borderlands in our brave new globalized world. The conceptual (and actual) "border" between Sierra Leone and Belgium can be found somewhere aboard the SN Brussels Airbus that takes six hours to fly between Freetown and Brussels twice a week—possibly in the toilet where smugglers can easily repackage their contraband before arriving in Belgium.

In what follows, we present a discussion of the methodological difficulties of studying this industry and the effects of an intervention by two non-governmental organizations which has forced a new level of transparency on this industry. The success of this regulatory effort remains to be seen. But first we introduce three scenarios to show that what transforms the trade in diamonds from a legal, if unregulated, industry into an illicit process are the routes and paths the diamonds take once extracted from a mine.

Scenario 1: The "Licit" Diamond Trail

Tamba Momoh is a seventeen-year-old high school dropout, living near the town of Jaiama Sewafe in the Eastern District of Sierra Leone. He digs diamonds with ten other young men on a lease held by Daniel Morlai. Morlai has been a diamond miner for a dozen years, although he does none of the digging himself. He pays the diggers a small daily wage and gives them a share of the proceeds from the diamonds they find. He buys them their equipment, some clothes, and rice, and he also pays their medical bills, as they often come down with malaria, bilharzia, or gastroenteritis as a result of working all day in swampy conditions. He pays his annual license fee to the government and sells the diamonds that Tamba and the others find to Nawaz Mansour, a diamond dealer in Kenema. Mansour, whose parents emigrated to Sierra Leone from Lebanon in 1951, buys from many miners and consolidates his purchases, taking them once a week to Freetown for sale to Mohammed Ibrahim, a diamond exporter. Mansour has a buying license; Ibrahim has an export license. Ibrahim takes the diamonds to the Government Gold and Diamond Office for valuation, where he pays a 3 percent export tax. The diamonds are then shipped to his cousin, Ali Ibrahim, who owns a company called Diagem in Antwerp. Diagem receives the diamonds and sorts them into two basic categories. The very small gems are sent to a cutting firm in Surat, India. Once they are polished, they are sold to Vales, a large retail jewelry chain in the U.S. While the

U.S. market consumes almost half of all polished diamonds every year, they tend to be lower-end goods. The better diamonds go to Ramat Gan in Israel. Once they are cut and polished, the best will be sold to European and American dealers for settings that will wind up in the showrooms of Cartier and Tiffany.

Scenario 2: The "Illicit" Diamond Trail

Tamba Momoh is tired of being sick and working in the blazing sun all day for the pittance paid by his boss, Daniel Morlai. He swallows the best diamonds he finds and takes them every week to a Lebanese diamond dealer in Kenema, Nawaz Mansour. Mansour gives him a better price than Morlai. Mansour, in fact, pays the best prices in town. He gives Tamba leones and can afford to pay higher than market prices because he makes huge profits on his real business, which is rice imports. He prices the rice to cover the cost of the diamonds he buys. Every month, Mansour drives to Freetown and then flies to Banjul, the capital of Gambia, after bribing the customs officers not to check his carry-on luggage. There he sells the diamonds to his brother Mohamed, who gives him the dollars he needs to buy rice on the world market. Mohamed or one of his associates make a diamond run to Antwerp once a month. They never declare the diamonds when they arrive in Brussels, and they have never been stopped or questioned. The diamonds are bought by Ali Ibrahim, who owns a company named Diagem. Ibrahim sorts and exports the diamonds to India and Israel, but in collusion with the buyers, he understates the value of the diamonds on the invoices. This will help him explain the volume-to-value ratio of his business if anyone asks—which is unlikely—and it helps his customers, who pay less tax in India and Israel as a result of the collusion.

Scenario 3: The "Conflict Diamond" Trail

Tamba Momoh is seventeen. At the age of twelve he was kidnapped by the Revolutionary United Front (RUF) after being forced to murder his uncle in front of the entire family. The RUF gives him a mixture of gunpowder and heroin which he rubs into a scrape on his forehead. This "brown-brown" gives him the energy he needs to dig for diamonds all day. He and the others are always guarded by armed RUF "Black Guards" who have instituted what they call a two-pile system. Technically Tamba is allowed to keep half of what he finds, but in reality the Black Guards take all the best diamonds themselves. Brima Conteh, known as "Brigadier Chop

Hands," is the regional RUF commander. He consolidates all the diamond finds in his area and takes them to RUF headquarters in Buedu once every two weeks. One of the more senior RUF commanders, General Rambo, takes a larger consolidation of diamonds across the border to Liberia. It takes him two days to reach the office of Khalil Khalil, once a gas station attendant in Lebanon and now known as the unofficial finance minister of Liberia. Khalil weighs and sorts the diamonds and tells General Rambo that he can ride back to Buedu on the Liberian government helicopter that will transport the weapons he has exchanged for the diamonds. Khalil's brother-in-law takes the diamonds to Antwerp once a month. They are handed over to a company named Diagem, which has instructions to transfer all payments to an account in the Isle of Man. Funds arriving in this account are automatically transferred to the Cayman Islands, to the account of Freedom Air, registered in the Central African Republic but based in Dubai. Freedom Air, owned by Viktor Crout (who has Russian and Israeli passports), buys used weapons on the open market in Bulgaria and Ukraine and flies them to Monrovia, via Sudan. He uses false flight plans and false Togolese or Nigerian end-user certificates to avoid detection by UN sanctions experts. Meanwhile, Diagem sends Khalil's diamonds to Israel and India for cutting and polishing, and within a few weeks they are in Vales windows in American shopping malls or in the showrooms of Tiffany and Cartier in Paris, London, and New York.

The Diamond Business

The value of gem diamonds is completely artificial. Diamonds, once rare, are now almost common. The world's diamond production multiplied ten times in the decade following the South African discoveries of the 1860s, and has multiplied forty times again since then. Over 500 tons of diamonds have been mined altogether, one third of them in the 1990s.[2] The value of diamonds, established when they were rare, has been sustained by the influence exercised over the worldwide industry by one company, De Beers. De Beers established its control in the nineteenth century and has never let go. Today, about 60 percent of global diamond production goes through De Beers offices, from mines owned or jointly owned by De Beers, or via direct arrangements with other mining firms. Half of the biggest and most lucrative diamond operation in the world—Debswana—is owned by De Beers, the other half by the government of Botswana (which, as a result, had a higher GNP growth rate than the Asian "tiger economies" throughout the 1980s and 1990s). Traditionally, De Beers has mopped up loose supplies and withheld diamonds from the market whenever prices were set

FIG 6.1. Illicit diamond diggers in Sierra Leone washing gravel. Photograph courtesy Partnership Africa-Canada.

to fall. It maintains its control and its prices in other ways. It sells to fewer than 100 selected "sightholders" on a preferential basis. These sightholders are made offers that cannot be refused. De Beers also creates demand. It spends almost US$200 million a year on advertising, and it expects its sightholders to advertise as well. And it cultivates new markets. Japan has in recent years provided a lucrative outlet for the growing supply.

The diamond trade is secretive, perhaps more secretive than any other. Multimillion-dollar deals are made on a handshake; tens of millions of dollars worth of diamonds are sent across borders and across continents on approval, with little or no paperwork. Some of this is traditional—a way of doing business in a trade that is heavily populated by small (and a few very large) family-run businesses, and by people who have known each other for generations. Some of it has to do with security and the transportation of high-value goods from one place to another. But there have been other reasons for secrets. In order to keep its control over the market, De Beers bought all the diamonds it could, no questions asked. And it had to deal in the 1950s and onward with a wide array of strange and incompatible bedfellows. Apartheid South Africa, the home of De Beers, was an inappropriate partner for newly independent diamond-producing nations elsewhere in

Africa—Congo, Tanzania, Sierra Leone, and Guinea. And it was an even more inappropriate partner for the Soviet Union after its discovery of diamonds in the 1950s. In addition, having dealt with the Portuguese colonists of Angola until the mid-1970s and the apartheid regime of Southwest Africa until the late 1980s, De Beers had some fancy and confidential footwork to do in making friends with the new management. Most of this was done very successfully, largely because the company avoided the spotlight of public attention.

By value, more than 60 percent of all gem diamonds are mined in Africa, and until recent discoveries in Canada, the percentage was much higher. As some African diamond-producing countries slipped into corruption and chaos during the 1960s and 1970s, diamond buyers remained on the scene but began to conduct their business in new ways. Formal diamond production in Sierra Leone, for example, fell from two million carats in 1970 to only 48,000 carats by 1988, courtesy of one of the most corrupt regimes on the continent's west coast. The same was true in the Democratic Republic of Congo (DRC), known from 1971 to 1997 as Zaire. There was no drop, however, in the overall supply of diamonds reaching the world's trading centers, of which Antwerp had become the most important. All that was required was a degree of secrecy, and few questions would be asked when the diamonds were declared on arrival at Belgian customs.

Between the 1950s and the mid-1980s, the diamond scene in Africa changed. A significant proportion of the production of countries like the Congo, Sierra Leone, Angola, and others was being hidden under a veil of secrecy, which cloaked a vast network of corruption, theft, and smuggling. Diamonds were also being used for money laundering—as a means of moving cash in cashless societies, or in economies where currency no longer had value. Lebanese traders in Sierra Leone, for example, have for decades smuggled diamonds out of the country as a way of repatriating profits or of obtaining the hard currency needed to buy imports for other commercial activities: rice and other foodstuffs, vehicles, petroleum products. Most of this was "illicit" behavior, deemed "illegal," as noted in the introductory chapter, in various ways by various governments, some of them increasingly predatory in their own behavior.

Most governments learned long ago that taxes on diamonds—even very low taxes—lead inevitably to smuggling, because diamonds can be so easily concealed and because the nature of the trade is so opaque. Export duties are typically set at about 3 percent in producing countries, and import duties are frequently zero in trading, cutting, and polishing countries. Other attempts at restricting trade are strenuously and effectively avoided as well.

A recent, dramatic example can be found in the Democratic Republic of Congo (DRC). An Israeli firm, International Diamond Industries (IDI), obtained an eighteen-month monopoly on diamond exports from the DRC in September 2000. The DRC minister of mines defended the monopoly at the time, saying, "This is the optimum way for the Congo diamond production to be marketed in a transparent manner that will inspire trust and confidence in the country's certificate of origin, which will accompany each and every parcel to be exported by IDI."[3] It did nothing of the kind, in part because it was little more than a thinly disguised attempt by then President Laurent Kabila to direct more of the industry's profits his way. He canceled the licenses of all the other dealers—bought earlier for US$100,000 each—and reportedly received a multimillion-dollar payment from IDI for the favor.[4]

Exports from the DRC, however, immediately fell, while across the river in Brazzaville, the capital of a country with no diamonds at all, there was a sudden and dramatic change. Belgian diamond imports from Brazzaville—which stood at zero in August of that year—jumped by October to US$37 million.[5] Congo Brazzaville has played this role for years, in part because of the massive corruption and predatory behavior of the DRC's longtime dictator, Mobutu Sese Seko. Under his leadership, formal diamond production in the Congo apparently fell from 18 million carats in 1961 to 12 million in 1970 and to only 8 million in 1980, finally leveling off at about 6.5 million carats in the 1990s. Production "apparently" fell to these levels, because these are the figures that were recorded. But Mobutu "informalized" much of the diamond industry, bringing it and its profits under his own control and that of his cronies. Miners, middlemen, and diamantaires devised a simple way to avoid his rapacious appetite and heavy system of informal taxation (otherwise known as "bribery"). They simply smuggled their product across the river to Brazzaville. The ups and downs of Belgian diamond imports from Brazzaville are, in fact, a relatively good barometer of war and corruption in the DRC. In 1997, when the DRC was undergoing the chaotic transfer of power from Mobutu to Kabila, Belgium imported US$454.6 million worth of diamonds from Brazzaville. By 1999, however, when things had settled down, and when it looked as though Kabila might actually be a new wind sweeping away the corruption and cronyism of the past, Belgium imported only US$14.4 million worth of diamonds from Brazzaville, and there was growth in imports from the DRC. By 2000, however, the blush was off the Kabila rose, and the volume from Brazzaville soared to US$116.6 million, almost doubling again in 2001 to US$223.8 million.[6]

Scale of the Problem

At least 20 percent of the world's trade in rough diamonds is marked by smuggling, tax evasion, money laundering, sanction busting, war, and state collapse. This represents approximately US$1.56 billion worth of illicit behavior in a rough diamond trade of about US$7.8 billion annually. The extent of the problem started to become clear in the late 1990s, when two NGOs—Global Witness in Britain and Partnership Africa Canada—exposed the relationship between diamonds and the wars in Angola and Sierra Leone. Here the issue was *conflict* diamonds, a subset of the larger problem, but infinitely worse in its effect.[7]

In March 2000, the UN Security Council Sanctions Committee expert panel on Angola confirmed what the NGOs had found, and for the first time in the history of the United Nations, sitting heads of state were named for their complicity in laundering diamonds and assisting in weapons sanction busting. Since then, there have been intense diplomatic negotiations aimed at creating a certification system for rough diamonds. More than fifty governments, along with NGOs and the diamond industry—in a series of meetings that became known as the Kimberley Process, described below—reached an agreement that came into effect on January 1, 2003, which saw sweeping changes in the way diamonds are protected, traded, counted, and tracked. Or so it seemed. The problem with the agreement is that it contains weak provisions for independent monitoring, and a year after startup it was still struggling to achieve basic, agreed minimum standards among participating countries. In an industry so infected by illicit behavior, independent monitoring might seem like an essential element, a *sine qua non* to the casual observer.

The problem, however, is that conflict diamonds represent a very small portion of the overall trade. A system designed to catch these diamonds would ultimately expose the much bigger traffic in illicit diamonds, and too many vested interests are at stake for this to be given up without a fight.

Some Definitions

Conflict diamonds, or "blood diamonds," are diamonds used by rebel movements to buy weapons and fuel war. The definition was made more restrictive by the Kimberley Process, which tied conflict diamonds to UN resolutions:

> Conflict Diamonds means rough diamonds used by rebel movements or their allies to finance conflict aimed at undermining legitimate governments, as

described in relevant United Nations Security Council (UNSC) resolutions insofar as they remain in effect, or in other similar UNSC resolutions which may be adopted in the future, and as understood and recognized in United Nations General Assembly (UNGA) Resolution 55/56, or in other similar UNGA resolutions which may be adopted in future.[8]

This definition eliminates Democratic Republic of Congo (DRC) diamonds from the calculation, because neither the Security Council nor the General Assembly have made any pronouncement on Congolese diamonds. This technicality notwithstanding, the connection between diamonds and conflict in the Congo has been well established by journalists, NGOs, UN expert panels, and the diamond industry itself. In a much-quoted estimate, Andrew Coxon, then director of De Beers diamond buying, calculated in 2000 that conflict diamonds in 1999 amounted to approximately 3.7 percent of the world's rough diamond production of US$6.8 billion.[9] The total was based on the estimates in Table 6.1. This 3.7 percent figure, rounded up to 4 percent, was widely quoted for several years. It has also been disputed. In earlier years, the figure was certainly much higher. In 1996 and 1997, the Angolan rebel movement (UNITA) alone exported as much as US$700 million annually—10 percent of world production. An April 2001 UN report on Angola estimated UNITA smuggling at US$300 million or more in 1999, double the figure in Table 6.1.[10] With the end of hostilities in Angola and Sierra Leone, however, the figure was probably less than 2 percent of world trade in 2004.

Illicit diamonds, however, have never been properly defined, in part because they are so rarely discussed. A brief definition is provided here for the sake of clarity.

> Illicit diamonds are diamonds that have been stolen, smuggled, or used for purposes of tax evasion and money laundering. Illicit diamonds include diamonds referred to as "conflict diamonds."

In its search for conflict diamonds from Sierra Leone, a UN expert panel noted the much greater volume of illicit diamonds. Part of the difficulty in understanding diamond statistics is that once rough diamonds arrive in Europe, Israel, and elsewhere, they are sorted, traded across borders, resorted and retraded—possibly many times—before they actually get to a cutting and polishing center. The report said,

> This obscuring of origins makes the diamond industry vulnerable to a wide variety of illicit behaviour. It is no secret that diamonds are stolen from virtually every mining area in the world. Diamonds have long been used as an unofficial hard currency for international transactions. As with other pre-

Table 6.1. Estimate of Conflict Diamonds
by Weight and Value, 1999

	Angola	Sierra Leone	Democratic Republic of Congo
Average Price per Carat	US$300	US$200	US$180
Number of Carats	433,000	350,000	194,000
Total	US$150 million	US$70 million	US$35 million

cious commodities, they lend themselves to money laundering operations. Because they are small and easily concealed, they are readily moved from one country to another for the purpose of tax evasion, money laundering or to circumvent trade agreements. Virtually all of these diamonds eventually find their way into the legitimate trade. And all of these illicit transactions are made easier by the industry's long history of secrecy. Secrecy in the diamond industry is understandable for security reasons, but secrecy also obscures illicit behaviour.[11]

When asked how conflict diamonds enter the system, dealer after dealer told the Panel that it happens in the same way that illicit diamonds enter the system. Someone brings them to a trading centre—Israel or New York, for example—either smuggling them past customs or making a false declaration. Either way, they will find a buyer. Or, a dealer will go to Africa and buy them from rebels, or from a third or fourth party. He will then take them to Europe, Israel, or New York, and smuggle them past customs or make a false declaration.[12]

Diamonds have always lent themselves to theft and smuggling, and they have served a wide variety of interests as a ready alternative to both soft and hard currency. They are small; they have a high value-to-weight ratio; they keep their value. And they are completely unregulated. Most governments gave up long ago trying to tax diamond exports and imports in any meaningful way because diamonds have been virtually impossible to trace and to police.

Customs departments in most countries can call on technical expertise to examine and assess diamonds. With the exception of Belgium and Israel, however, no non-mining country has in-house diamond expertise in their customs departments, and in any case, there the main purpose is valuation, not identification. Diamonds have passed unhindered and mostly unchecked across U.S., Swiss, British, and other EU borders, the value and origin recorded by customs departments as they are presented by the importer. Licensing and other regulations have been stringent in some producing countries—South Africa, Botswana, Namibia, Russia—but elsewhere, especially in major consuming countries such as the U.S., there have been none. Anyone can buy and sell diamonds; values are rarely checked; there is no reconciliation between what a dealer buys and sells.

The Volume of Illicit Diamonds

Before dealing with the global volume of illicit diamonds, there is another terminological issue that needs clarification. Many of the statistics in this chapter relate to the diamond trade between various countries and Belgium. This is partly because, as noted, more than 80 percent of the world's rough diamonds pass through Antwerp in a year. But the main reason is that Belgium has until recently kept and published very good statistics on its diamond trade. Most other countries have not. Diamonds statistics are either kept under lock and key—as in Russia where diamonds are treated as a "strategic mineral"—or they are simply not published out of neglect or lack of interest. Where statistics *are* available, however, they may bear no relation to reciprocal statistics in other countries. For example, Canadian diamonds exported to Belgium under one customs code are recorded as arriving in Belgium under another, making it difficult and sometimes impossible to reconcile the trade figures.[13] On top of that, there is not much reliable information on what a particular mining country is capable of producing in a year, so anomalies between actual production and exports may be difficult to track. This was not so difficult in the case of Liberia, which was stated as the origin of an astonishing US$2.2 billion in rough diamonds arriving in Antwerp between 1994 and 1999. Until this "anomaly" was pointed out by Partnership Africa Canada, however, nobody did anything about it. (The UN Security Council finally banned all "Liberian" diamonds eighteen months later, in May 2001.) The Kimberley Process Certification Scheme (KPCS) for rough diamonds deals specifically with the issue of statistics, requiring all participating countries to post quarterly trade statistics and semi-annual production statistics. A year after the KPCS began in January 2003, however, not a single statistic had yet been made public.

This statistical fog is part of a further subterfuge in the diamond trade, which distinguishes between country of *origin* and country of *provenance*. "Country of origin" means the country in which a diamond was mined. "Country of provenance" means the country from which it was last shipped.

Customs departments are usually only interested in the latter, which means that origin can be obscured simply by moving diamonds through a third country, such as Switzerland or Dubai—or Liberia.

The next six tables calculate the difference in value between the actual export of rough diamonds from five West African countries and the value of imports from these countries declared by Belgian importers over a six-year period between 1994 and 1999.[14] All figures are in millions of U.S. dollars.

Table 6.2. Sierra Leone

	1994	1995	1996	1997	1998	1999
Official Exports from Sierra Leone	30.2	22	27.6	10.5	1.8	1.2
Declared Belgian Imports from Sierra Leone	106.6	15.3	93.4	114.9	65.8	30.4
Difference	76.4	-6.7	65.8	104.4	64	29.2

Table 6.3. Côte d'Ivoire

	1994	1995	1996	1997	1998	1999
Official Exports from Côte d'Ivoire	3.1	2.9	2.4	4	3.6	4.6
Declared Belgian Imports from Côte d'Ivoire	93.6	54.2	204.2	119.9	45.3	52.6
Difference	90.5	51.3	201.8	115.9	41.6	48.0

Table 6.4. Liberia

	1994	1995	1996	1997	1998	1999
Official Exports from Liberia	No data available because of civil war, although no official exports are likely to have occurred.				0.8	0.9
Declared Belgian Imports from Liberia	283.9	392.4	616.2	329.2	269.9	298.8
Difference	283.9	392.4	616.2	329.2	269.1	297.9

Table 6.5. Guinea

	1994	1995	1996	1997	1998	1999
Official Exports from Guinea	28.6	34.7	35.5	46.9	40.7	40.2
Declared Belgian Imports from Guinea	165.7	26.2	83.6	108.1	116.1	127.1
Difference	137.1	-8.5	48.1	61.2	75.4	86.9

Table 6.6. Gambia

	1994	1995	1996	1997	1998	1999
Official Exports from Gambia	0	0	0	0	0	0
Declared Belgian Imports from Gambia	74.1	14.9	128.1	131.4	103.4	58.0
Difference	74.1	14.9	128.1	131.4	103.4	58.0

Table 6.7. Summary
Excess of Belgian Diamond Imports over
West African Exports (US $1,000,000)

	1994	1995	1996	1997	1998	1999
Sierra Leone	76.4	-6.7	65.8	104.4	64	29.2
Côte d'Ivoire	90.5	51.3	201.8	115.9	41.6	48
Liberia	283.9	392.4	616.2	329.2	269.1	297.9
Guinea	137.1	-8.5	48.1	61.2	75.4	86.9
Gambia	74.1	14.9	128.1	131.4	103.4	58
Total	662	443.4	1060	742.1	553.5	520

The difference between official rough diamond exports from these five West African countries and imports into Belgium during the period 1994–1999 averaged about US$663 million per annum. None of the countries in question is a diamond-*importing* country; in other words, there is no officially sanctioned import of rough diamonds, so the issue of "provenance" versus "origin" does not arise. There is, for example, no reason to declare Liberia or Gambia as a country of provenance except to disguise the true origin of the goods. While some of the diamonds declared as Gambian may well have passed through Gambia, it is unlikely that the US$2.2 billion noted in Table 6.4 ever went anywhere near Liberia, one of the most unsettled and dangerous countries on earth during the years in question. It may be assumed, therefore, that all of these diamonds were one of two things: diamonds produced in the countries recorded by Belgian import authorities and not recorded as exports (i.e., smuggled out); or diamonds produced elsewhere and imported into Belgium under false declarations.

The former could be possible to a certain extent in the cases of Sierra Leone and Guinea, although it is unlikely in the case of Côte d'Ivoire, where known production is significantly less than what was said to be imported into Belgium. The second explanation is the most likely, and can be the only one in the cases of Gambia and Liberia. Liberian diamond production has never been significant in either volume or quality, and Gambia has no diamonds whatsoever. All the diamonds mentioned in Table 6.7, therefore, are illicit diamonds, representing approximately 10 percent of annual world production.

Additional estimates of illicit goods can be added to these:

- the CEO of the Angolan Selling Corporation (ASCorp) has said that between US$350 and US$420 million in smuggled goods left Angola in 2000, representing about 5 percent of world supply;[15]
- most Belgian imports from Congo Brazzaville, a country without diamonds of its own (US$2.2 billion between 1994 and 1999, or US$377 million per annum on average; US$116 million in 2000 and US$224 million in 2001). The 1994–1999 average represents a further 5 percent of world supply;
- US$200–$250 million worth of diamonds of "questionable origin" in 2001 from South Africa: mine thefts along with smuggled goods from Angola, the DRC, and elsewhere;[16]
- the direct imports of West African diamonds into Britain, Israel, the U.S., Hong Kong, the UAE, Switzerland, and elsewhere. While these are not significant and may be backed by legitimate export documentation, the numbers would have the effect of inflating the Belgian figures;
- theft from mines and from places further along the trading chain; estimates vary: 30 percent from Namibia's Namdeb in 1999; 2–3 percent of Botswana's US$2 billion annual production;[17]
- laundering through, and/or theft from, other producing countries: Angola, DRC, South Africa, Namibia, Central African Republic, Brazil, Ghana;

- laundering and/or theft in or through other significant trading, cutting, and polishing countries: Israel, India, Switzerland, Britain, the U.S.;
- laundering and/or theft through smaller conduit countries such as Portugal and Germany. As noted above, exports of rough diamonds from the UAE (Dubai) to Belgium have increased exponentially in recent years: from US$2.5 million in 1997 to US$149.5 million in 2001. Large increases have been recorded in shipments from the UAE to Israel as well. Hong Kong rough diamond exports to Belgium increased by 370 percent between 1997 and 2001.

In addition, there is a phenomenon in Russia, known in the diamond trade as "submarining." As much as one-third of Russia's US$1.6 billion worth of diamonds are sold within Russia to Russian cutters and polishers. Many of these diamonds cannot be processed economically in Russia, and the surplus is "exported," escaping official statistics and agreements. Another term for this phenomenon is "leakage." Because these diamonds are laundered under other labels, the leakage does not show up in import figures elsewhere as diamonds of Russian origin.[18] Another word that might be used is "illicit."

There is undoubtedly double counting in some of these figures, made inevitable by the secrecy surrounding diamond statistics. Some of the smuggled Angolan goods may be counted in the figures of Brazzaville or countries in West Africa, for example. But these figures, and the potential in countries for which there are no figures, suggest that an estimate of 20 percent of world trade as illicit is more than possible, and that it may actually be conservative.

Why is the level so high? The reasons are simple enough: the value, portability, and accessibility of diamonds; the inherent secrecy of the trade, lack of government controls, an absence of data for checking even the most rudimentary movement of diamonds within and between countries; little detection; and few penalties. These "reasons" represent the *opportunity*. The *motivation* in the past was predominantly tax evasion and money laundering, and this continues. As noted above, where money laundering is concerned, diamonds offer an attractive alternative to hard currency, often in short supply in Africa. More recently, however, there have also been links to drug money and organized crime.[19] At the far end of the spectrum, conflict diamonds are essentially illicit diamonds taken one step further—to pay for weapons in rebel wars. And there is growing evidence that they have been used to benefit a wider terrorist network. An al-Qaeda diamond connection was first reported by the *Washington Post* in November 2001 (and subsequently much pooh-poohed by the industry).[20] More recently, the UN monitoring group established to deal with the UN Security Council's Counter-Terrorism Resolution (S1373) has also noted the diamond connection, saying that all nations involved in the rough diamond trade should join the Kimberley Process.[21] And the U.S. General Accounting Office has repeatedly warned about the use of diamonds in terrorist financing.[22]

Conflict Diamonds

The stage was thus set for a new phenomenon, one that came to be known as "conflict diamonds" or "blood diamonds." Diamonds and war are not recent bedfellows. The Portuguese fueled their anti-independence wars in Africa with the proceeds from Angolan diamonds. The Amal faction in Lebanon's civil war was funded in part by subscriptions raised among Sierra Leone's diamond-trading Lebanese community. But it was the Angolan rebel movement, UNITA, that developed the concept with a vengeance, taking it to spectacular heights in the 1980s and 1990s. Charles Taylor, the Liberian warlord, financed the early stages of his rampage to power by selling timber. The market for tropical hardwood is lucrative, and once he secured the Port of Buchanan, he had both the supply and the means to export. But diamonds would be even more lucrative. Taylor backed Sierra Leone's fledgling Revolutionary United Front (RUF), giving them a base, weapons, and an outlet for whatever they could steal in Sierra Leone. The RUF trademark was chopping the hands and feet off civilians, often small children. As a terror technique, it was extremely effective in clearing the alluvial diamond fields, providing the RUF and Taylor with a highly rewarding money machine.

In the Democratic Republic of Congo, another kind of conflict diamond was being invented. There the conflict was silent at first, fueled by greed, apathy, and corruption at the top, and sustained by the rapacious appetite of foreign firms for anything the Congo had to offer, including diamonds. When Mobutu's regime collapsed under the weight of its own depravity, it was succeeded by something that was little better. Laurent Kabila's foreign allies, however, fell to squabbling over the spoils, and by the late 1990s the DRC barely existed as a country, and the armies of Zimbabwe, Uganda, and Rwanda picked over the spoils and exported copper, cobalt, coltan, and diamonds back to their capitals.

Those selling conflict diamonds did not need to invent routes, buyers, or systems. These had long been established by the illicit trade. Conflict diamonds are simply illicit diamonds taken to their logical extreme. They are illicit diamonds that have gone septic.

The Kimberley Process: A Moment of Sudden Change

Conflict diamonds were first brought to the world's attention late in 1998 by a small British NGO called Global Witness. Global Witness had been started only five years earlier by three dropouts from the environmental movement who had seen that environmental and human rights problems were complex and interrelated and that in order to solve them, the source of the problem needed to be addressed. They began to look at the role of resources in conflicts, which at that time very few people had examined. The first issue they tackled was timber exploitation in Cambodia, and in 1998 they turned their attention to the war in Angola and found that diamonds were fueling the UNITA war machine. UNITA, which had long before lost any moral or political justification for its twenty-year war effort and which had lost the Cold War rationale needed for its American backing, was funded now almost exclusively through the sale of diamonds. In a December 1998 report entitled *Rough Trade*, Global Witness reported that between 1992 and 1998, UNITA controlled between 60 and 70 percent of Angola's diamond production, generating US$3.7 billion to pay for its war effort. Half a million Angolans died and many more were displaced, their lives ruined.[23]

A year later, in January 2000, a Canadian NGO, Partnership Africa Canada (PAC), released its own report on diamonds: *The Heart of the Matter: Sierra Leone, Diamonds and Human Security*. That report told the story of Sierra Leone's Revolutionary United Front (RUF), a rebel movement devoid of ideology, without ethnic backing or claims to territory. Between them, Global Witness and Partnership Africa Canada had put the diamond industry on notice and had singled out the giant De Beers conglomerate for special attention.

In 1999, the Security Council Sanctions Committee on Angola, chaired by Canada's UN ambassador Robert Fowler, fielded an expert panel to examine the connection between diamonds and weapons, first exposed several months earlier by Global Witness. When they reported to the Security Council in March 2000, they also had the benefit of the PAC report. Unable to ignore what the NGOs had already shown, for the first time a UN report named sitting heads of government as accomplices in the breaking of UN sanctions. The presidents of Togo and Burkina Faso were named as both diamond and weapons traffickers.

Worried that growing NGO awareness and publicity might spiral out of control, the government of South Africa called a meeting of interested governments, NGOs, and the diamond industry in May 2000. The meeting, held in the town of Kimberley, where South African diamonds had been discovered 135 years before, was ground-breaking, not least because of the eclectic mix of NGOs, government officials, and leaders of the diamond industry. This was the beginning of what became known as the "Kimberley Process," and through the rest of that year and the next, it grappled with the issue of how to ensure greater probity in an unregulated industry and how to end the phenomenon of conflict diamonds. The wider diamond industry joined the process and in July 2000 created a "World Diamond Council," which proposed a "chain of warranties" for rough diamonds as they moved from one dealer to another. De Beers and virtually every diamond bourse from Antwerp to Mumbai threatened to cut off any of its members caught dealing in conflict diamonds.

There were thirteen meetings of the Kimberley Process between May 2000 and November 2002, when an agreement was finally reached. The meetings were detailed, often tense, but always reasonably open. Industry representatives and NGOs participated on an equal footing with government delegations. In the end, the most contentious issues related to statistics and WTO compatibility. For some delegations, diamond statistics had been raised to the level of a state secret, but it was understood that without good production and trade data, no control mechanism could hope to succeed. It was finally agreed that quarterly trade statistics would be produced by all participating countries and semi-annual production statistics would be produced by all mining countries, both sets of statistics to be compiled within two months of the end of the reference period.

The Kimberley Process Agreement on Monitoring: New Regulatory Space?

Throughout the Kimberley Process meetings, the debate on monitoring was long and heated. Invariably, there were two sides to the issue. NGOs argued for regular, credible, independent monitoring of all national control systems for rough diamonds. Without this as the ultimate test, all systems would be suspect. Most of the governments that spoke on the issue, however, rejected the concept outright. Many others remained silent or said that "the time is not right." The text emerging from the final November 2002 meeting at Interlaken left monitoring to the discretion of the entire membership of the Kimberley Process at plenary meetings, to be triggered only by extraordinary need:

- "Participants at Plenary meetings, upon recommendation by the Chair, *can* decide on additional verification measures";
- "These *could* include . . . review missions by other Participants or their

representatives *where there are credible indications of significant non-compliance* with the international certification scheme";

- Review missions are to be conducted in an analytical, expert and impartial manner with the consent of the Participant concerned. The size, composition, terms of reference and time-frame of these mission should be based on the circumstances and be established by the Chair with the consent of the Participant concerned *and in consultation with all Participants*.[24]

As the assembled governments agreed on this hesitant wording, there were already "credible indications" that a wide variety of countries would be in "significant non-compliance" if permitted to join. Membership would be open to "all applicants willing and able to fulfill the requirements of the scheme"—in order to avoid a WTO challenge—but there was no mechanism established—short of a full plenary debate—to determine whether an applicant actually *is* able "to fulfill the requirements of the scheme." Membership criteria, however, tightened up during 2003, and several countries were removed from membership until they could demonstrate that they had appropriate laws in place to reflect agreed minimum standards in the system. Monitoring, too, advanced somewhat, with an agreement at the end of 2003 that participating countries might "volunteer" for review missions. But this fell considerably short of regular independent monitoring for all participating countries.

Some national systems will rely for much of their national diamond oversight on the proposed "chain of warranties" to be devised by the World Diamond Council, presumably in conjunction with interested governments. The World Diamond Council proposal will be underpinned by independent auditing and penalties for non-compliance, but—critically—it will be voluntary. And the World Diamond Council by no means represents all companies involved in the diamond trade.

In creating their World Diamond Council and describing their proposal for a certification system, the World Federation of Diamond Bourses and the International Diamond Manufacturers Association said in July 2000 that the "[k]ey to the whole process is monitoring."[25] The December 2001 United Nations General Assembly Resolution on conflict diamonds described a system which included the "need for transparency."[26] On July 23, 2000, the G8 Heads of Government Meeting in Okinawa, Japan, issued a communiqué which said, *inter alia*, "we have agreed to . . . implement measures to prevent conflict, including by addressing the issue of illicit trade in diamonds." Two years later, the G8 meeting in June 2002 stated in its *G8 Africa Action Plan*, "We are determined to make conflict prevention and resolution a top priority, and therefore we commit to . . . working with African governments, civil society and others to address the linkage between armed conflict and the exploitation of natural resources—including by . . . supporting voluntary control efforts such as the Kimberley Process for diamonds, and . . . *working to ensure better accountability and greater transparency with respect to those involved in the import or export of Africa's natural resources from areas of conflict.*"[27]

The Kimberley Process arrangements mock all these resolutions on monitoring and transparency. In fact the Kimberley Process wording on transparency is as follows: "Participants and observers should make every effort to observe strict confidentiality regarding the issue and the discussions relating to any compliance matter."[28]

The U.S. General Accounting Office, the investigative arm of the United States Congress, reviewed the Kimberley Process agreement in June 2002 and found it seriously deficient in the area of monitoring. "Even acknowledging sovereignty and data sensitivity constraints, the Kimberley Process scheme's monitoring mechanisms still lack rigor. . . . The scheme risks the appearance of control while still allowing conflict diamonds to enter the legitimate diamond trade and, as a result, continue to fuel conflict."[29]

The Kimberley Process international diamond certification scheme began officially on January 1, 2003, with more than fifty governments participating. The initial startup period was bumpy, and the issue of regular independent monitoring remained a matter of unfinished business for the NGO participants. But a significant international agreement had been achieved in relatively short order. Why did governments and industry move so far and so fast? It was in part because the impact of the illicit nature of the diamond industry had become so catastrophic that something had to be done. The inordinate death and destruction, and the concomitant cost in relief programs and UN peacekeeping missions, finally pushed the issue to the top of the Security Council agenda. Without the NGO research, publicity, and campaigning, however, it is questionable whether anything would have changed. It was the industry's fear of an NGO swarming, akin to the fur embargo of previous years, that provided the real impetus to move. By the end of 2001, the issue of "blood diamonds" had been aired by every television newsmagazine from Tokyo to London, every major consumer magazine from *Esquire* to *Vanity Fair* and the *National Geographic*. The story was featured regularly in the *New York Times*, the *Financial Times, Bloomberg News*, and CNN.

Why then have governments been so reluctant to move further on monitoring? Three reasons have been given, with different emphasis placed on them by different parties. The first is cost; the second is commercial confidentiality; the third is national sovereignty. The cost argument is disingenuous. The diamond industry already spends considerable sums to protect its interests. De Beers, for example, spends US$4 million a year on a Gem Defensive Program aimed at keeping synthetic diamonds out of the normal trade. If there were a levy on rough diamond transfers of one-tenth of 1 percent of a shipment's value, it would yield more than US$75 million a year—four times as much as the newly agreed Aviation Security Plan of Action and many times more than would be required for a respectable diamond monitoring system. Such a levy would add one-seventh of 1 percent to the cost of a diamond ring, or 75 cents to the cost of a US$500 luxury item, no great burden.[30]

The issue of commercial confidentiality arose frequently at Kimberley Process meetings. However, some of the same governments that worried about the possibility of breaking WTO regulations on free trade also defended monopolistic diamond industry practices, secrecy, and single-company dominance of trade in one country or another. That aside, monitoring is no more about publicizing commercial confidentialities than standard financial auditing is. All commercial firms are independently audited, and commercially sensitive information is protected. If the same cannot be done where diamonds are concerned, governments are essentially condoning the secrecy that has been used to hide and foster serious crimes against humanity. In any case, Kimberley Process monitoring should be about the effectiveness of systems, not the commercial confidentialities of legitimate business.

One Kimberley Process delegation leader said that there is no compulsory international monitoring mechanism in any agreement, so why now for diamonds? This is incorrect. The word "compulsory" does not exist anywhere in the Kimberley agreement. The entire agreement is voluntary, as are all its provisions. There are, or should be, penalties associated with failure to meet them. These may be costly, but any country is free to join or not join. If a country joins, it must observe the rules. If the rules include certificates, it must issue certificates. This is not an infringement of national sovereignty. It is part of the cost of doing business in the diamond trade. It is agreed to voluntarily. Regular independent monitoring can likewise be voluntarily agreed to. In the end, of course, no force on earth can compel a country to accept a monitoring mission if it refuses. But there would, and should, be consequences.

There were two additional and largely unspoken reasons for the resistance. The first was political. Russia and China said they would simply not accept independent monitoring—for the reasons given above. Other governments might well have pushed for independent monitoring but may have believed that it made more sense to get a tepid agreement which included Russia and China than a strong agreement without them. Hence the suggestion from some that "the time is not right."

The other unspoken reason has to do with the much larger issue of illicit diamonds. Some governments participating in the Kimberley Process have actively colluded with elements of the illicit trade. With effective monitoring, this would be exposed, and the benefits that flow from it would have to stop. Other governments may be concerned that an effective regulatory system would simply drive the business and the jobs it creates away from their bourses and cutting factories to those in countries that are less regulated. Belgium complains of losing business to Israel. Israel complains of losing business to India. China, Thailand, and Hong Kong are growing. And so on.

Whatever the reasons, a truly effective Kimberley Process would have a major impact on the illicit diamond trade. It would curb conflict diamonds, but it would also make major inroads into that part of the industry that has been used for money laundering, tax evasion, and worse.

When the global Kimberley Process system became effective on January 1, 2003, it became appreciably more difficult to launder illicit diamonds. All rough diamonds required a government export or re-export certificate, guaranteeing the origin and cleanliness of the goods. But many of the countries that were accepted into the system without demur had been laundering illicit and conflict diamonds for years. The addition of some new paperwork into the system was unlikely in the end to make a great deal of difference.

NGOs involved in the process vowed to continue pressing on the issue. The test in the months ahead will be the resolve of the governments that have the most to gain from a clean industry—Belgium, South Africa, Namibia, Botswana, Israel, India, Russia, Canada. And it will depend to a large extent upon the tradeoffs the diamond industry itself is willing to make—between what could be a difficult cleanup and a decline into further criminality and disrepute.

Epilogue

Many of the fears described in this chapter proved to be unfounded. The voluntary monitoring arrangement grew teeth during 2004. More than a dozen participating countries invited reviews. Teams, usually comprising representatives from three other governments, someone from the industry, and someone representing NGOs, carried out detailed compliance studies. The Republic of Congo (Brazzaville) was expelled from the Kimberley Process following a review which found that it could not account for the mining or importation of the diamonds it had been exporting. A dozen more reviews were planned for 2005, and only a small number of countries remained aloof from the process.

Statistics remained a problem and the subject of much debate. While countries such as Russia overcame their legal and commercial restraints, others refused or were unable to submit meaningful data. As of mid-2005, this remained one of the thorniest issues in Kimberley Process compliance.

By then, however, the diamond-fueled wars the Kimberley Process had sought to affect had ended. Sierra Leone, which had officially exported only a handful of diamonds in 1999, exported US$126 million worth in 2004, and the Democratic Republic of the Congo had its best year ever for diamond exports. Both governments acknowledged the Kimberley Process as a major contributor to the legalization of their diamond industries. The challenge for them now, and for the diamond industry at large, will be to ensure that the Kimberley Process can serve as prevention as well as cure and that diamonds can become an engine of growth and development rather than a resource for predators.

NOTES

1. These scenarios are completely authentic. The final scenario describes conditions prevailing until the end of the war in Sierra Leone in January 2002. Names have been changed.

2. Kevin Krajick, *Barren Lands* (New York: Times Books, 2001), 13.

3. Sharon Berger, "Congo Signs $700m Agreement with IDI Diamonds," *Jerusalem Post*, August 2, 2000.

4. Christian Dietrich, "Have African-based Diamond Monopolies Been Effective?" *Central Africa Minerals and Arms Research Bulletin* 2 (June 2001), available at http://www.diamondstudies.com/docs/online.html.

5. For a complete discussion of diamonds in Central Africa, see Christian Dietrich, *Hard Currency: The Criminalized Diamond Economy of the Democratic Republic of the Congo and Its Neighbours* (Ottawa: Partnership Africa Canada, June 2002).

6. Figures from the Diamond High Council, Antwerp, and *Diamond Intelligence Briefs*, Tel Aviv.

7. Global Witness, *A Rough Trade: The Role of Companies and Governments in the Angolan Conflict* (London: Global Witness, December 1998); Ian Smillie, L. Gberie, and R. Hazleton, *The Heart of the Matter: Sierra Leone, Diamonds and Human Security* (Ottawa: Partnership Africa Canada, 2000).

8. Kimberley Process, "Essential Elements of an International Scheme of Certification for Rough Diamonds," Kimberley Process Working Document no. 1/2002, March 20, 2002.

9. A. M. Coxon, untitled paper (De Beers, March 2000).

10. UN Security Council, Report S/2001/363 (New York: United Nations, April 18, 2001), para. 54.

11. United Nations, *Report of the Panel of Experts Appointed Pursuant to UN Security Council Resolution 1306 (2000), Paragraph 19 in Relation to Sierra Leone* (New York: United Nations, December 2000), 28.

12. United Nations, *Report of the Panel of Experts Appointed Pursuant to UN Security Council Resolution 1306*, 28.

13. For a discussion of this problem, see Ian Smillie, *Fire in the Ice: Benefits, Protection and Regulation in the Canadian Diamond Industry* (Ottawa: Partnership Africa Canada, 2002).

14. All figures have been produced by the governments of the countries in question, although only those for Belgium are currently in the public domain.

15. UN Security Council, S/2001/966 (New York: United Nations, October 12, 2001), para. 141.

16. "Diamond Pipeline 2001," *Mazal U'Bracha* 146 (June 2002).

17. Matthew Hart, *Diamond: A Journey to the Heart of an Obsession* (New York: Viking, 2001), 159–181.

18. Details of various Russian diamond frauds are contained in Hart, *Diamond: A Journey to the Heart of Obsession.*

19. Ian Smillie, L. Gberie, and R. Hazleton, *The Heart of the Matter*, 44–47; United Nations, Report S/2000/1195 (New York: United Nations, 2000), 32–40.

20. Douglas Farah, "Al Qaeda Cash Tied to Diamond Trade," *Washington Post*, November 2, 2001.

21. "Al-Qaeda terrorist operatives diversifying finances, UN Expert Panel Warns," *UN News Center*, New York, May 22, 2002.

22. U.S. General Accounting Office, *International Trade: Critical Issues Remain in Deterring Conflict Diamond Trade*, GAO-02-678 (Washington, D.C.: U.S. General Accounting Office, June 2002); U.S. General Accounting Office, *Terrorist Financing: US Agencies Should Systematically Assess Terrorists' Use of Alternative Financing Mechanisms*, GAO-04-163 (Washington, D.C.: U.S. General Accounting Office, November 2003).

23. Global Witness, *A Rough Trade*, 3.

24. Emphasis added.

25. World Federation of Diamond Bourses and International Diamond Manufacturers Association, Joint Resolution (Antwerp, July 19, 2000).

26. UN General Assembly, Resolution A/RES/55/56 (New York: United Nations, December 1, 2000).

27. G8 Heads of Government, "G8 Action Plan for Africa" (statement presented at G8 heads of government meeting, Kananaskis, Alberta, June 27, 2002).

28. Kimberley Process, "Essential Elements of an International Scheme of Certification For Rough Diamonds," Section VI, para. 15.

29. U.S. General Accounting Office, *International Trade: Critical Issues*, 21.

30. US$7.9 billion in rough diamond production in 2001 was converted into US$54.1 billion in diamond jewelry. A 0.1 percent levy on US$7.9 billion would represent, on average, a 0.15 percent levy on finished goods. US$500 x 0.15 percent = US$0.75.

seven

Small Arms, Cattle Raiding, and Borderlands

The Ilemi Triangle

Kenneth I. Simala and Maurice Amutabi

In this chapter we offer an analysis of how, in the border region adjoining Kenya, Ethiopia, Uganda, and Sudan, an area known as the "Ilemi Triangle," communal regulation broke down in the face of an upsurge in violence. Our primary focus is on the tensions between traditional authority and state power and on the transformation of cattle raiding among pastoral communities in this region, closely related to illegal cross-border traffic in small arms. We show how changes in this seemingly remote area are directly related to global events and how cattle raiding, once a culturally defined reciprocal activity among pastoralists, has been transformed into an uncontrollable, technologically sophisticated, and highly violent practice.

There are a variety of reasons why conflict among pastoralists in the Ilemi Triangle has recently taken on new and more violent dimensions. Incessant droughts have led to the death of livestock and reduced the availability of pasture and water. More sophisticated weaponry has added to the problem. Moreover, the demand for livestock has increased because of the existence of rebel encampments in Sudan, Ethiopia, and Uganda. Thus, a shrinking resource base, new technologies of violence, and new demands for livestock have provoked desperate struggles for survival among the pastoralists living in this borderland.

Traditionally, pastoralist customs, especially the requirement that young men have to provide dowry in the form of livestock, accounted for the practice of mutual cattle rustling. Former president Daniel Arap Moi of Kenya, who comes from a pastoralist community, has noted, "Traditionally, cattle rustling did not involve killing people."[1] In the past, rustled livestock replenished lost herds following drought or major outbreaks of disease. If elders from neighboring communities identified stolen herds, the matter was usually discussed jointly and livestock returned. This is no longer the case; reciprocity has been replaced by merciless plunder orchestrated by hired goons. A significant proportion of our interviewees were unanimous that cattle rustling did not explode in its present violent form until the 1970s.[2] Today the practice has evolved into novel forms that are better described as banditry and commercial raiding.

Small arms (and light weapons) have become so commonplace in eastern Africa today that some villages are better equipped with the latest weaponry and military hardware than local state security personnel. Further, these communities' nomadic lifestyles and relative lack of fixed assets have resulted in weak attachments to nations and states. Not surprisingly, despite increased state surveillance and policing in the region, trafficking in arms goes on unabated. As a result, the region is full of permanent and potential war zones.

On May 11, 2001, the *Daily Nation* carried a feature article on Baragoi, a pastoralist area close to the Kenya-Ethiopia border. Because of banditry, the area is one of the most dangerous in the country; the newspaper article described it as "Kenya's Kosovo." Baragoi is just a few kilometers from the Suguta Valley, an area that Kenya's security personnel and local people fear and dread because of its treacherous terrain and unbearable temperatures and humidity. The Suguta Valley is a nightmare for Kenya's security personnel and a haven for livestock thieves and bandits from Ethiopia, Kenya, and Sudan. "Even children know this. They welcome visitors chanting: 'Welcome to Kosovo! Baragoi is Kosovo!'"[3] In 1996, bandits in this region blew to smithereens a helicopter carrying senior Kenyan government officials together with the district commissioner of Samburu.[4]

The use of sophisticated weapons in cattle rustling has become more frequent than ever before in eastern Africa's history, and cattle rustling has turned into interethnic warfare. In the past decade, there have been constant clashes between various peoples in the Ilemi Triangle, especially the Nyangatom, Merille, Pokot, Toposa, and Karimojong. These incessant conflicts (e.g., between the Turkana and Pokot in Kenya, or the Sebei, Karimojong, and Iteso in Uganda) have resulted in numerous deaths and thefts of livestock.[5] The governments of the various adjoining countries, except Sudan, have responded by launching military operations aimed at containing the violence, without much success.

Commercial raiding has been brought about by a greatly expanded demand for meat by various rebel groups and combatants. Among them are warring factions in Somalia, the Oromo Liberation Front (OLF) in southern Ethiopia, Pokot livestock raiders in northern Kenya, the Sudan People's Liberation Movement/Army (SPLM/A), and rebels of the Lord's Resistance Army (LRA) in northern Uganda. Having depleted the area of its edible wild animals, rebel groups have turned to livestock as the only readily available food source; as a result their neighbors have been forced to build up their own military arsenal to survive. Warlords, professional raiders, rebel groups, belligerent youths, and egocentric vagabonds have appeared as violent protagonists in the pastoralist environment, causing many social and economic upheavals in the Triangle.

Violence in the Ilemi Triangle has been described variously as clan and ethnic skirmishes, raiding, banditry, cattle rustling, and warfare. The availability of small arms has introduced a new twist to the conflicts: armed pastoralists from the Triangle now terrorize non-pastoralists outside the pastoralist ranges. Non-pastoralists feel compelled to protect themselves by acquiring arms, leading to an escalation of violence.[6] Preliminary research done in Samburu indicates that the Samburu pastoralists began to arm themselves after being raided repeatedly by Turkana herdsmen. They claim that their arms are obtained from Pokot district in Kenya, SPLM/A camps in Sudan, Karamoja in Uganda, and Somalia.[7] Arms in Pokot are likely to be from Ugandan and Sudanese sources, but some arms also come from Isiolo via Somalia.[8] The Ilemi Triangle acts as the channel through which arms move across the pastoralist corridor that runs from Djibouti through Somalia, Ethiopia, and Kenya to Sudan and Uganda.

The scale of the arms trade, and the resulting violence, is constantly increasing. In the past ten years there has been a clear rise in the number of casualties from armed raids and the amount of livestock commandeered by armed raiders. State security forces have increasingly lost battles with raiders whenever the two sides have confronted each other militarily. Despite increased militarization in the Ilemi Triangle, nobody knows for sure the number of illegal arms in circulation here. To complicate matters, the Triangle is both a transit point and a market for small arms. At certain times of the year, and depending on various activities in other parts of the region, the Triangle handles hundreds of arms a day. This is particularly so during periods of drought when many pastoralists, seeking to replenish emaciated stocks, intensify their raiding. During ethnic conflicts and in preparation for cross-border livestock raids, thousands of arms are collected. At other times, especially during the rainy season when movement becomes difficult due to impassable roads, the circulation of arms and people is impeded. Conservative estimates have put the number of small arms in the Triangle at about one million. Our estimate, based on our own calculations, observations, and interviews, is higher: between 1.4 to 2 million.[9]

Borders and Borderlands in Eastern Africa

Little of the existing scholarly literature addresses borderland situations in Africa in concrete ways.[10] This is reflected in the inadequacy of formulations by Adeyoyin, who describes borderlands as "regions lying along and across the boundary separating one country from another,"[11] and Hansen, who sees them as "sub-national areas whose economic and social life are directly and significantly affected by proximity to an international boundary."[12] It has been argued that Africa no longer has traditional frontiers (areas outside national boundaries and not fully occupied by states), although it may be more accurate to note that there are "new" frontiers in eastern Africa, where governments with territorial claims over borderlands do not in fact have full control over them. Here government forces are permanently engaged in wars of attrition with bands of "warlords" and "bandits" for the control of these areas. Like most post-colonial areas, many African boundaries are clearly artificial and arbitrary. In the recent past, African elites have retained these colonial boundaries to exploit their citizens and to exercise political, economic, and fiscal policies over a given territory.[13] Those at the bottom of the exploitative hierarchy, such as those in borderlands, know this, hence their indifference to national issues.

In the Ilemi Triangle, the various ethnic groups share a sense of community with others across the border. These borderland citizens have not been co-opted into the national scheme of things. The national governments in Nairobi, Kampala, Addis Ababa, and Khartoum have relied excessively on control through state agencies and customs and immigration personnel, and they have allocated few resources to borderland development. Borderland citizens find ethnic and ancestral links far more meaningful than the political sovereignty of states. In other words, cross-border ethnic groups that share certain cultural aspects and understand each other's language feel greater closeness to their kin across the border than to fellow citizens within the artificial confines of official state territory. This complicates border problems in eastern Africa. We agree with Momoh when he says that boundaries in Africa and elsewhere are not only artificial but also arbitrary creations.[14]

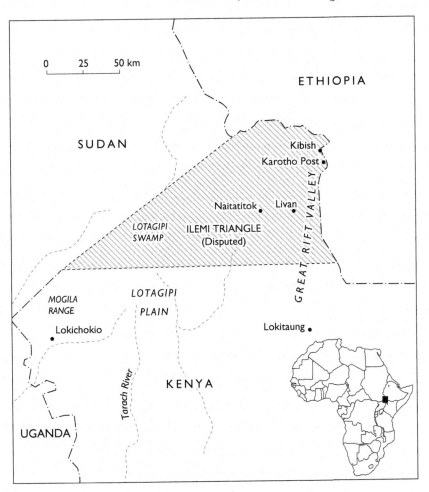

FIG 7.1. The Ilemi Triangle. Map by Bill Nelson.

Borders in Africa are porous, poorly policed, hated as irritatingly confining by ordinary citizens, and considered almost irrelevant to daily life.
Consequently, they serve not as boundaries but as interstate pathways, con-
duits for moving goods and movement of people, especially extra-legal ones.
In eastern Africa, the identical cultural environment prevailing on either
side of the colonial-imposed international borders provides a general cover
under which clandestine activities take place. Being strategically located
between Uganda, Kenya, Sudan, and Ethiopia, the Ilemi Triangle witnesses
these types of activities daily.

The Ilemi Triangle, Pastoralism, and State Policies

The Ilemi Triangle[15] lies at the intersection of the borders of Kenya, Uganda, Ethiopia, and Sudan. The region has permanent pasture as a result of rivers such as the Tarach that pour their waters into the Lotagipi Swamp in the Triangle. For this reason, colonial authorities, keen to minimize conflict between the pastoralists in the area, carved the Triangle out as a neutral buffer zone to reduce warring and rustling activities among cattle-keeping ethnic groups. Thus, the Toposa (Sudan), the Merile, Nyangatom, and Hamar (Ethiopia), and the Turkana (Kenya) were entitled to graze and water their livestock in the Triangle during times of extreme drought. This was under the supervision of the British authorities in Kenya.

It is estimated that some 500 to 600 million people live in the arid and semi-arid parts of the world and that some 30 to 40 million of them depend entirely on animals. Of these 30 to 40 million people, 50 to 60 percent are found in Africa. The Horn of Africa "is home to the largest remaining aggregation of traditional livestock producers in the world."[16] It also has the highest proportion of pastoralists in the world; Sudan has the highest percentage in the world, while Ethiopia ranks fifth. In Kenya, pastoralists occupy three quarters of the national land space and Uganda has significant numbers of pastoralists, prominent among them the Karimojong and Jie.[17] In typically pastoralist areas such as Karamoja in Uganda, Turkana in Kenya, Toposa in Sudan, and Merille in Ethiopia, as much as 80 percent of cash income is generated from livestock.[18] In Kenya, semi-arid and arid land constitutes 439,000 square kilometers, covering fourteen districts,[19] or 80 percent of Kenya's total land area.[20] This area supports 25 percent of Kenya's population and half its livestock.

The Ilemi Triangle and its surrounding areas are therefore home to one of the largest pastoralist economies in Africa. The incredibly rugged terrain, punishing climate, extreme temperatures, vegetation with needle-sharp thorns, rattlesnakes, centipedes, scorpions, and other wild creatures and animals typical of this entire region makes nonsense of international border demarcations. This makes policing pastoralist regions extremely difficult; not surprisingly, pastoralist border areas are more porous than other border areas.

During droughts, the Ilemi Triangle often provides sanctuary to pastoralists. The resident population then comes into conflict with transient populations over grazing rights, even though some of the transient populations (such as the Jie and Toposa) often only want to move across the Triangle to areas such as the Omo Valley in Ethiopia. Despite its natural endowments, the Ilemi Triangle is actually often the last resort for roaming pastoralists fleeing drought because it is so insecure and lacks government control and arbitration. The Triangle has a high concentration of arms, which makes raiding easy. Raided cattle are difficult to retrieve because they can easily be sneaked across international borders. Hence many pastoral groups avoid the Triangle until there is no other option open to them.[21] When such groups are raided and lose animals in the Triangle, they often become destitute and rarely recover economically. This is one factor that accounts for the large numbers of refugees and displaced and poor people from various countries who now live in the Triangle's urban areas.

In interviewing a wide range of elderly informants and examining government archives, we found that the Ilemi Triangle suffers from gross neglect and inappropriate government development policies stretching back into the colonial past. Policies pursued by successive colonial and postcolonial governments in Sudan, Uganda, and Kenya, as well as misguided actions by imperial Ethiopia, have tended not only to neglect the needs of pastoralists but also often to harm pastoralist interests and aspirations. The net effect of these policies, which were biased toward agriculturalists and modern rangers, have added to the problems and insecurities of pastoralist communities in the Triangle, particularly regarding access to water and pasture.

Colonial officials rarely appreciated the dynamics of land tenure and use in Africa and set into place policies that account for some of the problems encountered by pastoralists today. Sir Charles Elliot, a colonial commissioner of the East African Protectorate (later Kenya), had no reservations about displacing pastoralists from their traditional lands: "I cannot admit that wandering tribes have a right to keep other superior races out of large tracts of land merely because they have acquired the habit of struggling over more land than they can utilize."[22] The same official attitude obtained in Sudan and Uganda. It was the colonial policy to confine pastoralists in native reserves while colonial authorities appropriated much of their free-range space for other purposes. Throughout the colonial period, governments intervened in pastoral societies and economies to try to remedy problems by setting up commissions to advise on better—i.e., more efficient—ways of utilizing land. Before intervention by colonial officials, traditional practices allowed pastoralists to hold back their animals from wetter areas so as to keep the grass in reserve for the dry season. Many interviewees, such as Lekilam Sotie and Okuan Lupa, told us that the well-watered Ilemi Triangle was historically considered the refuge of last resort.[23]

Post-colonial governments have followed a similar approach. Policy planners and development activists assumed that part of the solution to the problem of arid and semi-arid lands was to dig wells and develop boreholes. But this exacerbated environmental damage to such an extent that the water table and pastoralists' ecosystems were damaged forever. In an oral interview, Ewalam Lokolak, eighty-three years old, noted that he had witnessed the drying up of literally hundreds of boreholes in the areas around Lokitaung in his lifetime, a fact confirmed by government officials and extension workers working in the area.[24] Some of the boreholes were sunk in fossil water, which could not be replenished, leading to the drying up of these wells forever. In other areas, the water table has been sinking, making it necessary to sink deeper and deeper wells and boreholes. The lack of water would in turn drive migration to new areas where water was still available.

Other state policies also affected pastoralists negatively. Policies aimed at animal improvement were accepted by pastoralists but led to dramatic increases in the numbers of animals, which exacerbated the problem of overgrazing. Policies directed toward changing pastoralist behavior in favor of agriculture or seeking to turn roaming herdsmen into town dwellers also failed. This was because arid and semi-arid areas were well suited to pastoralism as an economic activity and few other alternatives could succeed. This has led to a rise in numbers of internal refugees, victims not only of ill-conceived government policies in the past, but also prevented from re-entering their old way of life because of displacement and current state policies.[25]

Little wonder, then, that modern states, both colonial and post-colonial, are hardly popular with pastoralists in the Ilemi Triangle. Musa Ekuro felt that the governments across the region were not doing enough for pastoralists. Like many interviewees we spoke with, he believed that governments were interested only in collecting levies at markets and instituting taxes, but were otherwise absent most of the time. When reminded about the system of chiefs and assistant chiefs (in Kenya), he retorted, "We have never seen the government here. Show me, where it is?"[26] However, it is at the level of policy that one comes face to face with the greatest mistreatment of pastoralists by governments in the region.

In Kenya, the most recent changes in policy occurred in the 1990s and assumed that linking privatization, land registration, and titling with the provision of credit would lead to a "take-off" for pastoral development. The basic assumption was that individual control of land and resources would lead to more efficient production.[27] These policies were flawed from the very outset because they were derived from the belief that indig-

enous tenure systems impeded productivity and development. They took
no cognizance of the native population's indigenous knowledge systems,
their understanding of local conditions, or their practical solutions to herd
management. Privatization of land is not only ecologically inappropriate
but also antithetical to the pastoral nomadic way of life. Imposed individualization has led to factionalism and rivalries, leading to an increased use
of violence to gain access to water, pasture, and livestock. Development
policies undermined traditional systems of regulation without providing
viable alternatives.

The Decline of Traditional Authority

Fred Ejore, a Turkana elder, speaks three of the major languages spoken
on the fringes of the Ilemi Triangle besides his own indigenous Turkana:
Karimojong, Toposa, and Nyangatom. He pointed out that it was the jostl-
ing for the resources of the Triangle by the governments of Kenya, Uganda,
Sudan, and Ethiopia that had led the people in the Triangle not only to
become antagonistic toward each other but also to feel isolated and peripheralized. He insisted that many of the problems faced by pastoralists in the
Triangle today should be understood as colonial and post-colonial legacies.

> We have been told that we lived as happy people before the colonial powers
> came and told us that we are different. Many Toposa, Karimojong and some
> Atekur understand my language when I speak. I also understand when they
> speak. We have the same culture. We even intermarry. But [now] we are
> told that we are Kenyan, Ugandan, Sudanese, and Ethiopian, and this just
> causes a lot of hatred. I believe that we should all share the water, the graz-
> ing areas, and even land, but the problem is that the government soldiers
> from our countries think that we are always looking for ways of fighting
> each other. I am not bitter with anybody for having lost all my herds. Even if
> "Anyanya" [the Sudan People's Liberation Army (SPLA)] did not take them,
> maybe drought would have killed them. What I want is that we should not
> kill each other because of livestock. These people are even killing women
> and children and old men like me. The colonizer gave the *bunduki* [small
> arms] that they are using, right? He started all these problems. How many
> people can a spear kill? Even "Anyanya" would not kill many people if they
> used spears.[28]

Historically, it was elders who were responsible for the governance of the
community in pastoralist societies. Pastoralist communities had structures
for conflict resolution through councils of elders, traditional courts, and
peer- or age-group supervision, where each individual or group had to meet
certain social and cultural expectations. In Uganda among the Karimo-

jong, elders made important decisions through collective discussions and debates and solved communal conflicts.[29] In Ethiopia among the Oromo, and in Kenya among the Boran (the two are cousins and share similar structures), the village council and *Aba-Olla* (village head) had far-reaching political, social, and economic functions. The *Aba-Olla* was responsible, *inter alia*, for maintaining peace and order, for resolving disputes, for representing the village at meetings, for grazing and water management, and for reporting back to village households.[30] There were well-defined systems of utilization of the grazing areas through well-known migration routes and norms of access to pasture land and watering points. When there was a breakdown in these norms, groups negotiated peacefully.

Declining pastoralist authority structures account for some of the problems confronting pastoralists in the Triangle today. Pre-colonial coping strategies were an integral component of the pastoralists' socioeconomic system and included leaving land fallow, splitting families to better manage family herds, loaning and pooling resources, group herding, collective migration, and trade ties with businessmen.[31] These strategies were based essentially on the premise that a variety of resources were needed to provide access to pasture and water at different times of the year and particularly during periods of drought. Government policies, from the colonial to the post-colonial period, have consistently sought to alter, rather than build upon, pastoral production and coping systems. The failure to appreciate the logic of pastoral life has meant that development objectives have been defined on the basis of presumptuous and erroneous assumptions. These policies have been implemented with little regard to pastoralists' needs and have disrupted pastoral economies and traditional coping mechanisms. As a result, these mechanisms can no longer be relied upon to resolve conflicts in the region. They have been replaced by other power structures. Elders have lost their authority to leaders of raiding bands who have access to money and tools of violence such as sophisticated arms. As Tilam Lokwel, ninety, put it eloquently:

> When we were young, we respected our elders. Now we usually carry our own stools but this was done for elders in the past. A young man would carry his grandfather's seat for him. Nowadays things are different. When I came, did you see them giving me a seat? No. Things have changed very much. These young people no longer respect age. That is why they will continue killing each other. They even kill women and children. We never wanted to kill humans, leave alone women and children. Women and children were never killed in our days as youths do nowadays. Do women and children have spears, bows and arrows to defend themselves? No. Then why kill them? You see what I mean? We respected elders. We waited for elders to

give us the nod to marry. All my sons have married; all of them obeyed our choice of wife and decision for them. The elders gave us the cattle to give as dowry in marriage and we were obedient. Nowadays those who have arms are the ones who own many cattle. Sons steal and rob cattle from fathers. Brothers steal cattle from each other. The children of these days have no manners. They are killers. Those days when we were still warriors [young] we went far to raid for cattle. Elders knew where to get them. To be an elder was respectable. Elders were the wealthiest and most visible members of the family. But this is not the case any more. One of my grandsons has more cattle than I. Those days, if you disobeyed an elder, the clan punished you, and you agreed with them. You could not escape the verdict of elders. The elders had so much power that we really envied them and always hoped one day to become elders ourselves. We are now elders only in name, without wealth and power.[32]

The Transformation of Livestock Raiding

Traditionally, raiding among pastoralists was a social function and a cultural enterprise carried out by youths under the direction of elders. Raiding was used only to replenish depleted herds after extended drought or in the aftermath of a major outbreaks of disease. Following these catastrophes, pastoralists often negotiated for seed stock (live cattle loans) from their neighbors which they paid back after reaching herd stability. Raiding was a last resort when the loaning system[33] had failed or when the whole population was equally short of livestock.[34] This understanding differs remarkably from contemporary raiding missions that are primarily undertaken for commercial reasons.

Raiding involved reciprocity: groups came together to help each other in restocking through exchange or helping in raiding faraway areas.[35] Where captives were taken, assimilation, not annihilation, was usually the rule.[36] Raiding was thus relatively humane and carried out under the command of elders who ensured that ethical and traditional rules of engagement were maintained and adhered to. The loss of life was to be avoided at all costs. Women, children, and invalids were never killed during raids. Calves and other young animals were never taken in raids as they would often succumb on the way due to the long distances. Elders usually opposed young men's aggressive tendencies, which might lead to an unwelcome escalation or expansion of conflict and would undercut their authority and pre-eminence. As Paul Baxter has remarked, "War was too serious a matter to be left to the young," and the elders ensured that this remained the case.[37] The generation system therefore provided important ways elders could exert authority over truculent juniors and impose strict limitations on warfare itself.

Livestock rustling, a traditional activity among all plains pastoralists, is embedded in cultural traditions, especially songs and dances that are carried from one generation to another. Historical accounts preserved in oral traditions highlight the existence of cattle rustling before Europeans came to eastern Africa. Pastoral communities engaged in a cattle-rustling "culture," raiding weaker communities and taking away their animals as a means of expanding grazing lands, restocking livestock, and obtaining cattle for bride price.[38] When warriors returned from successful raids, ululation and other songs of praise welcomed them. Among the singers were the warriors' potential brides. Raiding was thus celebrated and occurred at specific times and seasons. A lot of planning went into it. Considerable care was taken to avoid human fatalities and casualties, as Lukuem Emuria, eighty-six, recalled:

> Raiding was not something to be entrusted with juveniles and youths. Elders decided it after intense consultations. Elders would tell the warriors before departing for raiding that the aim of the raid was to get livestock and not to kill fellow humans. If the owners of livestock that you had gone to raid threatened you, you were advised to inflict temporary and not permanent or fatal injury. The ones being raided also knew that death was not intended. But death did occur at times and in such cases cleansing was administered on the warrior who had occasioned the death. Calves were not taken. Women and children were never touched. Warriors raided far and wide beyond the ethnic area. If death occurred during the raid, extra cattle from the killer's family were given to compensate the victim. A *Moran* (warrior) who killed during armed conflict could not enter his *ekai* (homestead) and had to be cleansed at the nearest water point with blood from a slaughtered goat and intestinal contents smeared all over the body. The *Moran* would then be cleansed with water and had to stay alone in the bush overnight before being declared clean to enter the *ekai*. This rigorous ritual cleansing prevented *Morani* from killing during cattle raids. Nowadays warriors do not respect human life or the authority of elders; often, we see them corrupted by money and they even raid clansmen and fellow tribesmen. Money and these new arms have spoilt everything. Elders are not even consulted. When we were warriors, we were on full alert for the service of the community, protecting community property and not ready for hire for money as youths are today.[39]

The Turkana of Kenya, like their Karimojong neighbors in Uganda, had a distinctive clan-based customary system of governance derived from a progressive age-set system. Elders made decisions that guided raiding and decided when, where, and how to raid. The decisions of elders were also absolutely binding in arbitrating conflict. The elders played a major role in natural resource management and determined the modes of production, distribution, or sharing of food and other essential common property resources such as water, salt-licks, pasture, and livestock.

The status and functions of elders as resource managers have been eroded in recent years, partly because of the failure of governments to recognize the role of traditional institutions in management at the community level and partly because of changing property rights regimes in the legal systems of modern states. As a result of emerging individualization and privatization of land that was previously governed by a common property regime, the ability of traditional governance institutions to control conflict has weakened. Small arms have in turn fueled raiding that has escalated into banditry as non-pastoralists have joined the fray, for loot and as fortune seekers. "Eldership" can now be attained by wealth, and armed youth can attain wealth by raiding. This has added a completely new dimension to conflict which community elders have never had to deal with on such a scale before. Despite all this, traditional structures are still important in trying to understand conflict in arid and semi-arid areas of the Triangle. If state administrations had recognized and respected indigenous knowledge and cultural practices in the past, such structures could still have been used to resolve conflicts today. Peter Leliak reported:

> I lost all my cattle to sporadic raiding. Many of the people who raided me were Pokot and others who did not speak the Pokot language but Kiswahili. Our people [in the Triangle] do not speak a lot of Kiswahili. Several non-Turkana were among the raiders. We have been wondering how and why people from so far away were found among the dead or injured in these livestock raids. We have been seeing non-Turkana participate in livestock auctions as sellers of animals and yet they do not own livestock in this area. Where do these Kikuyu, Luyia, Luo, and Kalenjin get their livestock from, and why do they come all the way to Kibish to sell animals? Nobody asks them this question but I believe these are stolen animals. These are our animals. We have even seen many non-pastoralists living in the Triangle but if you ask them what they do for a living, they cannot answer. Where do they get money to pay rent and buy food? They are raiders and sellers of guns. Many of them are gone by night. Begin here [pointing to neighbor's house] and ask people who live in that block [pointing . . .] what they do for a living, and many will just look at you and laugh. I believe that even the police know that what these individuals do for a living si halali [is not honest]. These people are the ones who spoil our youth by hiring them as raiders.[40]

Lamphear avers that in the past "most military activity took the form of intermittent raiding rather than anything like large-scale campaigns and typically it stemmed from a desire to capture livestock, to gain access to natural resources."[41] The recent escalation of violence in the region and its increasing toll on human life is an indication of a breakdown in traditional practices, including reciprocity, and is marked by a reduced regard for the sanctity of human life. Contemporary raiding is sometimes carried out merely for military reputation and prestige.[42] A new hierarchy based on the capacity to amass and use modern arms has replaced the authority of the elders.[43]

The greater demand for livestock and livestock products has led to trading cartels and the entry of very aggressive middlemen. Because of a scarcity of livestock in traditional areas due to raiding, these cartels and middlemen organize and sponsor their own raids by hiring mercenaries and bandits to execute their schemes. Thus traditional raiding, where children and women were spared and male casualties limited, has been replaced by merciless raiding practices by private armies where a whole family or clan can be completely wiped out in a single raid. These mercenaries engage in banditry when not raiding for livestock, and reports of attacks carried out with uncanny military precision are legion in the region.

Recent attempts to restore and revive traditional power structures have been impeded by heavily armed individuals now residing within pastoralist societies. These "renegade youths" constitute rival centers of power. However, there has been some success at recuperating traditional power structures. This is where local efforts at disarmament have succeeded or where governments have allied their military clout with elders to counter the power of the renegade youths. This happened recently between the Karimojong and Turkana elders under the arbitration of Kenyan and Ugandan government officials.

The Ubiquity of Small Arms, or, a Bullet for Bus Fare

The Ilemi Triangle has seen arms used in the course of colonial and imperial expansion and control, but small arms in the hands of pastoralists increased substantially only in the 1930s, following the Italian invasion of Ethiopia. The Italo-Ethiopian war, which broke out in 1936, led Emperor Haile Selassie I to mobilize people at Mychew to confront the Italians. In the ensuing battle, the Ethiopians lost the war and the soldiers retreated. After the emperor left the country in 1936, some soldiers joined the patriotic forces, while others returned to their homes with their guns. The Italians' divide-and-rule policy was a critical factor in making arms more easily available in the area. The Italians occupied Ethiopia between 1936 and 1941 and they deliberately fomented hostility between the Amhara and Oromo. They favored the Oromo and armed them heavily in order to track down anti-colonial forces resisting Italian rule.[44] These forces, in turn, however, received smuggled arms from the French, who were hostile to the Italians.

The First and Second World Wars had a spillover effect in the Horn of Africa. During these imperial wars, Africans were recruited to fight in far-off places. Soldiers were conscripted from many countries in the region. On their return from the wars soldiers carried home mementos other than military regalia and insignia; they also often smuggled in small arms. Whereas the former are proudly and prominently displayed by surviving combatants, the latter can hardly be found, let alone talked about. Interviews with two such surviving World War veterans, Ezekiel Odaro and Francis Ombacho, suggest that the smuggled World War arms were easily sold off to willing buyers.[45]

Soon after the Second World War, the continent of Africa was engulfed in the agitation for independence from colonial rule. Protest and resistance to colonial administration took various forms. In order to take on the European imperialists, Africans, especially in Uganda and Kenya, came up with the idea of making their own weapons. Thus homemade guns emerged as weapons for defense and offense for Africans. Although the technology used was crude, the guns were quite effective and lethal. Over the years, the technology was improved to make guns and explosives of a superior quality and in large quantities. It is not uncommon even today to stumble on both old and new homemade guns being used in armed conflict. Thus the traditional pastoralist weapons used in cattle raiding—spears and bows and arrows—were superseded by more technologically advanced weaponry. Today the weapon of choice is the AK-47 or the M16.[46] A casual walk through the Triangle indicates the presence of small arms all over the place, at markets, in grazing fields, and in private homes. It is not at all uncommon to find large arsenals of small arms in private hands.

As a result of the proliferation of these arms, pastoralists living near the Kenya-Ethiopia, Kenya-Uganda, Kenya-Somalia, Kenya-Sudan, and Uganda-Sudan borders have found themselves victims of cattle rustling. Apiri Ekuam traces the genesis of small arms in the Triangle, and their connection to livestock rustling, to the Anyanya movement that emerged in southern Sudan in the 1950s. He suggests that the use of small arms intensified in the 1980s when the Sudan People's Liberation Army (SPLA) was born.

> *Anyanya* [the predecessors of the SPLA] are the ones who brought many dangerous guns here. The guns that the Italians left [behind in 1935] were too old. Anyanya were the first to bring Russian guns [in the 1950s] and they

started robbing us of our animals in large numbers, until we started to buy our own guns. And after the SPLA struggle started in Sudan, livestock were stolen in the thousands. Many heads of cattle would disappear without a trace, sometimes the livestock of entire villages. When the cattle population went down here, *wezi wa ng'ombe* [livestock thieves] . . . started hiring our youth and sending them to Pokot, Samburu and Karimojong to steal animals for them. The SPLA people have also been sending the Nyangatom and Merille, and Toposa to take our animals. Bad stealing [raiding], where everything is taken away and people are killed, has come about because of the SPLA and these other people who want to take over governments in Uganda and Ethiopia.[47]

Markakis confirms Ekuam's report that the proliferation of arms in the Ilemi Triangle is intimately and intricately intertwined with livestock rustling.[48] Tornay makes a connection between the availability of weapons across state borders and the rise of anti-state movements, when he reports that in 1991, "twenty five young Nyangatom (Merile) had been trained in an EPRDF (Ethiopia Peoples' Republic Democratic Front) camp in Awasa and they had been sent back to their country with Kalashnikovs, as purely tribal militia, committed to maintain local order under the guidance of their elders."[49] Tornay further reports that "the Sudanese Toposa have made an alliance with the Sudan People's Liberation Army (SPLA), from which they acquired automatic weapons."[50]

Meanwhile, arms are traded freely and openly in the Triangle. There are buyers who travel all the way from Kampala in Uganda, Nairobi in Kenya, and Addis Ababa in Ethiopia looking for illegal arms. Negotiations take place in hotels and lodgings. There are middlemen and middlewomen who spot potential buyers and link them to sellers. In Kibish, a guide led researchers to a house where they saw an array of arms on display, in a neighborhood not far from the police post and the Kenyan army outpost. They also met a young seller in one of the hotels by chance and he asked them if they wanted to buy arms. He proceeded to display his wares by lifting his overcoat; he was carrying at least five guns under that one overcoat. Almost every week, security personnel unearth arms caches hidden in all kinds of places. Weapons are often concealed in spare tires, fuel tanks, and even automobile engines.

In the Ilemi Triangle, border crossings are barely policed. Only Kibish post is registered as an official entry point, but there are a dozen other entry points that are more active in human and livestock traffic. The crossing at Kibish is scantily manned and the security personnel there are ill equipped. On January 17, 2003, between 2 and 4 P.M., researchers stationed just behind Kibish police post counted more than thirty people entering Kenya from Ethiopia with loads of various sizes. Several rode bicycles loaded with huge bags or suitcases. The researchers followed one of the cyclists to his residence. To a casual observer the cyclist appeared to be carrying charcoal but embedded in the bag of charcoal was an assortment of electronic goods and appliances. Also hidden in it were three AK-47 machine guns. If all thirty people were carrying arms, nearly 100 firearms entered Kenya in just two hours. What is more important is that none of the border crossers were stopped or inspected. It is easy to understand how small arms move between the states of eastern Africa without the knowledge of their respective governments.

The ubiquity of small arms is illustrated in other ways as well. In the Triangle a bullet can be used as bus fare or to buy a glass of beer or a bottle of Coca-Cola. At Loelli town we came across an open-air market where small arms were openly displayed with price tags marked in the currencies of Kenya, Uganda, and Ethiopia, as well as in U.S. dollars. We saw an assortment of pistols and guns. The AK-47 was the most expensive, followed by the M16. We were surprised that these illegal guns were displayed so openly and that they were so cheap. We were told that an AK-47 fetches five head of cattle (about 10,000 Kenya shillings, or 100 U.S. dollars) when offered for barter but costs almost half that price when cash is paid. We also learned that some guns can also be rented. Gun renters in the Triangle at times also double up as sellers. *The East African*, a Kenyan-based weekly regional newspaper, estimates that there are between 150,000 and 200,000 firearms in the Karamoja region of Uganda alone, and about 50,000 in Turkana, and many of these must have passed through the Ilemi Triangle. While the exact number of small arms in the hands of pastoral communities in the region is difficult to assess and actual figures impossible to get, it is clear that the threat posed by them is enormous.

Small arms have become a common medium of exchange in the pastoralist areas. In 2002, three to six cows could buy a gun in the Triangle. In Turkana (Kenya) and Karamoja (Uganda), bullet calibers and the names and types of various modern guns are common knowledge. The accuracy of local knowledge would put army recruits or unsophisticated security personnel to shame. Arms have become part of ordinary currency transactions among pastoralists in eastern Africa, as spears and arrows once were. The demand for small arms is made more complex by two new dimensions: the arrival of warlords and the commercialization of cattle rustling, whereby rich urban merchants fund raids in the pastoral communities.[51]

Small arms usually arrive in the Ilemi Triangle from distant civil wars or conflict zones, both legally and illegally. Sengile Fugicha, a Shangilla herdsman interviewed at Sololo on the Kenya-Ethiopia border, was bold enough to describe how arms are ferried across the border, reasoning that everyone knows how arms are moved across international borders:

> There are many ways through which these arms are moved across borders. The first one is the use of Shangilla herdsmen who cross the Kenya-Ethiopia border every day with their herds to carry the arms across, often concealed in the mobile homes atop camels. We do not have a permanent abode as we can move with our homes, stocks, and property across this border as many times as we want, and in many places without raising eyebrows. However, since commercial gun buyers and runners have increased their use of herdsmen to move arms across, security forces are beginning to discover our tricks. Also, the fact that many Turkana, Rendille, and Boran are nowadays masquerading as Shangilla in order to go unnoticed, it is becoming difficult to operate. People betray each other more often than in the past, usually to eliminate competition, and this has complicated matters and intensified rivalry. This is because they are hired by gun-runners and want to make as many trips as possible even when there is grass and water here, which are the excuses that we often use to justify our free movement. The new people are making crossing the border between Kenya and Ethiopia suspect. We use unofficial routes, usually unmanned border points and remote hills and forested areas. The police and army are only found where there are roads. Although this often makes for long routes and lasts for days, one is always sure to cross the border safely. Finally, we at times use our children and women to carry arms because security forces rarely inspect this category of individuals at the border.[52]

Rifles and pistols are small, easy to take apart, and consequently simple to conceal and transport. Small aircraft can deliver smuggled goods undetected to remote airfields. This has happened in the past in the case of one unused airfield in a ranch not far from Archer's Post Township in Samburu district. In March 2003, a light aircraft from Somalia made an unauthorized landing at Masinga dam airstrip, and only intervention by ordinary people made the security forces arrest its passengers and seize its cargo, but by then the aircraft had made a safe escape back to Somalia. Transporting by land, smugglers have to cope with border guards, customs officials, and/or the police. In the event that officials actually carry out freight checks, however, small bribes are usually sufficient to ensure safe passage for anything, including contraband goods. Ironically, the risk of being attacked by bandits or rebels is considerably greater. In order to defend themselves in such emergencies, smugglers must carry arms themselves.[53]

An NGO analyst's account of how weapons are smuggled into Africa tallies with this account of how small-arms proliferation takes place in the Ilemi Triangle:

They [governments] often collected weapons from the former Soviet Union and Eastern Europe, transshipped them through airports like Ostende in Belgium or Burgas in Bulgaria, filed false flight plans to Cairo, Kinshasa, or Lagos, and "secretly" delivered their lethal cargoes to UNITA rebels and Hutu perpetrators of Rwandan genocide based in Eastern Congo. They carried with them maps and diagrams of various clandestine airfields and depended on their well-greased relations with rogue officials to ensure the secure off-loading of their cargo as "farm machinery," but they were rarely, if ever, subject to cargo inspections. Circuitous air routes, forged export licenses and bills of lading, and fictitious end-user certificates to show to unsuspecting officials are all standard. Even humanitarian organizations can be trapped, not always unwittingly, into ferrying weapons into conflict-ridden zones. Planes under the supervision of the World Food Program, the UN High Commission for Refugees, and non-governmental relief organizations such as OXFAM have been commandeered. Chinese arms industries' weapons shipments—labeled "farm implements"—are carried on the same Chinese ships that bring beans and tools to needy Great Lakes Refugees.[54]

According to our interviewees, Lokichokio International Airport in Kenya is used for clandestine activities, including arms movement and livestock rustling from the Ilemi Triangle. Lokichokio is an ideal entry point for arms as it has reportedly been used by SPLA officials flying into southern Sudan (New Sudan). Airport security is not tight—there are huge gaps in the perimeter fence and a lack of personnel to man gates inside the airport. Lokichokio can serve as an ideal hideout and exit port for stolen livestock. Florence Etuko (a pseudonym) informed us that she had witnessed many suspicious activities at Lokichokio airport, especially at night, ever since she started working there as an air traffic controller five years ago. Particularly fascinating were her accounts of cargo planes that delivered and picked up cargo under tight security and closed cover. Florence suspected that planes brought in arms and took away livestock and other related products. It was noticeable that tensions were usually high at Lokichokio whenever researchers arrived at the airport for overnight vigil and other research activities. While the growth of Lokichokio town and airport owes its origins to the Cold War (in the form of war between Ethiopia and Somalia), today Lokichokio town bears the marks of contemporary conflicts and its status as the region's major refugee center.

Cross-Border Raids, Forced Migration, and Poverty

Long-distance and cross-border nomadic movements of peoples with their herds are a convenient cover for transporting small arms. Stolen animals are also brought together into what might look like genuine herds.

Droughts occurring frequently since the 1970s and 1980s have made matters worse. Not only have pastoralists in the Triangle had to compete for scarce resources, but the asset base of their livelihoods has also been seriously eroded.

An interview with one person, Elijah Lekulian, on the Kenyan side of the Triangle, dramatized how the people in the Triangle felt. He jokingly asked researchers who the president of Kenya was, and whether Idi Amin and Mengistu Haile Marriam were still presidents of Uganda and Ethiopia respectively, just to demonstrate how peripheralized and disinterested the pastoralists in the Triangle have become vis-à-vis the states in the region. Elections had been held four months previously, and Mwai Kibaki had just replaced Daniel Moi as president of Kenya in 2002. This was news that dominated the region, but Lekulian feigned ignorance concerning the political dynamics of the region to make his point. Lekulian is a Turkana, a former herdsman now living at Kibish as an urban refugee. He said that he lost most of his cattle to raiders from Sudan and Ethiopia. He was a sad man, poor and emaciated, and he blamed the Kenyan government for not allowing the people on their side of the border to acquire and own arms to protect themselves from well-armed raiders from neighboring countries.

Because of the marginality of this area, goods in the Ilemi Triangle often cost two or three times their prices in other parts of the surrounding countries. A 380-milliliter bottle of Coca-Cola costs sixty shillings in the Triangle but only twenty shillings in other parts of Kenya. Bread costs fifty shillings in the Triangle and twenty-five shillings in the rest of Kenya. Because of poor roads and a poor transport network, many NGO officials prefer to use light aircraft to move in their essentials. The communication network is also poor, with telephones found only in a few urban centers of the Triangle.

Destitution is widespread. There are hundreds of families that have lost their livestock to cross-border raiders and are forced to eke out a living by providing labor as hired herdsmen or other manual tasks. Others work as urban caregivers, domestic servants, shopkeepers, charcoal burners, and hawkers, and yet others rely on handouts from international NGOs such as OXFAM, CARE, World Vision, etc. Some families go as many as three days without a decent meal. There is a rise in the number of homeless and street families in towns in the Triangle, especially in Kibish. In spite of the difficulty of travel, many destitute families have moved out of the Triangle. For example, many destocked Turkana families are living right outside the United Nations High Commission for Refugees (UNHCR) camp at Kakuma. These families depend on handouts for survival; humanitarian relief has become their main source of sustenance. The *Daily Nation* of January

21, 2001, reported that more than 600 Burji, Gabra, and Boran families had fled their Moyale homes following invasions from the Ethiopian side of the border. Many ended up in Walda refugee camp, which houses refugees from Ethiopia and Somalia. Following the escalation of bandit attacks, the Member of Parliament from Moyale reported, "Six villages in my constituency are now desolate as residents have fled their homes and are camping at the Moyale divisional headquarters."[55]

Violence, cross-border raids, and forced migration since the 1990s have led to booming slums in the Triangle. Slum dwellings are mainly made from paper, cardboard, sticks, and grass. Every urban center in the Triangle has its share of these informal settlements that are increasingly sites of criminal activities. In some areas,[56] informal dwellings far outnumber formal settlements, and they have congested the town's social and economic infrastructure. There are no facilities for leisure such as playing fields, stadiums, or social centers. The only available playing field at Kibish Primary School has been so overused that its ground is barren. The Kibish Division District Officer uses this field during public holidays as a parade ground for march-pasts and military drills. It is therefore dusty and uncomfortable to play on.

The most vulnerable families are known as "cattle-less pastoralists," an even poorer group within an already marginalized community. They are found in town slums in the Triangle and are forced to engage in all kinds of activities, including prostitution, to eke out a living. Fedi Bayeswa, originally from Kelem, Ethiopia, is a businesswoman in Kibish and has seen girls turn into prostitutes because their families could no longer fend for them.

> These displaced pastoralist girls are victims of circumstance. When they arrive here, they are very shy and often begin as house-helps and domestic servants. When they realize that they cannot make enough money, they begin to sell sex. The worst are those who work for police officers and soldiers in the barracks. Since many soldiers do not have their wives here, they often seek satisfaction from these girls and before you know it, the girls have become full-time prostitutes. Others give birth to bastards and add to the problems of women. There are Ethiopian, Sudanese, Ugandan, Kenyan and even Somali women prostitutes here [in Kibish]. These girls are able to take care of their families, usually fathers, mothers and their siblings. The biggest problem now afflicting these girls is AIDS.[57]

Conclusion

Our analysis suggests the complexity of the dynamics that make up an African borderland, the Ilemi Triangle, located on the periphery of four East African states and at the crossroads of illegal trade in small arms and livestock. Although at first glance the Ilemi Triangle looks remote, its physical distance from recognized centers of power should not obscure the impact of global events, from imperial expansion to World Wars and the Cold War. This borderland provides an example of the intersection of multiple historical, geopolitical, and ecological scales, which in this case have produced a massive proliferation of small arms and a concomitant rise in violence, insecurity, and environmental degradation.

Traditional forms of authority in pastoral communities, while not preventing violence, did offer a relatively ordered and accepted system of rules that kept peace within and between communities that have now come to straddle one or more national boundaries. These forms of licit traditional authority have broken down under the pressures of new borders, alternative conceptions of development, massive ecological change, proximity to major conflicts, an increasing demand for meat and animal products, and the arrival in bulk of technologically superior weapons. New forms of authority have now replaced the old regulatory system that enjoyed great legitimacy and acceptability compared to the new arrangements. The population of the Ilemi Triangle does not see the governance of modern post-colonial states as licit. Many pastoralists hate the states' development policies that have continued to marginalize them; they abhor the military presence of these governments, detest international borders, loathe the policing rather than embrace it. This loss of regulatory cohesion is highlighted by the example of cattle raiding, once a culturally defined practice that was part of reciprocal relations between pastoral communities. Raiding has now been transformed into commercial plunder and warlordism. For the foreseeable future, there appears little chance for licit forms of authority to re-establish themselves in the Ilemi Triangle.

NOTES

1. R. Chesos, "(President) Moi Offers One Month Arms Amnesty," *Daily Nation*, April 18, 2001.

2. Interviews conducted in Kaabong and Loyoro in Uganda, Lokichokio, Kibish and Todentang, Lodwar, Maralal, Baragoi, Sololo in Kenya, Kelem, Mega, and Chelago in Ethiopia, and Lutuke, Nagpotpot, Kapoeta, Loeli, and Nagichot in Sudan. September 2 to November 30, 2002.

3. M. Agutu and J. Kariuki, "Welcome to Kenya's Kosovo," *Daily Nation*, May 11, 2001.

4. M. N. Amutabi, "Cattle Rustling among Pastoralists in Northern Kenya: The Genesis and the Truth," presented at the conference on *Community Education*, Isiolo (August 25–28, 1999).

5. M. Niamir-Fuller, "Conflict Management and Mobility among Pastoralists in Karamoja, Uganda," in *Managing Mobility in African Rangelands* (London: ITDG,

1999), 176. Also see D. Belshaw and M. Malinga, "The Kalashnikov Economies of the Eastern Sahel: Cumulative or Cyclical Differentiation between Nomadic Pastoralists," paper presented at the first workshop of the Study Group on Conflict and Security of the Development Studies Association (South Bank University, University of East Anglia, 1999).

6. M. N. Amutabi, "Banditry and Livestock Rustling in the Ilemi Triangle of East Africa," presented at the 2nd Edinboro University of Pennsylvania Conference on African Studies on "War, Refugees and Environment in Africa," Edinboro University of Pennsylvania, Erie, Pa., USA, (April 3–5, 2003).

7. M. N. Amutabi, "Cattle Rustling and the Proliferation of Small Arms: The Case of Baragoi, Samburu District in the Rift Valley Province of Kenya" (unpublished research report, Moi University, 2000).

8. Amutabi, "Cattle Rustling and the Proliferation of Small Arms." See also K. Mkutu and M. Marani, "The Role of Civic Leaders in the Mitigation of Cattle Rustling and Small Arms: The Case of Laikipia and Samburu" (Nairobi: African Peace Forum, 2001).

9. These figures are based on estimates from interviews, observation, and official governments records. There are about fifty rural villages in each given local area of administration, such as Kalokol Division of Turkana district of Kenya or Lake Stephanie division of Omo Valley region in Ethiopia. Based on the number of firearms in the hands of village vigilante groups as revealed by opinion leaders, firearms in the hands of known and suspected raiders based on confidential interviews with former raiders, and firearms officially given to home guards in border areas by governments, we estimated that each village would have about 200 firearms. There are about fifty administrative areas near the Triangle, each with about fifty rural villages, which when multiplied by 200 yields approximately 500,000 small arms. There are about twenty concentrated (urban) settlements in each of the fifty administrative areas, each with about 600 firearms in the hands of security forces (police and the military) usually based in these urban outposts, and others in illegal hands, plus those in the hands of the urban vigilante groups, which yields 600,000. Additionally, based on our visits to underground arms markets at Kibish, Loeli, Sololo, etc., and together with arms that pass through the Triangle in transit to rebel armies in Sudan, Uganda and Ethiopia, we estimated that this source would yield 300,000, giving us a grand total of 1.4 million.

10. For a review of the borderlands literature, see Willem van Schendel, chapter 1, this volume.

11. F. A. Adeyoyin, "Methodology of the Multi-disciplinary Problem," in A. I. Asiwaju and P. O. Ademiyi, eds., Borderlands in Africa: A Multidisciplinary and Comparative Focus on Nigeria and West Africa (Lagos: University of Lagos Press, 1989), 375.

12. N. Hansen, Border Economy: Regional Development in the Southwest (Austin: University of Texas Press, 1981), 340.

13. O. Akintola-Bello, "The Political Economy of Artificial Boundaries," in Borderlands in Africa, ed. Asiwaju and Ademiyi, 331.

14. C. S. Momoh, "A Critique of Borderland Theories," in Borderlands in Africa, ed. Asiwaju and Ademiyi, 58.

15. The Ilemi Triangle was named after Chief Ilemi (Ilembi, Melile, Chambar) of the Anuak, whose village was located on the Sudan bank of the Akobo River near the juncture of the River Ajibur and the Akobo.

16. J. Markakis, Resource Conflict in the Horn of Africa (London and New Delhi: Sage Publications, 1998), 41.

17. The semi-arid and arid areas in Kenya, Sudan, Uganda, and Ethiopia make up 70 percent of their total land area and provide 20 to 30 percent of the gross domestic product of these states, mainly through livestock and livestock products.

18. Cited in ILRI/ASARECA, "Coping Mechanisms and Their Efficacy in Disaster-Prone Pastoral Systems of the Greater Horn of Africa (GHA): Effects and Responses of Pastoralist and Livestock during the 1995–97 Drought and the 1997–1998 El Nino Rains" (Nairobi: ILRI/ASARECA, 1998).

19. The districts include Isiolo, Marsabit, Garissa, Mandera, Wajir, Baringo, Keiyo, Kajiado, Laikipia, Marakwet, Narok, Samburu, Turkana, and West Pokot.

20. Government of Kenya (GOK),"Recovery and sustainable development to the year 2000," Sessional paper no. 1 (Government of Kenya, Government Printer: Nairobi, 1995), 59.

21. For example, Turkana herdsmen would go as far as Kainuk, Isiolo, Maralal, and Baringo before they found themselves forced to enter the Triangle with their livestock. Many Karimojong herdsmen also go as far as Soroti and Kitgum in Northern Uganda, but when drought persists they also end up in the Triangle.

22. Quoted in the Report of the Kenya Land Commission of 1933, Kenya National Archives (1933–1934), Part II, Chapter 1, p. 185, paragraph 635 and 642.

23. Lekilam Sotie and Okuan Lupa, interview, Kibish, Ethiopia, October 19, 2002.

24. Interview with Ewalam Lokolak, interview, Lokitaung, October 7, 2002.

25. Numbers of "destocked" pastoralists are found in townships such as Kaabong and Loyoro in Uganda, Lokichokio, Kibish, and Todentang in Kenya, Kelem, Mega, and Chelago in Ethiopia, and Lutuke, Nagpotpot, Kapoeta, Loeli, and Nagichot in Sudan.

26. Musa Ekuro Kalemothia, interview, October 29, 2002.

27. I. Livingston, "The Common Property Problem and Pastoralist Economic Behaviour," *Journal of Development Studies* 23, no. 1 (1986): 5–19.

28. Fred Ejore, interview, Kibish, February 23, 2003.

29. M. D. Quam, "Creating Peace in an Armed Society: Karamoja, Uganda," *African Studies Quarterly* 1, no. 1 (1996): 15.

30. Niamir-Fuller, "Conflict Management and Mobility among Pastoralists in Karamoja."

31. Casper Odegi Awuondo, *Life in the Balance: Ecological Sociology of Turkana Nomads* (Nairobi: ACTS, 1990).

32. Tilam Lokwel, interview, Lokitaung, Turkana, Kenya, January 24, 2003.

33. Cattle-loaning is an ancient practice among pastoralists where one clan provided seed animals to a neighboring one for restocking. After herds recovered, an equal number of seed animals were usually returned to the lender. This was carried out between friendly pastoralist groups. Raiding was a last resort when such schemes had failed.

34. George Ekidor, interview, Kibish, February 15, 2003.

35. H. Muller, *Changing Generations: Dynamics of Generation and Age Sets in Southeastern Sudan (Toposa) and Northeastern Kenya (Turkana)* (Searbrucken: Breitenbach Publishers, 1989).

36. Amutabi, "Cattle Rustling among Pastoralists," 12, and J. Lamphear, "The Evolution of Ateker 'New Model' Armies: Jie and Turkana," in *Ethnicity and Conflict in the Horn of Africa*, ed. K. Fukui and J. Markakis (London and Athens, Ohio: James Currey and Ohio University Press, 1994), 69.

37. U. Almogor, "Raider and Elders: A Confrontation of Generations among the

Dassanetch," in *Warfare among East African Herders*, ed. K. Fukui and D. Turton (Osaka: Senri Ethnological Foundation, National Museum of Ethnology, 1979); Amutabi, "Cattle Rustling among Pastoralists"; P. Baxter, "Boran Age Sets and Warfare," in *Warfare among East African Herders*, ed. Fukui and Turton, 167–186; J. D. Galaty, "Form and Intention in East African Strategies of Dominance," in *Dominance, Aggression and War*, ed. Diane McGuinness (New York: Paragon House, 1987).

38. See Mkutu and Marani, "Role of Civic Leaders"; Amutabi, "Cattle Rustling and the Proliferation of Small Arms"; B. Novelli, "Aspects of Karimojong Ethno-sociology," *Museum Comboninium*, no. 44 (Comboni Missionaries: Kampala, 1988).

39. Lukuem Emuria, interview, Lodwar, Kenya, December 15, 2002.

40. Peter Leliak, interview, Kibish, November 29, 2002.

41. Lamphear, "Evolution of Ateker 'New Model' Armies," 69.

42. O.-L. Dent, "Manhood, Warriorhood and Sex in Eastern Africa," in *The Warrior Tradition in Modern Africa*, ed. Ali A. Mazrui (Leiden: E. J. Brill, 1977); Geoffrey Parker, *The Military Revolution* (Cambridge: Cambridge University Press, 1988).

43. M. N. Amutabi, "Challenging the Orthodoxies: The Role of Ethnicity and Regional Nationalism in Leadership and Democracy," presented at the conference on "Ethnicity, Nationalism and Democracy in Africa," May 28–31 (Kericho, UNESCO, 1995); Amutabi, "Cattle Rusting among Pastoralists."

44. Amutabi, "Cattle Rustling and the Proliferation of Small Arms."

45. Ezekiel Odaro and Francis Ombacho, interview, Kakamega, September 27, 2002.

46. Amutabi, "Cattle Rustling and the Proliferation of Small Arms"; Belshaw and Malinga, "The Kalashnikov Economies of the Eastern Sahel; K. Mkutu, "Banditry, Cattle Rustling, and the Proliferation of Small Arms: The Case of Laikipia and Samburu," Arusha report (Nairobi: African Peace Forum, 2000). See also S. Muiruri and W. Mugo, "Thirty Killed in Raids," *Daily Nation*, February 9, 2001, 1.

47. Apiri Ekuam, interview, Kokwo, November 23, 2002.

48. Markakis, *Resource Conflict in the Horn of Africa*.

49. S. A. Tornay, "More Chances on the Fringe of the State? The Growing Power of the Nyangatom, a Border People of the Lower Omo Valley, Ethiopia (1970–1992)," in *Conflicts in the Horn of Africa: Human and Ecological Consequences of Warfare*, ed. T. Tvedt (Uppsala: Uppsala University, Department of Social and Economic Geography, 1993), 151.

50. Tornay, "More Chances," 148.

51. Fred Ejore, interview, Kibish, February 23, 2003.

52. Sengile Fugicha, interview, Sololo, Ethiopia, December 18, 2002.

53. Amutabi, "Livestock War: Banditry and Livestock Rustling in the Ilemi Triangle of East Africa," 24.

54. Kathi Austin, *The New Field of Micro-Disarmament: Addressing the Proliferation and Buildup of Small Arms and Light Weapons* (Bonn: Bonn International Center for Conversion [BICC] and Monterey Institute of International Studies, June 1996), 35.

55. Quoted in the *Sunday Nation*, January 12, 2001. The affected villages were Kiltipe, Uran, Lataka, Uran Dida, Badanota, and Kicha on the Kenyan side of the border with Ethiopia.

56. Including urban centers such as Nagpotpot, Kaiemothia, Kokwo, Kibish, Lomuru Itae, and Todentang.

57. Fedi Bayeswa (Miss), interview, Kibish, January 26, 2003.

Consolidated Bibliography

Abduca, Ricardo. "De los yungas paceños al noroeste argentino: Nuevo enfoque sobre la producción de coca para consumo tradicional." Unpublished manuscript, ca. 1994.

Adams, M. "The Baggara Problem: Attempts at Modern Change in Southern Darfur and Southern Kordofan (Sudan)." *Development and Change* 13 (1982): 259–89.

Adas, Michael. "From Avoidance to Confrontation: Peasant Protest in Precolonial and Colonial Southeast Asia." *Comparative Studies in Society and History* 23, no. 2 (1981): 217–247.

Adeyoyin, F. A. "Methodology of the Multi-disciplinary Problem." In *Borderlands in Africa: A Multidisciplinary and Comparative Focus on Nigeria and West Africa*, edited by A. I Asiwaju and P. O Ademiyi. Lagos: University of Lagos Press, 1989.

Adler, Patricia A. *Wheeling and Dealing: An Ethnography of an Upper-Level Drug Dealing and Smuggling Community.* New York: Columbia University Press, 1985.

Aduana de la Coca. *Estadística general de la extracción de productos agrícolas de las provincias de nor y sud Yungas, Inquisivi, Larecaja, Caupolicán, Muñecas, Murillo y Loayza, cuya recaudación de impuestos corre a cargo de la Aduana de la Coca.* La Paz: Imprenta Nacional, 1949–1959.

Aglietta, Michel. *A Theory of Capitalist Regulation.* London: New Left Books, 1979.

Agnew, John. "The Territorial Trap: The Geographical Assumptions of International Relations Theory." *Review of International Political Economy* 1, no. 1 (1994): 53–80.

Agnew, John, and Stuart Corbridge. *Mastering Space: Hegemony, Territory and International Political Economy.* London and New York: Routledge, 1995.

Aguilar, I. M. "Reinventing Gada: Generational Knowledge in Boorana." In *The Politics of Age and Gerontocracy in Africa: Ethnographies of the Past & Memories of the Present*, edited by M. Aguilar, 257–279. Trenton, N.J., and Asmara, Eritrea: AfricaWorld Press, 1998.

Akintola-Bello, O. "The Political Economy of Artificial Boundaries." In *Borderlands in Africa: A Multidisciplinary and Comparative Focus on Nigeria and West Africa*, edited by A. I. Asiwaju and P. O. Ademiyi. Lagos, Nigeria: University of Lagos Press, 1989.

ALARM, SNV, Oxfam, World Concern, and Action-Aid. "Livestock marketing from Pastoral Areas of Kenya." ALARM in Conjunction with SNV/the Netherlands Development Organization (Kenya), Oxfam (GB) Kenya, World Concern and Action Aid, Nairobi, Kenya, 1999.

Albert, Mathias, David Jacobsen, and Yosef Lapid, eds. *Identities, Borders, Orders:*

Rethinking International Relations Theory. Minneapolis: University of Minnesota Press, 2001.

Alcaráz, Franklin, et al. *El Consumo Indebido de Drogas en Cinco Ciudades de Bolivia*. La Paz: Cruz Roja Boliviana, 1990.

Alcaráz, Franklin, et al. *La prevalencia del uso indebido de drogas en Bolivia (Población urbana)*. La Paz: Ministerio de Prevision Social y Salud Publica, Direccion Nacional de Prevencion (DINAPRE) 6, 1993.

Alcaráz, Franklin, et al. *La prevalencia del uso indebido de drogas en estudiantes urbanos de Bolivia (Ciclos intermedio y medio)*. La Paz: Secretaría Nacional de Salud, Dirección Nacional de Prevención Integral de Drogadependencias y Salud Mental, 1994.

Alcaráz, Franklin, Nilda Flores, and Joel Jutkowitz. *El uso indebido de drogas en Bolivia y uso tradicional de la hoja de coca*. La Paz: Centro Latinoamericano de Investigación Científica, 1993.

Alcaráz, Franklin, Rosse Mary Soliz, and Julia Zuazo. *Drogas en Bolivia (Comentarios y sugerencias de estudiantes urbanos)*. La Paz: Centro Latinoamericano de Investigación Científica, 1999.

Allen, Catherine J. *The Hold Life Has: Coca and Cultural Identity in an Andean Community*. Washington, D.C.: Smithsonian Institution Press, 1988.

Allen, T. "Ethnicity and Tribalism on the Sudan-Uganda Border." In *Ethnicity and Conflict in the Horn of Africa*, edited by K. Fukui and J. Markakis, 112–139. London and Athens, Ohio: James Currey and Ohio University Press, 1994.

Almagor, U. "Raiders and Elders: A Confrontation of Generations among the Dassanetch." In *Warfare among East African Herders*, edited by K. Fukui and D. Turton. Osaka: Senri Ethnological Foundation, National Museum of Ethnology, 1979.

Alverson, J. A. *Starvation and Peace or Food and War? Aspects of Armed Conflicts in the Lower Omo Valley, Ethiopia*. Uppsala, Sweden: Research Reports in Cultural Anthropology, 1989.

Amutabi, Maurice N. "Challenging the Orthodoxies: The Role of Ethnicity and Regional Nationalism in Leadership and Democracy in Africa." Paper presented at UNESCO Conference on "Ethnicity, Nationalism and Democracy in Africa," Kericho, Kenya, May 1995.

———. "Cattle Rustling among Pastoralists in Northern Kenya: The Genesis and the Truth." Research paper/report presented at conference on Community Education co-hosted by Action-Aid and Association for World Education (AWE), Isiolo, Kenya, August 1999.

———. "Cattle Rustling and the Proliferation of Small Arms: The Case of Baragoi, Samburu District in the Rift Valley Province of Kenya." Unpublished research report, Moi University, 2000.

———. "Livestock War: Banditry and Livestock Rustling in the Ilemi Triangle of East Africa." Paper presented at the 2nd Edinboro University of Pennsylvania Conference on African Studies on "War, Refugees and Environment in Africa," Edinboro University of Pennsylvania, Erie, Pa., USA. April 3–5, 2003.

Amutabi, Maurice N., and E. M. Were. *Nationalism and Democracy for People-Centered Development in Africa*. Eldoret, Kenya: Moi University Press, 2000.

Anderson, Benedict. *Imagined Communities*. 2nd ed. London: Verso, 1991.

Anderson, James, and Liam O'Dowd. "Borders, Border Regions and Territoriality: Contradictory Meanings, Changing Significance." *Regional Studies* 33, no. 7 (1999): 593–604.

Anderson, Malcolm. "The Transformation of Border Controls. A European Precedent?" In *The Wall around the West: State Borders and Immigration Controls in North America and Europe*, edited by Peter Andreas and T. Snyder. Lanham, Md.: Rowman & Littlefield, 2001.

Andreas, Peter. "When Policies Collide: Market Reform, Market Prohibition, and the Narcotization of the Mexican Economy." Chapter 5 in *Illicit Global Economy and State Power*, edited by H. Richard Friman and Peter Andreas. Lanham, Md.: Rowman & Littlefield, 1999.

———. *Border Games: Policing the U.S.-Mexico Divide*. Ithaca, N.Y., and London: Cornell University Press, 2000.

———. "The Transformation of Migrant Smuggling Across the U.S.-Mexican Border." In *Global Human Smuggling: Comparative Perspectives*, edited by David Kyle and Rey Koslowski, 107–125. Baltimore: Johns Hopkins University Press, 2001.

Andreas, Peter, and Timothy Snyder. *The Wall around the West: State Borders and Immigration Controls in North America and Europe*. Oxford: Rowman & Littlefield, 2000.

Appadurai, Arjun. *Modernity at Large: Cultural Dimensions of Globalization*. Minneapolis: University of Minnesota Press, 1998.

Appadurai, Arjun, ed. *The Social Life of Things: Commodities in Cultural Perspective*. Cambridge: Cambridge University Press, 1986.

Ardaya, Gloria. "Inserción socio-ocupacional de los inmigrantes bolivianos en la Argentina." Master's thesis, Facultad Latinoamericana de Ciencias Sociales (FLACSO), Buenos Aires, 1978.

Asamblea Permanente de Derechos Humanos de Bolivia. *La masacre de Todos Santos*. La Paz: Asamblea Permanente de Derechos Humanos, 1980.

Ashley, Richard. "The Poverty of Neo-realism." In *Realism and Its Critics*, edited by Robert Keohane. New York: Columbia University Press, 1986.

Asiwaju, J., ed. *Partitioned Africans: Ethnic Relations across Africa's International Boundaries, 1884–1994*. London: C. Hurst and Co. and Lagos: University of Lagos Press, 1984.

Astorga, Luis A. *Mitología del "narcotraficante" en México*. Mexico City: Plaza y Valdés, 1995.

———. *El siglo de las drogas: Usos, percepciones y personalidades*. Mexico City: Espasa-Hoy, 1996.

———. "Traficantes de drogas, políticas y policías en el siglo XX mexicano." In *Vicios públicos, virtudes privadas: La corrupción en México*, edited by Claudio Lomnitz, 167–93. Mexico City: CIESAS /Miguel Angel Porrúa, 2000.

Austin, Kathi. *The New Field of Micro-Disarmament: Addressing the Proliferation and Buildup of Small Arms and Light Weapons*. Bonn: Bonn International Center for Conversion [BICC] and Monterey Institute of International Studies, June 1996.

Awuondo, C. O. *Life in the Balance: Ecological Sociology of Turkana Nomads.* Nairobi: ACTS, 1990.

Baily, John, and Roy Godson. *Organized Crime and Democratic Governability: Mexico and the U.S.-Mexican Borderlands.* Pittsburgh, Pa.: University of Pittsburgh Press, 2000.

Barfield, T. J. *The Nomadic Alternative.* Prentice Hall, N.J.: Englewood Cliffs, 1993.

Barnes de Marshall, Catherine. *Revolution and land reform in the Bolivian Yungas of La Paz.* La Paz: Servicio Nacional de Reforma Agraria, 1970.

Barrios Morón, Raúl. "Guerra de las drogas: Operaciones sicológicas en Bolivia." *Presencia—Linterna diurna,* August 4, 1980.

Barthes, Roland. *Lo obvio y lo obtuso. Imágenes, gestos, voces.* Barcelona: Paidós, [1982] 1995.

Bascopé Aspiazu, René. *La veta blanca: Coca y cocaína en Bolivia.* La Paz: Ediciones Aquí, 1982.

Battistella, Graziano, and Maruja M. B. Asis. "Southeast Asia and the Specter of Unauthorized Migration." In *Unauthorized Migration in Southeast Asia,* edited by Graziano Batistella and Maruja M. B. Asis. Manila: Scalabrini Migration Center, 2003.

Baud, Michiel, and Willem van Schendel. "Toward a Comparative History of Borderlands." *Journal of World History* 8, no. 2 (1997): 211–242.

Baxter, P. T. W. "The Creation and Constitution of Oromo Nationality." In *Ethnicity and Conflict in the Horn of Africa,* edited by K. Fukui and J. Markakis, 167–186. London and Athens, Ohio: James Currey and Ohio University Press, 1994.

Baxter, P. "Boran Age-Sets and Warfare." In *Warfare among East African Herders,* edited by K. Fukui and D. Turton. Osaka: Senri Ethnological Foundation, National Museum of Ethnology, 1979.

Bayart, Jean-François, Stephen Ellis, and Béatrice Hibou. *The Criminalization of the State in Africa.* Oxford and Bloomington: James Currey and Indiana University Press, 1999.

Bazán, Avelino. *Voces del socavón: Relatos, vivencias y sucesos en El Aguilar.* Jujuy, 1986.

Beal, Frank. *The Inside of the White Slave Traffic.* Directed by Frank Beal, 1913. Film.

Behnke, R. H., et al., eds. *Range, Ecology at Disequilibrium: New Models of Natural Variability and Pastoral Adaptation in African Savannas.* London: Overseas Development Institute, 1993.

Bellone, Amy. "The Cocaine Commodity Chain and Development Paths in Peru and Bolivia." In *Latin America in the World-Economy,* edited by Roberto Patricio Korzeniewicz and William C. Smith. Westport, Conn.: Greenwood Press, 1996.

Belshaw, D., and M. Malinga. "The Kalashnikov Economies of the Eastern Sahel: Cumulative or Cyclical Differentiation between Nomadic Pastoralists." Paper presented at the first workshop of the study group on conflict and security of the Development Studies Association, South Bank University. University of East Anglia, 1999.

Belshaw, Deryke, Sean Avery, Richard Hogg, and Richard Obin. "Report of the Evaluation Mission: Integrated Development in Karamoja," Uganda project. New York: Overseas Development Group, Norwich and UNCDF, 1996.

Benencia, Roberto. "La horticultura bonaerense: Medianeros bolivianos." In *Inmigración limítrofe: Los bolivianos en Buenos Aires*, ed. Roberto Benencia and Gabriela Karasik. Buenos Aires: Centro Editor de América Latina, 1995.

Benencia, Roberto, and Gabriela Karasik. *Inmigración limítrofe: Los bolivianos en Buenos Aires*. Buenos Aires: Centro Editor de América Latina, 1995.

Berdahl, Daphne. *Where the World Ended: Re-unification and Identity in the German Borderland*. Berkeley and Los Angeles: University of California Press, 1999.

Berridge, Virginia, and Griffith Edwards. *Opium and the People: Opiate Use in Nineteenth-Century England*. New Haven, Conn.: Yale University Press, 1987.

Bertram, Eva, et al. *Drug War Politics: The Price of Denial*. Berkeley: University of California Press, 1996.

Bhabha, Homi. "The Commitment to Theory." In *Questions of Third Cinema*, edited by Jim Pines and Paul Willemen. London: British Film Institute, 1989.

Bigo, Didier. "The Mobius Ribbon of Security(ies)." In *Identities, Borders, Orders: Rethinking International Relations Theory*, edited by Mathias Albert, David Jacobsen, and Yosef Lapid. Minneapolis: University of Minnesota Press, 2001.

Bigwood, Jeremy. "Plan Colombia's Potential Impact on the Andean Cocaine Trade: An Examination of Two Scenarios." CIA Intelligence Report, DCI Crime and Narcotics Center, September 19, 2000. Available at http://jeremybigwood.net/FOIAs/2Scenarios-Colombia/CIA-2scenarios-Colombian_coca-2000.htm.

Birgegard, L. E. *Natural Resources Tenure: A Review of Issues and Experiences with Emphasis on Sub-Saharan Africa*. Uppsala: Rural Development Studies, Swedish University of Agriculture Science/International Rural Development Centre, 1993.

Black, David. *ACID: A New Secret History of LSD*. London: Vision Paperbacks, 1998.

Black, Jeremy. *Maps and Politics*. Chicago: University of Chicago Press, 1997.

Blunt, Alison, and Gillian Rose. *Writing Women and Space: Colonial and Postcolonial Geographies*. London: Guilford, 1994.

Bollig, M. "Ethnic Conflicts in North-west Kenya: Pokot-Turkana Raiding 1969–1984." *Zeitschrift für Ethnologie* 115 (1990): 73–90.

Bonner, Raymond. "Murky Life of an International Gun Dealer." *The New York Times*, July 14, 1998.

Botelho Gozálvez, Raúl. *Coca*. La Paz-Cochabamba: Los Amigos del Libro, [1941] 1981.

Bourgois, Philippe. *In Search of Respect: Selling Crack in "El Barrio."* Cambridge: Cambridge University Press, 1995.

Boutwell, Jeffrey, and Michael Klare. "A Scourge of Small Arms." *Scientific American* (June 2000): 48–53.

Consolidated Bibliography

Bovenkerk, Frank. *La Bella Bettien*. Amsterdam: J. M. Meulenhoff, 1995.

———. *Misdaadprofielen*. Amsterdam: J. M. Meulenhoff, 2001.

Brenner, Neil. "Beyond State-Centrism? Space, Territoriality, and Geographical Scale in Globalization Studies." *Theory and Society* 28 (1999): 39–78.

———. "The Limits to Scale? Methodological Reflections on Scalar Structuration." *Progress in Human Geography* 25, no. 4 (2001): 591–614.

Brook, Timothy, and Bob Tadashi Wakabayashi. *Opium Regimes: China, Britain, and Japan, 1839–1952*. Berkeley: University of California Press, 2000.

Brzezinski, Matthew. "Re-engineering the Drug Business." *New York Times Magazine*, June 24, 2002.

Bucchi, Kenneth C. *C.I.A.: Cocaine in America? A Veteran of the C.I.A. Drug Wars Tells All*. New York: Spi Books, 1994.

Burgos, Fausto. *Coca, chicha y alcohol: Relatos puneños de pastores, arrieros y tejedoras*. Buenos Aires: Editorial Tor, 1927.

Camporesi, Piero. *Bread of Dreams: Food and Fantasy in Early Modern Europe*. Chicago: Chicago University Press, 1989.

Carter, William E., and Mauricio Mamani. *Multidisciplinary Study: Traditional Use of the Coca Leaf in Bolivia*. La Paz: Museo Nacional de Etnografía y Folklore, 1978.

———. "Patrones del uso de la coca en Bolivia." *América indígena* 38, no. 4 (1978).

———. *Coca en Bolivia*. La Paz: Editorial Juventud, 1986.

Cassinelli, Lee V. "Qat: Changes in the Production and Consumption of a Quasi-legal Commodity in Northeast Africa." In *The Social Life of Things*, edited by Arjun Appadurai, 236–257. Cambridge: Cambridge University Press, 1986.

Castells, Manuel. *The Information Age: Economy, Society and Culture*. Vol. 3: *End of Millennium*. Oxford: Blackwell, 1998.

Castles, Stephen. "Migration and Community Formation under Conditions of Globalization." *International Migration Review* 36, no. 4 (Winter 2002): 1143–1168.

Chabal, Patrick, and Jean-Pascal Daloz, eds. *Africa Works: Disorder as Political Instrument*. Oxford: James Curry/Bloomington: Indiana University Press, 1999.

Chaktow: Het verhaal van een drugsdealer. Utrecht: Het Spectrum, 1995.

Chantavanich, Supang. "Recent Research on Human Trafficking in Mainland Southeast Asia" (review essay). *Kyoto Review*, Center for Southeast Asian Studies, Kyoto University (October 2003). Available at http://kyotoreview.cseas.kyoto-u.ac.jp/issue/issue3/article_282.html.

Chattopadhyay, Suhrid Sankar. "Waiting to Go Home." *Frontline* 18, no. 10 (May 12–25, 2001): 10.

Cheater, A. P. "Transcending the State? Gender and Borderline Constructions of Citizenship in Zimbabwe." In *Border Identities: Nation and State at International Frontiers*, edited by Thomas M. Wilson and Hastings Donnan, 191–214. Cambridge: Cambridge University Press, 1998.

Chin, Ko-lin. *Smuggled Chinese: Clandestine Immigration to the United States*. Philadelphia: Temple University Press, 1999.

Clawson, Patrick, and Rensselaer W. Lee III. *The Andean Cocaine Industry*. New York: St. Martin's Press, 1996.

Cohn, Bernard S. "The Census, Social Structure and Objectification in South Asia." In *An Anthropologist among the Historians and Other Essays.* New York: Oxford University Press, 1987.

Comisión de Justicia y Paz. *La masacre del Valle.* La Paz: Cuadernos de Justicia y Paz, 1975.

Constantinous, B. T. "Alternative Natural Resources Management Systems: Processual and Strategic Dimensions in Governing the Environment." In *Political Change and Natural Resource Management in Eastern Africa and Southern Africa,* edited by H. W. O. Okoth-Ogendo and G. W Tumushabe. Nairobi: ACTS, 1999.

Cooper, Frederick. "What Is the Concept of Globalization Good For? An African Historian's Perspective." *African Affairs* 100, no. 399 (2001): 189–213.

Coppock, L. *The Borana Plateau of Southern Ethiopia: Synthesis of Pastoral Research, Development and Change, 1980–91.* Addis Ababa: International Livestock Center for Africa (ILCA), 1994.

Cornelius, Wayne A., Philip L. Martin, and James F. Hollifield, eds. *Controlling Immigration: A Global Perspective.* Stanford, Calif.: Stanford University Press, 1994.

——. "Spain: The Uneasy Transition from Labor Exporter to Labor Importer." In *Controlling Immigration: A Global Perspective,* edited by Wayne A. Cornelius et al., 2nd ed. Stanford, Calif.: Stanford University Press, 2004.

Cotler, Julio. *Drogas y política en el Perú.* Lima: IEP, 1999.

Courtwright, David T. *Forces of Habit: Drugs and the Making of the Modern World.* Cambridge, Mass.: Harvard University Press, 2001.

Cousins, B. "Conflict Management for Multiple Resources Users in Pastoralist and Agro-pastoralist Contexts." *IDS Bulletin* 27, no 3 (1996): 41–54.

Cox, Kevin. "Spaces of Dependence, Spaces of Engagement and the Politics of Scale, Or: Looking for Local Politics." *Political Geography* 17, no. 1 (1998): 1–23.

Cranna, M., ed. *The True Cost of Conflict.* London: Saferworld, 1994.

Crummey, Donald. "Introduction: 'The Great Beast.'" In *Banditry, Rebellion and Social Protest in Africa,* edited by Donald Crummey, 1–29. London and Portsmouth, N.H.: James Currey and Heinemann, 1986.

——. "Banditry and Resistance: Noble and Peasant in Nineteenth-Century Ethiopia." In *Banditry, Rebellion and Social Protest in Africa,* ed. Donald Crummey, 133–149. London and Portsmouth, N.H.: James Currey and Heinemann, 1986.

Currie, Elliott. *Reckoning: Drugs, the Cities, and the American Future.* New York: Hill and Wang, 1993.

David, Fiona. "New Threats or Old Stereotypes? The Revival of 'Trafficking' as a Discourse." Paper presented at the History of Crime, Policing and Punishment Conference, Canberra, December 9–10, 1999.

——. "Human Smuggling and Trafficking. An Overview of the Response at the Federal Level." Australian Institute of Criminology. Research and Public Policy Series no. 24. Canberra, 2000.

Davis, David Bryan. *The Problem of Slavery in the Age of Revolution.* Ithaca, N.Y.: Cornell University Press, 1975.

De Franco, Mario, and Ricardo Godoy. "The Economic Consequences of Cocaine in Bolivia: Historical, Local and Macro-Economic Consequences." *Journal of Latin American Studies* 24, no. 2 (1992): 375–406.

De Genova, Nicholas P. "Migrant 'Illegality' and Deportation in Everyday Life." *Annual Review of Anthropology* 31 (2002): 419–447.

Dent, O.-L. "Manhood, Warriorhood and Sex in Eastern Africa." In *The Warrior Tradition in Modern Africa*, edited by A. Mazrui. Leiden: E.J. Brill, 1977.

Derrida, Jacques. *On Cosmopolitanism and Forgiveness*. London: Routledge, 2001.

Desrosieres, Alain. *The Politics of Large Numbers: A History of Statistical Reasoning*. Translated by Camille Naish. Cambridge, Mass.: Harvard University Press, 1998.

Dietrich, Christian. "Have African-Based Diamond Monopolies Been Effective?" *Central Africa Minerals and Arms Research Bulletin* 2 (June 2001). Available at http://www.diamondstudies.com/docs/online.html.

———. *Hard Currency: The Criminalized Diamond Economy of the Democratic Republic of the Congo and its Neighbours*. Ottawa: Partnership Africa Canada, June 2002.

Dillon, Michael. *Politics of Security: Towards a Political Philosophy of Continental Thought*. New York: Routledge, 1996.

Doezema, Jo. "Loose Women or Lost Women. The Re-emergence of the Myth of 'White Slavery' in Contemporary Discourses of 'Trafficking in Women.'" *Gender Issues* 18, no. 1 (Winter 2000): 23–50. Available at http://www.walnet.org/csis/papers/doezema-loose.html.

Donnan, Hastings, and Thomas M. Wilson. *Borders: Frontiers of Identity, Nation and State*. Oxford and New York: Berg, 1999.

Douglas, Mary. *Purity and Danger: An Analysis of the Concepts of Pollution and Taboo*. London: Routledge & Kegan Paul, 1966.

Downs, Roger M., and David Stea. *Maps in Minds: Reflections on Cognitive Mapping*. New York: Harper & Row, 1977.

Driessen, Henk. "The 'New Immigration' and the Transformation of the European-African Frontier." In *Border Identities: Nation and State at International Frontiers*, edited by Thomas M. Wilson and Hastings Donnan, 96–116. Cambridge: Cambridge University Press, 1998.

Duke, Steven B., and Albert C. Gross. *America's Longest War*. New York: Putnam's Sons, 1993.

Dummett, Michael. *On Immigration and Refugees*. London: Routledge, 2001.

Dunn, Timothy J. *The Militarization of the U.S.-Mexico Border, 1978–1992: Low-Intensity Conflict Doctrine Comes Home*. Austin: Center for Mexican American Studies, University of Texas at Austin, 1996.

Eisner, Bruce. *Ecstasy: The MDMA Story*. Berkeley, Calif.: Ronin Publishing, 1994.

Epstein, Edward Jay. *Agency of Fear: Opiates and Political Power in America*. Rev. ed. New York: Verso, 1990.

Eschbach, Karl, Jacqueline Hagan, Néstor Rodríguez, Rubén Hernández, and Stanley Bailey. "Death at the Border." *International Migration Review* 33, no. 2 (1999).

Federación Especial Campesina del Trópico Cochabambino. "Coca." Paper presented at the Foro Nacional sobre la Problemática Coca-Cocaína, under the auspices of Comité Cívico Pro-Cochabamba. Cochabamba: Editorial Arol, 1988.

Fekete, Liz, and Frances Webber. "The Human Trade." *Race and Class* 39, no. 1 (1997).

Fingarette, Herbert. *Heavy Drinking: The Myth of Alcoholism as a Disease*. Berkeley: University of California Press, 1989.

Finkenauer, James. "Russian Transnational Organized Crime and Human Trafficking." In *Global Human Smuggling: Comparative Perspectives*, ed. David Kyle and Rey Koslowski, 166–186. Baltimore: Johns Hopkins University Press, 2001.

Foner, Eric. *Free Soil, Free Labor, Free Men*. Oxford: Oxford University Press, 1970.

Foucher, Michel. *Fronts et frontières: Un tour du monde géopolitique*. Paris: Fayard, 1991.

Frears, Stephen. *Dirty Pretty Things*. Directed by Stephen Frears, 2002. Film.

Freitag, Ulrike, and William G. Clarence-Smith, eds. *Hadrami Traders, Scholars and Statesmen in the Indian Ocean, 1760s–1960s*. Leiden: Brill, 1997.

Freud, Sigmund. "Craving for and Fear of Cocaine" (July 1887). Chapter 15 in *Cocaine Papers*, edited by Robert Byck. New York: Stonehill Press, 1974.

Friedmann, Jonathan. *Cultural Identity and Global Process*. London: Sage, 1994.

Friman, H. Richard. *NarcoDiplomacy: Exporting the U.S. War on Drugs*. Ithaca, N.Y.: Cornell University Press, 1996.

Friman, H. Richard, and Peter Andreas. *The Illicit Global Economy and State Power*. Lanham, Md.: Rowman & Littlefield, 1999.

Fugich, W. "The Role of Gada in Decision-Making and Its Implication for Pastoral Development and Poverty Alleviation among Borana." Paper presented at conference on community education co-hosted by Action-Aid and Association for World Education (AWE). Isiolo, Kenya, August 1999.

Fukui, K. "Conflict and Ethnic Interaction: The Mela and Their Neighbors." In *Ethnicity and Conflict in the Horn of Africa*, edited by K. Fukui and J. Markakis, 33–47. London and Athens, Ohio: James Currey and Ohio University Press, 1994.

Fukui, K., and D. Turton, eds. *Warfare among East African Herders*. Osaka: Senri Ethnological Foundation (National Museum of Ethnology), 1979.

Fukui, K., and J. Markakis, eds. *Ethnicity and Conflict in the Horn of Africa*. London and Athens, Ohio: James Currey and Ohio University Press, 1994.

Furedi, F. *The Mau Mau War In Perspective*. Nairobi: Heinemann Publishers, 1989.

Gagliano, Joseph A. *Coca Prohibition in Peru: The Historical Debates*. Tucson: University of Arizona Press, 1994.

Galaty, J. D. "Form and Intention in East African Strategies of Dominance." In *Dominance, Aggression and War*, edited by Diane McGuinnes. New York: Paragon House, 1987.

Galaty, J. G., and D. L. Johnson, eds. *The World of Pastoralism: Herding Systems in Perspective*. London: The Guilford Press, 1990.

Galaty, J. G., and Pierre Bonte, eds. *Herders, Warriors, and Traders: Pastoralism in Africa*. Boulder: Westview, 1991.

Gallagher, Anne. "Human Rights and the New UN Protocols on Trafficking and Migrant Smuggling: A Preliminary Analysis." *Human Rights Quarterly* 23, no. 4, (2001): 975–1004.

Gallagher, Anne, and Susu Thatun. "The US Government Report—A Critique." *Step By Step*, newsletter of the UN Inter-Agency Project on Trafficking in Women And Children in the Mekong Sub-Region, Third Quarter, 2001. Available at http://www.un.or.th/TraffickingProject/Publications/Number4.pdf.

Gallant, Thomas W. "Brigandage, Piracy, Capitalism, and State-Formation: Transnational Crime from a Historical World-Systems Perspective." In *States and Illegal Practices*, edited by Josiah McC. Heyman, 25–61. Oxford and New York: Berg, 1999.

Gereffi, Gary, and M. Koreniewicz, eds. *Commodity Chains and Global Capitalism*. Westport, Conn.: Greenwood Press, 1994.

Giddens, Anthony. *The Nation-State and Violence*. Berkeley: University of California Press, 1987.

Giorgis, Marta. "Y hasta los santos se trajeron: La fiesta de la virgen de Urkupiña en el boliviano Gran Córdoba." Master's thesis, Universidad Nacional de Misiones, Argentina, 1998.

Gironda, Eusebio. *Coca inmortal*. La Paz: Plural, 2001.

Global Witness. *A Rough Trade: The Role of Companies and Governments in the Angolan Conflict*. London: Global Witness, December 1998.

Goffman, Erving. *Estigma: La identidad deteriorada*. Buenos Aires: Amorrortu, [1971] 1998.

Gonzáles Casanova, Pablo. "El colonialismo interno." In *Sociología de la explotación*. México: Siglo XXI, 1969.

Goode, Erich. *Drugs in American Society*. 2nd ed. New York: Knopf, 1984.

———. *Between Politics and Reason: The Drug Legalization Debate*. New York: St. Martin's Press, 1997.

Goodman, Jordan. *Tobacco in History: The Cultures of Dependence*. New York: Routledge, 1993.

———. "Excitantia: Or, How Enlightenment Europe Took to Soft Drugs." In *Consuming Habits: Drugs in History and Anthropology*, edited by Jordan Goodman, Paul E. Lovejoy, and Andrew Sherratt. New York: Routledge, 1995.

Gootenberg, Paul. "Between Coca and Cocaine: A Century or More of U.S.-Peruvian Drug Paradoxes, 1860–1980." *Hispanic American Historical Review* 83, no. 1 (February 2003): 123–53.

———. "Secret Ingredients: The Politics of Coca in U.S.-Peruvian Relations, 1915–65." *Journal of Latin American Studies* 36, no. 2 (2004).

———. "Cocaine in Chains: The Rise and Demise of Global Commodity, 1860–1950." Manuscript for *Latin America and Global Trade*, ed. S. Topik, C. Marichal, and Z. Frank. Durham, N.C.: Duke University Press, forthcoming.

Gootenberg, Paul, ed. *Cocaine: Global Histories*. New York: Routledge, 1999.

Gottmann, Jean. *The Significance of Territory*. Charlottesville: University Press of Virginia, 1973.

Gray, Mike. *Drug Crazy*. New York: Random House, 1998.

Graycar, Adam. "Human Smuggling." Paper presented at the Centre for Criminology, the University of Hong Kong, February 19, 2000.

Grimal, Jean-Claude. *Drogue: L'autre mondialisation*. Paris: Gallimard, 2000.

Grimson, Alejandro, ed. *Fronteras, naciones e identidades: La periferia como centro*. Buenos Aires: Ediciones CICCUS-La Crujía, 2000.

———. "Introducción ¿Fronteras políticas versus fronteras culturales?" In *Fronteras, naciones e identidades: La periferia como centro*, ed. Alejandro Grimson, 9–40. Buenos Aires: Ediciones CICCUS-La Crujía, 2000.

———. "La migración boliviana a la Argentina." In *Migrantes bolivianos en la Argentina y los Estados Unidos*, edited by Alejandro Grimson and Edmundo Paz Soldán. Cuaderno de Futuro, no. 7. La Paz: Programa de las Naciones Unidas para el Desarrollo, 2000.

Gufu, O. *Assessment of Indigenous Range Management Knowledge of Boran Pastoralists of Southern Ethiopia*. Neghelle: Report to the GTZ Boran Lowland Pastoral Development Program, 1998.

Guha, Ranajit. "La Prosa de Contrainsurgencia." In *Debates postcoloniales. Una introducción a los estudios de la subalternidad*, comp. Silvia Rivera and Rossana Barragán. La Paz: Historias-SEPHIS-Aruwiyiri, 1997.

Guillermoprieto, Alma. *The Heart That Bleeds*. New York: Knopf, 1994.

Gulliver, P. H. *The Family Herds: A Study of Two Pastoral Tribes in East Africa: The Jie and Turkana*. London: Routledge and Kegan Paul, 1955.

———. "Nomadism among the Pastoral Turkana of Kenya." Nkanga Makerere: Institute of Social Research, 1972.

Gusfield, Joseph R. *Contested Meanings: The Construction of Alcohol Problems*. Madison: University of Wisconsin Press, 1996.

G8 Heads of Government. "G8 Action Plan for Africa." Statement presented at G8 heads of government meeting, Kananaskis, Alberta, June 27, 2002.

Habermas, Jürgen. *The Postnational Constellation: Political Essays*. Cambridge: Polity Press, 2001.

Hacking, Ian. *The Social Construction of What?* Cambridge, Mass.: Harvard University Press, 1999.

Hadley, J. *Pastoralist Cosmology: The Organizing Framework for Indigenous Conflict Resolution in the Horn of Africa*. Harrisonburg, Va.: Eastern Mennonite University, 1997.

Hansen, N. *Border Economy: Regional Development in the Southwest*. Austin: University of Texas Press, 1981.

Harding, Geoffrey. *Opiate Addiction, Morality and Medicine: From Moral Illness to Pathological Disease*. Houndmills Basingstoke, Hampshire: Macmillan, 1988.

Hart, Matthew. *Diamond: A Journey to the Heart of an Obsession*. New York: Viking, 2001.

Haugerud, Angelique, M. Priscilla Stone, and Peter D. Little, eds. *Commodities and Globalization: Anthropological Perspectives*. Lanham, Md.: Rowman and Littlefield, 2000.

Healy, Kevin. "The Coca-Cocaine Issue in Bolivia: A Political Resource for all Seasons." In *Coca, Cocaine and the Bolivian Reality*, edited by Barbara Léons and Harry Sanabria, 99–115. New York: State University of New York Press, 1997.

Healey, Lucy. "Gender, Aliens and the National Imaginary in Malaysia." Paper presented at the annual meeting of the Australian Asian Studies Association Meeting, Brisbane, 2000.

Helland, J. "Institutional Erosion in the Drylands: The Case of the Borana Pastoralists." *Eastern Africa Social Science Review* XIV, no. 2 (1993).

Hendrickson, D., R. Mearns, and J. Armon. "Livestock Raiding among the Pastoral Turkana of Kenya." *IDS Bulletin* 27, no. 3 (1996): 17–30.

Heyman, Josiah McC., and Alan Smart. "States and Illegal Practices: An Overview." In *States and Illegal Practices*, edited by Josiah McC. Heyman, 1–24. Oxford and New York: Berg, 1999.

Hinojosa, Alfonso. "El viaje, la residencia y el retorno." Paper presented at Curso de Metodologías Cualitativas, Universidad de La Cordillera, 2000.

Hinojosa, Alfonso, Guido Cortéz, and Liz Pérez. "Estrategias migratorias: Tarijeños en la Argentina, vidas fronterizas." *T'inkazos. Revista boliviana de ciencias sociales* 6 (May 2000): 49–65.

Hinojosa, Alfonso, Liz Pérez, and Guido Cortéz. "Idas y venidas: Campesinos tarijeños en el Norte Argentino." Programa de Investigación Estratégica en Bolivia (PIEB) Final Report. La Paz: Instituto de Investigaciones Socio Económicas, 2000.

Hobsbawn, Eric J. *Bandits*. 2nd ed. New York: New Press, 2000.

Hobsbawm, Eric J., and Terence Ranger. *The Invention of Tradition*. Cambridge: Cambridge University Press, 1983.

Hopkins, Terence, and Immanuel Wallerstein. "Commodity Chains: Construct and Research." In *Commodity Chains and Global Capitalism*, ed. Gary Gereffi and M. Koreniewicz. Westport, Conn.: Greenwood Press, 1994.

Howitt, Richard. "Scale as Relation: Musical Metaphors of Geographical Space." *Area* 30, no. 1 (1998): 49–58.

Huanca, Bernardo. "Cronología de un hecho social: La expulsión de la Fuerza de Tarea Conjunta del vivero de Evenay, Chamaca y Totora por los campesinos de La Asunta." Thesis (in preparation), Universidad Mayor de San Andres, Bolivia, n.d.

Hubert, Annie. "Introduction." In *Opiums: Les plantes du plaisir et de la convivialité en Asie*, edited by Annie Hubert and Philippe Le Failler, 7–12. Paris: L'Harmattan, 2000.

Hurtado Gumucio, Jorge. *Cocaína: En busca del paraíso perdido*. Santa Cruz, 1987.

Ibn Khaldūn. *The* Muqaddimah: *An Introduction to History*. Translated by Franz Rosenthal. London: Routledge and Kegan Paul, 1958.

ILRI/ASARECA. "Coping Mechanisms and Their Efficacy in Disaster-Prone Pastoral Systems of the Greater Horn of Africa (GHA): Effects and Responses of Pastoralist and Livestock during the 1995–97 Drought and the 1997–1998 El Nino Rains." ILRI/ASARECA, 1998.

Instituto Indigenista Interamericano. *La coca . . . tradición, rito, identidad*. México: Instituto Indigenista Interamericano, 1989.

International Commission on Intervention and State Sovereignty. "The Responsibility to Protect." Report of the International Commission on Intervention and State Sovereignty. Ottawa: Canadian Foreign Ministry, 2002.

International Organization for Migration (IOM). "Overview." Available at http://www.iom.int/en/who/main_policies_trafficking.shtml#chap0.

Interpol. "People Smuggling." Available at http://www.interpol.int/Public/THB/PeopleSmuggling/Default.asp.

Jackson, Robert H. *Quasi-States: Sovereignty, International Relations and the Third World.* Cambridge: Cambridge University Press, 1990.

Jelin, Elizabeth. "Epílogo II: Fronteras, naciones, género: Un comentario." In *Fronteras, naciones e identidades,* edited by Alejandro Grimson, 333–342. Buenos Aires: Ediciones Ciccus, 2000.

Jessop, Bob. *State Theory: Putting the State in Its Place.* University Park: Pennsylvania State University Press, 1991.

Jokisch, Brad, and Jason Pribilsky. "The Panic to Leave: Economic Crisis and the 'New Emigration' from Ecuador." *International Migration* 40, no. 4 (2002).

Jones, Katherine T. "Scale as Epistemology." *Political Geography* 17, no. 1 (1998): 25–28.

Jones, Sidney. "Making Money Off Migrants: The Indonesian Exodus to Malaysia." Hong Kong: Asia 2002 Ltd., and Centre for Asia-Pacific Transformation Studies, University of Wollongong, 2000.

Kaggia, B. *Roots of Freedom.* Nairobi: East African Publishing House, 1975.

Kaihla, Paula. "The Technological Secrets of Cocaine Inc." *Business,* July 20, 2002.

Kanogo, T. "Kikuyu Women and the Politics of Mau Mau." In *Images and Women in Peace and War: Cross-Cultural Historical Perspectives,* edited by S. MacDonald et al., 123–138. London: Macmillan, 1987.

Karasik, Gabriela. *Formas de sociabilidad de un grupo de migrantes andinos en el Gran Buenos Aires.* Buenos Aires: Consejo de Investigaciones Científicas y Tecnicas (CONICET), 1987.

———. "Trabajadoras bolivianas en el conurbano bonaerense. Pequeño comercio y conflicto social." In *Inmigración limítrofe: Los bolivianos en Buenos Aires,* edited by Roberto Benencia and Gabriela Karasik. Buenos Aires: Centro Editor de América Latina, 1995.

———. "Tras la genealogía del diablo. Discusiones sobre la nación y el Estado en la frontera argentino-boliviana." In *Fronteras, naciones e identidades. La periferia como centro,* edited by Alejandro Grimson. Buenos Aires: La Crujia, 2000.

Keire, Mara L. "The Vice Trust: A Reinterpretation of the White Slavery Scare in the United States, 1907–1917." *Journal of Social History* 35, no. 1 (2001): 5–41.

Keller, E. J. "A Twentieth Century Model: The Mau Mau Transformation from Social Banditry to Social Rebellion." *Kenya Historical Review* 1, no. 2 (1973): 189–205.

Kerven, C. "Customary Commerce: A Historical Reassessment of Pastoral Livestock Marketing in Africa." ODI Agricultural Occasional Paper no 15. London: Overseas Development Institute, 1992.

Kimberley Process. "Essential Elements of an International Scheme of Certification For Rough Diamonds." Kimberley Process Working Document no. 1/2002, March 20, 2002.

Kinyatti, wa M. *Thunder from the Mountains: Mau Mau Patriotic Songs.* Nairobi: Midi-Tera Publishers, 1980.

Kinyatti, wa M., ed. *Kimathi's Letters: A Profile of Patriotic Courage.* Nairobi: Heinemann, 1986.

Kitching, G. *Class and Economic Change in Kenya: The Making of an African Petite Bourgeoisie, 1905–1970.* Nairobi: East African Publishers, 1970.

Klein, Bradley. *Strategic Studies and World Order: The Global Politics of Deterrence.* Cambridge: Cambridge University Press, 1994.

Kohn, Marek. *Narcomania: On Heroin.* Boston: Faber and Faber, 1987.

———. *Dope Girls: The Birth of the British Drugs Underground.* London: Lawrence & Wishart, 1992.

Kopytoff, Igor. "The Cultural Biography of Things." In *The Social Life of Things,* ed. Arjun Appadurai. Cambridge: Cambridge University Press, 1986.

Krajick, Kevin. *Barren Lands.* New York: Times Books, 2001.

Kyle, David. *Transnational Peasants: Migrations, Networks, and Ethnicity from Andean Ecuador.* Baltimore: Johns Hopkins University Press, 2000.

Kyle, David, and John Dale. "Smuggling the State Back In: Agents of Human Smuggling Reconsidered." In *Global Human Smuggling: Comparative Perspectives,* edited by David Kyle and Rey Koslowski, 29–57. Baltimore: Johns Hopkins University Press, 2001.

Kyle, David, and Rey Koslowski. "Introduction." In *Global Human Smuggling: Comparative Perspectives,* edited by David Kyle and Rey Koslowski. Baltimore: John Hopkins University Press, 2001.

Kyle, David, and Rey Koslowski, eds. *Global Human Smuggling: Comparative Perspectives.* Baltimore and London: Johns Hopkins University Press, 2001.

Labrousse, Alain. *La droga, el dinero y las armas.* Siglo Veintiuno, 1993. Originally published in Paris, 1991.

Lamphear, J. "The Evolution of Ateker 'New Model' Armies: Jie and Turkana." In *Ethnicity and Conflict in the Horn of Africa,* ed. K. Fukui and J. Markakis, 63–94. London and Athens, Ohio: James Currey and Ohio University Press, 1994.

Laserna, Roberto. *20 Juicios y Prejuicios sobre Coca-Cocaína.* La Paz: Clave, 1996.

Lee, Martin A., and Bruce Shlain. *Acid Dreams: The CIA, LSD and the Sixties Rebellion.* New York: Grove Press, 1985.

Lefebvre, Henri. *The Production of Space.* Translated by Donald Nicholson-Smith. Oxford: Blackwell, [1974] 1991.

Lema, Ana María. "The Coca Debate and Yungas Landowners during the First Half of the 20th Century." In *Coca, Cocaine and the Bolivian Reality,* edited by Barbara Léons and Harry Sanabria, 99–115. New York: State University of New York Press, 1997.

Lenson, David. *On Drugs.* Minneapolis: University of Minnesota Press, 1995.

León, Federico R., and Ramiro Castro de la Mata. *Pasta básica de cocaína: Un estudio multidisciplinario*. Lima: Centro de Información y Educación para la Prevención del Abuso de Drogas, 1988.

Léons, Barbara. "Changing Patterns of Social Stratification in an Emergent Bolivian Community." Ph.D. thesis, University of California, Los Angeles, 1966.

———. "After the Boom: Income Decline, Eradication and Alternative Development in the Yungas." In *Coca, Cocaine and the Bolivian Reality*, edited by Barbara Léons and Harry Sanabria, 139–167. New York: State University of New York Press, 1997.

Léons, Barbara, and Harry Sanabria, eds. *Coca, Cocaine and the Bolivian Reality*. New York: State University of New York Press, 1997.

Léons, Madeleine B., and William Léons. "Land Reform and Economic Change in the Yungas." In *Beyond the Revolution: Bolivia since 1952*, edited by James M. Malloy and Richard S. Thorn. Pittsburgh: University of Pittsburgh Press, 1971.

Liang, Zai, and Wenzhen Ye. "From Fujian to New York: Understanding the New Chinese Immigration." In *Global Human Smuggling: Comparative Perspectives*, edited by David Kyle and Rey Koslowski, 187–215. Baltimore: Johns Hopkins University Press, 2001.

Livingston, I. "The Common Property Problem and Pastoralist Economic Behaviour." *Journal of Development Studies* 23, no. 1 (1986).

Lohman, María, ed. *Coca—Cronología. Bolivia: 1986–1992*. Cochabamba y La Paz: Centro de Documentación e Información (CEDIB) and Instituto Latinoamericano de Investigaciones Sociales (ILDIS), 1991.

Lomnitz, Claudio, ed. *Vicios públicos, virtudes privadas: La corrupción en México*. Mexico City: CIESAS/Miguel Angel Porrúa, 2000.

Lotuai, D. "The Causes and Consequences of Cattle Rustling among Pastoralist Communities." APA Paper no. 47/97. Nairobi: KIA, 1997.

Lucassen, Leo, Wim Willems, and Annemarie Cottaar. *Gypsies and Other Itinerant Groups: A Socio-historical Approach*. Houndmills: Macmillan/New York: St. Martin's Press, 1998.

Ludden, David. "History Outside Civilization and the Mobility of South Asia," *South Asia* 17, no. 1 (June 1994).

———. "Presidential Address: Maps in the Mind and the Mobility of Asia." *Journal of Asian Studies* 62, no. 4 (November 2003): 1062.

Luke, Timothy W., and Gearoíd Ó Tuathail. "The Fraying Modern Map: Failed States and Contraband Capitalism." *Geopolitics* 3, no. 3 (1999): 14–33.

Malamud-Goti, Jaime. *Smoke and Mirrors: The Paradox of the Drug Wars*. Boulder, Colo.: Westview Press, 1992.

Mamdani, M, P. M. B. Kasoma, and A. B. Laatende. "Karamoja: Ecology and History." Working Paper no. 22. Kampala: Centre for Basic Research: Kampala, 1992.

Manderson, Desmond. "Metamorphosis: Clashing Symbols in the Social Construction of Drugs." *Journal of Drug Issues* 23, no. 4 (1995): 799–816.

Mandivamba, R. "Land Tenure and Sustainable Development in Africa: Experiences from Community Based Natural Resource Management—Models for 21st Century Africa." Conference paper, African Studies Centre, World

Resource Institute, Co-sponsored by Ministry of Foreign Affairs and HIVOS, Netherlands, 8–10 September 1999.

Mann, Michael. *States, War and Capitalism: Studies in Political Sociology.* Oxford: Blackwell, 1988.

Manning, Chris, and Pradip Bhatnagar. "Coping With and Managing Temporary Labour Migration in Southeast Asia: The Role of 'Markets' versus International and Regional Economic Agreements." Paper presented at the conference on Migrant Labour in Southeast Asia: Needed Not Wanted, Armidale, December 1–3, 2003.

Mansilla, H. C. F. *Repercusiones ecológicas y éticas del complejo coca/cocaína: La percepción de la problemática por los involucrados.* La Paz: SEAMOS and Centro Boliviano de Estudios Multidisciplinarios (CEBEM), 1994.

Markakis, J. *National and Class Conflict in the Horn of Africa.* Cambridge: Cambridge University Press, 1987.

———. *Resource Conflict in the Horn of Africa.* London and New Delhi: Sage Publications, 1998.

Markakis, J. ed. *Conflict and the Decline of Pastoralism in the Horn of Africa.* London: Macmillan, 1993.

Marston, Sallie A. "The Social Construction of Scale." *Progress in Human Geography* 24, no. 2 (2000): 219–242.

Martinez, Sanjuana. "Psicosis por la Ley de Extranjeria. Espana-Ecuador: La guerra migratoria." *Proceso,* no. 1267 (February 11, 2001).

Marx, Karl, and Frederick Engels. *The Communist Manifesto.* London: Verso, [1848] 1998.

Massey, Douglas S. "Why Does Immigration Occur? A Theoretical Synthesis." In *The Handbook of International Migration,* edited by Charles Hirschman, Philip Kasinitz, and Josh deWind, 34–52. New York: Russell Sage Foundation, 1999.

Massey, Douglas S., Jorge Durand, and Nolan J. Malone. *Beyond Smoke and Mirrors: Mexican Immigration in an Era of Economic Integration.* New York: Russell Sage Foundation, 2002.

Massing, Michael. *The Fix.* New York: Simon & Schuster, 1998.

Matthe, Rudi. "Exotic Substances: The Introduction and Global Spread of Tobacco, Coffee, Cocoa, Tea, and Distilled Liquor, 16th–18th Centuries." In *Drugs and Narcotics in History,* edited by Roy Porter and Mikulas Teich. Cambridge: Cambridge University Press, 1995.

Mbembe, Achille. "At the Edge of the World: Boundaries, Territoriality and Sovereignty in Africa." *Public Culture* 12, no. 1 (2000): 259–284.

McAllister, William B. *Drug Diplomacy in the Twentieth Century: An International History.* London: Routledge, 2000.

McCoy, Alfred E. "Heroin as a Global Commodity: A History of Southeast Asia's Opium Trade." In *War on Drugs: Studies in the Failure of U.S. Narcotics Policy,* edited by Alfred McCoy and Alan A. Block, 237–255. Boulder, Colo.: Westview Press, 1992.

———. *The Politics of Heroin: CIA Complicity in the Global Drug Trade.* Rev. ed. Chicago: Lawrence Hill Books, 2003.

McDowell, Linda. *Gender, Identity and Place: Understanding Feminist Geographies*. Minneapolis: University of Minnesota Press, 1999.

Middelburg, Bart. *De Godmother: De criminele carrière van Thea Moear, medeoprichter van de Bruinsma-groep*. Amsterdam/Antwerpen: L.J. Veen, 2000.

Mintz, Sidney W. *Sweetness and Power: The Place of Sugar in Modern History*. New York: Penguin Books, 1985.

———. "The Forefathers of Crack." *NACLA Report on the Americas* 22, no. 6, March 1989.

Mkutu, K. "Banditry, Cattle Rustling and the Proliferation of Small Arms: The Case of Baragoi Division of Samburu District." Arusha report. Nairobi: African Peace Forum, 2000.

Mkutu, K., and M. Marani. "The Role of Civic Leaders in the Mitigation of Cattle Rustling and Small Arms: The Case of Laikipia and Samburu." Nairobi: African Peace Forum, 2001.

Molins, W. Jaime. *Bolivia: Crónicas Americanas*. Buenos Aires: Libro Primero, 1916.

Momoh, C. S. "A Critique of Borderland Theories." In *Borderlands in Africa: A Multidisciplinary and Comparative Focus on Nigeria and West Africa*, edited by A. I. Asiwaju and P. O. Ademiyi, 51–61. Lagos: University of Lagos Press, 1985.

Monge, Carlos. *Acclimatization in the Andes: Historic Confirmation of "Climatic Aggression" in the Development of Andean Man*. Baltimore: Johns Hopkins University Press, 1948.

Morales, Edmundo. *Cocaine: White Gold Rush in Peru*. Tucson: University of Arizona Press, 1989.

Morgan, John P., and Lynn Zimmer. "The Social Pharmacology of Smokeable Cocaine: Not All It's Cracked Up to Be." Chapter 7 in *Crack in America: Demon Drugs and Social Justice*, edited by Craig Reinarman and Harry G. Levine. Berkeley: University of California Press, 1997.

Morris, L. "Globalization, Migration and the Nation-State." *British Journal of Sociology* 48, no. 2 (1997): 192–209.

Morrison, John, and Beth Crosland. "The Trafficking and Smuggling of Refugees: The End Game in European Asylum Policy?" New Issues in Refugee Research working paper no. 39. UNHCR, 2001. Available at http://www.unhcr.ch/refworld/pubs/pubon.htm and http://www.jha.ac/articles/u039.pdf.

Mukhopadyay, Baskhar. "The Rumour of Globalisation: Subaltern Imaginaries of Consumption and the Rhetoric of Temporality." Paper presented at the Sephis Workshop, Kuala Lumpur, Malaysia, June 14–16, 2002.

Muller, H. *Changing Generations: Dynamics of Generation and Age-Sets in Southeastern Sudan (Toposa) and Northeastern Kenya (Turkana)*. Searbrucken: Breitenbach Publishers, 1989.

Mundlak, Y., and F. S. Singer, eds. *Arid Zone Development: Potentialities and Problems*. Cambridge, Mass.: Ballinger, 1975.

Muriuki, R. "Livestock Marketing from Pastoral Areas of Kenya: A Strategy for Pastoral Development." Arid Lands Resource Management Organization (ALRMP) in conjunction with SNV, the Netherlands Development Organization (Kenya), Oxfam (GB and Kenya), World Concern and Action Aid, 2000.

Musto, David C. *The American Disease: Origins of Narcotic Control.* Expanded ed. New York: Oxford University Press, 1987.

Nadelmann, Ethan. "U.S. Drug Policy: A Bad Export." *Foreign Policy* 70 (1988): 97–108.

———. "Global Prohibition Regimes: The Evolution of Norms in International Society." *International Organization* 44, no. 4 (1990): 479–526.

———. *Cops across Borders: The Internationalization of U.S. Criminal Law Enforcement.* University Park: Pennsylvania State University Press, 1993.

Naím, Moisés. "Five Wars of Globalization." *Foreign Policy* (January/February 2003): 28–36.

Nangulu-Ayuku, A. "Politics, Urban Planning and Population Settlement: Nairobi, 1912–1916." *Journal of Third World Studies* XVII, no. 2 (Fall 2000): 171–204.

Nasution, M. Arif. "Aliran Pekerja Indonesia Malaysia: Kes Tentang Pekerja Indonesia dalam Sektor Pembinaan di Kuala Lumpur, Malaysia." Ph.D. dissertation, Jabatan Geografi, Fakulti Sains Kemasyarakatan dan Kemanusian, Universiti Kebangsaan Malaysia, 1997.

National Council of Churches of Kenya (NCCK). "The Update on Peace and Rehabilitation." Nairobi: NCCK, June 30, 2000.

Naylor, R. T. *Wages of Crime: Black Markets, Illegal Finance, and the Underworld Economy.* Ithaca, N.Y., and New York: Cornell University Press, 2002.

Nevins, Joseph. *Operation Gatekeeper: The Rise of the "Illegal Alien" and the Making of the U.S.-Mexico Boundary.* New York and london: Routledge, 2002.

Newman, David. "Boundaries, Borders and Barriers: Changing Geographic Perspectives on Territorial Lines." In *Identities, Borders, Orders: Rethinking International Relations Theory,* edited by Mathias Albert, David Jacobsen, and Yosef Lapid, 137–151. Minneapolis: University of Minnesota Press, 2001.

Niamir-Fuller, M. "Conflict Management and Mobility among Pastoralists in Karamoja, Uganda," in *Managing Mobility in African Rangelands.* London: ITDG, 1999.

Nnoli, O. "Ethnic Conflicts in Eastern Africa." In *Ethnic Conflicts in Africa,* edited by O. Nnoli. Dakar: CODESRIA, 1998.

Nora, Pierre, ed. *Les lieux de mémoire.* 3 vols. Paris: Éditions Gallimard, 1997.

Nordstrom, Carolyn. *Shadows of War: Violence, Power, and International Profiteering in the Twenty-First Century.* Berkeley and Los Angeles: University of California Press, 2004.

Noriega, Chon A. "Requiem for Our Beginnings." *Aztlan: A Journal of Chicano Studies* (published by Chicano Studies Research Center, Los Angeles) 25, no. 2 (Autumn 2000).

Novelli, B. "Aspects of Karimojong Ethno-sociology." *Museum Comboninium,* no. 44. Kampala: Comboni Missionaries, 1988.

Nugent, Paul. "Power versus Knowledge: Smugglers and the State along Ghana's Eastern Frontier, 1920–1992." In *Frontiers and Borderlands: Anthropological Perspectives,* edited by Michael Rösler and Tobias Wendl, 77–99. Frankfurt am Main: Peter Lang, 1999.

———. *Smugglers, Secessionists & Loyal Citizens on the Ghana-Togo Frontier: The*

Lie of the Borderlands since 1914. Athens: Ohio University Press/Oxford: James Currey/Legon: Sub-Saharan Publishers, 2002.

Organización de las Naciones Unidas. "Informe de la Comisión de Estudio de las Hojas de Coca." Actas Oficiales. Duodécimo Período de Sesiones. Nueva York: Organización de las Naciones Unidas, 1950.

Orleans, Peter. "Differential Cognition of Urban Residents: Effects of Social Scale on Mapping." In *Image and Environment: Cognitive Mapping and Spatial Behavior,* edited by Roger M. Downs and David Stea, 115–130. Chicago: Aldine Publishing Company, 1973.

Ott, Jonathan. *Pharmacotheon: Entheogenic Drugs, Their Plant Sources and History.* Kennewick, Wash.: Natural Products Co., 1993.

Paasi, Ansi. "Boundaries as Social Processes: Territoriality in the World of Flows." *Geopolitics* 3, no. 1 (1999): 669–680.

Pacini, Deborah, and Christine Franquemont. "Coca Chewing and the Botanical Origins of Coca (Erythroxylum spp.) in South America." In *Coca and Cocaine: Effects on People and Policy in Latin America,* edited by Deborah Pacini and Christine Franquemont. Peterborough, N.H.: Cultural Survival and Cornell University, 1986.

Padrón, Ricardo. "Mapping Plus Ultra: Cartography, Space and Hispanic Modernity." *Representations* 79 (2002): 28–60.

Painter, James. *Bolivia and Coca: A Study in Dependency.* Boulder and London: Lynne Rienner, 1994.

Parker, Geoffrey. *The Military Revolution.* Cambridge: Cambridge University Press, 1988.

Pendergrast, Mark. *For God, Country and Coca-Cola: The Unauthorized History of the Great American Soft-Drink and the Company That Makes It.* New York: Scribner's, 1993.

Perner, C. "'The Reward of Life Is Death': Warfare and Anyuak of the Ethiopian-Sudanese Border." In *Conflicts in the Horn of Africa: Human and Ecological Consequences of Warfare,* edited by T. Tvedt, 125–142. Uppsala: Uppsala University, Department of Social and Economic Geography, 1993.

Pickles, John. "Texts, Hermeneutics and Propaganda Maps." In *Writing Worlds: Discourse, Text and Metaphor in the Representation of Landscape,* edited by Trevor J. Barnes and James S. Duncan, 193–230. London and New York: Routledge, 1992.

Polanyi, Karl. *The Great Transformation.* Boston: Beacon Press, 1944.

Pollan, Michael. *The Botany of Desire.* New York: Random House, 2001.

Pomeranz, Kenneth, and Steven Topik. *The World That Trade Created: Society, Culture, and the World Economy, 1400–the Present.* Armonk, N.Y.: M.E. Sharpe, 1999.

Poole, Deborah. *Visión, raza y modernidad: Una economía visual delmundo andino de imágenes.* Lima: Sur, 2000.

Poser, Patricia R. "The Role of Gender, Households and Social Networks in the Migration Process: A Review and an Appraisal." In *The Handbook of International Migration,* edited by Charles Hirschman, Philip Kasinitz, and Josh deWind, 53–70. New York: Russell Sage Foundation, 1999.

Prasertkul, Chiranan. *Yunnan Trade in the Nineteenth Century: Southwest China's Cross-Boundaries Functional System.* Bangkok: Institute of Asian Studies, Chulalongkorn University, 1989.

Prashad, Vijay. *Fat Cats and Running Dogs: The Enron Stage of Capitalism.* Monroe, Maine: Common Courage Press, 2003.

Pratt, Mary Louise. *Imperial Eyes: Travel Writing and Acculturation.* London: Routledge, 1992.

Preston, Brian. *Pot Planet: Adventures in Global Marijuana Culture.* New York: Grove Press, 2002.

Quam, M. D. "Creating Peace in an Armed Society: Karamoja, Uganda." *African Studies Quarterly* 1, no. 1 (1996): 15.

Quiroga, José Antonio. *Coca/cocaína: Una visión boliviana.* La Paz: AIPE/PROCOM-CEDLA-CID, 1990.

Rabey, Mario. "Legalidad e ilegalidad del coqueo en Argentina." In *La coca . . . tradición, rito, identidad,* Instituto Indigenista Interamericano, 35–78. México: Instituto Indigenista Interamericano, 1989.

Raffestin, Claude. "From Text to Image." In *From Geopolitics to Global Politics: A French Connection,* edited by Jacques Lévy, 7–34. London and Portland, Ore.: Frank Cass, 2001.

Raffestin, Claude, Dario Lopreno, and Yvan Pasteur. *Géopolitique et Histoire.* Lausanne: Éditions Payot, 1995.

Ragas, Ed. *Baarle op de grens van twee eeuwen: Enclavedorpen in beeld.* Baarle: Bruna, 1999.

Raghavan, V. R. *Siachen: Conflict without End.* New Delhi: Viking/Penguin, 2002.

Raikes, Philip, Michael Friis Jensen, and Stefano Ponte. "Global Commodity Chain Analysis and the French Filière Approach: Comparison and Critique." CDR Working Paper 00.3, Centre for Development Research, Copenhagen, 2000.

Reeves, Jimmie L., and Richard Campbell. *Cracked Coverage: Television News, the Anti-Cocaine Crusade, and the Reagan Legacy.* Durham, N.C.: Duke University Press, 1994.

Reinarman, Craig, and Harry G. Levine. "The Cultural Contradictions of Punitive Prohibitions." Chapter 16 in *Crack in America: Demon Drugs and Social Justice,* ed. Craig Reinarman and Harry G. Levine. Berkeley: University of California Press, 1997.

Reinarman, Craig, and Harry G. Levine, eds. *Crack in America: Demon Drugs and Social Justice.* Berkeley: University of California Press, 1997.

Relyea, Scott. "Trans-State Entities: Postmodern Cracks in the Great Westphalian Dam." *Geopolitics* 3, no. 2 (1998): 30–61.

Rengert, George. *The Geography of Illegal Drugs.* Boulder, Colo.: Westview Press, 1996.

Republic of Kenya National Archives. "Kenya Land Commission of 1933." Kenya National Archives (1933–1934): 185.

Republic of Kenya. *The 1969 Population and Housing Census.* Nairobi: Government Press, 1969.

Republic of Kenya. *The 1979 Population and Housing Census*. Nairobi: Central Bureau for Statistics, 1979.

Republic of Kenya. *The 1989 Population and Housing Census*. Nairobi: Central Bureau for Statistics, 1989.

Republic of Kenya. *The 1999 Population and Housing Census*. Vol. 2. Nairobi: Central Bureau for Statistics, 2001.

Richard, Amy O'Neill. "International Trafficking in Women to the United States: A Contemporary Manifestation of Slavery and Organized Crime." Center for the Study of Intelligence, 2000. (Dated November 1999, made public in April 2000.) Available at http://www.cia.gov/csi/monograph/women/trafficking.pdf.

Rivera Cusicanqui, Silvia. *"Oprimidos pero no vencidos": Luchas del campesinado aymara y qhichwa, 1900–1980*. La Paz: HISBOL-CSUTCB, 1984.

———. "Sendas y senderos de la ciencia social Andina." *Autodeterminación* 5 (1992).

———. "Mestizaje colonial andino: Una hipótesis de trabajo." In *Violencias encubiertas en Bolivia*, vol. 1: *Cultura y política*, edited by Silvia Rivera y Raul Barrios. La Paz: HISBOL-Aruwiyiri, 1993.

———. "Pachakuti, los horizontes históricos del colonialismo interno." In *Violencias encubiertas en Bolivia*, vol. 1: *Cultura y política*, edited by Silvia Rivera y Raul Barrios. La Paz: HISBOL-Aruwiyiri, 1993.

———. *Wut Walanti: Lo Irreparable*. Written and directed by Silvia Rivera Cusicanqui. 17 min. 1993. Videocassette.

———. "En defensa de mi hipótesis sobre el 'mestizaje colonial andino.'" In *Mestizaje: Ilusiones y realidades*, comp. Alison Spedding. La Paz: Museo Nacional de Etnografía y Folklore, 1996.

———. "Palabras mágicas." *Lecturas de la Prensa*, September 2000.

———. *Las fronteras de la coca*. Directed by Silvia Rivera Cusicanqui. 29 min. 2001. Videocassette.

Roldan, Mary. "Colombia: Cocaine and the 'Miracle' of Modernity in Medellín." Chapter 8 in *Cocaine: Global Histories*, edited by Paul Gootenberg. New York: Routledge, 1999.

Romano, Ruggiero. "Alrededor de dos falsas ecuaciones: Coca buena, cocaína buena; cocaína mala, coca mala." *Allpanchis* 19 (1986): 237–252.

Ronell, Avital. *Crack Wars: Literature, Addiction, Mania*. Lincoln: University of Nebraska Press, 1992.

Rösler, Michael, and Tobias Wendl, eds. *Frontiers and Borderlands: Anthropological Perspectives*. Frankfurt am Main: Peter Lang, 1999.

Roth, Erick, and Raúl Bohrt. *Actitudes de la población de La Paz hacia la producción y consumo de la hoja de coca*. La Paz: Centro Interdisciplinario de Estudios Comunitarios (CIEC), 1987.

Rudgley, Richard. *Essential Substances: A Cultural History of Intoxicants in Society*. New York: Kodansha International, 1994.

Sadler, Louis R. "The Historical Dynamics of Smuggling on the U.S.-Mexican Border Region, 1550–1998: Reflections on Markets, Cultures and Bureaucracies." In *Organized Crime and Democratic Governability: Mexico and the*

U.S.-Mexican Borderlands, edited by John Baily and Roy Godson. Pittsburgh: University of Pittsburgh Press, 2000.

Sáenz, Luis N. *La coca: Estudio médicosocial de la gran toxicomanía peruana.* Lima: Miranda, 1938.

Salgado, Wilma. "La crisis en el Ecuador en el contexto de las reformas financieras." *Ecuador Debate* 51 (2000): 7–22.

Samaddar, Ranabir. *The Marginal Nation: Transborder Migration from Bangladesh to West Bengal.* New Delhi: Sage Publications, 1999.

Samers, Michael. "The Political Economy of Illegal Immigration and Informal Employment in the European Union." Paper presented at the conference on International Migration: New Patterns, New Theories, Nottingham Trent University, September 11–13, 2000.

Sanabria, Harry. "The Discourse and Practice of Repression and Resistance in the Chapare." In *Coca, Cocaine and the Bolivian Reality,* edited by Barbara Léons and Harry Sanabria, 169–193. New York: State University of New York Press, 1997.

Sandford, Stephen. *Management of Pastoral Development in the Third World.* London: John Wiley & Sons, 1983.

Sassen, Saskia. *Losing Control: Sovereignty in an Age of Globalization.* New York: Columbia University Press, 1996.

Sayer, G. "Kenya Promised Land." Oxfam Country Profile. London: Oxfam, 1998.

Schivelbusch, Wolfgang. *Tastes of Paradise: A Social History of Spices, Stimulants and Intoxicants.* New York: Vintage Books/Random House, 1992.

Schuck, Peter. "Law and the Study of Migration." In *Migration Theory: Talking across Disciplines,* edited by Caroline B. Brettell and James F. Hollifield, 187–204. New York: Routledge, 2000.

Schultes, Richard Evans, and Albert Hoffman, *Plants of the Gods: Their Sacred, Healing and Hallucinogenic Powers.* Rochester: Healing Arts Press, 1992.

Scoones, I., ed. *Living with Uncertainty: New Directions in Pastoral Development in Africa.* London: Intermediate Technology Publications, 1995.

Scott, James C. *Seeing Like a State: How Certain Schemes to Improve the Human Condition Have Failed.* New Haven, Conn., and London: Yale University Press, 1998.

Scott, Peter Dale, and Jonathan Marshall. *Cocaine Politics: Drugs, Armies and the CIA in Central America.* Berkeley: University of California Press, 1991.

Secretaría de Salud del Gobierno de la Provincia de Jujuy. *Encuesta sobre el consumo de hoja de coca en la Provincia de Jujuy.* San Salvador del Jujuy: Secretaría de Salud, 2000.

Sen, Amartya. "On Corruption and Organized Crime." In United Nations International Drug Control Programme (UNIDCP) *World Drug Report,* 150–153. Oxford: Oxford University Press, 1997.

Seymour, Christopher. *Yakuza Diary: Doing Time in the Japanese Underworld.* New York: Atlantic Monthly Press, 1996.

Silverblatt, Irene. *Luna, sol y brujas: Género y clases en los Andes prehispánicos y coloniales.* Cusco, Peru: Centro Bartolomé de las Casas, 1990.

Simala, Kenneth I., and Maurice N. Amutabi. *Indigenous Social Mechanism of Conflict Resolution in Kenya: A Contextualized Paradigm for Examining Conflict in Africa.* Eldoret: Association for World Education, 2001.

Singer, Audrey, and Douglas S. Massey. "The Social Process of Undocumented Border Crossing among Mexican Migrants." *International Migration Review* 32, no. 3 (1998): 561–592.

Sivak, Martín. *La dictadura elegida: Biografía no-autorizada del Gral. Bánzer.* La Paz: Plural, 2001.

Skrobanek, Siriporn, et al. *The Traffic in Women: Human Realities of the International Sex Trade.* London: Zed, 1997.

Small Arms Survey. *Small Arms Survey 2001: Profiling the Problem.* Geneva: Graduate Institute of International Studies/Oxford: Oxford University Press, 2001.

———. *Small Arms Survey 2002: Counting the Human Cost.* Geneva: Graduate Institute of International Studies/Oxford: Oxford University Press, 2002.

Smart, Alan. "Predatory Rule and Illegal Economic Practices." In *States and Illegal Practices,* edited by Josiah McC. Heyman, 99–128. Oxford and New York: Berg, 1999.

Smillie, Ian. *Fire in the Ice: Benefits, Protection and Regulation in the Canadian Diamond Industry.* Ottawa: Partnership Africa Canada, 2002.

Smillie, Ian, L. Gberie, and R. Hazleton. *The Heart of the Matter: Sierra Leone, Diamonds and Human Security.* Ottawa: Partnership Africa Canada, 2000.

Smith, Michael L., et al., *Why People Grow Drugs: Narcotics and Development in the Third World.* London: Panos Institute, 1992.

Smith, Neil. "Contours of a Spatialized Politics: Homeless Vehicles and the Production of Geographical Scale." *Social Text* 33 (1992): 55–81.

Smith, Steve. "The United States and the Discipline of International Relations: Hegemonic Country, Hegemonic Discipline?" *International Studies Perspectives* 4, no. 2 (2002).

Soguk, Nevzat. *States and Strangers: Refugees and Displacements of Statecraft.* Minneapolis: University of Minnesota Press, 1999.

Solo de Zaldivar, Victor Breton. *Cooperacion al desarrollo y demandas etnicas en los Andes ecuatorianos.* Quito: FLACSO and Universitat de Lleida, 2001.

Soux, María Luisa. *La coca liberal: Producción y circulación a principios del siglo XX.* La Paz: Cocayapu and CIDES, 1993.

Spaan, Ernst. "*Taikongs* and *Calos:* The Roles of Middlemen and Brokers in Javanese International Migration." *International Migration Review* 28, no. 1 (1994): 93–113.

Spedding, Alison. *Wachu Wachu: Cultivo de coca e identidad en los Yunkas de La Paz.* La Paz: Hisbol, Cocayapu and CIPCA, 1994.

———. "The Coca Field as a Total Social Fact." In *Coca, Cocaine and the Bolivian Reality,* edited by Barbara Léons and Harry Sanabria. New York: State University of New York Press, 1997.

———. "Cocataki, Taki-Coca, Trade, Traffic and Organized Peasant Resistance in the Yungas of La Paz." In *Coca, Cocaine and the Bolivian Reality,* edited by Barbara Léons and Harry Sanabria, 47–70. New York: State University of New York Press, 1997.

Consolidated Bibliography

———. *La estructura de la represión: Origen social y situación jurídica de las detenidas y procesadas bajo la Ley 1008*. La Paz: Instituto de Investigaciones Sociológicas, 2000.

———. "Batallas Rituales y Marchas de Protesta: Modos de Apropiarse del Espacio en el Departamento de La Paz." Unpublished manuscript, 2001.

Spedding, Alison, comp. *Mestizaje: Ilusiones y realidades*. La Paz: Museo Nacional de Etnografía y Folklore, 1996.

Spillane, Joseph F. *Cocaine: From Medical Marvel to Modern Menace in the United States, 1884–1920*. Baltimore: Johns Hopkins University Press, 2000.

Stares, Paul B. *Global Habit: The Drug Problem in a Borderless World*. Washington, D.C.: Brookings Institution, 1996.

Sterling, Claire. *Crime without Frontiers: The Worldwide Expansion of Organised Crime and the Pax Mafiosa*. London: Little, Brown and Co., 1994.

Stevens, Jay. *Storming Heaven: LSD and the American Dream*. New York: Atlantic Monthly Press, 1987.

Swyngedouw, Erik. "Excluding the Other: The Production of Scale and Scaled Politics." In *Geographies of Economies*, edited by Roger Lee and Jane Wills, 167–176. London: Arnold, 1997.

Taussig, Michael. *Shamanism, Colonialism and the Wild Man: A Study in Terror and Healing*. Chicago: University of Chicago Press, 1987.

Taylor, Arnold H. *American Diplomacy and the Narcotics Traffic, 1900–1939*. Durham, N.C.: Duke University Press, 1969.

Taylor, Peter. "Embedded Statism and the Social Sciences: Opening Up to New Spaces." *Environment and Planning A* 28, no. 11 (1996): 1917–1928.

Temu, A. J. *British Protestant Missions*. London: Longman, 1972.

Thoumi, Francisco E. "Why the Illegal Psycho-Active Drugs Industry Grew in Colombia." *Journal of Inter-American Studies and World Affairs* 34 (Fall 1992): 37–63.

———. *Economía política y narcotráfico*. Bogotá: Tercer Mundo Editores, 1994.

Tilly, Charles. "War Making and State Making as Organized Crime." In *Bringing the State Back In*, edited by Peter Evans, Dietrich Rueschemeyer, and Theda Skocpol, 169–191. Cambridge: Cambridge University Press, 1985.

Tornay, S. A. "Armed Conflict in the Lower Omo Valley, 1970–1976: An Analysis from within Nyangatom Society." In *Warfare among East African Herders*, edited by K. Fukui and D. Turton. Osaka: Senri Ethnological Foundation, National Museum of Ethnology, 1979.

———. "More Chances on the Fringe of the State? The Growing Power of the Nyangatom—A Border People of the Lower Omo Valley, Ethiopia (1970–1992)." In *Conflicts in the Horn of Africa: Human and Ecological Consequences of Warfare*, edited by T. Tvedt, 143–163. Uppsala: Uppsala University, Department of Social and Economic Geography, 1993.

Torpey, John. *The Invention of the Passport: Surveillance, Citizenship and the State*. Cambridge: Cambridge University Press, 2000.

Tórrez Reque, Omar. *La Diosa del Chapare*. Cochabamba: Editorial FINSA, 1990.

Tovar Pinzón, Hermes. *La coca y las economías de exportación en América Latina.* Santa María de la Rápida: Universidad Hispanoamericana, 1993.

Tucker, George Loane. *Traffic in Souls.* Directed by George Loane Tucker, 1913. Film

Turton, D. "'We Must Teach Them to be Peaceful': Mursi Views on Being Human and Being Mursi." In *Conflicts in the Horn of Africa: Human and Ecological Consequences of Warfare,* edited by T. Tvedt, 164–180. Uppsala: Uppsala University, Department of Social and Economic Geography, 1993.

———. "Mursi Political Identity and Warfare: The Survival of an Idea." In *Ethnicity and Conflict in the Horn of Africa,* edited by K. Fukui and J. Markakis, 15–32. London and Athens: James Currey and Ohio University Press, 1994.

Twomey, Patrick. "Europe's Other Market: Trafficking in People." *European Journal of Migration and Law* 2 (2000): 1–36.

United Nations. Convention against Transnational Organized Crime, the Protocol against the Smuggling of Migrants by Land, Sea and Air, and the Protocol to Prevent, Suppress and Punish Trafficking in Persons, Especially Women and Children, November 15, 2000.

United Nations. *Report of the Panel of Experts Appointed Pursuant to UN Security Council Resolution 1306 (2000), Paragraph 19 in Relation to Sierra Leone.* New York: United Nations, December 2000.

United Nations. Report S/2000/1195. New York: United Nations, 2000.

United Nations. Report of the Panel of Experts on the Violations of Security Council Sanctions against UNITA, S/2000/203, March 10, 2000.

United Nations General Assembly. Resolution A/RES/55/56. New York: United Nations, 1 December 2000.

United Nations High Commissioner for Refugees. *The State of the World's Refugees: Fifty Years of Humanitarian Action.* New York: Oxford University Press, 2000.

United Nations High Commissioner for Refugees. *Statistics.* Available at www.unhcr.org.

United Nations International Drug Control Programme. "The Illicit Drug Industry: Production, Trafficking and Distribution." Pt. 4 of *World Drug Report.* Oxford: Oxford University Press, 1997.

United Nations International Drug Control Programme. Introduction to *World Drug Report.* Oxford: Oxford University Press, 1997.

United Nations Security Council. Report S/2001/363. New York: United Nations, April 18, 2001.

United Nations Security Council. S/2001/966. New York: United Nations, October 12, 2001.

United States Department of Labor Report. *Migrant Farmworkers: Pursuing Security in an Unstable Labor Market.* Research Report 5, Washington, D.C., May 1994.

United States Department of State. *International Narcotics Control Strategy Report.* Washington, D.C., March 2000.

United States General Accounting Office. *International Trade: Critical Issues*

Remain in Deterring Conflict Diamond Trade, GAO-02-678. U.S. General Accounting Office, Washington, D.C., June 2002.

United States General Accounting Office. *Terrorist Financing: US Agencies Should Systematically Assess Terrorists' Use of Alternative Financing Mechanisms.* GAO-04-163. U.S. General Accounting Office, Washington, D.C., November 2003.

Van der Torre, Edwin. *Drugstoeristen en kooplieden: Onderzoek naar Franse drugstoeristen, Marokkaanse drugsrunners en het beheer van dealpanden in Rotterdam* Deventer: Kluwer, 1996.

Van Schendel, Willem. "Easy Come, Easy Go: Smugglers on the Ganges." *Journal of Contemporary Asia* 23, no. 2 (1993): 189–213.

———. "Stateless in South Asia: The Making of the India-Bangladesh Enclaves." *The Journal of Asian Studies* 61, no. 1 (2002): 115–147.

———. *The Bengal Borderland: Beyond State and Nation in South Asia.* London: Anthem Press, 2005.

Vásquez, Calixto. "La Prosa Antidrogas. Discursos estigmatizadores y formas de resistencia de los jóvenes consumidores de marihuana en El Alto." Work in progress for a thesis in the Department of Sociology, Universidad Mayor de San Andrés, La Paz, n.d.

Volkov, Vadim. *Violent Entrepreneurs: The Use of Force in the Making of Russian Capitalism.* Ithaca, N.Y.: Cornell University Press, 2002.

Wald, Elijah. *Narcocorrido: A Journey into the Music of Drugs, Guns, and Guerrillas.* New York: Rayo/Harper Collins, 2001.

Waldorf, Dan, Craig Reinarman, and Sheila Murphy. *Cocaine Changes: The Experience of Using and Quitting.* Philadelphia: Temple University Press, 1991.

Walker, Andrew. *The Legend of the Golden Boat: Regulation, Trade and Traders in the Borderlands of Laos, Thailand, China and Burma.* Honolulu: University of Hawai'i Press, 1999.

Walker, R. B. J. *Inside/Outside: International Relations as Political Theory.* Cambridge: Cambridge University Press, 1993.

Walker, William III. *Drug Control in the Americas.* Rev. ed. Albuquerque: University of New Mexico Press New Mexico, 1989.

Walker, William III, ed. *Drug Control Policy: Essays in Historical and Comparative Perspective.* University Park: Pennsylvania State University Press, 1992.

Walton, John, and David Seddon. *Free Markets and Food Riots: The Politics of Global Adjustment.* Oxford: Blackwell Press, 1994.

Washington Office on Latin America. *Clear and Present Dangers: The U.S. Military and the War on Drugs in the Andes.* Washington, D.C.: Washington Office on Latin America (WOLA), 1991.

Weil, Andrew. *The Natural Mind: An Investigation of Drugs and the Higher Consciousness.* Boston: Houghton-Mifflin, 1972.

Weil, Andrew, and Winifred Rosen. *From Chocolate to Morphine.* Boston: Houghton-Mifflin, 1994.

Wendl, Tobias, and Michael Rösler. "Introduction: Frontiers and Borderlands—The Rise and Relevance of an Anthropological Research Genre." In *Frontiers and Borderlands: Anthropological Perspectives,* edited by Michael Rösler and Tobias Wendl, 1–27. Frankfurt am Main: Peter Lang, 1999.

Widgren, Jonas. "Multinational Co-operation to Combat Trafficking in Migrants and the Role of International Organisations." Paper presented to the 11th IOM Seminar on International Responses to Trafficking in Migrants and Safeguarding of Migrant Rights, Geneva. October 26–28, 1994.

Williams, Phil. "Transnational Organized Crime and the State." In *The Emergence of Private Authority in Global Governance,* edited by R. B. Hall and T. J. Bierstecker. Cambridge: Cambridge University Press, 2003.

Wilson, Suzanne, and Marta Zambrano, "Cocaine, Commodity Chains, and Drug Politics: A Transnational Approach." In *Commodity Chains and Global Capitalism,* edited by Gary Gereffi and Miguel Korzeniewitz. Westport, Conn.: Greenwood Press, 1994.

Wilson, Thomas M., and Hastings Donnan, eds. *Border Identities: Nation and State at International Frontiers.* Cambridge: Cambridge University Press, 1998.

Wolf, Eric R. *Europe and the People without History.* Berkeley: University of California Press, 1982.

Wong, Diana. "The Semantics of Migration." *Sojourn* 4, no. 2 (1989): 275–285.

———. "The Recruitment of Foreign Labour in Malaysia: From Migration System to Guest-worker Regime," Paper presented at the Conference on Migrant Workers in Southeast Asia. Needed, Not Wanted, Armidale. December 1–3, 2003.

Wong, Diana, and Gusni Saat. "Trafficking of Persons from the Philippines into Malaysia." Unpublished report submitted to United Nations Interregional Crime and Justice Research Institute, 2002.

Wong, Diana, and Teuku Afrizal Teuku Anwar. "*Migran Gelap:* Irregular Migrants in Malaysia's Shadow Economy." In *Unauthorized Migration in Southeast Asia,* edited by Graziano Battistella and Maruja M. B. Asis. Manila: Scalabrini Migration Center, 2003.

World Federation of Diamond Bourses and International Diamond Manufacturers Association. Joint Resolution. Antwerp, July 19, 2000.

Zaitch, Damián. "Traquetos: Colombians Involved in the Cocaine Business in the Netherlands." Ph.D. dissertation, University of Amsterdam, Amsterdam School of Social Science Research, 2001.

Zinberg, Norman. *Drug, Set and Setting.* New Haven, Conn.: Yale University Press, 1984.

Zolberg, Aristide R. "Matters of State: Theorizing Immigration Policy." In *The Handbook of International Migration,* edited by Charles Hirschman, Philip Kasinitz, and Josh deWind, 71–93. New York: Russell Sage Foundation, 1999.

Zorn, Elayne. "Coca, Cash and Cloth in Highland Bolivia: The Chapare and Transformations in a 'Traditional' Andean Textile Economy." In *Coca, Cocaine and the Bolivian Reality,* edited by Barbara Léons and Harry Sanabria, 71–98. New York: State University of New York Press, 1997.

Contributors

Itty Abraham, former program director for the South Asia and Global Security and Cooperation programs at the Social Science Research Council, is now a fellow at the East-West Center, Washington, D.C. He is author of *The Making of the Indian Atomic Bomb: Science, Secrecy and the Postcolonial State.*

Maurice Amutabi is Lecturer at Moi University, Kenya, where he has been teaching since 1992. He is co-author of *Nationalism and Democracy for People-Centred Development in Africa.*

Paul Gootenberg is Professor of History and Director of Latin American and Caribbean Studies at Stony Brook University. His books include *Between Silver And Guano; Imagining Development*; and the edited volume *Cocaine: Global Histories.*

David Kyle is Associate Professor of Sociology at the University of California, Davis. He is author of *Transnational Peasants: Migrations, Networks, and Ethnicity from Andean Ecuador* and co-editor of *Global Human Smuggling: Comparative Perspectives.*

Silvia Rivera Cusicanqui is Professor at the Universidad Mayor de San Andrés, Bolivia. She is author of *Oprimidos pero no vencidos* (*Oppressed but not Defeated*) and *Las fronteras de la coca* (The frontiers of coca) and producer of a video of the same name.

Kenneth I. Simala is Senior Lecturer in the Department of Kiswahili, Maseno University, Kenya. He has published articles on nationalism, ethnicity, conflict, democracy, development, globalization, and poverty.

Christina A. Siracusa is Lecturer in Political Science and International Relations at the University of California, Davis.

Ian Smillie is an Ottawa-based consultant and writer. A leader in the campaign to end "conflict diamonds," he has served on a United Nations Security Council expert panel on this topic and as Research Coordinator for Partnership Africa Canada. He is a member of the intergovernmental Kimberley Process, which created and operates a global diamond certification system. Among his books is *The Charity of Nations: Humanitarian Action in a Calculating World* (with Larry Minear).

Willem van Schendel is Professor of Modern Asian History at the University of Amsterdam and head of the Asia Department of the International Institute of Social History. His publications include *The Bengal Borderland: Beyond State and Nation in South Asia.*

Diana Wong is a senior fellow at the Institute of Malaysian and International Studies (IKMAS) at Universiti Kebangsaan Malaysia in Bangi. Her publications include *Peasants in the Making: Malaysia's Green Revolution; Vom Exil zur Diaspora: Asyl in einer deutschen Stadt; Memory Suppression and Memory Production: The Japanese Occupation of Singapore;* and *Migran Gelap: Irregular Migrants in Malaysia's Shadow Economy.*

Index

Index

Index

Index

169–173, 176n64. *See also* Coca leaf, legal status of

Legality, 4, 9, 17, 31; boundaries of, 23

Ley de Extranjería (Spanish immigration law), 165–166, 171

Liberia, 20, 27, 178–179, 187–190

Libya, 1, 5

Licit, 18, 20, 22, 25, 29. *See also* Illicit

Licitness, 23, 31; defining, 8, 25, 27

Livestock, 202, 206, 209, 211–213, 220; demand for, 201, 203, 214; theft of, *see* Cattle raiding

London (Great Britain), 117

Lorca accident (Spain), 165–167

Lord's Resistance Army (LRA) (Uganda), 203

Los Mercenarios (Devil's Dance group), 145, 149

LSD, 102, 105

Mafia, 2, 115; and Pax Mafiosa, 51; state as, 164

Mahuad, Jamil (Ecuadorian President), 160, 163–164, 175n34, 175n35

Malaysia, 29–30, 70, 72, 81–83, 85–88, 91, 93–96

Manzanilla, Juan Carlos (Ecuadorian spokesman), 169–170

Maps: cognitive, 55–57; of illegal flows, 41–43; political, 59

Marijuana, 18, 102–103, 107–108, 118–119; medical, 120

Market, 1, 3, 136, 141, 163; black, 1, 22, 24, 107; border, 48, 56; coca leaf, 130, 139–140, 143, 151n15; diamond, 179–182; drug, 110, 114; global, 70, 161; labor, 85–88, 165; small arms, 49, 203–204, 217

Marx, Karl, 2

Mayor, Jaime (Spanish Minister of Interior), 167–168

Mbembe, Achille, 11, 90–91

Media, 1–2, 22, 69, 81; and coca leaf, 143, 130; and diamonds, 196; and drugs, 118; and smuggling, 154–155; and trafficking, 77–78. *See also* Campaigns; Images

Memory sites, 49–50, 65n25

Menem, Carlos (Argentinean President), 9

Mercenaries, 214

Merille region (Ethiopia), 206; people of, 202, 206, 216

Methamphetamines, 102

Mexico, 155, 172; borders of, 24, 47–48, 53, 65n25, 66nn35,44, 103, 111; and drugs,

108–109, 114–115, 121; and migrants, 13–14, 161

Migrant labor, 85, 165, 170, 172. *See also* Migrants, labor

Migrant-exporting schemes, 36n57, 155–161, 165, 167–168, 170–172

Migrants, 70–71, 86, 133, 156–157, 159; agency of, 72, 87; control over, 153; dangers to, 158; experiences of, 135, 163, 165–166; discourse on, 81, 171–173; female, *see* Women, migrant; illegal, 24, 74–75, 86–88, 96, 97n17, 157; labor, 26, 81, 83, 128, 130, 132, 141, 148, 154, 166–168, 172, 175n48 (*see also* Demand, labor); legal status of, *see* Legal status, migrant; international, 26, 29, 81, 138, 151n18; 165–166, 169; perspectives of, 82, 155, 157, 161–162, 164–167, 169–173; rituals of, 144–145; as victims, *see* Victims, migrants as. *See also* Agency, migrant; Smuggling, human

Migration, 9, 71, 85–86, 157, 208, 210; commodification of, 167; control over, 29, 69; costs of, 160; criminalization of, 89; distress, 91; female, 73–74; forced, 12, 221; illegal, 14, 30, 72, 81, 89, 155–156, 161; international, 12–13, 73, 159–160, 171; labor, 26, 60; mass, 29, 70, 159, 161, 164; patterns of, 154; risks of, 158, 171; safe, 78. *See also* Movement, population

Migration industry, 172

Migration merchants, 158, 167. *See also* Coyotes; Snakeheads; Wolves

Migration services, 155–158, 172. *See also* Migrant-exporting schemes

Migration theory, 12–13

Militarization, 203

Mobility, 11, 13, 23–25; control over, 26, 83–84, 171; labor, 70; social, 156, 172

Mobuto Sese Seko (Congolese dictator), 183, 192

Moeller, Heinz (Ecuadorian Minister of Foreign Affairs), 169–170

Moi, Daniel Arap (Kenyan President), 202, 220

Money, 210, 212; drug, 114, 191; laundering of, 3, 15, 20, 182, 184–186, 191, 198. *See also* Currency

Monrovia, 180

Moral panic, 100n72, 112, 118

Mores, social, 5, 12, 15, 19–20

Morphine, 117

Movement, 11–13, 29, 42–43, 59; anti-state,

Index

Index

United States (U.S.), 31, 60, 72–73, 78–79; and asylum, 75–76; borders of, 24, 47–48, 53, 65n25, 66nn35,44, 103, 110–111; Coast Guard, 161; Congress, 69; Department of Justice, 80; and diamonds, 178, 186–187, 190–191, 196; and drugs, 108–116, 118–120; General Accounting Office, 192, 196; and law, 18; and migration, 1, 13–14, 160–161, 168; and trafficking, 88

Uranium, 51

Urban legends, 112–113

Venezuela, 9

Vice industry, 81, 82–84, 87, 93–95

Victims, 27, 29–30, 76, 208, 215, 221; accident, 165; drug, 117–118; migrants as, 87, 89, 154, 167, 170–171; white slavery, 72–73

Vienna process. See Organized crime, United Nations Vienna Convention Against

Villazón (Bolivia), 129–130, 133–136, 144–145

Violence, 14, 16, 21, 28, 57, 132, 151n18, 201–202, 209–210, 221–222; and drugs, 121–122; escalation of, 203, 213; international, 4; legitimate, 13

Wages, 86, 161, 165, 168, 170

War, 183, 191, 199, 211; of attrition, 204; civil, 188, 192, 217; border, 160; and diamonds, 184, 192–193; and drugs, 30, 107, 109, 111–114, 119–120, 122; interethnic, 202; Italo-Ethiopian, 214; limitations on, 211; opium, 104; and terror, 31. See also Cold War; Conflict zones

War crimes, 17

War zone, 202

Warlords, 204, 217

Weapons, 27, 180, 184, 191, 201, 215; nuclear, 18. See also Small arms

West Bengal (India), 55, 68n63

White slavery, 71–73

Wolf, Eric, 38

Wolves (human smugglers), 47

Women, 218; Coalition of Trafficking Against (CATW), 77; and coca chewing, 138–140, 143; Global Alliance Against Traffic in (GAATW), 77; migrant, 29, 73, 85, 96, 161; trafficked, 30, 74, 77–78, 80–84, 93–95

Work permits, 168–169, 175n48. See also Documents, legal

Workers, 106; foreign, 75, 86, 97n8; mine, 145–149; undocumented, 14, 155, 165–166. See also Migrants, labor; Policies, guest worker

World Bank, 78, 163, 173

World Diamond Council, 194–195

World Food Program, 219

World Trade Organization (WTO), 194–195, 197

World Vision, 220

Yemen, 5, 13, 16, 18–19, 151n15

Yerba-mate, 107

Youth, 118, 214

Yugoslavia, 75

Yungas region (Bolivia), 131, 137–138

Zaire. See Democratic Republic of Congo

Zimbabwe, 192

Zolberg, Aristide, 13

TRACKING GLOBALIZATION

Illicit Flows and Criminal Things: States, Borders, and the
Other Side of Globalization

Edited by Willem van Schendel and Itty Abraham